JOHN WESLEY

A Theological Biography

MARTIN SCHMIDT

JOHN WESLEY

A Theological Biography

VOLUME II
John Wesley's Life Mission
PART I

Translated by

NORMAN P. GOLDHAWK

Tutor in Church History and the History of Christian
Doctrine at Richmond College, Surrey

ABINGDON PRESS
NEW YORK   NASHVILLE

PRINTED IN GREAT BRITAIN
BY EBENEZER BAYLIS AND SON, LTD.
THE TRINITY PRESS, WORCESTER, AND LONDON

Contents

Translator's Preface

THIS translation consists of the first half of Professor Martin Schmidt's second and final volume on John Wesley. Part II will appear in due course. As in the previous English volume quotations from John Wesley's *Journal*, *Letters* and *Sermons* have been reproduced according to the text of the Standard Edition.

In the preface to the original German edition Dr Schmidt, who is now Professor at the University of Heidelberg, explained his method of procedure in the following words: 'The author has found it necessary to treat Wesley's main activity, to which this second volume is devoted, under subjects, instead of giving a chronological narrative—such as was done in the classical English biography by John S. Simon, to whose expert elucidation of many separate points, careful discussion of complicated and debated questions, and clear descriptions from intimate knowledge of actual places, he is deeply indebted, even when he differs from him. The reason for this subject-treatment can be stated simply, as appears in the opening sentences of the final chapter: John Wesley's course remained constant after his conversion on 24th May 1738. But within the discussion of the different spheres of his activity the attempt has been made to treat each subject as far as possible chronologically, although the balance of the subject sometimes made it necessary to depart from this temporal order, especially in chapter 5, which deals with the opposition against Methodism. It might be objected that the portrait given of John Wesley has been too severely isolated, so that he is made to stand, like a monument, upon a pedestal. But this answers to the conviction, which was increasingly forced upon the author during the course of his work, that Wesley was influenced only comparatively little by other people, whether they were his teachers, friends, fellow-workers, or opponents. He derived by far the most from his constant preoccupation with the Bible (particularly the Greek New Testament), with individual Fathers of the church, and with biographies, not to mention the constraint of the historical moment, which he interpreted by means of scripture. The words of his successor, Thomas Coke, based upon a reference to Athanasius of Alexandria, "Wesley contra mundum", give expression to a most important truth.'

Professor Schmidt dedicated the volume to the theological faculties of the Wartburg Theological Seminary of the American Lutheran Church in Dubuque (Iowa), U.S.A., and the Friedrich-Alexander-University, Erlangen-Nürnberg, Germany, which gave him honorary doctorates, and to the memory of two European Methodist bishops, J. W. Ernst Sommer and Ferdinand Sigg.

RICHMOND COLLEGE

The Beginnings of the Evangelistic Movement: John Wesley and the Moravians

ON 16TH SEPTEMBER 1738, a Saturday, John Wesley returned from Germany to London, and straightway threw himself into his work. The following day he preached three times and spent the evening in one of the important groups of the religious societies.[1] He first expounded a biblical text and then related his experiences at Herrnhut. On Monday he visited the prisoners in Newgate Gaol and preached to them the gospel of the free grace of God for sinners. That and the succeeding evenings he devoted almost without exception to the religious societies. Among them he had his most important experiences and found guidance for his actions. An habitual drinker, who suffered desperately from his craving, and who had taken part in the normal services, sacraments and prayers of the Church without receiving any help from them, and who at first vigorously opposed him, found from his preaching and from praying with him forgiveness of sins.[2] On 20th October he began pastoral work in a religious society made up of soldiers in Westminster.[3] But above all he undertook once again the leadership of a newly-formed religious society, which had been started on 1st May 1738, and which became the centre of his activity in London. It was this society which met at 32 Fetter Lane, in a meeting-house which had belonged to a nonconformist congregation,[4] a fact which has symbolic significance, for through John Wesley's advent and leadership a nonconformist congregation was brought back into the Church of England, without having to give up its peculiar characteristics. Just before Peter Böhler left, and by means of his active co-operation, this group had been newly constituted by combining in a powerful way features of a religious society, German Moravianism and early Methodism. A new model was thus brought into being, the chief characteristic of

9

which was, as compared with the older pattern of Horneck and Woodward, that membership was not confined to adherents of the Church of England. For the first time the opportunity was given for nonconformists to enter into close fellowship with members of the established church, and this was to lead to such unforeseen results in England at large as united service by the churches and the Evangelical Alliance.

The central feature of this particular fellowship was the Herrnhut idea of 'bands' of five to ten persons who openly shared their temptations and difficulties, shortcomings and afflictions. From 25th September 1738, it met as often as twice a week, and the members entered into a remarkably close relationship. In the punctuality in beginning the meeting and the requirement of standing up to speak and of obtaining the consent of the others before going on a journey, in the censure for absence without good reason and the obligation to put membership of the fellowship before any other to which a person might belong, in the method of acceptance which implied a thorough interrogation and two months' probation, and finally in the exclusion for disobedience to the brethren's regulations, lay the root of a strict organization which went right against the spirit of the century and the British tradition. It is not difficult to detect the influence of Count Zinzendorf. There is no doubt that as soon as these circumstances passed beyond the select circle opposition was aroused.

In the meetings themselves most of the time was given to prayer and singing, while the reading and exposition of Scripture are scarcely mentioned, although that was taken for granted. Similarly no reference was made to the obligation of attendance at worship and the sacrament, since these belonged essentially to the type of religious society associated with Horneck and Woodward. Every fourth Saturday was to be given to general intercession, the hours of 12 to 2, 3 to 5 and 6 to 8 being devoted to continuous prayer. On the following Sunday there was a Herrnhut 'love-feast', a service with personal testimonies, from 7 to 10.

It is surprising that such a reorganization of an established Anglican phenomenon was so thoroughly effected. It is doubly surprising, because it had a foreign, Herrnhut origin.[5] Two reasons may have been responsible. The old religious societies must at that time have been in a state of some exhaustion, such as had distressed John

Wesley's friend and admirer, the young bookseller, James Hutton, who was stimulated to form new ones. But above all there was within the Herrnhut movement a vitality and aggressiveness which owed a great deal to Böhler's leadership. In the rules of the Bands a strong attempt to revive the design and form of monasticism in the soil of the Reformation can be discerned.

Difficulties were soon experienced in these circles in which John Wesley moved. Differences appeared, although not so much through the strict organization to which reference has been made, and which perhaps was only gradually transferred to the older religious societies, as through the preaching itself. The trouble could have been overcome through charity and understanding, but within a short time both Wesley and his brother were forbidden to conduct services in the majority of Anglican churches.

In such a small way the life-work of this man began, a work which was to assume such large proportions. Nevertheless in the events of these few weeks nearly all the characteristics of that enterprise were evident: the energetic zeal with which its supporters went to work, a fellowship of like-minded friends,[6] the leading position it gave to preaching, the emphasis on the Pauline gospel of justification, forgiveness of sins and the new birth, the urge to concentrate this message on personal experience of salvation and talk about faith. At the same time there was the beginning of resistance which threatened it both externally and from within,[7] the obligation of protecting itself from Herrnhut, the strong association with the religious societies, the particular kind of love which was to develop into a strong social class, and the difficulty of building all this into a strong organization. What was still missing was the appeal to the masses. As before in the student group at Oxford John Wesley quite naturally became part of that evangelistic activity which others, his brother Charles first, with his associates, James Hutton, John Hutchings and James Habersham, had begun. Charles had passed through a conversion experience while ill in bed three days before John—also under the influence of Peter Böhler—although he was a less dominant character, quite different from John. In his case also Luther played a leading part, although not through the preface to Romans, which was not well known in England, but through the Commentary on Galatians, familiar since the time of Elizabeth and especially prized by John Bunyan. His brother's sermon on 3rd June 1738, in St Mary's

Church, Oxford, on Salvation by Faith expressed his own experience also. He too refused to capitulate before opposition, and like John had the satisfaction of seeing those who had opposed him being shaken out of their self-confidence by sudden unexpected events, and showing repentance and a desire for forgiveness. He was more sensitive than his brother, and it was natural that he should become the true poet and lyricist of the experience of salvation, the author of strongly biblical hymns of faith. The similarity in the fortunes and works of the two brothers is as striking as the difference. Unlike Charles it was characteristic of John that he was influenced by the idea of mission and by missionary work.[8]

John could not contemplate staying long in the capital and its surroundings. His objective was Oxford, his spiritual home. There he visited his college, his circle of students, and the Holy Club, which since his acquaintance with Böhler was somewhat uncertain of him,[9] and the prisoners. For the rest he gave his time to the religious societies and the Fox and Compton families, which took a leading part in them. In the following months he stayed either in London or Oxford. He constantly tried to enlarge his work in the university city, to keep the Fox family there, although for economic reasons they wanted to move to London, and to bring his friends Kinchin and Hutchings there.[10] Although his activity in the calm of the little circle was proceeding smoothly, it was noted and objected to, because it went against the spirit of the time and the easy-going atmosphere of normal Anglicanism.[11] During his first journey to Oxford he had read the account of the great revival movement, published by the congregational minister Jonathan Edwards about his work in Northampton in North America (1703–58). He had been so gripped by this that he immediately passed on to a friend in a letter long extracts from it.

In the midst of this energetic outward activity he did not in any sense overlook his inner needs. The tortuous questions connected with his conversion in London and his visit to Herrnhut were not settled or laid to rest. The title 'The Weak in Faith' which he gave the account of Jonathan Edwards was an indication of a similar agitation in himself. The answer he received to the letter brought the ferment to a head, and it dismayed him. As always he found help in the Bible, above all in the prayer of Jabez for God's blessing (1 Chronicles 4[10]) and then again in the classical text for the Puritan

theology of conscience, which was the Sunday evening lesson:
'Examine yourselves, whether ye be in the faith' (2 Corinthians
13⁵).[12] Obedient to this summons he undertook a calm analysis of
himself, the method of which was entirely in line with Puritan
sermons and devotional books. Immediately following the text he
wrote out the favourite quotation of the whole Pietist movement, the
Pauline word: 'If any man be in Christ, he is a new creature: old
things are passed away; behold, all things are become new'
(2 Corinthians 5¹⁷). To do justice to the claim of this statement as
a whole he described the change from the old to the new man in
five points, in his judgements, his designs, his desires, his conversation and his actions. It was not intellectualism which led him to put
the consideration of a man's judgements first, for everything follows
from them. They are a true indication of the regenerate man. They
comprise his judgement about himself, his idea of happiness and of
holiness, and so indicate the range of his inner strivings.[13] As to
judgement about himself Wesley says of the regenerate man that he
judges himself to be altogether fallen short of the glorious image of
God, to have no good thing abiding in him, but all that is corrupt and
abominable. Wesley represents himself therefore as earthly, sensual,
devilish, a motley mixture of beast and devil.[14] This radical condemnation of himself was a result of the new creation, a judgement
of faith, not to be reached apart from faith.[15] When he turned to his
idea of what constitutes happiness he was clear that the attempt to
find it in riches, honour, pleasure or any earthly thing must miscarry,
since it does not consist in any of these things. There is no happiness
except in the enjoyment of God, he said, expressing the tradition of
Anglicanism in the manner of Augustine. Such joy is the foretaste
of the blessedness of heaven. He thus recognized the difference
between the old and the new man as a change from orientation upon
this world to the other. Accordingly the new man knows that the
point is not, as he thought when unregenerate, to follow the commandments of God, avoiding evil and doing good, but to have the
life of God in the soul, maintaining the image of God fresh stamped
on the heart, so that every temper and thought, speaking and acting
is affected. This conception of holiness might be called mystic-
spiritualistic in the tradition of Scougal and Law, but the significant
thing is that the words 'Do good', which were written all round the
activities of the Oxford student circle and with which John Burton

had won Wesley for service in Georgia, are now expressly rejected. In his relationship with God he had reached a dimension beyond the ethical, one which concerned holiness, not consecration. So much as to his thoughts concerning judgements.

His views about the designs of the regenerate man also correspond in a new way with his understanding of holiness. False and true ideals stand in sharp distinction to each other: the new man does not want to heap up treasures upon earth nor to gain the praise of men nor to indulge the desires of the flesh, the eye or the pride of life; but to regain the image of God and to have the life of God replanted in his soul. These new desires constitute what being a new creation means. It is not merely his desires however but the whole train of his passions and inclinations which are set on heavenly things—his fear and sorrow, his hope and love. Wesley goes on to say that he cannot claim to be a new creature in all these respects, for other desires arise in his heart. Yet he immediately comforts himself with the assertion that they do not reign, for through Jesus Christ, who strengthens him, he puts them under his feet. Here he gives expression to a favourite distinction in Pietism between a ruling sin and the sin of weakness.

Again the conversation of the regenerate man is new. It is 'seasoned with salt' (Colossians 4[6]) and fit to 'minister grace to the hearers'. New also are his actions, since all aim at the glory of God. Every deed springs from the love of God and of man. Paul says the fruit of the spirit is love, peace, joy, long-suffering, and temperance, but although Wesley can find a measure of these in himself, not all are present. More than anything he lacks love to God, the love which was in Jesus Christ and which came forth from Him. Accordingly he confesses his wandering thoughts in prayer and the shortcomings of his devotion at communion. In the same way he lacks settled joy in the Holy Ghost and a peace which excludes fear and doubt. For these reasons he is often not sure whether he has true faith, and then he finds relief in prayer and the Bible. Even when he finds that for his part he has not fulfilled all the requirements of scripture, he still trusts in the fact that God has accepted him. The handwriting that was against him has been blotted out and he is reconciled to God. In this way Wesley overcame the subjective[16] attitude at the decisive point and reached an objective foundation, avoiding the danger of an egocentric orientation.

14

It was always the Bible which was the determining factor in his own religious concerns. Two weeks later, when he was once again troubled about himself by the word of Jesus about the kingdom of God being within (Luke 17^{21}), he was comforted by the description given of Joseph of Arimathea: 'He himself also waited for the kingdom of God' (Mark 15^{43}). He asked further whether he ought not to wait in silence and retirement, and received the answer: 'Seest thou not how faith wrought together with his works? And by works was faith made perfect' (James 2^{22}). Preaching and the care of his own soul went hand in hand, the Bible supplying the connecting link. It is significant that the message to condemned criminals in the prison time and again demonstrated its power. There it was unmistakably clear and compelling. This situation was able to bring to expression as no other the original meaning of Paul's words about grace and the fulfilment of the law. Impelled by inner necessity Wesley went on to extract for printing the doctrine of justification by faith as contained in the reformed Homilies of the Church of England.

Outward events contributed towards his depression and disquiet. A man who wanted to be his pupil committed suicide, if not before his eyes, yet very near. His friend, Charles Delamotte from Georgia, was struck by the change in him, but expressed doubts about his standing as a Christian with a directness of expression to which his close friendship gave him a right. He found in Wesley a righteousness based on self, a simplicity of his own making, but no real faith in Jesus Christ. Wesley knew of no other way than again and again to turn to the Bible and let individual texts speak to him. On one occasion it was the word from the end of the Epistle to the Galatians: 'As many as walk according to this rule, peace be on them, and mercy, and upon the Israel of God' (Galatians 6^{16}), and shortly afterwards Jesus's reply to His mother at the wedding in Cana: 'My hour is not yet come' (John 2^{4}). While he was staying the second time in Oxford in December 1738 he received two letters, the contents of which gave contradictory advice. The one urged him to publish his account of Georgia, the other sought just as urgently to dissuade him from doing so, because it would bring much trouble upon him. He consulted the Bible and read the words which God addressed to the prophet Ezekiel, commanding him to be a watchman over the people of Israel (Ezekiel 33$^{2-6}$), and also the exhortation to Timothy: 'Thou therefore endure hardship, as a good soldier of Jesus Christ' (2 Timothy 2^{3}).

His *Journal* does not say whether the texts made him uncertain or directed him to a particular course of action, but it contains every time the concise remark: 'I opened my Bible at these words.'[17] On the whole the majority of references seem to have come from the New Testament.

Much time was taken up by correspondence, which was of a more pastoral nature than it had previously been. People in the religious societies looked up to him as their spiritual father, as was common among Romanic mystics. Under his guidance they apparently passed through experiences similar to his and they expressed them in words derived from the biblical language of Herrnhut: God justifies the ungodly, the blood of Jesus is the guarantee of reconciliation, faith is the means by which it is received. The source of cleansing appeared in actual visionary form as the open wound in the side of the Saviour.[18] And even when the experience itself lay further back in the past and happened quite independently of himself, he is still able to express it in terms of Paul's doctrine of justification.[19]

On 30th November 1738, George Whitefield arrived back from Georgia, and Wesley hurried with his brother to London on 11th December in order to consult with him. This young man, who was born almost ten years after John Wesley, had joined the Oxford student group in 1734 while at Pembroke College, but had not at first said much about himself. Unlike John Clayton and William Morgan he had not taken the initiative in taking on a new sphere of work. It was in the religious societies themselves that he apparently found the first incentive to develop a certain independence. With resolution he set about raising the standards for reception into membership in order to attain a genuine fellowship of saints, no matter if the numbers should be reduced. Afterwards he had been the only one to take seriously John Wesley's call to go to Georgia. On the very day that the one left to come home the other set out. At the last moment John Wesley had news of this and in a letter tried to stop him, so disillusioned was he over the colony.

In the discussions with the trustees in London Wesley found broad agreement as against the magistrate of Savannah. The despotism of the burgomaster Causton and the council, which had caused the dispute to be brought to the trustees, was strongly censured. On the other hand Wesley created the impression that he was a very difficult man, who, disliked by the majority of the population of the colony, understood very well how to turn them against the authorities, and therefore appeared as an unpleasant combination of enthusiast and pharisee. His resignation from the pastorate of Savannah on 26th April 1738 was accordingly accepted with genuine satisfaction, since it seemed to ease all the difficulties.[20] His brother Charles kept his position as secretary to General Oglethorpe a while longer, but abandoned on medical advice his original intention of returning to Georgia. In this way this episode in his career was expressly and emphatically closed for John Wesley. He regarded the colony as a completely unfruitful spot, which God would punish by a lack of His word. On 2nd January 1738, Charles wrote to him that these attacks were preparing him in an unforeseen way for going to the heathen, and that the time was now ripe to turn to them since the gospel had been refused by the 'Jews'. His own feelings in the matter took him to the same conclusion, and only from this point of view can his attempt to prevent Whitefield from going be understood. But this did not make Whitefield change his mind; he was already displaying a noticeable independence which later had a decided effect upon the fate of the Methodist movement.

His visit to Georgia was significantly brief, and lasted only four months. It was more like a preliminary experiment than a settled undertaking. The Salzburgers in Ebenezer impressed him so powerfully that he made collections for the building of their church and orphan-house.[21] Next he immediately joined the Wesley brothers in their evangelistic work in England. The ancient Church of St Mary in the London district of Islington became the scene of a whole series of daily preaching and communion services during Christmas week. John Wesley was in a state of some spiritual distress[22] and he was physically ill, so that Charles feared he would die. Both yearned for Oxford, in order to have the quiet of a settled sphere of work. Charles became a candidate for the vacant living of the nearby village of Cowley at the beginning of 1739, but without success.

John Wesley had still a further interest, that of hymnody. From his first meeting with the Herrnhuters this had become a leading concern, and it had been strengthened and confirmed when the Salzburgers drew his attention to the Halle hymns. While in Charlestown he published his first collection of hymns; then in 1738 the second appeared. This second collection was made up of material from the first one plus some new items. The German influence was less and was supplemented by the best of recent English authors: Isaac Watts, George Herbert, John Norris and Thomas Ken. Among German hymns the mystical writers were more strongly represented: there were Johann Scheffler's 'Thou, Jesu, art our king' ('Dich, Jesu, loben wir'), Adam Drese's 'Bridegroom, Thou art mine' ('Seelenbräutigam, du Gottes Lamm'), Zinzendorf's 'All glory to the Eternal Three' ('Schau von deinem Thron'), Tersteegen's 'Thou hidden love of God' (Verborgene Gottesliebe, du'), and Johann Joseph Winckler's 'Shall I, for fear of feeble man' ('Sollt ich aus Furcht für Menschenkindern'). There was also the Spanish hymn, 'O God, my God, my all Thou art'.[23] Apparently this collection of hymns also helped to lessen the influence of the visit to Herrnhut. So ended the very significant year 1738. The powerful movement had not yet declined, nor had it found its definite form. Uneasiness and vacillation were still the order of the day.

The new year began significantly. The religious society at Fetter Lane in London celebrated on 1st January a love-feast with about sixty people, who presumably all belonged to the Church of England. They continued long together, and at 3 o'clock in the morning, as they continued in prayer, some of them went into an ecstasy. Many fell to the ground like the Hernnhuters, and cried out for joy.[24] When the rest had recovered from their first feelings of amazement they broke out in words which were familiar because they were in the Anglican service, 'We praise Thee, O God; we acknowledge Thee to be the Lord.' Yet John Wesley relates this almost as a spectator. He was still troubled about his own spiritual condition. Once again he made an acute analysis of himself and found that he lacked the marks of a true Christian, namely the fruits of the Spirit. He could not discover any love for God in himself. Instead he had to confess, in the face of the harsh alternatives contained in the First Epistle of St John (2^{15}), that he did not belong to God, because his heart was at least half filled with the love of the world, friends, eating and drinking. He could find no lasting victorious joy, no real supernatural peace, but only a quite natural peace derived from his very comfortable situation. He had indeed given up much, given his goods to the poor, endured much, denied himself, and taken up his cross; yet this did not make him a Christian, for he did not have the fruits of the Spirit. Once again the supreme concern of his spiritual life, which had been given him in early childhood, came to the fore: perfect love to God.[25]

The unusual psychological phenomena continued to be experienced in the meetings. At length Wesley gave way to those who had long desired him to visit a 'French prophetess', a Camisard, who as a refugee was causing quite a sensation in London. Wesley was not at all impressed by her.[26] But there were further unusual happenings. A middle-aged married woman suddenly started to cry out during the exposition of the Bible in a devotional meeting. When he spoke to her on her own the next day he found out that for a number of years she had been oppressed with the sense of unforgivable sin. She had received medical treatment, which was a false diagnosis, and now for the first time she received hope of genuine healing under the influence of the powerful Word, which was sharper than a two-edged sword (Hebrews 4[12]).

People came to believe that Wesley's prayers and faith could work miracles among spiritually sick children.[27] Crowds thronged his preaching, signs of its freeing effects were undeniable, demons appeared to be driven out of tormented people.[28] Primitive Christianity, which he had consciously and emphatically striven to reproduce, and in which he had been immersed in the Herrnhut community, seemed really to be present in these occurrences. When hostility showed itself, when the recently founded religious society in Reading was dispersed because the local minister vigorously upset the members, when in Oxford the leading woman-member of the group was excluded from Holy Communion because she maintained that she had first found true faith in Jesus Christ in the religious society, when a real theological dispute developed between John Wesley and one of his fellow-workers in the presence of the congregation about the Holy Spirit and the fruits of justification, he quoted the words of the Lord to Peter about the gates of hell not prevailing against the Church (Matthew 16[18-]) [29].

The deep joy he felt over the actualization of primitive Christianity did not blind him to the needs of the present. The constitution of the religious societies which he had taken over in the form drawn up by James Hutton failed to satisfy him at several points. The way was open to deviate from the style of the German Herrnhuters in accordance with a deeply felt Anglican sentiment. It was of secondary importance whether the women were to take part in the general meeting or meet together separately in order to prevent unsavoury gossip. Wesley agreed, after initial difference of opinion, with

Hutton's separation of the sexes. What was more fundamental was the position of the 'monitors' in the bands. Wesley objected to these as a separate office by saying simply, 'Every man in my band is my monitor, and I his.' As a result he developed the band-idea differently from his Herrnhut guides. The basic principle which he expressly put into effect was the mutual responsibility which no one could transfer to, or take from, another. To reprove one another was a commandment of God, and it applied to all. To confine this action to particular people would contradict the commandment and restrict the freedom with which Christians ought to deal with one another. Wesley could support his point of view by referring to the occasion when he had been reproved in Savannah by the Salzburg Pastor Boltzius, although his own properly appointed 'monitor' had said nothing. If however it should be urged from the Herrnhut side that there must be a particular monitor appointed by God as having authority over all, such a person already exists in the regularly constituted priest or deacon of the Church. When there was any question of limiting formal obedience to the Church of England John Wesley firmly acknowledged the classical Anglican position that bishops, priests and deacons are of divine appointment and that at this point the agreement with the national and the primitive Church must be unconditionally preserved. He recognized quite clearly the difference in the point of view of the German Brethren.[30]

Thus in this connexion also there is a foreshadowing of future developments. John Wesley was opposed to any influence which pointed in the direction of a free church. Faced with the choice he would forego his connexion with the Moravians rather than his allegiance to Anglicanism. It is remarkable how early all later developments were anticipated. Just as his evangelistic work in the religious societies in London and Oxford comprised those essential characteristics which were repeated later in his great life's work, so the decision he made in this particular discussion anticipated his attitude in the future.

He was still completely occupied with his duties in London when a letter reached him at the end of March 1739 from the 25-year-old George Whitefield, who urged him to come to Bristol, then the second city in England. Whitefield had gone there on 14th February while on his journey given to preaching and collecting money; it was near his own home, and his sister actually lived there. He had tried to get permission to preach in the great church of St Mary Redcliffe, whose Gothic splendour was to lead the young Thomas Chatterton at the end of the century to rediscover the Middle Ages and to introduce the English romantic period. Whitefield had been refused the licence to preach because the reports of his somewhat over-excitable and aggressive manner made the clergymen of the city hesitant. As a result, with the radicalism of youth, he had gone to the other extreme, turning to prison work and joining himself to the religious societies. His passionate style led to unexpected results, especially in nearby Kingswood among the coal-miners, who were regarded as the heathen savages of England.[31] On 17th February 1739, out of affection for them, he preached in bitter cold on the plain called Hanham Mount to about 200 listeners so movingly that many were in tears. This unheard-of action and its unexpected success for a time opened to him several churches in the city, including St Mary Redcliffe, but by the end of the month they were again closed to him. Field-preaching recalled Cromwell's revolutionary period, which nobody wished to see returning. Whitefield himself was pressing on with his companion William Seward to Wales, and for this reason wanted a successor for Bristol because he said many were ready to become members of bands. John Wesley was taken completely by surprise at the invitation, and it could scarcely have come at a more inopportune time. In addition to his full programme in London he was troubled by his health, often feeling so weak that the thought of death pressed in on him. His brother Charles felt the same hesitation about this new task. Nevertheless in obedience to the rules, which he took very seriously,[32] John laid the letter before the society in Fetter Lane, so that they might decide about the journey. They cast lots and the answer came in the affirmative; the Bible texts which they consulted spoke of persecution and suffering; hence he left the capital on 29th March on horseback and in the evening of the 31st he met Whitefield in Bristol.

At that time the city had 30,000 inhabitants, while London had almost twenty times as many, so great was the difference between it and every other centre of population. Bristol could boast that in June 1497 it had been the place of departure for those who had first planted the British flag on North American soil—a year before Columbus reached the continent. Because of its trade with the New World it continued steadily to expand. Since the Peace of Utrecht

(1713), which significantly had been concluded on the British side by the Bishop of Bristol, Dr John Robinson, acting for the government, Great Britain had been awarded the monopoly of supplying the Spanish colonies with negroes, and Bristol was chief port for this trade. It bordered on the counties of Somerset and Gloucestershire, and this gave it at the same time the character of a country-town with busy markets. On the high ground in the neighbouring villages of Kingswood and Brislington there had been during the last hundred years a growing number of coalmines which belonged to private owners, who, in contrast to the Continent, had according to British law the mining rights also.

The living conditions of the miners were the worst in the land. A deep gulf separated them not only from their masters but also from the rest of the population; they could look upon themselves as the lepers of the eighteenth century. To be sure the great industrial revolution was still to come, but it threw its shadows backwards over these miners, and looked forward to the age of coal and the rise of the proletariat. So Bristol was a combination of a growing city with overseas connexions, a continuing rural and provincial centre, and a growing proletariat. This unique mixture, reflected in a harbour which was continually being enlarged and always overcrowded, until it reached right into the market-place and the narrow streets, dirtied by rain and mostly blocked by country-carts, gave to the city a peculiar attraction, enhanced by its surrounding hilly landscape. At the same time it was still enclosed within medieval walls. In every way it was a most interesting place, and this applied also to its ecclesiastical constitution. But Bristol was not a stronghold of the Church of England. The bishopric is still the lowest endowed in the country, and it invited its occupant to change quickly for another or to take an additional office. Between 1718 and 1738 Bristol had had seven bishops. Amongst them was Thomas Secker, later Archbishop of Canterbury, who during his short stay in Bristol also had a prebend in far-away Durham and a living in the city of Westminster. His successor, Sir Thomas Gooch, was even richer: he held a prebend at Canterbury and another at Chichester, where he was also director of the famous old people's home, St Mary's Hospital. In the Middle Ages the Benedictine monks had received permission to erect a market, and had accordingly determined the commercial character of the city. The business folk represented a new and growing class, a liberal, industrious group of citizens who for personal and external reasons tended towards nonconformity. From an ecclesiastical point of view the city was significant because in the seventeenth century the Quakers became well established in it. Less than a hundred years before James Naylor had made his entrance into the city as King of Zion. During the Civil War under Cromwell the passions of the opposing parties had reached their climax, but then came the time of revenge in the early period of the Restoration. The Glorious Revolution under William of Orange again aroused deep conflicts between the majority of the population, who supported the new order, and their Jacobite opponents, the fanatical partisans of the Stuarts. The Baptists opened in the city their first and most important teaching institution on English soil. The sea-port attracted the usual vices, amongst which drunkenness was the most common; but it also aroused a powerful determination to guard against these curses and to improve things. It was a place full of fruitful tensions; it was also predominantly youthful.[33]

As usual John Wesley used the ride to Bristol to speak of the Gospel on the journey and in the hostels, but not without opposition from his fellow-travellers, an opposition he resolutely refuted. In the city itself he naturally went first to Whitefield's evening devotional meeting, where about 100 people met in the Weavers' Hall. Afterwards that night the two men held a long discussion on the rights and wrongs of preaching in the open-air. At first Wesley was not convinced; his strong sense of order and his devotion to the Church of England detected an ominous and revolutionary step. On the other hand he did not oppose his young friend whom he greatly admired and he accompanied him on the following Sunday morning and afternoon to hear him preach at the Bowling Green, Hanham Mount and Rose Green, where the congregation was extremely large. When on the midday of Monday 2nd April Whitefield left Bristol and left Wesley alone to continue his work, Wesley expressed the hope that, in the words of the prophet Elisha, a part of his spirit might be given to him.[34] On the Sunday evening Whitefield had preached to a society in Baldwin Street, where the crowd was so great that it was only with the help of a guide that he had been able to get into the room over the tiling of the next house. At the same time Wesley was with another smaller society in Nicholas Street, where he expounded the Sermon on the Mount, which struck him immediately as a powerful precedent of field-preaching.[35] During the following days he began to do the same thing himself, and this was in addition to his daily morning-service at Newgate, the keeper of which was one of Whitefield's first converts. Naturally the number of his listeners did not equal those of his young associate, yet it did run into thousands. It is significant that during these days he used the Epistle to the Romans and the parable of the Pharisee and the Publican,[36] showing that he was preoccupied with the theme of sin and forgiveness. He preached in the same places as Whitefield, and occasionally visited Bath also; at the same time he went to the prison and the society in Baldwin Street, where Whitefield had preached his last sermon. Under Wesley's leadership new societies and bands were formed, in which men and women from differing walks of life joined together, although the majority were either tradesmen or women. Among the men there was a doctor, a small business man, a haberdasher, a carpenter, and a distiller. Once again there were cases of nervous excitement, tremblings, outcries and fainting fits among men and women, but after continuing prayer by the congregation the individuals entered into the freeing experience of the joy of sins forgiven.[37] These manifestations showed themselves especially in the Newgate prison, where the offer of the free grace of God for all sinners broke through the curse of hopelessness. In another meeting a physician who was present expressed his doubts about these attacks, but admitted that he was convinced when he actually witnessed someone set free. A Quaker who thought that what he saw was all dissimulation, himself fell down as if thunderstruck, and then cried out, 'Now I know that thou art a prophet of the Lord.'

But the greatest impression was no doubt that created by the weaver, John Haydon, who tried to persuade all his acquaintances that these things were a temptation of the devil, and who while reading John Wesley's great sermon on 'Salvation by Faith'—not in a meeting but in his house, where his being alone excluded all possibility of his being affected by others—underwent so violent an attack that his neighbours hurried to help. His wife would have kept them out, but he cried, 'No; let them all come; let all the world see the just judgement of God!' When John Wesley himself went in the man immediately turned to him, confessed that he had been guilty of a devilish delusion, and spoke to the demon which possessed him and which he felt weaken before Jesus the conqueror.[38] Again

Wesley experienced something similar in Bristol. At a meeting on 21st May 1739, a young man fell to the ground, thrown hither and thither as if shaken by the devil, so that even six men could not hold him. His name was Thomas Maxfield and he later became a leading Methodist lay-preacher; but through his wilfulness he was also to bring Wesley a lot of trouble. In this instance too and in the future Wesley entertained a sober reserve about these attacks. He emphasized that they were no more signs of God's favour than were dreams or visions, yet they must be accepted as facts. They are probably to be seen as peculiar to the time, since they were experienced all over Europe and America by the newly converted, that is by those who were convinced of their sins. Therefore Wesley said that he neither encouraged nor hindered them.[39] He often went to the city Poorhouse, where people worked, and where hundreds crowded inside and even more outside. Even pouring rain could scarcely affect the numbers. Once in Bath they did not expect him because of the wet, and so he says he had 'only' a thousand or twelve hundred listeners,[40] and he was not fatigued by preaching three or four times on the same day.

The excitable manifestations in his meetings brought him many cautions, not least from his elder brother Samuel, the schoolmaster in Devon. John Wesley felt himself under an obligation to recognize the facts which had happened before his own eyes, and wrote back to him in a manner which showed that he had to acknowledge their reality. He could not get away from the fact that the people he had met had been fundamentally changed. A drunkard had become sober, a violent lion a lamb, a whoremonger a moral man. But he also relentlessly pursued his questioning and asked why God permitted such ecstasies, finding the answer in the point that they happened because the hardness of men's hearts requires such sensible signs. God condescends to the weakness of his creatures.[41]

The content of Wesley's message was always the same. Almost without exception he preached Jesus Christ as wisdom and righteousness, sanctification and salvation. He could well have applied to himself Paul's word that he knew nothing but Jesus Christ and Him crucified, and he felt as he expounded the second chapter of Acts the power of the early Christian community life to be so near that he thought it must be felt even by those who heard it unwillingly.[42] On one occasion he preached in Pensford near Bristol in a brickyard on the words, 'The hour is coming, and now is, when the dead shall hear the voice of the Son of Man, and they that hear shall live' (John 5[25]), the very words which he had expounded a year before in the chapel of Lincoln College in Oxford, and to the record of which in his *Journal* he had added the comment, 'I see the promise; but it is afar off.'[43]

A little over a month after he began field-preaching Wesley took the opportunity which came to him of securing a new place in the Horsefair in the middle of the city. This was a piece of ground on which the 'New Room' was to be built, and which was to be *the* centre of the work in and around Bristol. The early Christian open-air preaching, which produced such unexpected results, was never intended to be the normal way of proclaiming the Gospel, and probably not even the predominant way. Whitefield had already built the ground-floor of a house in Kingswood, although this was not in the first instance intended as a room but a school, where the children of the poor colliers, as well as adults, might receive instruction.[44] This was in line with the practices of the religious societies, who through the Society for Promoting Christian Knowledge had started a great movement for the establishment of schools for the poor. Now the New Room was to combine both; it was to be a room for the two separated religious societies which met in Nicholas Street and Baldwin Street, and for a school. John Wesley himself wished to have nothing to do with its construction and financing, and had left both matters to a board of eleven trustees selected by himself; but it was soon evident that this was impossible. The debt, which he had to transfer immediately to his own name, amounted to four times the sum promised, and his friends in London, especially Whitefield, pressed him to discharge the trustees; otherwise they would not agree to contribute towards the building. So the whole affair devolved upon him personally, and it is possible to see here the historical beginning of that personal leadership which he increasingly came to accept and maintain in his movement. His whole background led him to prefer common action rather than individual assertion; up until this moment he had not started anything on his own initiative. His most significant decision, the mission to the heathen in Georgia, had been discussed in the student group, and even then had been undertaken only because he was able to take with him three companions. When they lay off Cowes in the Isle of Wight on the voyage to America the four friends had made a solemn vow to take no step independently but to refer everything to a common decision, and if there was no clear majority, to consult the lot.[45] Hence John Wesley had been able to submit to such a stern discipline as that demanded by the rules of the Fetter Lane society. Now however the building of the New Room required that he must for the first time stand completely on his own; and this he did. Like August Hermann Francke he relied upon God to provide him with the means, and after one month it was possible to hold the first meeting in the unfinished building. On this occasion the new hymn book of 1739 first came into use. The rapidity with which it was built made its reconstruction necessary in the year 1748.[46]

Near Bristol lay Kingswood, the home of the depressed coal-miners. They were notorious on account of their brutality, drunkenness, ignorance and filthiness. According to many contemporaries they lived more like animals, without any awareness of a higher existence. Whitefield's and Wesley's sermons in the open-air, which at first were regarded merely as sensational diversions, brought about a complete change. After about a year scarcely any swearing was heard, and drunkenness was no longer the order of the day. Where once men had bitterly quarrelled and fought, there was now peace, love and discipline. Obviously they regarded it as quite remarkable that anyone should concern themselves over them, and it is recorded that they were so affected that tears ran down their faces as John Wesley preached to them the love of God and the forgiveness of their sins. A school for poor children was built by the Methodists as a centre for their work, and watch-night services after the early Christian pattern were held in it as counter-attractions to the nights of debauchery in the tavern.[47]

The spiritual content of the work became more defined as the external characteristics developed. On 26th April 1739 John Wesley for the first time touched upon the critical subject of predestination and reprobation when preaching to the prisoners at Newgate, and he repeated it on the following Sunday, the 29th, at the Bowling Green in Clifton. On the first occasion the listeners were deeply affected, and some of them passed through the familiar experience of fear to a sense of freedom. When Wesley asked his friend Purdy whether he should continue to speak on the subject, the lot was consulted and they received the answer: 'Preach and print!' It is apparent that the use of the lot meant that they did not confine themselves to biblical texts, but made a free choice between various alternatives. A few days previously Wesley had received a long anonymous letter which branded him a false teacher who denied predestination—even although he could not remember having yet spoken about it! So everything turned upon one definite point, and the signs were that there would be a struggle. His emphasis upon the unconditional love of God, which he was fond of concluding from 1 Corinthians 13 or from the word of Jesus: 'The Son of Man is not come to destroy men's lives, but to save them', brought forth opposition. He had to defend treating the subject to James Hutton, since his friends, especially Whitefield, had agreed not to mention it in Bristol. But then he met Howell Harris, the unattached evangelist from Wales, who had already begun a revival there at the time of his voyage to Georgia. He was a determined advocate of an extreme doctrine of predestination. Surprisingly he declared himself in cordial agreement with Wesley after he had heard him preach, although the subject had not been the controversial point at issue.[48]

The dispute centred around a single article of doctrine, but John Wesley's authority in general was attacked, although at first to be sure by an outsider. There was indeed the instance when during the first days he had written of how the Bristol clergy opposed him, 'aiming at us with gladiatorial intent'. But when the churches in general—with exceptions such as Clifton—were closed to him, quiet reigned, and the great movement was able to develop without hindrance in the meeting-places of the religious societies and in the open air. It was in Bath on 5th June 1739, and not in Bristol, that one of the first hostile encounters occurred. He met Beau Nash, the director of gaming and entertainments, now 65 years of age, who after an adventurous career had made the city wealthy and fashionable. He intended to charge the young disturber of the peace under the Conventicle Act passed during the period of the Restoration (1664), but John Wesley reduced him to embarrassment and won the day. Nash had accused him of causing a seditious assembly, but Wesley denied this and inquired of him in return whether he had ever heard him preach. When Nash answered in the negative Wesley pronounced him incapable of passing judgement; after pausing for a while Nash said that he wished to know why these people came there, and received the answer that he cared for their bodies but that they came for food for their souls.[49]

Yet the opposition was not always so ineffective. At the earnest request of his London friends on 11th June Wesley left Bristol for a week and returned to them, still deeply under the influence of the unusual depth of feeling which he had found in his new sphere of work. In London he immediately encountered greater opposition, for he had to try and settle the differences in which the Fetter Lane Society was embroiled. In London too he preached before a great crowd, although a number turned away from him. He was attracted again to the virgin soil of Bristol, where joy was predominant. Certainly on his return he found some troubles there, but under the influence of his personality and by united prayer they were almost immediately resolved.[50]

Certain differences which had become evident in his conversations in London appeared more sharply and painfully in correspondence. This was the case with his one-time Oxford pupil and friend, James Hervey, who had so admired him when he went to Georgia. Going to the heathen had seemed to him at the time like Noah coming out of the ark, since a new country lay before both of them, full of promise but also of uncertainty. Everything which he, Hervey, was or had, he ascribed to Wesley's great example, and as late as the year 1747 he praised the kindness which the learned Fellow had shown towards his simple students. After Wesley's return from Georgia and Herrnhut Hervey had been perplexed by reports concerning Wesley's teaching about the sufficiency of faith without works and also concerning his alleged disregard for the ministerial office by the use of lay preachers. Now he asked Wesley quite correctly how his unrestricted activity could be reconciled with the prescribed parish ministry of the pastoral organization of the Church of England. A much more important issue in fact lay behind his question, and this was the deeply-felt Anglican historical consciousness, which in its realistic attachment to the order of creation held to the historical procedure as an essential ingredient of the mission of Christianity.[51] John Wesley replied in a letter which has become famous because it includes the sentence, 'I look upon all the world as my parish.'[52] The limits which Hervey would have wished him to acknowledge Wesley regarded as man-made, whereas his commission to instruct the ignorant, to summon the wicked to turn, and to strengthen the believers, came from God. Wesley was supported in his attitude by some of the strongest words from the early Church: 'We ought to obey God rather than men' (Acts 5[29]) and 'Necessity is laid upon me;

yea, woe is unto me, if I preach not the gospel!' (1 Corinthians 9[16]). In view of this radical obligation what is to be said about the tidy division of the world's inhabitants, both Christian and pagan, into distinct ecclesiastical units? The answer is that Wesley saw the whole world as his parish. This does not mean, as might popularly be supposed, that he had the right to go to properly appointed clerical administrative bodies and seduce their members from allegiance to their church; it implies rather that wherever he might be he ought to be living witness to the good news. In Wesley's view ordination did not confine a man to any definite place or to one distinct congregation, but that it was essentially universal. It was bound up with mission, and to this extent the idea of mission had from his Georgia days determined his understanding of the pastoral office. The congregation was a mission-field and a mission-congregation, because the situation of 'the old man' before acceptance of the gospel-message was in no way different from that of the heathen; both stood in need of the same 'new birth'.[53] Of course he was himself in an unusually favourable position, for Dr Potter, the Bishop of Oxford, who ordained him, expressly stated as early as 1734–5 that ordination did not authorize him to exercise the ministerial office within a particular congregation, and his College, to which Hervey referred as his natural sphere, did not need him in this capacity. Accordingly he was free to preach where he wished, and he interpreted this freedom as an opportunity for reviving the office of the primitive travelling apostolate. The basic endeavour of his whole life, namely that of making primitive Christianity contemporary, once again came into play. When Hervey objected that by so doing he encouraged evil reports against himself he asked in return if he had forgotten that the disciples of Jesus were to be hated by everyone for His Name's sake.

In this manner Wesley overcame one kind of authority by another; the content of the commission claimed precedence over the manner in which it was carried out, the charismatic idea of the Church gained the victory over the legalistic. A distinction was made such as has arisen time and again in the history of the Church, such as for example the early Christian tension between spirit and office, the rivalry between monasticism and the regular ministry in east and west, and the Reformation critique of the canonical Church, or Pietism's encounter with orthodoxy.

The course the problems were to take soon became evident. Back in the autumn of 1738, on 8th October, John and Charles Wesley had been cross-examined by the Bishop of London, Edmund Gibson; the questioning had been conducted in a very friendly way. Among the various complaints which had been openly made against the Methodists were questions of both doctrine and order, typical of genuine Anglicanism. The 70-year-old bishop had scarcely any reservations about assurance and justification by faith as taught by the two brothers, but as one with a good knowledge of canon law he rejected baptism, mostly of adults, when it had already taken place in one of the nonconformist churches. He gave it as his opinion that the religious societies were not conventicles in the sense of the Conventicle Act, and assured the brothers that an accusation against them would have to be based upon the witness of at least two or three persons. Finally he dismissed them with the assurance that they had at any time free access to him.[54] On 21st February 1739, in connexion with an audience with the Archbishop of Canterbury at Lambeth Palace, a second conversation with the Bishop of London took place. The archbishop, Dr John Potter, who as Bishop of Oxford had ordained the Wesley brothers, was very friendly. In a fatherly way he admonished them about their manner of expressing things, warned them to keep to the doctrines of the Church and professed his own allegiance to justification by faith. In a similar way the Bishop of London warned them against antinomianism and complete rejection of law.[55] But the matter did not rest in this favourable state. The first definite rejection from the Anglican side, which arose from deep mistrust, was James Hervey's letter, which led to a cooling-off of the concord between them. Islington Church in London was refused the brothers, and it is probable that the Bishop of London, once so well-disposed, was behind this. But the real crisis came in Bristol, for the suspicious signs noticeably increased there. During the same week in which John Wesley was in London an event took place which went contrary to Anglican feeling and which was fatally reminiscent of the disorder of the Cromwellian revolution. An enthusiastic member of the religious societies, John Cennick, a layman from Reading,[56] had responded to an invitation to preach to the coal-miners, and both preacher and hearers had a good time. It was soon urged that the Lord's Supper should be celebrated in the meetings. Both lay-preaching and lay administration of the sacrament appeared to threaten the whole structure of Anglican Church order.

31

The reports of the misdemeanours in the meetings went further. It is not surprising that a serious situation was created, and on 3rd June 1739, John Wesley's permission to preach in Newgate Gaol was withdrawn. There is no doubt that this was due to the interposition of the bishop. On 16th August 1739, Wesley came face to face with him for the first time.

Joseph Butler, who was then 47 years of age, had been bishop for one year. His father was a tradesman, a draper from Wantage in Berkshire, not far from Oxford, who belonged to the Presbyterian Church. Like John Wesley's father Butler's son received a liberal education in two dissenting academies, an education which included natural science.[57] He soon developed an independence in spiritual matters. As a 21-year-old student he carried on a personal conflict against the celebrated theologian of the early Enlightenment, Samuel Clarke (1675–1729), the founder of a rationalistic supranaturalism, who strove to defend the truths of the Christian faith by natural reason. Butler's opposition greatly impressed his contemporaries, and he was recognized as a worthy adversary by his opponent. He brought the same critical faculty to his own nonconformist theological position and like Wesley's father reached the point where he rejected it and went over to the Church of England. At the age of 22 he went up to Oriel College, Oxford. His sermons are very few. Renouncing simplicity and attractiveness of presentation they set forth abstract arguments around the important points. Accordingly they not only won the approval of his own age; they also attained a position not since reached by any literature of this kind. They are philosophical classics and have maintained this position into the twentieth century. Prominent Englishmen during the nineteenth century, in spite of fundamental differences between them, were one in the praise of these sermons; people like John Henry Newman, who revived Anglo-Catholicism, John Stuart Mill, the utilitarian moralist, and William Ewart Gladstone, the Liberal statesman, who occupied his leisure hours with reflections on theological subjects. The sermons reached only a restricted number of people, and were probably more read than listened to. The precision and meticulous character of their style was in keeping with the requirements of the time. The deist criticism of traditional Christianity, which radically removed what could not measure up to their idea of what constituted natural religion, demanded a frank and powerful demonstrative method. After the young scholar had so successfully entered the lists against Samuel Clarke much could be expected of him when he crossed swords with the Deists. In contrast to John Wesley's father he was highly gifted as a constructive philosopher. His ecclesiastical awareness was entirely subordinated to his intellectual purposes. Butler was quite free from that fanaticism in condemning his past allegiance which the elder Samuel Wesley at least sometimes showed.[58]

His major work, *The Analogy of Religion according to the Course and Constitution of Nature* (1736), led to his appointment as private secretary to Queen Caroline. This exalted lady, who followed the religious movements of the time with extraordinary understanding and zeal, allowed the young celebrity in the last year of her life to give her a philosophical grounding in, and interpretation of, the truth of the Christian religion. Butler knew how to marshal a wealth of ideas in a strict and at the same time unpretentious way, while keeping his readers' attention fixed inexorably upon the problem. He left no gaps in his argument and he anticipated all possible objections. The book may well claim to be the most conclusive demonstration of the idea of analogy between the temporal and the eternal world, and between experience and reason on the one side and revelation on the other. It is one of the great examples of a theology of synthesis. In line with natural theology it began with the immortality of the soul, and sought to demonstrate its probability, not only by observations from the transformations which take place in the world of plants and animals, but also from the psychological consideration that when an elderly man looks back to his youth he sees it as a completely different world in which he himself nevertheless remains the same.[59] In a similar way the observation that well-being and discomfort are dependent upon his behaviour should point to the moral order of the eternal world, where virtue and happiness finally go together.[60] An important place is occupied in Butler's argument by the unresolved enigma of human knowledge, and this indicates the necessity of revelation and miracles. Therefore the declarations of the Christian faith are not to be limited to those of natural religion, as the representative of the Deists, Matthew Tindal, desired, but on the contrary the limitations of natural religion demonstrate the truth of revealed religion. It is the Christian faith which gives support and meaning to natural religion. The same relationship, which Thomas Aquinas demonstrated in classical manner between reason and revelation, appears in the form of gradations, in which the one is referred to the other in a relationship in which both are intimately bound together, but in which the content of revelation receives the greater emphasis. Butler's method was enriched by the new discoveries of natural science, but at the same time it was hampered by being confined to the Deists' polemical statement of the problems. It was from the start forced to be somewhat superficial, since the whole problem was conceived as taking the form of an intellectual exercise in logical deduction. Since it left out of consideration the fact of sin it discovered everywhere parallelism and continuity, and was not able properly to take into consideration discontinuity and contradiction.[61]

The greatness of Butler lay in his caution. He did not aim at exact proof, such as his mathematical and scientific age required, but he was satisfied with probability, uncertainty and suggestiveness;[62] he did not break with tradition but contributed towards the affirmation of it in a refined form. Analogy provided him with the essential point of his thought. The careful trustworthiness of the movement of his thinking, the cosmological breadth of his viewpoint, and the moral energy of his spiritual purpose were directly typical of the British character. All his writings inspired confidence. The effect of his work rested upon the fact that he inverted the relationship between revealed and natural religion and once again gave precedence to the former, as did Schleiermacher two generations later in his *Discourses on Religion addressed to its Cultured Despisers*, although the later man was of course less sympathetic to natural religion. Butler was able to put an end to the disquiet which the Deists had introduced into the period, because he introduced once again a sense of proportion. Naturally the shortcomings in his attempt were even greater than those which later adhered to that of the German theologian. Because he failed to perceive that sin was the essential fact in the human situation he was not really able fully to incorporate into his system the redeeming work and mediatorship of Jesus Christ, although he of course held fast to them himself. Accordingly, as in his sermons, conscience and moral responsibility occupied the central place.[63] In the message of salvation moral education leading to the goal of perfection was the principal point. The teleological standpoint which was part of the principle of analogy governed the whole presentation.

Thus Butler was a significant but essentially solitary figure, a thinker rather than an orator, not at all disposed to any personal fame or show, one who concentrated entirely upon the matter in hand, guided by prudence. Consequently he was devoted to the well-being of his dioceses, by no means only a retiring scholar but a spiritual and ecclesiastical leader in the best tradition of Anglicanism. He did not conform to the image of the time either by the grandeur of his bearing or in the cultivation of the Court or political affairs.[64] Would this man, who held none of the usual prejudices of the Church of England against nonconformity, show understanding for John Wesley, eleven years younger than himself, or would he dismiss him as an excitable preacher from an insignificant sect? Would the sensational success of the little tyro make this bishop, the man who understood how to put presumptuous claims into simple words, distrustful towards him?

Their conversation, which John Wesley did not include in his *Journal*, is recorded only fragmentarily in a note which he wrote. Apparently from the first it proceeded unsatisfactorily. Wesley seems to have started straightway with his main interest, justification by faith alone. This meant nothing to the bishop, and he found the subject an embarrassment, which he unsuccessfully concealed with the usual objections raised in the Enlightenment. The words justification and faith do not appear at all in either his *Analogy* or his *Sermons*. He therefore argued that if God should declare the sinner free when he has nothing to show except his misery, then He is acting arbitrarily. Ideas of this kind make Him into a tyrannical Being. Faith, which Butler understood in the sense of the medieval, scholastic tradition exclusively as a human virtue, is seen rather as a good work. The distinction between faith and works therefore actually prevents any serious consideration of the relationship between God and man. Butler's inability to appreciate the Reformation way of stating the problem gave Wesley a trump card; he was able to hold against Butler the Homilies of the Church of England, with their strong Reformed emphasis, and with which the bishop was obviously not familiar. So he abruptly ended discussion of this point, and charged Wesley with possessing the arrogant self-assurance of George Whitefield, who maintained that the promises were to be fulfilled in his own person. Wesley found it easy to dissociate himself from responsibility for the utterances of his fellow-worker, and the bishop's added warning against claiming special revelations and spiritual gifts did not really apply. The conversation then turned to the administration of the sacrament in the meetings and the paroxysms suffered by some of the members. Wesley dismissed the first objection as untrue.[65] As to the second he replied that through prayer he was often able to control such manifestations. At this point the bishop found himself on familiar ground; he repeated his warning against claiming extraordinary divine powers and abruptly dismissed Wesley from his diocese. Following the Anglican tradition he was moved to reject the Donatist view that the efficacy of ecclesiastical action is dependent upon the condition of the holder of office, taking the view that it is not the minister but the office of the ministry which is determinative. "Wesley met him with the same arguments which three months previously he had used against his friend James Hervey. Following 1 Corinthians 9[16] he claimed that he was under an obligation to preach the Gospel, and in addition that he did not contravene any ecclesiastical discipline, since as a Fellow of a College he was not bound as a preacher to any one congregation, but held a commission in the Church of England as a whole. The similarity to Luther's reliance upon his doctorate as giving him the right to teach in the Church at large is clear.[67] Faced with the sharpness of the bishop's attitude Wesley brought his reply finally to the point of Peter's question as to whether he should obey God or man.[68]

After this somewhat violent encounter both men were ready and determined not to trouble each other any further.[69] So the most able bishop in the Church of England and the leader of its coming great movement for renewal separated from each other and went their different ways, without ever really having come in sight of one another. It may be that on Butler's side there was an element of disdain, strengthened by irritation with an embarrassing subject; and on Wesley's side there was a narrowness caused by his recognizing the importance of only one question. In spite of all the unfortunate misunderstanding in the circumstances and the shortsightedness in the way the conversation went, it must not be overlooked that two fundamentally different points of view were meeting each other, and that accordingly it was understandable that John Wesley should immediately raise, in the question of justification by faith, the irreconcilable opposition between God's offer of grace and the moralism of the natural man. The scholarly bishop's failure to understand the heart of the Pauline message was a failure of the period as a whole. There was a conflict between the theology of a divine-human correspondence and the biblical one of an invasion of grace;

and such a conflict was necessary in order to determine the form of preaching in the Church of England.[70] So the little scene had a significance for the history of the Church as a whole. It was a dialogue which the eighteenth century held with primitive Christianity, although not of course a genuine dialogue, since it really consisted of two monologues. It lacked any real effort at conciliation, and therefore the true possibility of persuasion. It resembled rather a cross-examination of an accused by an accuser with the latter desiring only the corroboration of his position. The spirit of the eighteenth century, which spoke through Butler, remained unchanged, with the same self-assurance as that of primitive Christianity, whose spokesman Wesley was. Neither was able to come to terms with the other, and even Wesley failed to do real justice to the problem, although, since he represented the biblical point of view, he had the greater right on his side.

The bishop was not alone during the discussion. Among those clergy who attended on him, such as the dean, the chancellor and the chaplain, the young clergyman Josiah Tucker stood out; he was later to make a name for himself for a synthesis, characteristic of the Enlightenment, between theology and political economy. Two years later Butler commissioned him to write an anti-Methodist polemic, which turned out to be of a more dogmatic character than was customary in England. This also indicated how little Butler was himself inclined to give his own attention to the principles of the Methodists. On the other hand he showed his desire for justice, since Tucker was originally friendly towards Methodism.

Shortly afterwards John Wesley left the city and returned to London, and his brother Charles replaced him. The adverse decision of the bishop could not stop the progress of the movement. An attempt in the municipal council to prohibit the religious societies did not secure the necessary majority. Bristol remained the first great success of the young movement. That success was seen far afield and implied that it would continue. Wesley's boldness led to his calling his friend and opponent James Hervey from the solitude of his country parish into the new area which was bearing such unexpected harvest. In this masterful way he gave his answer to the reproof which the former had administered to him for overstepping parish boundaries. In place of the controversy about fundamental principles, which he had not modulated, he now summoned the other, as Philip

37

had challenged the hesitant Nathaniel: 'Come and see!' (John 1[46]). Naturally Hervey retained his opposition to the new-fangled methods and was not prepared to admit that itinerant preaching was in line with the practice of the early Church: rather he found that at that time a settled congregational ministry was already indicated.[71] Anglicanism and Methodism, stability and hazardous enterprise, tradition and mission, were already being distinguished in the very close circle of friends in a way which was prophetic of the future.

The trouble which threatened the Methodist movement during these early days also determined the external circumstances of its leading personalities. As if shaken through a sieve they exchanged places. The same day on which John Wesley stood before Bishop Joseph Butler, George Whitefield left, renewed, for Georgia, leaving Charles Wesley alone in London. Unfortunately the latter was suffering from a deep depression, to which he was often subject. Accordingly he was moved to the more congenial atmosphere of Bristol, which gave promise of so rich a harvest, while John himself undertook the work in the capital. This strengthens the impression that from the first the direction of events lay to a surprising extent with Whitefield, that youthful and exuberant character. Was it not he who began the promising work in Bristol, who ventured into field-preaching, who started the school in Kingswood? Now once again it was his withdrawal which determined the further division of the work. Without doubt his removal from the English scene brought John Wesley into the position of leader. While in Bristol Wesley had accommodated himself to the opinions, proposals and arguments of his young friend, without being completely convinced by them, now he himself had to make the decisions and bear the responsibility for them all. Already one has the feeling that in the long run there was not room for both of them in the same movement.

His return to London brought John Wesley into close touch with his mother. We recall that she had remained somewhat cool towards his conversion experience, since she was under the influence of her eldest son, Samuel, who in the spirit of the age strongly repudiated John's attitude. The correspondence between the brothers had made a growing estrangement increasingly obvious, with the result that John in the end brought it to an end.[72] All the more must he have rejoiced that his mother had surprisingly come over to his side, because she had had an experience similar to his. It was characteristic of her loyalty to the Church that the experience came to her while she was receiving the sacrament: at the words of institution about the cup she had heard a direct word about the forgiveness of sins.[73] She then took up evangelistic work, and a distinguished personality, Selina, Countess of Huntingdon (1707–91), was associated with her. The Countess had her summer residence at Donnington Park in the north of England, not far from Birstall and Newcastle-on-Tyne, but in the winter she lived in London and visited the religious society in Fetter Lane. It is probable that she had been brought into association with Methodism and the Moravians for quite personal reasons. Benjamin Ingham, Wesley's friend who accompanied him to Georgia and who became the missionary to the Indians, had on 12th November 1741 married the sister of the Countess's husband, although she was socially his superior and twelve years older than he. The evangelistic work which, presumably on a small scale, he did in the neighbourhood of Birstall, was shared by his wife. She also seems to have won the co-operation in this of her sister-in-law, who in turn stimulated John Wesley to extend his activity to the coal-miners around Newcastle-on-Tyne.[74]

Two great tasks awaited him in London. He had to regulate his relationship with the Moravians and to establish a new centre in the great city. These tasks were closely connected; the new centre for the work was necessary because the fellowship with the Moravians was breaking up. But the second task was the easier. After an open-air gathering on 11th November 1739, at which Wesley estimated there were 6,000 people, he came into possession of the old Foundery, a ruined building in Upper Moorfields. It was in a desolate working-class area, but it symbolized in a dramatic way the social mission of the Methodist movement. As early as 9th September thousands had assembled there.[75] To his great satisfaction his mother and his sister Emily, who had already returned into the family as a widow, were able to find a modest accommodation in the building.

The situation in the Fetter Lane Society was not very satisfactory, owing to pharisaic pride and lack of love. Wesley found it necessary to counsel loyalty to the Church, since many fondly believed themselves to have grown beyond it. Once again he succeeded in healing the schisms,[76] but soon afterwards there broke out the great dispute which led to the separation of the Methodists from the Moravians. After a short interval in Oxford, where he found only remnants of the once flourishing work,[77] and after an excursion into the mountainous region of Wales, the quiet beauty of which deeply affected him, although there was a pressing need of the people for evangelization,[78] he was able to turn to the Fetter Lane Society. When on 1st November 1739 he met a woman who had been a faithful member of the society there, he, to his dismay, heard her commending mystical 'stillness' and—in the manner of the Quakers—silent waiting upon the testimony of grace. This 'quietness' was not directed, as in the mystical tradition, against the manifold activities of everyday life, but as in Quietism of the French type, against the institutions and practices of the Church, worship, sacrament and bible-reading. None of these were to be used before true faith was present. Wesley recognized in these principles, which had been introduced into the Fetter Lane Society a short while before by a young Moravian from Alsace, Philipp Heinrich Molther, that dangerous tendency to separate from the Church which he always opposed with such vigour.[79] He was pained to discover that Spangenberg, his counsellor and confidant in Georgia, also shared these opinions. Having returned from the separatist groups in Pennsylvania, he accepted only too willingly the emphases which recalled his youth in Jena and Halle.[80] After Wesley had taken part in a meeting in which, awaiting the coming of grace, an hour of complete silence was kept, and after he had given himself time to assess the effect of these principles, he held a long conversation with Spangenberg on 7th November. It is noticeable from his account that he wished to find agreement as far as he possibly could. Common to them both was the desire for Christian perfection, but a difference immediately became evident. Wesley could not agree that a person should abstain from using any of the Church's means of grace until he possessed the full faith which frees him from sin. For Spangenberg and Molther this point of view, which was rejected by Wesley, was but another expression of the doctrine of justification. Stillness signified renunciation of one's own works, and in the tradition of mystical radicalism this became a normal feature in its piety. Wesley noticed that many people, especially women, had lost their faith or deliberately abandoned it as a result of such influences, or were at least thrown into great doubt. He tried by every possible means to put them to rights, and seizing upon the catchword he distinguished between true and false 'stillness'. On one occasion he refuted one of his friends, the Anglican clergyman George James Stonehouse of Islington, who maintained in accordance with Molther's theology that nobody has any faith until he is perfect, by means of the contrary testimony of Stonehouse's own servant. Wesley asked this servant, 'Esther, have you a clean heart?' She replied, 'No, my heart is desperately wicked; but I have no doubt or fear. I know my Saviour loves me, and I love Him; and I feel it every moment.' Wesley then turned to her master and said, 'Here is an end of your reasoning. This is the state the existence of which you deny.'[81]

Nevertheless he succeeded with only some of the members. The majority, under the leadership of James Hutton, Matthew Clarke, Thomas Bray and Edmonds, with Molther, Spangenberg and even Zinzendorf himself in the background, aimed at the establishment of a genuine Herrnhut church on English soil[82]—and then when this had been proved impossible, at embodying the spirit of the Moravians in the Church of England through the religious societies. During the following months no decision was reached, but on the last day of the year 1739 Molther and Wesley spoke with each other expressly about all aspects of the subject, and the latter wrote down the details as fully as he could. He perceived that the primary difference between them was over the conception of faith. Molther thought in dogmatic terms, even in a doctrinaire way, and recognized as full faith only that which involved the renewal of the whole man, whereas Wesley thought psychologically and spoke of degrees of faith as they were represented principally in the progression from justification to the indwelling of the Holy Spirit. He saw the work of the Spirit in the joy and consciousness of victory.[83] His view followed from his own experience and possessed an existential importance because of it; his conversion and what had preceded it and followed necessitated this, and accordingly could not be allowed to contradict it. Naturally, behind the dogmatic discussions personal ambitions were also at work. James Hutton wrote to Count Zinzendorf on 14th March 1740 that John Wesley wanted to do everything on his own and accordingly was bound to fall out with the Herrnhuters,[84] and an historical review of the development of the Herrnhut groups in England which was written in the year 1747, signed by the leading Moravians, Benjamin Ingham, John Gambold, John Cennick and Francis Okeley, stated that if only Molther had made room for John Wesley as head of the Fetter Lane Society, he would have been able to do anything with him.[85] This was certainly a misjudgement, but the Herrnhut party obviously saw things in this way, even though the document was written later and played down the real differences between the two groups. Molther must have gone on to maintain, always in Wesley's hearing, that previous to his arrival nobody in the Fetter Lane Society had true faith, while Wesley traced back the beginnings of true faith to the work of Peter Böhler. In Wesley's eyes the contrast was not between Molther and himself, but between Molther and Böhler. For him it was a matter of having to defend the classic Pauline-Lutheran ideas about justification, represented by Zinzendorf and Böhler against a Herrnhuter of the younger generation,[86] and of recognizing that the difference was in the opposition between a piety located in the Church and orientated in the Bible and prayer, and a free, solitary, silent mysticism. Corresponding to this there were differences in moral judgement. Wesley would have nothing to do with dishonesty in any form, while Molther considered that a measure of dissimulation in the cause of the propagation of the Gospel was allowable. Speaking the whole truth and half of the truth were contrasted with each other, but Wesley believed that he could appeal to Paul in defence of the principle of unreserved openness.[87] He fought for the right of those weak in the faith to be within the Church and supported his argument by the 'little faith' of the disciples, whom Jesus in no sense rejected. To him it seemed that Molther only cared for the strong. The attitude of pastoral responsibility and readiness to serve was set against a dogmatic one-sidedness; dynamic and static conceptions of perfection stood in opposition to each other.

During these debates John Wesley left the capital from time to time and returned to Bristol. On 8th December 1739 he went on a preaching-tour from there to Oxford, via Malmesbury and Burford. He visited Lincoln College and made use of his room, which was still at his disposal there. He was forcibly reminded that it was from it four years before that he had left for Georgia, and he began to think of all the things which had happened to him since. He was moved to open his New Testament. His eyes fell upon the closing verses of Romans 9: 'What shall we say then? That the Gentiles, which followed not after righteousness, have attained to righteousness, even the righteousness which is of faith. But Israel, which followed after the law of righteousness, hath not attained to the law of righteousness. Wherefore? Because they sought it not by faith, but as it were by the works of the law.' Wesley not only accepted the words as renewed confirmation of the Pauline justification doctrine, but also as a summons continually to reflect upon it, and to lay hold of it ever more persistently. So the words which still bound him to his missionary resolution of 1735 became full of significance for his missionary activity in his homeland and for theological understanding of the basic truth of his message. The following days immediately offered an occasion to pursue these thoughts further. A serious learned man came to him and maintained that the difference between holy and godless men was mere outward appearance. In reality all, the good and respectable, the dishonest and evil, are under the same con-demnation because they are both motivated by self-will, and a desire for wealth and applause determined their action, leading them to seek their life-fulfilment in this world. They had not experienced a genuine love for God, so that they were really equally far from Him. Wesley had to agree with him. In the matter of justification, which in virtue of other conversations he considered and formulated by himself alone, he sharply distinguished his own point of view from the prevailing opinion that faith and works must work together. At the same time he rejected the commonly held view that justification is a double act in which the first part takes place in the present and presupposes only faith, whilst the second is at the last day and requires works. But for John Wesley there was only *one* justification. It guaranteed final salvation now, it was received by faith alone, and faith was begotten only through grace.[88]

When he again stayed in London he took up the discussion once more with Molther, but without agreement coming any nearer. On the contrary the estrangement between them increased. Provocation between them led to the loss of all sense of proportion, and John Wesley was insulted as being a child of the devil and a servant of corruption, having eyes full of adultery and being unable to cease from sin.[89] The dispute was not confined to London. The most talented member of the former student circle in Oxford, John Gambold, who was now the clergyman at Stanton Harcourt near Oxford, had joined the group around Molther and Spangenberg, as had also Wesley's notoriously untrustworthy brother-in-law, Westley Hall, who probably only made use of the new situation to pursue the old hostility.[90] But even Benjamin Ingham was perhaps no longer quite certain. On 18th June 1740, he defended the ecclesiastical ordinances and the right of those weak in faith, but not long afterwards he strongly advocated 'stillness' in Molther's sense, but never really attached himself to the Moravians, although he handed over to them the religious societies he had gathered together.[91] Even Charles Wesley later dallied with quietism, if only fleetingly and probably under the influence of John Gambold, Westley Hall and Peter Böhler; he was quickly brought back by both the Countess of Huntingdon and his brother John.[92] Thus the mystical understanding of justification was widespread. It is certain that the early Methodist-Herrnhut movement was seriously threatened in its foundations and its leading personalities. Wesley preached incessantly against neglect of the means of grace and morality. His favourite topics were the Epistle of James, Jesus's attitude to the law, which He desired to fulfil, not destroy (Matthew 5[17]), His invitation to observe the sacrament in memory of Him, the words of the Epistles of John, which place love to Jesus alongside obedience to His commandments, and the warning of the Epistle to the Hebrews not to throw away their confidence.[93] Finally one day he discovered to his surprise that a woman had an old book about which she asked him, since it commended stillness and renunciation of ecclesiastical ordinances almost in Molther's words. It proved to be *The Mystic Divinity of Dionysius the Areopagite*.[94] Wesley straightway read an extract from it to the Fetter Lane Society and invited their judgement upon it. 'It is right; it is all right,' came the reply, and when he disputed this others supported him. In the further course of the debate someone wanted to prevent Wesley from preaching in the Fetter Lane room, using the threadbare argument that it was for the Germans' use. At this controversy broke out. Some asked whether the Germans had in fact converted a single person here in England and had not rather created dissension, the end of which could not be seen, and whether God did not use the much-abused John Wesley as His instrument to heal the discord when all were in confusion. At the word 'confusion' others again denied that it had ever been so among them. The dispute went on without any conclusion being reached until eleven o'clock at night, when Wesley left. This took place on 16th July 1740. The next day but one he took counsel with Benjamin Ingham and Selina, Countess of Huntingdon. All were clear that the critical moment had been reached and that some action was called for. The following Sunday, 20th July 1740, brought the decision, and John Wesley himself was responsible for it. During the evening meeting in Fetter Lane, which took the form of a 'love-feast', at which people shared their own personal experiences, he remained silent. At the close he read out a declaration, which once more set out the main points of the dispute, the alleged harmfulness of using the means of grace when faith is incomplete, which could only promote works-holiness, and the denial that there is such a thing as weak faith at all. He pointed out that for nine months he had borne patiently with this mystical perfectionism, but now it could go on no longer. All his admonitions and warnings had been without effect. He must now give over his opponents, in whom he could only see false doctrine, to God. Let those who were of the same opinion follow him. Without saying any more he left the meeting-place with eighteen or nineteen sympathizers. A week later his followers met in the old Foundery, after a Mr Chapman, returning from Germany, had brought back a communication for the Wesley brothers, instructing them to give over the pastoral care of souls to the Moravians.[95] It cannot be established whether or no this came from Zinzendorf.

In spite of this John Wesley had for long maintained his connexion even with his real opponent, Molther, and this extended to actual doctrinal questions. It is remarkable that Wesley submitted to him for examination and approval his translation of the hymn 'Now I have found the ground wherein, Sure my soul's anchor may remain', written by Johann Andreas Rothe, the Herrnhut minister of Berthelsdorf.[96]

Wesley was resolved to pursue the matter and accordingly wrote a long letter to Herrnhut on 8th August 1740,[97] where just two years before he had had so happy and rewarding a stay. It is noteworthy that he did not send to Zinzendorf in Marienborn; for he was disposed to acknowledge like the Moravians the primacy of the Count in his community. The letter was written with unusual care and shows how seriously Wesley regarded the dispute, how deliberately and comprehensively he considered the problems, and how earnestly he sought for clarity about the basic questions concerning salvation. But the letter was also a statement of inexorable precision and frank honesty. Wesley addressed himself first to the subject of salvation, then of faith and the way to it, then to the Moravians' understanding of the Church and its discipline, and finally to their attitude to the Mystics. This order was his own, and shows what was of greatest concern to himself. It was a matter of a *present* salvation, its content and the way to it. The Herrnhuters denied that salvation took away sins or set one free from evil thoughts or implied assurance of final acceptance in eternity. But it could mean for them freedom from God's commandments and the right to be conformed to the world as well as the avoidance of persecution, while a man who saw another's sins need not reprove them and he might exercise subtlety and dissimulation instead of free, open behaviour. Concerning faith some of the Herrnhuters said it was either possessed completely or not at all, or that a man might possess it without being aware of the fact. It might be obtained without using the Church's means of grace, such as the reading of Scripture, prayer, or sacrament. To seek salvation through these was work-righteousness, which runs contrary to justification. Faith is attained apart from works, and Jesus Christ has not ordained any means of grace in His Church; even had He done so they would not be binding, for a man is dead before he possesses full faith, and as such cannot do the smallest work. All his would-be activity rests upon self-deception. With regard to their understanding of the Church Wesley in the first place complained about the excessive self-assurance of the Moravians. They rank their fellowship high above all others, actually regarding it as infallible, and this leads to an unchristian contempt for other Churches. In fact their Church discipline is novel and contrary to the primitive pattern, for their bishops have declined into mere shadows, so that it must be concluded that their institution of this office will only deceive those Churches which give importance to it. In actual fact the Eldest— Count Zinzendorf himself—is their bishop, although he corresponds only to half of the pattern from the primitive Church. The offices of presbyter and deacon they have split up, the former into Lehrers, Aufsehers and Ermahners, the latter into Hilfers, Krankenwarters and Dieners. Their episcopal ordination does not in fact count for anything, since their constitution is really congregational, depending upon the community and not upon the office—although even then two main characteristics of it are not in conformity with this, namely, the disclaiming of any divine right for the system in general, and the position of the Count in particular. The power of his office may be compared with all the following added together: the bishops and priests in the ancient Church, the king and Convocation, the representatives of the clergy in the Church of England combined, the

General Assembly of the Presbyterian Church of Scotland, and the Roman Catholic Pope as well. In the whole history of ecclesiastical organization there is hardly another example of excess of episcopal, regal or papal power such as is exercised by the Count when, at the election of the Eldest, he causes the lot to be cast repeatedly if it has not favoured him.

In this judgement on the ecclesiastical order there speaks the convinced Anglican. Understandably enough the whole of his point of view was derived from his own circumstances. But although he could become so passionate in his argument his real concern was still the way in which salvation and faith were understood. Therefore he returned once again to this subject with the comprehensive objection that the Moravians saw in the Mystics—and particularly because he knew that the Anglican Church gave a high place to the Greek and Syrian monastic mystics in the ancient Church, he emphasizes the *modern Mystics*—the best interpreters of Scripture. Hence they are misled into making an unbiblical divorce between nature and grace, which not only makes them blind to the natural feeling of joy, but even weakens ordinary brotherly love and, worse still, throws suspicion upon all joy in the Holy Ghost and all sensible comforts from God. In this way they do despite to the simplicity of the new-born babes in Christ, who in their zeal are anxious to bear witness to others to the great things God has done in their lives. Their error is seen further in their veto on good works. Because these are to be done only where there is a particular inner urge so to do, they are not regarded as an integral part of the Christian life, and a believer is no more under any obligation to them than a subject of the King of England is to the law of the King of France. So Wesley concluded his letter. He then added a note drawing attention to the deliberate artless manner in which he had written. He had disclaimed all refinement of expression in order that the matter itself should stand out clearly. If his words created an effect, it ought not to be attributed to him but only to the power of God.

Even though this letter was written in such sharp terms it did not mean the end of their friendship. The reply from Marienborn which arrived a few weeks later[98] allayed some of his fears, but only some. He was pleased to learn that the disowning of the commandments by believers applied only to their character as commands; their actual content as promises for the new man remained as a description

47

of the believers' new situation, an indicative, with a future reference. On the other hand the distinction which the Herrnhuters, following Luther, drew between the spiritual and earthly realm—expressed by the celebrated doctrine of God's two 'kingdoms' and 'spheres of powers'—went right against Wesley's ideas. He could not allow that a man's conduct in his vocation, and above all in his work, ought to be determined by the state's authority, which would imply other than scriptural standards. It went right against his conviction that the attitude of the heart, which was the real concern of the Church, should not be open to question, and that a Christian acting in the Name of God could be content that all external activities should be the concern of the civil power. Such a point of view lay behind the fact that Zinzendorf preferred to 'discourse out of the newspaper than chatter about holy and spiritual things to no purpose', because 'a regular human action' has more value than 'misusing or taking the Name of God in vain'.[99] At this point the Count became extremely sharp, unnecessarily so with such a critic as Wesley. An important difference lay behind this. Almost all the objections which Wesley raised arose from Zinzendorf's conviction that sinfulness continues in the justified. The Count had stated conclusively: 'We believe that sin remains in our members, but that it cannot reign over us', and he had summarily based this on the assertion: 'because it stands thus in scripture.'[100] He vigorously rejected Wesley's claim that grace covers life only in the present and not the future, and he asserted that the greatest saint could become tomorrow the greatest sinner if he thinks anything of his holiness.[101] To the harsh objection that the Herrnhuters avoided persecution, he replied that according to the Saviour it is not necessary to seek it. He warded off all pride in martyrdom. On the subject of the means of grace and faith he distinguished between the faith of the heart and intellectual belief in miracles, and based this upon 1 Corinthians 13[2]: 'And though I have the gift of prophecy, and understand all mysteries, and all knowledge, and though I have all faith, so that I could remove mountains, and have not charity, I am nothing.'[102] Only faith of the heart should allow a man to receive communion, which ought not to be offered indiscriminately to unbelievers and the unconverted; this was in line also with the injunctions of Paul in 1 Corinthians 10 and 11. In this way, of course, Wesley's real question, which arose from Molther's idea of mystical 'stillness', was not answered but evaded.

As to 'religion' and 'church' Zinzendorf made a distinction between them, understanding from the standpoint of a purely mystical spiritualism under 'religion', 'an assembly which teaches and expounds Holy Scripture according to a prescribed method which many or few profess'. Such was a 'religious party', as the spirituals said, or a 'society', as the apostles of the Enlightenment liked to express it.[103] Contrary to the spirituals the Count gave it a positive meaning and allowed no room for doubt that the 'Church' was essentially superior to it.[104] A church was for him 'an assembly . . . of sinners who have received grace, and forgiveness of sins in Jesu's blood'.[105] Belonging to it are apostolic orders and constitutions with apostolic authority and powers. There can be no doubt that he conceived his creation, the Herrnhut Moravians, as a renewed community of the United Brethren in these terms and also justified his own position in it in a way with which Wesley rightly found nothing comparable in the history of the Church. But the Count guarded against giving expression to this, and instead put it diplomatically and moderately in the following words: 'That the one Sub-Senior of all the congregations is held in particular esteem in our churches, given filial honour by the bishops and his office of the Spirit in the church is recognized by him, this is a particular soon to be demonstrated to modest and truth-seeking people, but which does not belong to such a letter as this.'[106] In other words he demanded that his particular position of authority should be unique. Accordingly from the start and for ever he deprived himself of the possibility of removing one of the chief troubles in his Church. Moreover he emphasized with full determination and unmistakable anger that obedience in every human society is absolutely necessary—or, as he forcibly put it: 'in every church, in every stall, in every barn.'[107] Without this the human family would completely disintegrate in chaos. That this reply could only strengthen John Wesley in his opposition is obvious. Zinzendorf seems to have been aware of this, for he tried in what followed to make 'the power of the Count' historically and legally explicable. He made four points. In Herrnhut he was at first the civil authority, but he renounced this and became 'Superintendent of the Church', although subordinate to the Eldest. In 1737 he became bishop in accordance with the Moravian Church order, and so the office of superintendent ceased to be. In addition, however, he is 'the father of a very scattered Domestico', which is in accordance with the

D

Lutheran Church order. The repetition of the lot, about which Wesley had objected as an indication that he assumed absolute authority, was misunderstood by Wesley. The lot was never cast twice in Herrnhut in the case of an Eldest, but it was normal practice that one selected by a preliminary lot from the chosen candidates should be confirmed by a second lot. On the whole it is to be noted that the congregation did far more independently of the Count's will than he would have wished or could prevent.

The Count strenuously denied any predilection for either ancient or modern mystics. On the contrary he claimed that the Moravians were anti-mystic. He eloquently justified their emphasis upon joy by reference to the feeling of the woman who found the lost coin in the parable of Jesus. He conceded that this might go too far. Among the Brethren also good works are done naturally and as a matter of course, and are done on their own account and not because they are commanded. Anyone who does not do them is not for this reason brought under suspicion, but shows through his own situation that he is not in the right condition to do them.[108]

Over against this Wesley believed that reprehensible acts ought to incur brotherly censure. For him there was too great a freedom in the ethical teaching of Herrnhut, a freedom the notorious mis-use of which among his own circle of acquaintances he could not overlook. His chief concern was always the same; he wanted to see evidence of the new man in the experience of salvation and in sanctification, in justifying faith, in loyalty to the Church, and in unbounded brotherly fellowship. In spite of this he did not claim any certainty based upon his own point of view. Time and again he set out the opinions of the Herrnhuters and came to the conclusion that they contradicted the clear sense of Scripture. He let himself be guided in particular by 1 Timothy 5[21]: 'I charge thee before God, and the Lord Jesus Christ, and the elect angels, that thou observe these things, without preferring one before another, doing nothing by partiality.'[109] He detected in the good works of the Brethren self-esteem and partiality. That his brother-in-law and fellow-worker, Westley Hall, was a man like this was a painful confirmation of his constant mistrust. He bitterly lamented this to his sister and recalled the happy times at Oxford.[110] John Cennick, who had been introduced to him by Charles Kinchin in Reading, and whom Whitefield had especially approved, had by now become one of his severest critics. He had, as his brother Charles put it, taken him as a 'son in the Gospel' to the colliers in Kingswood and given him the role of lay-preacher. There Wesley met him again on 16th December 1740, but he was cold and uncommunicative, as if he were a stranger. Only a few days later after repeated questioning he explained his change of attitude by differences over predestination, which he held to be true doctrine and by which the Wesley brothers were damned. In this way the controversy over the mystical 'stillness' led on to a second dispute about election.

Two months later, at an Herrnhut love-feast in Bristol, the matter was brought into open discussion. Cennick and his friend Thomas Bissicks (or Beswicks) charged John Wesley with preaching, as an opponent of predestination, that righteousness lay in man. They, on the contrary, regarded themselves as witnesses to the sole righteousness of God, which remains at His disposal and is in no sense dependent upon man. As a result the opposition between them was brought to a climax. The greater part of the assembly agreed with Cennick against Wesley, who recently had several times preached to only two or three people where not two years before thousands had listened to him.[111] A private letter from Whitefield to Wesley, which defended predestination,[112] was printed without the knowledge of either of them and distributed among the members of the Fetter Lane Society in London. John Wesley tore it up in view of the company, but this brought him no more than a momentary success, although all others who had copies followed his example. When a few weeks later, on 28th March 1741, he was himself speaking with travellers who had just returned from Georgia, the effect was even worse. He found in Whitefield a man embittered by severe disappointments, and when he came back to England these recoiled on him. His publisher James Hutton refused to do anything for him in the future because of his teaching on predestination. His friend William Seward was dead, the first martyr of Methodism; struck down by a furious rabble in a Welsh village, he had later died from the wounds. The literary attacks which Whitefield himself made against the well-loved Puritan devotional book, *The Whole Duty of Man*, and against the equally esteemed Archbishop John Tillotson of the previous century, because neither taught justification by grace through faith, had offended many erstwhile admirers.[113] John Cennick threw himself passionately into the quarrels in Kingswood, naturally upon Whitefield's side. Everything combined to turn him against John Wesley. Their first meeting was unexpectedly abrupt. Whitefield declared that they preached two different gospels and that this constrained him openly to oppose the Wesley brothers. When John Wesley reminded him through his companion Westley Hall, whom he had surprisingly taken with him, that a few days before he had promised to abstain from publicly arguing against him, Whitefield ascribed the pledge as due merely to human weakness.[114]

Wesley's whole work was threatened. He could not count upon either London or Bristol, and Oxford had for a long time been uncertain. But he was not the sort of man to capitulate. Instead he embarked upon a new course which was to have important results. On 24th February 1741, he laid before the assembled 'Bands', the little groups in Bristol, the whole disordered situation, read out the names of all members and found out the attitude of each one by means of a judicial examination. To those who passed the test without fault he gave membership tickets, to the others he granted time for further thought and the opportunity of discussion. He repeated the same procedure four days later at Kingswood. In this way he won back the larger part of the people. It was the mark of the born leader to have undertaken the control of so complicated and almost desperate a situation, and not without satisfaction he noted in his *Journal* the surprise which his initiative occasioned, especially when he made known the names of those to be excluded from membership. His chief opponents, John Cennick and Thomas Bissicks, and also a woman, Ann Ayling, were shocked, and tried to make out that their differences were entirely matters of doctrine, reproaching him with 'Popery' because of his rejection of predestination. In spite of this they were willing to remain with him if *he* was so prepared.

Yet Wesley was not able to maintain this initial success. In the following weeks he conferred with several members about the next steps. Again, on 7th March 1741, he openly addressed the whole society and told them plainly what he thought was wrong. There were three points. The first was their despising the minister and slighting God's ordinances, by which he presumably meant putting mystical self-conceit above worship and prayer as much as offences against moral stability, and above all failures in love of the brethren. Secondly there was the mystical 'stillness' which waited for a special inner impulse before speaking or praying. Finally came the separation from the brethren and the formation of a new society. He was not willing to let this go on any longer and he desired an immediate decision. The speaker for the opposition was Thomas Bissicks; he again referred to predestination as the decisive point and reproached Wesley with having begun the separation because of this, to which the latter replied that although he was himself of a different opinion he tolerated predestinarians in his societies both in London and Bristol. Bissicks then demanded that he should employ John Cennick as an independent helper, as before; Wesley, however, laid down the condition that Cennick should repent of the wrong which he had done by his continual speaking against Wesley. When Cennick declined to do this, since he was not conscious of any guilt in the matter, Wesley closed the issue by observing that no course seemed possible other than that each should choose the society to which he ought to belong. In this way he followed the natural bent of his character, which sought sharp and clear distinctions, and he gained clarity by separation. Perhaps he acted hastily and gave way too easily to his natural sensitivity, which showed itself when his claim to leadership was contested. It is easy for those who come afterwards to think in this way, but the fact is that he was willing that the breach should deprive him of some followers. Probably what counted in his judgement as more serious than personal considerations and differences of doctrine was the threatened indifference towards the Church, in which now as ever was his true home and which he wished to retain. He thought that he could detect sectarian tendencies and he wanted to stop this disastrous process in all circumstances. We cannot consider all the consequences, but in the meeting to which reference has been made half of the members immediately left the room with Cennick, and in Kingswood 52 people separated from Wesley, 90 remaining with him.[115]

These events took place in Bristol. The situation in London remained exceedingly strained. At the end of March 1741 Wesley's old friend Peter Böhler returned there from America. Did this not augur well for the desired understanding? Wesley hastened to him with the urgent questions. At their first meeting neither mentioned the problem, and there was only aroused once again in Wesley the old desire for full fellowship with Herrnhut. Four weeks later, on 2nd May 1741, there followed a conversation between Wesley, Spangenberg and Böhler in the house of Nanny Morris, one of the female members, and this lasted for several hours. Spangenberg took the lead and the subject was the 'new creature'. Whatever Wesley may have anticipated from the discussion he was now talking with the very men, who, next to the Bible, had been his most important help. Yet his *Journal* betrays no sign of his concern. It is written in exactly the same terms as the doctrinal discourses of Zinzendorf in Marienborn and the sermons of Christian David in Herrnhut. Wesley reported the doctrinal statements concisely and prosaically, carefully and clearly, as only he could do. Spangenberg's point of view was as follows: the moment of justification is that in which a new creature comes into being and is put into a man. But this new man does not displace the old, which exists until the moment of death, and in it is the old heart with its corrupt and abominable nature. Inward corruption remains in the soul as long as the soul remains in the body. Yet the heart of the new man is clean, and since the new man is stronger than the old it maintains itself against the old nature, although not of itself but only because it ever looks to Jesus Christ. So the believer experiences a continual struggle between the old man and the new, in which the victory belongs not to himself but to Jesus Christ. This conception of the Christian life, which corresponded exactly to that which Zinzendorf derived from Luther,[116] greatly disappointed Wesley and many in the Fetter Lane congregation. But this can only be read between the lines in the account in his *Journal*. He asked Spangenberg about his own experience and wanted to know if the corruption he had described was still in his heart, to which Spangenberg replied, 'In the heart of my old man there is; but not in the heart of my new man.' Wesley wished to know further whether the experience of his brethren agreed with this, and Spangenberg confirmed that it did for the whole of his Church. Wesley then appears to have been silent, but several members of the society spoke up about their own different experience of salvation. Thereupon Spangenberg spoke to them with great emotion, his hand trembling, and warned them against self-deception. There was no higher state than that which he described. When they supposed that their inner corruption was taken away, they were in error, since it was only covered over and would only cease when the body lay in the dust. So ended the discussion. It is only in his *Journal* that Wesley raises the question whether there was this inward corruption in Jesus himself, and if not, whether the disciple cannot be as his Master?

As if to answer this he preached the next day, a Sunday, from 2 Corinthians 5^{17} on the new creature in Christ for whom old things are passed away and all things are become new. But soon after when he tried to convince Peter Böhler by telling him of the testimony of a dying woman about the unbroken presence of Jesus Christ and the sensible virtue of the Holy Spirit in her heart, he was unable to get him to agree. Böhler used the example of the old nature in a man being like an old tooth which may well break but never disappear or cease to ache so long as it is not removed.

The conversation with Spangenberg and Böhler over these questions must have affected Wesley and his followers a great deal. On the following Wednesday, 6th May 1741, they desired to explore in prayer God's will about reuniting with the Fetter Lane Herrnhuters. The result, which was probably obtained with the help of a scriptural lot, although this is not stated, was to the effect that the time was not yet ripe. Their critics had not renounced their errors, and they had many times failed to speak about them in a clear way, so it was not possible to say what they really believed or rejected.[117]

The summer of 1741 saw this unsatisfactory state of things continuing. Everything went on more or less under the shadow of this doctrinal controversy, both with regard to the people with whom John Wesley spoke, and also not less to the books he read. To his chagrin he could not find in the society at Nottingham, which had reckoned itself Methodist for more than a year, so that he had been able to build on its foundations, either a Bible or a Methodist hymn-book, but in their place plenty of Herrnhut song-books and the Count's sermons. He was not helped when Peter Böhler's former interpreter, Richard Viney, admitted to him that the Bible contains many commands of God and that the Lord's Supper, the Bible and public and private prayer were the normal means of grace, but that at the same time the *Sixteen Discourses* of Count Zinzendorf were as widely disseminated as if all truth were contained in them alone. But even more significant was the fact that John Wesley at this time happened upon Luther's large *Commentary on the Epistle to the Galatians*, written in 1531–5, the one book of the German reformer which in its English version had gone through the largest number of editions. It had been instrumental three years before in converting his brother Charles and his friend William Holland. Yet in his present state of mind he could only find fault with it, and this he did with unusual warmth. He found it both shallow and confused. He found it shot through with mysticism; first in its condemnation of reason, which Luther regarded as the irreconcilable enemy of the Gospel; then in its rejection of the law, which Luther condemned as a means of salvation; and also in its neglect of good works, which he excluded from the Christian life. Was not this the 'stillness' and 'passivity' of the Herrnhuters and which must necessarily lead to moral arbitrariness and to the dissolution of all traditional ordinances of Christianity in its developed and ordered forms? How could Luther so perversely couple the law with sin, death, hell and devil? If Jesus Christ freed His own in the same way from all these powers then He has also freed them from holiness and heaven. Against such exaggerations should one not set the word from the Epistle of James: 'Who art thou, that speakest evil of the law, and judgest the law?' (James 4[11f]) So Wesley considered that it was his duty expressly to warn his society against Luther's *Commentary on Galatians*. With some justification he recognized in Luther the source of the mystical indifference of the Herrnhuters, which caused him so much concern.[118]

So prepared he went to the final conversation with Zinzendorf himself on 3rd September 1741. A more cheerful experience, however, preceded the meeting. In a long conversation which he had with Benjamin Ingham on 1st August 1741, the two agreed about the close practical relationship between justification and good works. Both were of the opinion that if a justified person neglected these he would lose the grace which he had received. But Ingham was not prepared to agree to Wesley's claim that before justification a person ought to do good works and to wait for faith in such an attitude. In other words he denied that the law was a preparation for justifying faith.[119]

Then came the meeting with Zinzendorf himself. Once again the two natural leaders faced each other as they had done previously on German soil, but how different was the situation from three years before! At that time Wesley was a beginner, who admired the Count like a schoolboy under the guidance of an older fellow-scholar. Now the storms and disappointments had turned him into an acute observer and made him into a mature man of action with a striking independence of judgement. It could almost be foreseen that the conversation would come to no positive conclusion. For if Spangenberg and above all Böhler with their advantage of personal friendship and their claims on his gratitude had not been able to convert Wesley to their doctrine of the meaning of the faith, how much less likely that the almost unknown Count should succeed—unless he were able to develop greater clarity and sensitivity of feeling between Wesley and himself. Obviously neither option was really open to him.

The conversation took place in the gardens of Gray's Inn, one of the Inns of Court. Wesley recorded it in Latin from memory, and perhaps this made it seem harsher than it actually was; nevertheless it is corroborated by Zinzendorf, since he reproduced it in his *Büdingische Sammlung*.[120] The Count began with the question: 'Why have you changed your beliefs?' Wesley immediately denied this, and wanted to know how Zinzendorf had come to this extraordinary view.

The Count referred to the long letter of 8th August 1740, in which Wesley dissociated himself from the idea of 'glorious sinfulness'. From this it must follow that Christians were the most miserable sinners to the moment of death, and that anything else was deception and seduction; while Wesley was denying to the Brethren the peace which they desired. So the Count treated his companion like a disloyal subordinate whom he was taking to task. In Zinzendorf's eyes Wesley seemed like the assailant who as a matter of course had put himself in the wrong. When Wesley came back with his questions in surprise, the Count's reproaches only increased. If the first letter from Georgia had won over the Count's full support for Wesley, the personal meeting in Marienborn had shown Zinzendorf that the confused ideas which he had perceived in him from the start had increased. Then Wesley returned to England and Zinzendorf heard shortly afterwards that the Herrnhut Brethren were engaged in controversy with him. Whereupon he, the Count, sent Spangenberg to make peace, and following the latter's report had instructed the Brethren to ask Wesley's pardon, because they had been unjust to him. But Spangenberg informed him that Wesley did not desire any reconciliation. Wesley agreed that he had declined the apology as unnecessary, because there was nothing to forgive; he had never in fact been angry with them. To be sure he had been afraid that they taught and lived falsely, and for this reason he diverted the conversation from the personal to the factual plain, so that it then turned entirely on Christian perfection. Questions about the means of grace and the regulations of the Church, which had in addition been raised, were dropped. Zinzendorf would have nothing to do with any kind of perfection which was a human possession. All holiness rests entirely upon Jesus Christ, and perfection does not mean anything other than faith in the blood of Jesus Christ. When Wesley asked whether the new man did not have love for God and his neighbour, and whether he did not bear in himself the image of God in a restored form, Zinzendorf replied that this was a holiness of legal degrees, whereas evangelical holiness consisted entirely of faith. At this point Wesley asked his protagonist if they were not disputing merely about words. He, Wesley, did not want to contend for anything more than the position that the believer loves God with his whole heart and serves Him with his whole strength, but Zinzendorf denied this and asserted again that this had no meaning in his conception of holiness. Wesley then asked in surprise if the Count would deny that the new man grew in love and accordingly in holiness? He referred to the Pauline word that the inner man is renewed from day to day (2 Corinthians 4[16]), and went on to ask whether the apostles did not possess a greater holiness after Pentecost than previously, since they had received the Holy Spirit. Zinzendorf replied again in the same vein that this had nothing to do with holiness, since the Holy Spirit merely gave them power to perform miracles. Wesley then put forward, apparently somewhat timidly, the question whether believers do not by their daily self-denials die to themselves and live to God, but Zinzendorf rejected this with his favourite idea that self-denial, as something legalistic, contradicts the freedom of the Gospel.[121] He affirmed: 'As believers, we do as we please and nothing else. No purification is a prerequisite to love's perfection.' Wesley ended the conversation with the assurance that he would consider what Zinzendorf had said. It would appear that he did not consider the parting final, but it may have been different with Zinzendorf. He saw in the doctrine of Christian perfection, as held by John Wesley, a dangerous heresy, and he was convinced that the brothers John and Charles were leading their followers astray. Only when they gave it up would he be prepared to renew his relationship with them.[122]

So ended an association which was unique in the history of the Church for the intensity of mutual understanding, assistance and enrichment between its participants. Did it have to come about? Was there a genuine clash? Was the breach in fact an indication that the Methodist movement, which up to this point had been like a scholar dependent upon his teacher, had come to maturity? Undoubtedly Wesley and Zinzendorf spoke about salvation with different accents. Both agreed that justification was realized by grace alone through the sacrificial death of Jesus Christ, that it was received by faith and was the source of the new man. Both affirmed that God Himself was the Creator of this new man through the new birth. It was only from this point that the difference between them began to appear. This had nothing to do with the conception of God or of His particular activity; it concerned only their understanding of the human aspect. Zinzendorf, like Luther, saw the new man as existing from the beginning, depending entirely upon God;[123] Wesley conceived him rather in terms of advancing to a goal, and coming to completion with God's help. The image of God, which was conceived as likeness to Jesus Christ, accordingly implied for Wesley a profound transforming work in the believer. Zinzendorf in no way denied this, and indeed his ethic of the imitation of Christ gave an important place to it.[124] But he opposed the final decisive implication of this proceeding. He thought dogmatically; following the pattern of the Reformation he was concerned with the legal aspect of salvation. Wesley thought psychologically in the manner of the eighteenth century, and he was concerned with the empirical facts of a situation and with the effect of salvation. For this reason he tried more than once to trace the difference back to a mere dispute about words. On the other hand Zinzendorf detected in Wesley's words the classic interests of Pietism in the new man, which he, under the influence of Luther, had grown out of. Quite logically he missed in Wesley the difference between law and gospel as the fundamental categories in the relationship of man with God. On the other hand Wesley felt that Zinzendorf's rejection of the law went beyond Paul's teaching and bordered on antinomianism, and the practical consequences of indifference to worship and ethics demonstrated this all too clearly to him.[125] Two epochs stood in contrast to each other: Wesley was the modern thinker, Zinzendorf the man who thought in the categories of the Reformation.

The overall impression is that of a tragic breach. Many factors contributed to this. There was the slender acquaintance of the two men with each other, their claims to authority which made it difficult for either to give way, the practical experience of Wesley contrasted with Zinzendorf's dogmatism; in addition there were their different ways of thinking, one derived from the Reformation emphasis upon God's action, God's judgement, God's law, the other from Pietism, which looked for the effect of God's working in a man. Other differences, like the exaggerated estimate of their own Church on the part of the Herrnhuters and attachment to the Anglican tradition by Wesley, were kept in the background. The importance of the dispute lay in the fact that, as in all great periods in the history of the Church, doctrine conceived as the expression of the truth was taken with such great seriousness.[126] At the root of it there was a different under-standing of Scripture.

Nevertheless it must be deplored that this ecumenical encounter, which had begun so promisingly and produced such profound results, came to an end in this fashion, and still more, that it happened so painfully. But it had not been without its fruits. The message of the justifying grace of God remained for Wesley and Methodism at the centre of their preaching. This would not have happened apart from the association with Herrnhut, for there were no influences in the theology or ecclesiastical life of the Anglican Church of the time to encourage it. Thus for Dr George Cheyne, a medical doctor from Bath, who had studied divinity for thirty years, the idea of the forgiveness of sins was a new concept.[127] It is this which confirms the view that the significance of John Wesley's conversion was derived from his encounter with Luther.[128] For three years no subject had occupied Wesley's attention to such an extent as this. Everything was subordinated to it, including even his much-loved book, the biography of Count de Renty, the origin and purpose of which was very different. The French mystic became for him a bearer and example of faith, and Wesley even found in him the gospel of grace and the effect of God's sole working.[129] Yet it seems that the stimulus to this, which German Pietism was able to provide, exhausted the contents of this contribution. The Methodist movement from this moment found its own way. It was impossible to transfer the actual forms of the Herrnhut Moravian Church to a greater extent on to English soil. The close relationship with the Church of England demanded a form, which had to develop according to its own law. The liturgical, sacramental and ecclesiastical structures of this Church and its extraordinarily close relationship with the community to which it ministered, its emphasis upon the primitive Christian tradition, and the richness of its inheritance, were values which neither John Wesley nor his followers were able to cast on one side.

In spite of this it would have been unnatural had the connexions between the two communities been ended at one stroke or forcibly broken. They were continued, yet in a sporadic way. Many members hovered backwards and forwards between Methodism and the Herrnhuters; men like Richard Ridley[130] and Benjamin Ingham, who always had fault to find and settled nowhere;[131] and John Cennick, who changed his allegiance, not from Wesley but from Whitefield to Count Zinzendorf. In the nature of the case unfavourable judgements were passed upon these happenings and by one side at least they were harsh. The most severe was perhaps that which John Wesley made about John Cennick,[132] the man who after his work with Kingswood colliers helped to found Methodism in the south of Ireland.[133] Others tried to maintain the connexion, without entering obviously into the disputed points. James Hutton's house in Islington near London remained for a long time a meeting-place and a centre of general confidence, which even John Wesley now and then visited. Benjamin Ingham's fellow-worker at Birstall in Yorkshire, John Nelson, went from there straight to the Foundery to comply with the summons of Wesley, who asked him in February 1744 for support and assistance during his preaching-tour to Bristol and Cornwall.[134]

There also the corset-maker Richard Viney, a founder-member of the Fetter Lane Society, sought refuge when in November 1743 Spangenberg, after a bitter quarrel, excluded him by the lot from the Brethren community as an 'enemy of the good order of God and His church' and as 'Satan'.[135] His impressible, woebegone, melancholic, even hysterical and hypochondriac nature,[136] which made him incapable of standing alone, so that he constantly sought the support of a group, requiring strong leadership,[137] cannot afford any real evidence in itself, yet his journal from the year 1744 gives some unique intimate insights into the troubled temper of the period after the breach, so that his own personal fate may be taken as representative of the whole experience, particularly as he was filled with a passionate desire to preach the gospel and to work among people,[138] thus priding himself on sharing the primary concern of Methodism.

Within a period of six years Viney had become quite prominent in the Herrnhut community. Whether his first visit to Germany in the year 1736 was in connexion with the Herrnhut settlements cannot be determined. He seems to have stayed for a considerable time, for he acquired such a facility in the spoken as distinct from the written language, that from 1738 he was able to act as interpreter for Peter

Böhler and other Germans. It is possible that he was present at the memorable meeting on 24th May 1738, in Aldersgate Street in London, at which John Wesley experienced his conversion. He accompanied Wesley on the journey to Herrnhut and Marienborn which followed this, and throughout remained his close associate. When in the year 1739 he stayed in Herrendyk-Ysselstein, the Dutch settlement of the Herrnhuters, he felt that he was called to warn the Methodists in a pamphlet against 'irregularities'. Accordingly even before Molther's arrival in England Viney had gone over to the Herrnhuter's side, and it is possible that his pamphlet was the first indication that a breach was beginning. Nevertheless, as Charles Wesley testifies, in March 1740 he still had not accepted Molther's and Spangenberg's view of salvation, nor had he as leader of the little fellowship group in Oxford given up the ordinances of the Church.[139] In October 1741 he was superintendent of the London Moravians, by 1742 he was governor of the Herrnhuter's international school for the children of missionaries at Broad Oaks in Essex, and on 27th June 1743, he was the preacher and superintendent of the Herrnhut community in Yorkshire, where he was brought close to Benjamin Ingham. In the autumn of that year he had come to the final collision with Spangenberg, after he, Viney, who had earlier shown 'papistical' tendencies, had refused to give unconditional obedience to the Count; because of this he had even offered his resignation, which the Brethren at first refused to accept. Spangenberg could not tolerate this. He excommunicated him and expected that he would humble himself, apologize for everything, and beg to be taken back. But there could be no question of this. He was ready for reconciliation with the Brethren, but not with Spangenberg himself.

He considered whether, as the Herrnhut Brethren Töltschig and William Holland advised, he should seek the personal pardon of Zinzendorf by travelling to Germany, but he rejected this idea too, because at the same time this would have involved bringing an accusation against Spangenberg.[140] Another possibility was to join himself to John Wesley. This he did, reluctantly, in obedience to the lot, by means of which he inquired on Sunday, 29th January 1744, about God's further designs for him, having posed the following five possibilities: try to settle the affair with Count Zinzendorf; continue the effort to come to terms with Wesley; look for a new sphere of work, where nobody had as yet been; remain quiet, and wait upon further enlightenment; first and foremost humble thyself before accepting other schemes. To be quite safe he added a sixth lot, which was empty. He drew the second on the list, which directed him to Wesley. On 19th February, having waited so long, he twice repeated the inquiry through the lot and received the instruction: take up without further delay full association with Wesley! Then at last he prepared for the preliminary conversation, which came the day after the drawing of the decisive lot; not, however, before Hutton and his wife and the other Brethren had wept copiously, pointing out what a great sacrifice he was about to make.[141] In reality he wanted to stay with the Herrnhuters, with whom he felt most at home.[142] When he compared the two leaders, Zinzendorf and Wesley, he noticed the same pride, the same self-conceit, the same seeking after dominance, and an equal harshness in the two men, just as he found the same characteristics in Ingham. He allowed that John Wesley, whom he found to be the more irascible, had a certain mastery which was lacking in Count Zinzendorf. Accordingly Wesley could be hypo-critical, while the Count always remained natural. But further reflection upon the difference between the two men led him to see that a phlegmatic, sanguine and melancholy character, which he counted himself to be, according to Robert Burton's famous *Anatomy of Melancholy* (1621), was not the man to inaugurate or sustain a religious revival, and that since God is served not by perfect angels but mortal men, choleric characters, by means of their natural energy, are always His best instruments. Such considerations led him to come to terms with the failures in the leaders which he deplored.[143] His debt to the Herrnhuters remained so real that he wished to require from John Wesley as the condition of joining his society the promise that he would no longer reproach the Herrnhuters or preach Christian perfection in the form in which they rejected it. To be sure he doubted whether this would be successful, since Wesley could in fact not agree to this.[144]

John Wesley received him coolly, but he did not repulse him. He left him absolutely free to remain or to return to the Herrnhuters.[145] Viney did not feel very happy, for Wesley told him with his usual blunt directness that his brother Charles frequently reproached him for his credulity with former critics,[146] and Viney[147] felt that he was under suspicion as an Herrnhut spy, especially as John Wesley had straightway granted that something of this kind was a possibility.[148]

On the other hand Wesley displayed a remarkable confidence in him when he immediately discussed with him a very significant favourite project, the realization of which he intended to give him, and which followed on from his former activity with the Herrnhuters. He was considering setting up an orphan-house, similar to that of August Hermann Francke in Halle, which in a similar way would serve as a Christian focal-point, bringing together an international school, an orphanage, and a work-house for the poor. The school was to be a social counterpart to the workmen's school at Kingswood, serving the higher classes. Once again it becomes evident what a deep impression his short visit to Halle in the year 1738 made upon him. In the background probably was the design to revive the primitive Christian idea of sharing possessions. At any rate he discussed it with Viney, who raised many practical objections, although not disagreeing in principle.[149]

Following on this Viney served John Wesley at first by acting as his personal secretary, and as such received many indications of the confidence placed in him. With Wesley he read through Zinzendorf's accounts of his Pennsylvanian synods, listened to the fourth part of Wesley's *Journal*, which included the dispute with the Herrnhuters, was invited to a conference with Wesley's leading helpers and shared in preparing the agenda for this.[150] But, as John Wesley had foreseen, he was not a man given to great constancy. In the midst of all this he had even begun to write an explanatory memorandum to the Archbishop of Canterbury, in which he tried to include all his complaints against the two movements which were already at enmity with each other. It was only through the vigorous intervention of Benjamin Ingham that this denunciation was not sent.[151] But this was only a tactical success, for Viney himself was not brought round. His complaints against the two movements reached their climax when he asserted that in the last resort it was the same whether a man belonged to them or to the Church of Rome. So he honestly believed it was his duty to warn the leaders of the Church of England against the prime danger of the process of Romanizing. Even after he had given up his letter of complaint he asked himself if it would not be better if the Herrnhuters were to abandon all their activity in England. He seriously doubted whether it was the work of God at all. Accordingly he considered whether he should not seek ordination in the Church of England in order to bring back the Methodists to it.[152]

On 17th April 1744, he acknowledged that, more than ever before, he felt completely committed to Wesley. A month later, on 16th May, he again changed his mind. Wesley surprised him, as he said, by inviting him to accompany him to Newcastle, so that in the first flush of his surprise he was not in a position to decline. The too-ready assent he gave aroused in him regret and distress. He was not in doubt about himself but of Wesley, and he planned, as already said, a completely private life somewhere in quietness,[153] although he was willing to wait upon further directions from God. When Wesley took a further opportunity of again criticizing the Herrnhuters and expressed his indignation very freely, Viney opposed him and wanted to go away. He continued to waver until June, although in reality he knew full well where he belonged. On the other hand, as he recognized, Wesley in a quite straightforward manner put him again under an obligation, in that he invited him to state his complaints before the coming conference in London. Since, however, that would have meant strengthening the ties between them, he felt no inclination to do this and wished rather to send his opinions in writing.[154] In this way he brought about the final separation. Wesley's patience with this man can only be wondered at. To be sure he did say of him later that like Lot's wife he became a pillar of salt, because having left Sodom he looked back. Viney then thought of his future in terms of the director of a school, since he felt that he was specially called to work among children, and he considered building an educational establishment in Hull, Halifax or Dukinfield, and in this he was supported by Charles Delamotte, Wesley's companion in Georgia.[155]

The agenda of the London conference included a consideration of the future relationship of Wesley with the Herrnhuters. One item was devoted expressly to the question: 'What can we adopt from other churches?' Wesley gave the first place to Count Zinzendorf, putting him before both Whitefield and the Quakers, and he named expressly the following institutions: helpers, bands, societies, schools.[156]

When Wesley came to the actual differences and systematically summarized them in the letter[157] of 27th November 1750 to the former Vicar of Islington, George James Stonehouse, who had gone over to the Herrnhuters,[158] it still remained true that he asserted his unity with them and desired to take it further. On 2nd August 1745, through James Hutton in the newspaper *Daily Advertiser*, Zinzendorf had inserted a declaration that he dissociated himself from John and Charles Wesley because they taught false doctrine, and at the same time he declined to enter into a theological dispute with either of them, should such a controversy ensue. Wesley replied on 6th September 1745, and condemned clearly the injustice of stating differences without allowing the opportunity of refuting them, and then stressed the fact, not without irony, that Zinzendorf had nothing to fear from him since, although he had been wronged, he would not himself begin any controversy. Zinzendorf's unusual conduct could not hinder him from still embracing him with love.[159]

In the long letter of 24th June 1744, with which Wesley prefaced the fourth part of his *Journal*, written chiefly to that part of the Moravian Church in England, the expressions of personal sympathy and agreement on actual points of detail still greatly outweigh his hesitations about them. The concurrence between them was not merely expressed in general terms but was based upon the soundness of their teaching about justification through the free grace of God received by faith, their brotherly love and the excellence of the Herrnhut ecclesiastical discipline. To be sure this was also accompanied with the desire that they should separate the good and the bad in their own midst.[160] In the letter to Ingham, written on 8th September 1746, he amplified the usual objections against the Herrnhuters in detail, their teaching about 'stillness', their falsifying historical facts when setting forth their grievances, the dishonesty in their ways of expressing things. But he also said that there was not a day in the last seven years when he had not desired full union with them.[161] When writing to Stonehouse he limited the positive judgement principally to the preceding year and said that the difference between them was that Stonehouse admired the Herrnhuters, while he loved them.[162] He gave a detailed explanation of why he was not able to admire them. He began with the name they give themselves. The word 'Brethren' must give the impression that they were the only Church with the right to bear this early Christian name, and so they slighted other Christian communities. Similarly their other title, the 'Moravian Church', was false, for not a tenth part of Zinzendorf's followers had anything to do with that Church, which was found now in Poland, with no contact with Herrnhut or Marienborn. Moreover the Count taught and represented a number of doctrines, which were completely unknown to the Moravian Church. Then Wesley opposed the Herrnhut teaching about justification, sanctification and faith as being unscriptural, just as he did in the conversation with Zinzendorf in 1741. Once again he disagreed with the idea that in the New Testament there is only one explicit commandment, the command to believe. Their moral attitude he also condemned in the familiar terms, calling it conformity with the world, avoiding the scandal of Christ, and hypocrisy. But two objections were new, namely that they cared only for their own people, and that their treatment of their opponents, especially those who wrote against them, was contemptuous and without feeling. How could this be reconciled with Christian humility and love? He deeply deplored the effects which followed from their teaching. According to his own observations it had destroyed for many their faith, their unaffected love for God and their neighbour, and their Christian humility. It had turned simple, straightforward people into arrogant folk, who despised the Church in which they had been brought up, together with their former teachers. He claimed to know examples where even only a short attendance on their preaching had destroyed the listeners' basic Christian virtues of gratitude, justice, mercy and truth.

This was a dark picture—and yet Wesley desired to hold fast to his love for them. Was he being two-faced? Was he deceiving himself? It is difficult to avoid questions of this kind, especially in connexion with this letter, because he concludes rather offensively by suggesting that his correspondent is probably an example of this sort of person. Yet he avoids making this precise charge by going on (in the very last sentence) to point out that if Stonehouse is not a self-deceiver he ought to go the next Sunday and, as Wesley disapprovingly puts it, hear the Germans, presumably in order to learn the truth. Probably in spite of everything he was striving after love as he understood it, and a union which held good in spite of unbiased censure. But he was also like every man, subject to the fluctuations of temper and highly impressionable; when Richard Viney's characterization of him as a choleric man is remembered, everything becomes more understandable.

The year 1750 was the lowest point in the relations between Wesley and the Herrnhuters. Expressions of bitter disapprobation were very common and took on a new tone of acrimony. They lost the affectionate note with which, by gentle irony, he had disarmed Count Zinzendorf's criticisms as recently as September 1745. There is no doubt that he now regarded the Herrnhuters as a grave threat to serious Christianity.[163] But they also mistrusted him from now on for a long time. He was now not able to repeat the opinions expressed in February 1745 and September 1746 that as a closely-knit community they were, next to the genuine disciples in the Church of England, the best Christians in the world.[164] In the same year 1746 he very reluctantly said that their teachers were a kind of Protestant Jesuits, although he exempted the ordinary members from any such charge.[165] But now they were all wolves, against whom the sheep could not be too loudly warned.

In 1749 a Parliamentary decision had given recognition to the Brethren as an independent Church in Britain. A collection of historical documents under the title 'Acta Fratrum Unitatis in Anglia' had been published, which gave an historical statement of their position. It was published in a limited edition and is not generally available. A commentary upon it appeared, written by 'A lover of the light'. It has been assumed that John Wesley was the author, and this is strengthened by the fact that George Lavington, the Bishop of Exeter, who was an opponent of both sides, attributed it to him, a fact which Wesley did not deny.[166] This commentary is in point of fact a very harsh document, in which all the previous objections are repeated and some new ones added. Since it follows closely the order of the original it is more difficult to trace the inner unity than in the case of earlier statements, yet it is clear that in it the chief concern is also with the question of doctrine. Wesley feels that with the Herrnhuters he is in a theatre, in which they appear as dreamers.[167] Their whole manner of speaking about Jesus and the work of salvation, the affected obscurity of their expressions, their blood and wounds theology, their peculiar hymns in honour of the Lamb, with incomprehensible Hebrew words, are all so far removed from the simple gravity of the Bible, that he can do no other than resolutely oppose them.[168] Their coquetry with sin, together with the boasting of their frankness and their freedom, convinces him of their fatal antinomianism.[169] Their teaching about marriage, with its unrestrained expressions, must cause the hearers to have evil thoughts, quite apart from the fact that it is exalted to a sacrament in a way foreign to protestantism.[170] In other respects also he feels that they include Roman Catholic elements. Their doctrine of the sacrament reminds him of transubstantiation, and similarly their reverential attitude towards the baptismal water indicates to him a Roman Catholic streak.[171] Their fondness for titles, their requirement of praise, which sustains the highly-placed, wealthy members, and the fantastic figures they give for their riches, run counter to the early Christian spirit which they claim for themselves. Counter to that same spirit are their constant self-praise and over-estimation of their own Church.[172] Their appeal to the Augsburg Confession is only partially justified, since in their obedience to the worldly authority they refuse to take an oath or bear arms, and so only follow it in an attenuated way. They are accordingly remiss, if not completely deceitful. On the other hand the Synod of Berne, which they represent as the basic writing for their reformed tradition, in the darkness and indecisive nature of many of its points, actually corresponds better with their position, as Wesley could not resist ironically mentioning.[173] Also they boast without justification about the ancient Moravian tradition, for John Hus would turn in his grave if he could see them claiming to be his successors.[174]

Wesley regarded Count Zinzendorf as the plan upon which the whole building was based. Under all the many disguises and veilings in the Herrnhut organization Wesley discovered his control. Since that control was thought of as extending throughout his lifetime, and included the right to name his successor, it is reminiscent of the position of an earthly monarch. For the Brethren Community he is the emperor who moves the universe. So much does his authority seem to Wesley the decisive characteristic of the whole concern, that the Brethren are to be regarded as his private undertaking in the name of Christ, which, with the Christian, is placed in absolute subservience to himself.[175] Moreover he condemns the practice of the ministry, by which the Brethren elevate simple artisans to the position of ecclesiastical dignitaries, because this must destroy natural modesty and engender false pretensions.[176] When finally they lament that they have been persecuted for the last thirty years, he replies with emphasis that they harvest opposition, not because of their confession of Jesus Christ, but on account of their peculiarities.[177] The pride in their pedigree prevents them, as he sarcastically says, from having any connexion with the Methodists in the past or the future,[178] therefore they are not in a position to give a true account of the Methodists' teaching; indeed they can only falsify it with their own tarnish.[179] As a Methodist he can only appeal to them to turn back to the Bible, to see through and repent of their dangerous situation.[180]

Well nigh every sentence of this book expressed his resolute opposition. The author ruthlessly exposed all the weaknesses and defects of the Brethren, leaving nothing good. At least so it appeared; but this was not in fact the case. He still found some things to praise, above all the fact that they accepted the Augsburg Confession; its clarity and general attitude to the Church he too found acceptable.[181] Besides, this book was not the last word on the subject. Between 1753 and 1756 Heinrich Rimius, a former councillor from Brandenberg in Prussia who was living in London, wrote four weighty volumes against the Herrnhuters, providing many unsuspecting folk with an insight into the follies of their sifting-time at Büdingen. But Wesley did not make use of these books; he remarked shortly that Rimius had not been able to teach him anything new. He was also led to say that God's judgement against these works of darkness was imminent, and that no one capable of impartiality would have anything more to do with such wicked men.[182] Shortly afterwards he learned from a former member of the Brethren that Rimius had not told the worst about their 'marriage economy' with its deceptive practices, far exceeding the shocking customs of barbarous peoples.[183] Wesley contented himself with condemning these, without pursuing them in any more detail.

Had he finished with the Moravians and finally given them up? In no sense was this so. Although it seems remarkable, at the same time and apparently in contradiction to all this he was endeavouring to get closer to them. Quite openly he felt an affectionate responsibility towards those from whom he had not been set free. On 8th December 1745, together with his brother Charles, he sent to the Synod of the Moravian Brethren at Marienborn a proposal for union,[184] or at least a request that they should join in a serious discussion about their differences, but it appears that he received no reply. When he met John Gambold again on 5th November and 16th December 1763, he wrote the moving words: 'Who but Count Zinzendorf could have separated such friends as we were? Shall we never unite again?'[185] He felt just the same when in December 1771, after an interval of twenty-five years, he once more met James Hutton.[186] Actually in the years 1785 and 1786 a deliberate attempt was made to restore the unity. The spokesman on the Herrnhut side was the former Baptist preacher Benjamin La Trobe, who had had a share in the beginnings of Methodism in Dublin, while the Methodist representative was Thomas Coke, the North American superintendent and 'bishop of missions', the man who after Wesley's death became the leader of Methodism.[187] John Wesley was himself passed over, because the Herrnhuters considered him to be autocratic. It was La Trobe who cruelly said that he doubted whether the leader of the Methodist movement had ever regarded himself as a sinner or thought of Jesus as his Saviour.[188] For this reason Charles Wesley was brought in. The proceedings led to no tangible results so far as organization or doctrine were concerned, but they were significant in themselves. Both groups rightly recognized that through the theme of justification and new birth they continued to belong to each other, and that they were not merely under obligation to one another only for their beginnings.

TWO

The Progress of the Evangelistic Movement

GREATLY as John Wesley was involved in doctrinal controversies he did not allow himself to be totally confined to them. In the severe winter of 1740–1, by organizing collections, he saw that the poorest members of his societies received bread, food and warmth. He appointed fast-days and days of prayer, at which the collections helped to provide clothing and shoes, and in this way drew attention to the invasion which the French were threatening, which might well shortly make such charitable enterprises impossible. In this way he showed that he stood in direct opposition to that attitude of increasing disregard for the needs of others which was tending to develop. For him the awakening of the spirit of love and readiness to give help was part of the restoration of primitive Christianity.[1]

In the midst of his unceasing evangelical activity he fell victim to a fever, which forced him to go to bed. He at once used the time to read books and recorded his opinions about them: Turretin's *History of the Church* seemed to him dry and heavy, the *Theologia Germanica*, which he now finally dismissed in favour of the plain words of the apostles and prophets, the *Ecclesiastical History* of Eusebius, which on account of its uncritical admiration of Constantine and Constantinian Christianity he could only censure, and Laval's *History of the Reformed Churches in France*, which he found contained much evidence for God's interventions.[2] But he did not permit himself any rest, and as soon as it was possible he allowed the members of his societies to come to his bedside, in order that he might help them as their pastor. In the course of one day fifty or sixty people availed themselves of the opportunity.[3] He knew everyone by name, and this was a remarkable help in keeping the societies together.

From the very beginning Wesley was severe in the exercise of discipline over his members, and also in the choice of his fellow-workers. Although it caused him pain he did not hesitate to exclude more than thirty members in Bristol, because they had brought disgrace to the Gospel.[4] He did not accept the offer of help from a minister who had returned from North America until he had tested by the apostolic standard whether the aspirant to the position really held all things dung and dross to win Jesus Christ.[5] He revived the liturgical use of the night watch, as practised in early eastern and western monasticism; first among the coal-miners of Kingswood, where he put it in the place of the Saturday nights which, after being paid, they spent in noisy drinking; and then soon afterwards also in London, and later in many other places.[6] In the meetings the familiar phenomena showed themselves, joy and exultation in the saving presence of Jesus Christ and in freedom from the burden of sin, and the sudden conversion of blasphemers, who had even sworn to ridicule and attack them, and went so far as to hurl stones at them. Among his members the female element was in the majority.

The work spread ever farther afield. Wesley passed hurriedly through Cornwall and the further parts of Wales. But more important was the opening to him in the north of Newcastle-upon-Tyne of a third independent area alongside London and Bristol; this northern area was a centre of the coal industry. To a certain extent Benjamin Ingham, the brother-in-law of the Countess of Huntingdon, had worked there previously, since he had preached in the neighbourhood of Birstall and obtained the services of the stonemason John Nelson as a lay-preacher.[7] Naturally this was scarcely to be compared with the great and successful activity of George Whitefield in Bristol, who in a unique manner had prepared the way there, while Newcastle had then not yet been reached. But the similarity between the two must not be overlooked. The work was begun by another, while it was John Wesley who continued it and increased it to large proportions. He went to Newcastle, not on his own initiative, but at the instigation of the Countess of Huntingdon, who got to know of the situation in the neighbourhood.[8] Wesley made his first journey there in May 1742. Riding his horse to the town he read Xenophon's *Memorable Things of Socrates* and found it instructive to note—in distinction to Plato's admiring description—how many shadows lay over the brightest picture of all heathen antiquity.

The town itself seemed to him a vulgar example of modern paganism, since there was so much cursing and swearing, not only from drunken folk, but even from the mouths of little children. He doubted whether he had ever heard so much in so short a time. The place seemed ripe for Him who would call, not the righteous, but sinners to repentance. Accordingly he began on the Sunday at seven in the morning at Sandgate, the worst part of the town, and with his companion John Taylor stood in the street and sang Psalm 100, 'Make a joyful noise unto the Lord, all ye lands!' Three or four people came out of their houses, curious to see what was happening. Within a brief period the two singers were surrounded by several hundred folk. Wesley preached on the suffering servant from Isaiah 53: 'He was wounded for our transgressions, He was bruised for our iniquities: the chastisement of our peace was upon Him; and by His stripes we are healed.' At five in the afternoon he stood in the same place and expounded the text: 'I will heal their backsliding' (Hosea 14[5]), before a huge crowd, and at the end his congregation would not let him go. A religious society, which had ceased to meet, provided the starting-point for a new one, the original members being joined by those listeners who had been recently awakened. On his further journeyings in the county of Yorkshire he repeatedly went to places where Moravians had already been before him. It was impossible to avoid controversies and divisions. Mr and Mrs Holmes, who lived at Lightcliffe near Halifax, with whom Richard Viney often made his home, were divided in their sympathies, and although a more serious cleavage was avoided, their house, under the stronger influence of the wife, subsequently became the chief centre solely of Methodism in the neighbourhood.

Wesley now continued his way to Epworth, the village where his own home had been. He was curious to know whether any would still recognize him, and so on Saturday, 5th June 1742, he went to an inn in the centre of the village, where an old servant who had worked for his father soon spoke to him. When he inquired of her if there were any people who really desired to be saved, he received the reply that not only she but also many others did, and that they claimed the forgiveness of their sins. But his father's successor, who was a confessed opponent of Methodism, not only refused him the pulpit but declined him a share in any part of the church service, at which Wesley had offered to assist—for example, in the reading of the prayers. From the text: 'Quench not the Spirit' (1 Thessalonians 5[19]) the rector directed his sermon at the Methodists, for, according to his exposition, the Spirit can be quenched by enthusiasm. However, he did not prevent John Taylor after the service, in which all the Methodists, led by John Wesley, had shared, from announcing in the churchyard that Wesley would preach there at six o'clock. A great crowd assembled for this. The preacher, who stood upon his father's gravestone, cried to them: 'The kingdom of heaven is not meat and drink; but righteousness, and peace, and joy in the Holy Ghost' (Romans 14^{17}). The following evening he preached in a private house and found even there evidence of the confusion which the Herrnhut teaching about 'stillness' had produced. Writings of Jakob Böhme, principally his commentary on Genesis entitled *Mysterium magnum*, had been circulated among his listeners. The opposition against Wesley sometimes took on amusing forms. The opponents of the Methodists had drawn a wagon-load of the 'new heretics' before a justice of the peace in Crowle, George Stovin, and when he asked what they had done he was told first that they prayed and sang from morning until night. But then an old man cried: 'They have *convarted* my wife. Till she went among them, she had such a tongue! And now she is as quiet as a lamb.' 'Take them away,' replied the justice, 'and let them convert all the scolds in the town!'

Wesley stayed in the neighbourhood of Epworth for a week. The subjects of his sermons were as at all times sin and justification, law and faith, the new birth and sanctification. John Whitelamb, who was the incumbent of his father's other church at Wroot was much more kindly disposed than his successor at Epworth. He offered him his church almost as a matter of course, and it was not able to hold all those who came. This willingness, however, was in no sense due to any real sympathy between them. It came, rather, from their personal relationship. Whitelamb was honouring his tutor from Oxford, who had been like a father to him, and who was also the son of the man who had inducted him into his living and had given him his daughter in marriage. This companionship had, to be sure, lasted only a short time, owing to the early death of the young wife, but the esteem in which the two clergymen, the elder and the younger, held each other had continued undiminished. It can be seen in the fervour with which Samuel Wesley supported Whitelamb's application to General Oglethorpe to become a missionary to the heathen in Georgia, before either John or Charles Wesley had decided to do the same. Samuel Wesley, who desired to go himself, had his age made it possible, recognized the young man as his spiritual son.[9] Now, in the year 1742,

John Wesley made a similar impression upon Whitelamb as Count Zinzendorf had made upon Wesley in 1738; he seemed to him to belong to another world, a man who ought to be approached only with reserved respect. And yet the same Whitelamb, like the rest of his generation, thought that the goings-on of Wesley's followers amounted to enthusiasm, the product of an over-heated fancy, although he expressly excluded the leaders from this judgement.[10]

John Wesley's farewell sermon in the Epworth churchyard on 13th June 1742 was heard by as great a number as when he preached in the church at Wroot. The text was the blessedness of the Sermon on the Mount. It filled him with deep gratitude that he now saw the seed of the Word bearing fruit in the soil on which his father had worked for nearly forty years.[11] After that he was occupied, mainly in his old centres of London and Bristol, for six months, but on 13th November 1742 he was again in Newcastle. The Society had kept together, and he expounded the Acts of the Apostles and the Epistle to the Romans to surprisingly large congregations. Yet the numbers did not prevent him from thinking that his words went no deeper than the surface. He was only persuaded of the effectiveness of his preaching when a woman came to a conviction of sin, accompanied by the witness of the love of God. But soon in this place also unmistakable signs of religious enthusiasm showed themselves. A certain John Brown from the neighbouring place of Tanfield Lea came riding through the town, driving the people before him, crying out that God had revealed to him that he was a king who would tread all his enemies under his feet. Wesley sent him back straightway to his work, and advised him to cry day and night to God that He might give him a lowly heart, so that Satan might not have any power over him. The admonition was apparently successful, for nine months later Wesley was able to say that Brown's rough, strong, though artless words had brought many people in Lower Spen, near Newcastle, to faith and the reading of the Bible.[12]

On the same day as this occurrence, which might so easily have brought the whole movement into disrepute, a merchant offered John Wesley a piece of ground; his neighbour assisted the transaction, and within four days the contract was signed, and this secured for Wesley a large building plot for the small sum of thirty pounds. After this agreement he was left with only one pound and six shillings, and with this he was himself to undertake the building. But then a letter from an unknown Quaker arrived, saying that he had seen Wesley in a dream, surrounded by a large flock of sheep; with the letter the writer sent one hundred pounds because he wished to ensure the erection of a meeting-place. Wesley was reminded by this remarkable beginning of August of Hermann Francke's orphan-house in Halle, and for this reason he called the new building 'the Orphan House'. Previous to this they had met in a rented room, which had been given the Old Testament name of 'Tabernacle'. Shortly before Christmas, on 20th December 1742, the foundation-stone of the new building was laid in bitterly cold weather, and several times John Wesley had to break off preaching because of spontaneous outbursts of thanksgiving. When his chief assistant Thomas Meyrick, who was so desperately ill that his doctor had given him up, was restored to consciousness and was able to speak, continuing to make progress through prayer made at his bedside, everyone regarded this as a miracle, performed as a sign of God's blessing.[13]

At the beginning of the next year, 1743, Wesley came again to Epworth. On the way he had an unpleasant experience which warned him that this time he would have a bad reception. A drunken traveller, whom he overtook while riding, plied him with so many questions that this man recognized who he was. Wesley was then charged with having forsaken his father's religion and founding a completely superfluous new sect. It was Saturday evening when Wesley reached his native village. At five on Sunday morning he preached to a group of people and at eight once again from his father's tomb. When it was proposed by those who had gathered together that they should all receive the Sacrament, he agreed, but on condition that they obtained the agreement of the curate, Romley. However, this was not forthcoming. Romley, who significantly did not come and say it himself, sent word through a messenger that he would have to refuse John Wesley himself the Sacrament, since he was not worthy of it. Hence the Sacrament did not take place. But more significant was the way in which Wesley took this refusal. Instead of brooding over the obvious insult to himself he recognized God's hand at work in it, and interpreted it as a typical outworking of a situation similar to that in which Paul found himself. He saw Epworth as the place where according to the straitest sect of our religion he had lived strictly, following the law (Acts 26[5]), and therefore there was no other place so appropriate in which he should learn a different way. It was God

Himself who cancelled the law and directed him to grace.[14] Later on he was again to find no joy in Epworth. When he was once more there on 11th May 1751, he met a congregation of 'poor, dead, senseless people'. He discovered that several of his own preachers had worked against him, and had not only picked up and retailed all evil reports about him, but had also given up all the Methodist rules and hymns. He could only ascribe it to the power of God that any spiritual life was still to be found there.[15] Moreover the curate Romley was mentally ill and died in a lunatic asylum.

Wesley's activity was characterized by early Christian experiences, at least in his own eyes. In addition to persecution his work was accompanied by signs and answers to prayer. In the neighbourhood of Stratford-on-Avon, Shakespeare's town, there lived a mentally-disturbed, middle-aged woman, who had acted like the devil incarnate towards a minister who had been summoned during one of her attacks. When she heard of Wesley's approach she desired to see him, especially as he had appeared to her in a dream so clearly that she would certainly recognize him again. Wesley went to her house, told those who were with him to remain below, and went with only one woman to her bedside. The sick woman fixed her eyes upon him, addressed him by name, and stated with conviction that she would now be better. Already she felt quite different. In the previous weeks the devil had threatened to tear her into pieces before Wesley should come, but later he had predicted that so long as Wesley remained with her, she would feel free from all her torment. Wesley sang and prayed with his associates at her bedside, and she suffered a frightful attack, from which she quickly recovered.

In Stratford he afterwards preached on the word of Jesus: 'The Son of Man hath power upon earth to forgive sins' (Mark 2[10]), and had an experience similar to that of Paul in his Areopagus speech in Athens: most remained unmoved, others mocked, and a few believed.[16] At Poppleton near York he made the acquaintance of a girl who was quite indifferent to him, who was not prepared to read the Bible to an old illiterate woman, but who suddenly, as one who had been converted, listened eagerly to his words.[17] Similarly Wesley explained in primitive Christian terms the nervous reactions to his preaching, such as constantly broke out in those who listened, and which earned him the reputation of a fanatic or enthusiast. He himself was extremely critical of such phenomena and every time tried to find out exactly whether the subjects of these hysterical outbursts had had similar attacks before. To his surprise he established that in Newcastle they were all completely healthy people. The answers he received from them agreed that the Word of God came to them in a bodily, physically experienced form, indeed that it had actually broken in upon them, unexpectedly and with pain, as if from a sword running through them or like a weight crushing them. Accordingly he had to say that it was a repetition of the biblical situation, in that the Word of God came as an active event, a real conflict between Jesus Christ and Satan.[18] It could only strengthen him in his evangelistic zeal. Without ceasing he passed hurriedly through the country to his various destinations and used even the most unlikely opportunity for proclaiming the Word of God, such as the conversation with the farrier who re-shod his horse.[19] Month after month of this ceaseless strenuous activity passed by, without there being in him any sign of natural weariness.

At the same time the scope of his activity widened. In May 1743 the opportunity unexpectedly came to purchase a church-building in London, the West Street Chapel, which had originally belonged to a Huguenot congregation. It could seat up to a thousand people, and next to it was a dwelling-house. On 29th May 1743, John Wesley held his first service in it, and administered the Sacrament to about a hundred communicants. Was this a decisive step towards an independent ecclesiastical community? Up to this point he had always stressed the fact that his meetings were only preparatory to Anglican services, not substitutes for them. He had indeed preached and offered free prayer, and allowed others to do the same. In so doing he had weakened to a small degree the liturgical pattern, in particular by not reading the Gospel for the Sunday and generally by preserving other things only as rigidly as was essential. But now he deviated from this, and since he was brought up according to the strong liturgical and hierarchical tradition of the Church of England it can only be assumed that he chose the new course consciously. Indeed, he inquired from Thomas Secker, the Bishop of Oxford, whether he should do this. Secker, who was the nearest ecclesiastical authority for Wesley as Fellow of Lincoln College, came from a nonconformist background, and he was in agreement. But his predecessor, who had ordained Wesley and who was now Archbishop of Canterbury, Dr John Potter, also concurred, and the Bishops

Edmund Gibson of London and Dr Robert Lowth of St David's were of the same mind. Neither of them regarded the proceedings as dangerous, and none believed that they would lead to separation[20]—a clear indication that they shared in the short-sightedness of their times, a period with a weakened sense of the Church.

The county of Cornwall was a world of its own in the England of that time. The Celtic background had been maintained comparatively pure in this countryside of choice beauty. The appearance of Methodism was prepared for by a remarkable experience of a clergyman, George Thomson, who from his first living had made a journey to the North American colonies and had then become incumbent of Jacobstow. He was deeply affected by a remarkable dream in which it seemed to him that the time was advanced by a month and he stood before God's throne to render an account. The dream occurred twice in the same night, and so he took it as an omen. He gave up his work and went into solitude to prepare himself for death. Study of the Bible only brought him words of condemnation. Then he turned to the Epistle to the Romans and realized that Jesus died not only for the sins of the whole world but also for his own sins. When the particular day arrived he expected the end, but it was not so; indeed he felt spiritually reborn, and so returned to his living. Thus six years before the Wesley brothers, he found an experience similar to theirs through the same document, the Epistle to the Romans, although without the mediation and confirming influence of Luther. Since that time he had preached, although within narrower limits, the message which had brought him to life again, soon assisted by John Bennett, an older clergyman. From this preaching small groups, religious societies of the older type, were formed. Then Charles Wesley made contact with these in St Ives. Straightway he was accepted by John Bennett and the members, but from the majority of clergymen he encountered the most severe opposition. He himself listened to their sermons against the new sect, the enemies of the Church, the false prophets, the Pharisees. He took them to task, without accomplishing anything. The next day the mob took the matter into their own hands. It forced its way into the room where the Methodists were meeting, smashed the window-panes, put out the candles, trampled on the seats, molested the women and made such an uproar that the service became impossible. This sort of thing was repeated three, four and five times. Charles Wesley did not allow himself to become embittered, but remained calm and continued to pray. In this way he countered the outburst of hatred and conquered it. It did not happen immediately, but after about ten days the town became quiet. It was true that he had the mayor, who was a Presbyterian, on his side. The opposition of the ministers and the inflamed mob was not, however, the whole story. Tin-workers and miners listened eagerly to the new preacher and his message of the justification of sinners. In the neighbouring place of Pool a churchwarden demanded to see Charles Wesley's ordination certificate and said that he was not satisfied with his Oxford authorization. With a group of people he drove him out of the village. On the way back they called at an inn, and in the church register there is the actual entry of one shilling spent in Anne Gartrell's tavern at the expulsion of the Methodists.[21]

When shortly afterwards, on 29th August 1743, John Wesley undertook his first journey through Cornwall from Exeter it began with what might have been a disaster. By sunset he had not yet reached his destination at St Ives, and found himself with his companions on a moor without any path, but the church bell from the nearby village of Bodmin set them to rights. In St Ives and the surrounding places many listeners gathered together almost every time he preached, but in spite of being truly moved in a general way the effect on his hearers went no deeper.[22] At the same time he experienced also surprising responses. On 21st September 1743, between three and four o'clock in the morning many tinners assembled, who waited, singing hymns, until he should preach the Gospel to them. He chose the text: 'Believe on the Lord Jesus Christ. and thou shalt be saved' (Acts 16[31]). The evening before he had already spoken to a huge crowd in the open air on Jesus Christ as wisdom and righteousness, sanctification and redemption (1 Corinthians 1[30]), and despite increasing darkness had found such close attention that he, the Anglican priest so deeply rooted in the services of the Church, felt that in this temple not made with hands God was truly worshipped in the beauty of holiness.[23] From St Ives he also visited the isolated Isles of Scilly to preach. He did this in the open air, since the clergyman denied him the use of the church. The inhabitants, who were mainly soldiers and defence-workers, listened attentively. Wesley, who could not see any sense in the strong military garrison, thought rather naïvely that he could detect God's purpose in bringing together so many people, namely, that they who would not otherwise have done so should hear the Gospel. During the stormy voyage to the islands he sang with his companions the hymn:

> *When passing through the wat'ry deep,*
> *I ask in faith His promised aid.*

In this, as in everything, he related all his experiences, down to the smallest detail, to his missionary work with a strange persistence, demonstrating thereby his continuing sense of obligation.[24] It is probable that he was calling to mind the joyful singing of the Herrnhut Brethren on the voyage to America.

His visit to Cornwall was brief. In the lay-preacher John Nelson he had a most trustworthy fellow-worker, to whom he could leave the continuance of the enterprise. Also in this year 1743 he reached for the first time the full extent of his undertaking and the limits of his capabilities for action. On 2nd October he remarked that he was not in a position to preach more than four times a day,[25] but from then onwards this number seems to have become the rule.

Cornwall soon belonged to the most successful areas for Methodism and it required attention similar to that demanded by London, Bristol and Newcastle. As early as April 1744 John Wesley returned there, and this was repeated in June and July 1745, in September 1746, and September 1748. His experiences were very varied. On the whole he found willing audiences in great numbers. At Gwennap the mayor suddenly snatched him away from his listeners and led him a long way off, after he had vainly tried to incite the crowd against him. The mayor then shouted that he would take him to serve His Majesty the King, and went on to tell him what wicked fellows belonged to the Methodist societies. His anger then cooled, and at Wesley's request he rode with him back to his people. But in Falmouth things went far worse. A great crowd there bellowed out against him in such a way that preaching or meeting was out of the question. The tumult seemed to him like the raging of the sea. They cried out: 'Bring out the Canorum!'—an allusion to the Methodists' love of singing. They smashed in the door and brought Wesley into the road, where he could only speak to a small crowd. Finally he was freed from his unhappy situation by the local clergyman, who asked his parishioners if they were not ashamed to treat a stranger in this way. He was constantly being suspected of political espionage as an agent of the Jacobite Pretender to the throne, who was expected from France or

Spain.[26] Forty-four years later in the same spot there was actually prepared for him a royal welcome.[27]

As early as 15th October 1739 he had responded to Howell Harris's urgent invitation to go to Wales. This young man, deeply disappointed by the immorality of the Oxford undergraduates, had left the university after one term. He was constantly refused ordination into the ministry and so had become a free evangelist. Through frequent field-preaching in South Wales he had founded in a short time thirty societies. From an understandable desire to join with the Methodist movement he sought out John Wesley on 19th June 1739 in Bristol, after he had already made contact with Whitefield in March. Both Whitefield and Wesley were very favourably impressed by him. Whitefield praised his courage, by which he defied all the hostility directed against him by village magistrates, alehouse musicians and landlords, with whose trade he interfered.[28] Wesley called him a faithful soldier of Jesus Christ and pointed out that none of the evil reports about himself had prevented Harris from coming to him.[29]

John Wesley's first preaching-tour in Wales lasted a bare week, and took place in severe frost. He gained the impression that the inhabitants of this country were ripe for the Gospel, but only in the sense of desiring preaching and teaching, since those whom he had got to know were as ignorant as the Indians of North America, in spite of the fact that they could repeat the Creed, the Lord's Prayer, and the Catechism.[30] Subsequently there followed eight equally brief visits to this particular area, between the years 1740 and 1746; presumably because of difficulties of language they were confined to South Wales.[31] The ninth journey from the 4th to the 7th of August 1747 went further: it took place when he was making for Ireland.

In Ireland George Whitefield, when he returned the first time from Georgia, had already found in 1738 a ready welcome from the Archbishop of Armagh and the Bishop of Londonderry, and he had preached in the cathedral at Limerick and in various Dublin churches. Then in 1745 a soldier, whose name is unknown, founded a religious society, the direction of which was taken over by a young Baptist, Benjamin La Trobe, who later became a Herrnhut minister. In 1746 John Cennick had great success there. By this time he belonged to the Herrnhuters. About the same time Thomas Williams was also very successful as a revivalist in Dublin. He was a young man who was converted by Charles Wesley, and who during his unregenerate days had committed all sorts of misdemeanours, in particular because of his delight in attacking the clergy. He was instrumental in forming a society with 280 members and they extended an eager welcome to Wesley. They met in a building which had originally been provided as an Evangelical-Lutheran church for immigrant Germans; it held about four hundred people. In the evening the numbers were so large that John Wesley asked himself if he or his brother by continuous work could not form there a larger society than in London. He was particularly surprised that his sermon on St Paul's severe word, 'The Scripture hath concluded all under sin' (Galatians 3[22]), was received so calmly. But this was not all. The Anglican curate of St Mary's Church, Moses Roquier, invited him to preach, and Wesley was able to present himself to the Archbishop; in a conversation which lasted two or three hours he was able to clear up all sorts of questions about the Methodists.[32] But he also retained his sense of proportion. He was not blind to the fact that almost without exception the Irish Protestants were only recently transplanted there from England, and that the actual Irish Roman Catholic population was touched neither by the Anglican Church nor by him, and could not be touched, since the British policy of penal laws and acts of Parliament against Roman Catholicism excluded any possibility of attracting them. Although the curate Roquier was well disposed towards him it could scarcely be hoped that there could be any lasting friendship between them, because the former expressed himself strongly against lay preachers.[33] John Wesley's cautious and uncommitted attitude was to find its justification a little later. When his brother Charles and his friend, the Anglican clergyman Vincent Perronet, set foot in Dublin on 9th September 1747, they found that there had arisen opposition against the young Methodist congregation from both the Roman Catholic and Anglican sides. It had become the target for the street mob, which gave powerful expression to all the characteristically Irish love of conflict.[34]

The second time that John Wesley went to Ireland was nine months later, and he stayed ten days until 17th May 1748.[35] The first thing which struck him in Dublin was that the membership of his society had been greatly exaggerated; it was therefore a time to advocate an attitude of critical, sober judgement, and respect for truth.[36] It is necessary to extend the same caution towards his own assessment of numbers! Elsewhere he found things different; surprisingly there was a response among people of good standing,[37] and even among Roman Catholics.[38] With the latter he could have very different experiences. Sometimes their priests came to listen;[39] at other times they fetched their people away;[40] or again they decried him as a liar.[41] Roman Catholics and Quakers even joined together in the Methodist societies.[42] In Ireland also he instituted what was quite unusual there—a service at five o'clock in the morning; moreover it proved successful.[43] A night without sleep was not able to diminish the vigour of his preaching.[44] His opinions about the people varied considerably, oscillating between high praise and severe censure. He appreciated their receptive attitude and readiness to listen;[45] therefore he was not surprised at the quick and ready hearing the Gospel found in the country.[46] He could say of the people in Kilmoriarty in his characteristic way, which delighted in superlatives, that they combined the best natural qualities of each of the British peoples. They had the softness and courtesy of the Irish, the seriousness of the Scots, and the openness of the English.[47] When he time and again came upon ruins in the countryside he was forcibly reminded of the uprisings and punitive expeditions and the destruction they caused. But just as often the decayed buildings spoke to him of the instability and neglect of the builders, who simply left off what they had begun because they had lost the will to persevere. He was even led to the serious conclusion that God had a controversy with the land because it was defiled with so much blood.[48] On the other hand he found some confirmation of this in the fact that in the history of the conversion of the country in the early Middle Ages there had been no experience of the Cross but only success, among high and low, kings, nobles and people alike.[49]

The next two visits in the years 1749 and 1750 took place at what was now the usual time, and they lasted from the beginning of April until the middle of June. Similar experiences were repeated; but they were supplemented by one important feature. From this time onwards soldiers formed a characteristic part of Methodist membership. In May 1756 this went so far that Wesley was permitted to preach in the barracks.[50] On 28th and 29th June 1760 he stood as a preacher of the Gospel in the barrack-yard in Sligo before the colonel and other officers, and in the following years the series of sermons in this style went on without interruption.[51] Limerick in particular was an outstanding place.[52] So Wesley felt that this was his special task. He said: 'Still, in Ireland, the first call is to the soldiery.'[53] On 12th May 1773, in Clare, the only folk who came to listen to him were soldiers. Afterwards he conversed with the commanding officer and then put up for the night in the barracks itself, since this was the only place in this wretched little town in which the Methodist society had greatly declined.[54]

Yet another world swung into his horizon. In the immediate neighbourhood of Limerick there had been since 1709 several settlements of people from the Palatinate which had in many ways retained their German character. Since they had no pastor they had sunk lower than the Irish around them; their drunkenness, cursing, swearing and their complete indifference to Christian worship had earned them a dismal notoriety, until a lay-preacher, Philip Embury, who had been won by Wesley's preaching in Limerick in 1752, brought about a change in them. On 16th June 1756, John Wesley himself visited the society which had been formed in Ballingarrane by Embury and was very favourably impressed by the plain, serious people he met there.[55] Two years later he stood in the yard of the preaching-house in the neighbouring village of Courtmatrix before these folk, because the room could not hold more than half of the congregation.[56] Then when he again came to them two years afterwards he noted only praiseworthy characteristics; no cursing, drunkenness, or Sabbath-breaking, but only orderliness, diligence and a frugality which stood out in sharp contrast to the luxury enjoyed by their landlords. He had a keen appreciation of the social problem which was already resulting in a growing emigration to North America.[57]

Altogether John Wesley went to Ireland twenty times in forty-three years. He was fascinated by the Emerald Isle, and all his life he felt a strong attachment to it.[58] Its stormy history, the influence of Roman Catholicism with all its merits and weaknesses,[59] the childlike openness of the people, which expressed itself in affection and gambling on the one hand and in indolence and sudden anger on the other, seemed to him to provide special opportunities for the proclamation of the Gospel and for the building up of his societies. In spite of the ancient religious tradition it was all virgin soil. In addition to this he greatly appreciated the peaceful beauty of the countryside. Everywhere, over nature, people and their habitations, lay the spell of an unspoiled world. The summons of his preaching in church and under open sky awakened it to a deeper life.

A review of the records of his Irish journeys discloses a highly coloured picture: large and small gatherings, flourishing and then languishing societies, mockery and expressions of enmity, from the throwing of mud, eggs and stones to the spilling of blood;[60] from Roman Catholic priests there was every type of attitude from open opposition and baiting in secret to friendly advances and interested attention; from the Anglicans came mainly support, but also indifference. Only one thing was different from earlier times. The personal experiences of members, the confession of sins and the testimony to salvation, and the excited outcries of the new converts, strikingly were no longer prominent. There is hardly one account which is like those of the first meetings in Bristol and London. From this point of view the proceedings were more normal.

What was the situation in Scotland, the remaining part of the British Isles? Not until 24th April 1751 did Wesley first set foot on Scottish soil, and he did so reluctantly. With reluctance also he began to preach there, since he supposed that he was under no necessity to do so. This feeling of strangeness was understandable. In Scotland neither the familiar Church of England nor even Roman Catholicism were in the majority, but Presbyterian Calvinism, with which he was in theological disagreement. The attitude of the congregation during service was characteristically different from his own. He could not sufficiently extol Anglican reverence in comparison with the easygoing behaviour of Presbyterians.[61] The Presbyterian service of the 'Kirk' in contrast to the Anglican 'Church' seemed to him poor and tedious, like weak new wine, which the taste of the genuine old article renders insipid. He was still of the same opinion twenty years later. Nevertheless his presentiment that his preaching would be unwelcome immediately proved to be untrue. Whether from curiosity or because they were really affected the assembled crowd listened as if enchanted, in contrast to the chatter and laughing which, as he had been informed, was the order of the day in Presbyterian services. This happened in Musselburgh near Edinburgh. In the town, to which he had been invited by an officer, he discovered a willingness to listen, a fact which contradicted the commonly held opinion about the Scots and their shyness to strangers; he even received an invitation to remain from one of the baillies of the town and one of the elders of the church. They wanted to provide him with a larger place than the school in which he had preached, but he had to decline because his duties called him back to Newcastle. Perceptive as ever he took note of the features of his new environment. Besides the dirt, for which Edinburgh seemed to him to surpass all other cities, not excluding Cologne on the Rhine, there was an air of antiquity in the towns. It spoke of the rich memories from the national history, which was closely bound up with the hilly landscape; this he found particularly pleasing. But he also praised the very friendly attitude of the people, and, down-to-earth man as he was, noted gratefully the good, abundant and cheap hospitality in the inns.[62]

In June 1757 he preached in the environs of Glasgow, where he had a warm friend in the Presbyterian minister, Dr Gillies, who accompanied him everywhere and introduced him. The crowds which assembled, especially in Musselburgh, caused him to wonder whether the time had not come when even these wise Scots should become fools for Christ's sake.[63] Two years later, in May 1759, he nevertheless found that the little society which had been formed in Glasgow was in a state of dissolution, so that he no longer wished to spend much time over it. Only if it showed any likelihood of continuing would he want to return.[64] Similar unfortunate experiences took place in April 1765 in Dunbar, Edinburgh, and again in Glasgow. Moreover literary attacks had added to the confusion.[65] In the following year differences between him and the Presbyterian ministers came to a head, especially when Wesley was staying in Edinburgh at the time of the General Assembly. In contrast to Whitefield he found the behaviour of the ministers unbecoming and inappropriate, and he was of the same opinion about their thundering sermons.[66] Further, when he read the account of the Scottish Reformation written by its leader John Knox, and when later he saw for himself the fanaticism of the reformer in the destruction of great medieval churches,[67] his unfavourable impression was finally confirmed. How could a Church with such beginnings of bitterness, excess and pride develop the qualities of Christian compassion, joy and humility? But deeply as he felt this, and though he both rebelled against it and suffered from it, he nevertheless avoided reference to his membership in the Church of England as a point of difference; this was, for Wesley, a change of attitude. Instead he stressed the fact that he preached, practised and inculcated the religion of the Bible only.[68] It is clear that his idea of the religion of the Bible, namely full communion with God, which he understood with 2 Peter 1[4] as participation in the divine nature, was enough in itself to make him feel that the formal orthodoxy of the Calvinists was insufficient.[69] On 18th April 1772 he preached powerfully in Glasgow against their bigoted over-estimation of their opinions and forms and modes of worship.[70] Even in his old age, when in Scotland once again, he emphasized that the Methodist societies, unlike all other churches in Christendom, maintained a unique openness in opinions and modes of worship and went further than any others in granting liberty of conscience.[71]

Wesley was in Scotland eleven times between 1767 and 1790, going every two or three years. He always undertook the journey from Newcastle and stayed for about three weeks. He therefore lacked nothing in zeal, but the result was not commensurate with all this effort. The societies which he founded principally in Edinburgh, Glasgow, Aberdeen, Perth and Leith did not grow; on the contrary they declined, strikingly so in Edinburgh, where in two years (1768–1770) the numbers fell from 150 to 60.[72] There he was impressed by the fact that through contention within the societies the devil does his work among the children of God.[73] He continually asked himself why the results were so meagre, and discovered all kinds of causes. In the first place he blamed the indolence of his preachers, because, tired of itinerating, they remained too long in the same place and so could not keep the attention of their listeners.[74] Then he charged them with being too cowardly in their preaching and—like the whole Presbyterian Church of Scotland—failing to apply personally the truth of salvation or relate it to the lives of themselves or their people.[75] For this reason the Scots were very hard to move[76] and had a false estimate of themselves, as if they were wise. This inverted good sense blocked even the way to the hearts of his listeners.[77] Only one place proved to be an exception, and that was the little town of Arbroath. There he wrought a profound change; from a wilderness, which was notorious for its wickedness and immorality, a fine garden of true virtue and order had developed.[78] He could say of the members of his society that nobody in England excelled them in simplicity of heart and love.[79] Ten years later, in May 1784, he called them a model Methodist society, because perfection in love was the bond which united them.[80] But there had been a decline in between these dates. On 2nd June 1779 he discovered that, owing to the influence of the heretical John Glass, they had been persuaded of a merely notional faith, and that this prevented any real progress in the work of God.[81] But he could also speak quite differently, and in a surprisingly favourable way, of Scotland. A large assembly of people in Dumfries in 1788, where a new preaching-house was being built, led him to comment: 'Surely the Scots are the best hearers in Europe!'[82]

The attitude of the various official representatives to Wesley himself varied between two extremes. The towns of Perth and Arbroath in 1772 both gave him the freedom of the city[83]—while in Edinburgh in 1774 because of a deposition he was arrested.[84] Representatives of both the Church of Scotland and the Episcopalian Church quite on their own initiative placed their buildings at his disposal,[85] and in the Port of Glasgow he was able to preach in the Freemasons' Lodge, and chose, since many wealthy and light-hearted people were present, the subject of judgement.[86] Proceedings in Scotland were less dramatic than in Ireland. There were no riots; there was nothing unusual by way of enthusiastic reception or rejection. As a whole the country was very hard soil and retained an attitude of great reserve. People were willing to accept John Wesley, although with hesitation, and they showed respect to him; but they did not give themselves over to him. Viewed as a whole the failures were greater than elsewhere; and they were of a lasting character. Methodism has never really been able to get a footing in Scotland. It has only warmed the coolness of Calvinism and softened its austerity. The reformed principle of congregational life, the connexion between the minister and the individual congregation, proved too strong, so that the itinerant preacher, exclusively responsible to the leader of the movement, found no support.[87] This responsibility, which was characteristic of Methodism, implied not only an authoritarian element but a condition of the whole Church in its set-up, and thus it stood in two-fold opposition to Presbyterianism. For the latter, church means congregation; and the very close relationship to political development gave the local congregation a characteristic stability and self-sufficiency to which the further splitting-up into Herrnhut-Methodist 'bands' or 'societies' ran contrary. Thus in content and form, in 'theology' as well as organization, Methodism in Scotland has remained a foreign body. John Wesley's first reserved attitude to this land was a parabolic foreshadowing of the fate of his movement.

So John Wesley touched some part of each country in the British Isles. Did he also see a task awaiting him in the North American colonies? Was it not made insistently clear to him by the course his own life had taken? Had he not left Georgia in 1737 with the lament: 'I took my leave of America, though, if it please God, not for ever'?[88] His attention and sense of obligation were once again turned to the New World by the young Swedish Embassy Pietist pastor, Dr Carl Magnus Wrangel (1727–99), who had worked in Pennsylvania from 1758 to 1768.[89] Wrangel had made friends with the Halle Pietist, Heinrich Melchior Mühlenberg (1711–87), who had asserted his position against Count Zinzendorf and become patriarch of German-speaking North American Lutheranism; Wrangel also became the close friend of George Whitefield, so that combining in church services and theological exchanges naturally became common —to the displeasure of his orthodox Lutheran superiors at home. On the return journey to Sweden he visited John Wesley in Bristol on 14th October 1768, and even preached on 18th October to the Methodist congregation in the New Room. The leader of the society made a deep impression upon him, as did also the work among the Kingswood workmen.[90] In 1771 he founded in Sweden the *Societas pro Fide et Christianismo* on the pattern of the religious societies in England. He now asked Wesley to send some preachers to America to gather together the sheep who were without a shepherd.[91] And so once again from outside came the stimulus to undertake work in a new field.

Owing to Wesley's own very extensive activity it was of course quite clear that he could not soon go there himself. It could only be a question of help in the form of money and preachers. On 1st August 1769 he raised both points in the Conference in Leeds, relying upon reports from the two large towns of New York and Philadelphia. Two young preachers, Joseph Pilmoor and Richard Boardman, offered to go over straightway. They were to take with them fifty pounds as a gift of brotherly love from the homeland.[92] On 26th December 1769, they reported from America that a great movement had begun. The Methodist societies in both New York and Philadelphia soon had memberships of one hundred.[93] It was typical of John Wesley that immediately he planned to go there himself. He first mentioned this tentatively on 25th January 1770, rather more definitely on 17th February; four days later he had apparently made up his mind when writing to Whitefield, to whom he mentions his unimpaired health, which was then no different from twenty-five years previously, and finally on 14th December of the same year he actually refers to the coming spring. In this last letter he declares that he is as ready to go to America as to Ireland. All places are alike to him; he is attached to none in particular. He lives only for today. Wherever the work of the Lord is to be carried on, that is the place for him; it is not for the Christian to take thought for tomorrow.[94] The proposed journey did not materialize. In the near future lay the estrangement brought about by the Declaration of Independence and the War of Independence. When on 30th October 1784, now 81 years of age and having just recovered from a severe illness, Wesley was once again urged by one of the preachers just returned from America to go and see the work for himself, he resolutely refused; he said that there was only one new world which he would yet see.[95]

So the Methodist movement in America developed without Wesley's immediate influence. Its chief supports were his English preachers, whom from 1st September 1784 he ordained for North America, although only after overcoming serious hesitations.[96] The step was unavoidable if the connexion between the Methodism of the homeland and the former colonies was to be maintained. On the point at issue, John Wesley's main concern was with purity of doctrine. He feared lest heresy should creep in and be promulgated by preachers who were not regularly authorized, whether they came from England or America itself. He had in mind principally the Calvinist doctrine of predestination. He considered it his duty to prepare against this, and the medieval-Anglican conception of the bishop, which he undoubtedly accepted himself, so dominated his thinking that he expected it to be an effective protection against deviations in doctrine. The British administrative system no longer existed after the Declaration of Independence in 1776 and the victorious war. Accordingly neither was there any episcopal authority; everyone could teach in the name of Jesus Christ what he wished.[97] Since John Wesley had definitely opposed the Declaration of Independence the new situation of the American Methodists provided evidence of his standing with them; it was imperative that they should not seize this new situation as a welcome opportunity to dismiss him as leader and make themselves fully independent. On the other hand he saw that the development of Methodism into a peculiar church would be hastened unless it was given independence.

The ups and downs of the Methodist movement can be seen in the different countries. John Wesley, much as he overestimated his numbers and loved superlatives, was temperate enough to retain a clear sight of other aspects. A few examples will suffice. Between 30th December 1742 and 12th March 1743, seventy-six members left his society in Newcastle, and he investigated the reasons with great care in each individual case. Fourteen, as members of other churches, had been threatened by their ministers with exclusion from Holy Communion, nine were opposed by their husbands, twelve by their parents, five by their employers. Seven had been enticed away by acquaintances, five were influenced by the bad things said about the Methodist society, nine were not willing to be laughed at, three left because they feared they would lose their poor allowance, three more because they could not spare the time; for two the distance was too great, one woman was afraid of falling into fits, another gave up because people were rude in the street. Two could not abide an apparently important member,[98] one felt that by taking part he was turning back upon his baptism, one disapproved because all the group were known to be under an obligation to the Church of England, and another believed he could postpone until later the serious turning to God. So light-heartedness, indolence, the fear of other people, external pressure and genuine scruples were united in motley array against the new movement. The list shows the sort of burdens a person took upon himself when he wished to belong to it.

But the opposite situation occurred, in that members were excluded from the societies. This happened to sixty-four people in the same place during the same period. In this case also Wesley details the reasons and provides in miniature a picture of common behaviour. In the case of twenty-nine members general lightness and careless-ness were given as the ground; seventeen were dismissed for drunkenness, two for retailing spiritous liquor, four for railing and evil-speaking, three for habitual, wilful lying, three again for quarrel-ling, two for habitual Sabbath-breaking, two others for cursing and swearing, one for laziness, and another for beating his wife. This is a measure of the care he took to preserve the identity of a society of convinced Christians. It indicates the absence of illusions in the strictness of his judgement and his procedure when he showed surprise that after a thorough purging of his society in Bristol more than seven hundred members remained.[99]

One thing is noteworthy in the expansion of the Methodist area of activity: it never took place as a result of the personal initiative of John Wesley. He did not take the lead as commander-in-chief or conqueror, in the way Johann Gottfried Herder spoke about Count Zinzendorf.[100] He allowed himself to be called. It was always a case of responding to an invitation, whether it came from a layman or preacher. The dominant influence of the idea of calling, which had driven him away from his beloved Herrnhut in August 1738, asserted itself here also. His natural endowment of course was a help to him; he was more of an optimist than a pessimist, and for him hope outweighed fear.[101] This meant that he had an unshakeable conviction that Christian truth would overcome every opposition. In all conflicts and disappointments he felt that neither hypocrisy nor bigotry, neither the rationalistic arguments of unbelievers nor the shameful lives of Christians, could weaken it.[102]

The opposite was also true. If there were no invitation from the field itself, even if the offer came from among his own circle, it was rejected. That happened on 14th February 1784, when at a conference of his preachers it was discussed whether anyone should be sent to the East Indies as a missionary.[103]

If the reasons for the extraordinary effect of John Wesley's preaching and that of his associates are sought, it is its content which must be held primarily responsible. For the majority of people in England at that time it was a completely surprising message. Repentance, confessions of sins, forgiveness of guilt, new birth, new life through sanctification, righteousness by grace through faith in the sacrificial death of Jesus Christ, and a personal faith-relationship to Jesus Christ Himself were unfamiliar to a generation which on the one hand was satisfied with a traditional type of church life without real reflection, and on the other, if it did pause to think, put questions about divine providence, or the agreement of natural and revealed knowledge, or the establishment of morality in the centre. At best, faith in Jesus Christ was added as supplementary.[104] One further thing may be said. The Puritan culture of individualism and observation of the self had long since ceased to apply to all. For a large part of Anglican Church adherents the religious life was confined to maintaining a correct relationship with the Church. Institutionalism, which every Church closely bound up with authority necessarily produces, was in this instance particularly rife, and it seemed difficult to break through it with the particular means provided by this Church. Moreover, among the Methodists there was another distinctive feature. Whilst the Anglican clergy read their sermons out of a book without any animation, the Methodists proclaimed the biblical truths in free, lively speech, accompanied by personal witness.[105]

THREE

John Wesley as Organizer of the Methodist Movement

IN ADDITION to the preaching of John Wesley the Methodist movement owed much of its abiding effectiveness to its carefully planned structure, which was so resolutely carried through. According to John Wesley's account[1] its chief feature, the class system, developed from no plan, but sprung up spontaneously, without design or direction. People who had been affected by his preaching asked him to watch over their spiritual life. They felt impelled to do this because by accepting the totally unusual message of justification by faith they placed themselves at once in very sharp contrast to their environment. Everything seemed against them; their nearest associates, parents, brothers and sisters, neighbours, friends and acquaintances thought they were almost crazy. Threatened by complete isolation they not only bound themselves together in the one fellowship which offered them support, but they also desired a regular way of being strengthened by the man who had brought them into this situation.[2] John Wesley responded to their wish; every Thursday evening they met in London to take counsel together and for exhortation, and to pray together for each other. So it was that the decisive impulse towards organization came from the preaching; it was both the determining factor and the fashioning principle. Wesley's movement once again showed itself as a preaching movement.

Soon it became evident that it was only through such close fellowships that people continued in the faith. Those who did not join the 'Society' sooner or later fell back into their former careless life. But the growing numbers were too great for John Wesley. He could see no other solution than the division of his 'Society' into groups of ten to twelve people. These were the classes. Men and women, old and young, without distinction met together in them;[3] it is possible that people met simply with those who lived near, for it was the leader's responsibility to inquire into the spiritual condition of each member at least once a week. He was to see how they advanced in the faith and according to each one's spiritual state to counsel, rebuke, console or admonish them. On the other hand he had to report to the minister of the society, that is, John Wesley himself, cases of sickness or even unruly members. Finally, following the proposal first suggested by a Captain Foy on 15th February 1742 in Bristol to help meet the cost of the New Room, it was his duty to collect a penny a week for the poor and to hand over the money to the stewards of the society. Soon, however, the house visitation proved to be impractical, since it was generally unfavourable towards real spiritual conversation. Those visited were not alone when they talked, and in cases of dispute only one side of the argument was heard, while some of those living in the house did not allow visits of this kind to take place at all. Accordingly the members of the classes came to meet together, and so a real encounter and true exchange between the members was assured. People shared experiences with each other, bore the burdens and cares of a brother, spoke openly with each other and so nipped in the bud rumours and evil gossip. People prayed and sang with each other. In spite of certain, quite understandable opposition the class-meeting became established. Wesley himself dealt energetically and patiently with its critics, who felt that their freedom was threatened, or that they were forced to speak in an unusual way before other people, or that the whole thing was an unnecessary novelty.[4] A more serious objection was that the leaders were not equipped for the task, and in this case Wesley was prepared immediately to replace anyone by a more suitable person, if such were available; however, he warned against over-hasty condemnation and pointed out that until then God had blessed the work in spite of their inadequacy.[5]

But even the 'society' and the 'classes' were not enough on their own. Many folk desired an even deeper and stricter fellowship through which they could not only seek strength for their faith, but also speak without reserve of their remaining spiritual struggles and temptations, without fear of confessing their backsliding into former sins. Such a need gave rise to the 'bands'.[6] In these, people were arranged according to age and sex. They met on one evening a week and each member gave without reserve a full account of the condition of his heart, his actions, his experiences, his thoughts, feelings and desires. The leader began the proceedings along these lines and then

G

acted as guide. Originally all the men's bands met with John Wesley every Wednesday evening, and the women met together every Sunday evening for prayer and exhortation. In addition he spoke with each member individually at least once a quarter in order to know personally how they were advancing in the faith.[7] These things took place, however, not only at the desire of the members, for Wesley himself wanted to have a special group in which he could completely confide.[8] In the matter of pastoral care and oversight he put the emphasis upon joint responsibility.

John Wesley derived the impulse towards the organization of the classes and bands, as well as their names, from Herrnhut.[9] They had started with Peter Böhler in Oxford, and it was there and in the place of their origin in August 1738 that Wesley had been able to become acquainted with them. Their naturalization on English soil was made easier because for two generations experience of something similar had been provided by the religious societies of Horneck, Smithies and Beveridge. In spite of this John Wesley did not consider taking over absolutely the Herrnhut arrangement of them. He criticized particularly the Herrnhut office of 'Ermahners' (monitors) for a whole series of reasons. They had no scriptural warrant. They ran contrary to the real purpose of the 'bands', according to which particular stress was laid upon the mutual responsibility of the members. As a definite 'office' they restricted the mutual freedom which pastoral care essentially requires. Further they could lead to the situation in which some might be deprived of their brother's admonition, and so to the violation of the biblical commandment, 'Thou shalt in any wise reprove thy brother.' This had been his own experience, and this reference to himself gave his objection particular weight. According to the judgement of the Herrnhut Brethren, he himself had sinned in Savannah. But nobody reproved him. The first time this had lasted seven months, the second time five. When eventually the Salzburg minister Johann Martin Bolzius had spoken to him of his own accord he himself had been reproved for taking on the task for which he was not commissioned.[10] But all these objections sprang from one chief consideration concerning pastoral care. Wesley added to them still one more which had to do with ecclesiastical order, and which was important to him as an Anglican. The 'monitor' as a particular office in his view implied the beginning of the splitting up of the real spiritual office into separate functions, and accordingly its undermining as a basic activity of the Church. As such he could not agree with it, especially as he was convinced that bishops, priests and deacons go back to the divine arrangement.[11] He resisted a laicization of the Church.

In addition to the influence derived from Herrnhut and the religious societies John Wesley brought with him further personal considerations. As an Oxford tutor he had kept an exact account of the young men entrusted to him and had divided them into classes. When he in doing so expressly recognized scholarship as a Christian virtue and required a true concern for method and industry,[12] he was foreseeing the close relationship between the control of learning and religion. The leadership of his group, sarcastically called the Holy Club, and particularly the pastoral responsibility for one of its members, William Morgan, had made this abundantly clear to him. Nevertheless one thing turned him decisively away from the Herrnhut model. In the latter case a social and economic organization of groups which had both a considerable outer and inner dynamic developed from the classes (or as they were later called, 'choirs'), because they actually created a completely new, independent communal life which was bound to have great vitality;[13] John Wesley for his part confined the classes to their original function, mutual edification in faith. Materially he left his followers in their original situations. This was a fundamental difference from German Pietism, which set out to make the rebirth or new creation of the whole man and humanity visible in an adequate external form and to extend the work of God into the material sphere,[14] the community of Brethren determining the social structure. Wesley gave full right to the order of creation. Revolutionary change of structure of the whole situation from the inner centre outwards and conservative recognition of what was already in existence were in this way set in opposition against one another. It would be tempting to say with extreme caution that this is another instance of a basic difference between the German and English temperament.

So John Wesley ensured that his movement not only had the possibility of developing within the regular structure of the national Church, but he saved it from many of the weaknesses which necessarily resulted from the improvised and essentially experimental character of the Moravian settlements in Herrnhut and Herrnhag. But in the one essential aim, counselling and confirmation through reciprocal oversight, he remained unmoved. It was an instance of his firm adherence to the essential principle, and by this concentration upon that which was really important he showed his natural capacity for leadership.

In the year 1741 at the latest he went over to distributing membership tickets for the societies.[15] It is significant that he did not understand these simply as statistical evidence of belonging to his movement, but he wished them to be taken strictly in the early Christian sense of letters of commendation, of which also his own signature was an essential part. The ticket was a distinguishing mark which could be withdrawn if the occasion should arise that the holder was refused its renewal. It guaranteed the right of hospitality to the brother who went on a journey.[16] The oldest examples follow no regular pattern. They might carry simple symbols in light baroque design: an angel, a crown, a scroll, and later even the Crucified, or on the other hand exclusively scriptural texts with some important message like 'Now is the accepted time' (2 Corinthians 6[2]), 'Lord, increase our faith' (Luke 17[5]), 'If ye love me, keep my command-ments' (John 14[15]), 'By grace are ye saved through faith; and that not of yourselves: it is the gift of God' (Ephesians 2[8]), and 'He that cometh to me shall never hunger' (John 6[35]). In the twenty-four years between 1742 and 1765 no less than thirty-eight different types of this very modest format were used[17]—so little did Wesley care about uniformity. Only one feature was carried clearly through: the scrip-tural texts took the place of the symbols, which either were moved to the edge or disappeared altogether. There could hardly be a clearer indication that Methodism was a scriptural preaching-movement than this little thing.

The bands and classes formed the smallest units in Methodism, and that means they were an expression of its very heart. Everything depended upon the fact that they should be rightly used. It was essential to avoid constraint and inquisitiveness, to exclude fear and self-display, and at the same time to prevent them becoming rigorously systematized, which would have transformed the whole proceeding into an empty formalism. Freedom and openness, natural-ness and confidence were the essential requirements for a fruitful development. For this reason John Wesley selected the leaders with a very great sense of responsibility.

It is evident that through such a three-pronged structure, in which the pastoral point of view was always decisive, an unusually profound nurture of people could take place. What was its content, what tasks were set, what principles were central? The answers to these questions are given chiefly in the 'Rules of the United Societies' of 23rd February 1743.[18] A single but central condition of entrance was stated briefly but clearly. It was the desire—in the words of John the Baptist—to flee from the wrath to come and to be saved from their sins. Therefore a knowledge of self, derived entirely from God's judgement, was required; God's wrath and personal sin are the governing factors; they form the starting-point, but God's grace and personal purity are the goal. The individual enters upon a life-process of great strength and fullness, since it is the movement from death to life and from annihilation to fulfilment.

After this basic position had been stated the rules passed to separate, quite commonplace applications, so that a catalogue of Christian virtues was developed, which was almost a social ethic. The contrast between the great introduction and its detailed application could scarcely be greater. Can this be said to be a weakness? The answer must be definitely in the negative. It is a mark of John Wesley's wisdom that he made visible and effectual that which was decisive and significant in everyday, concrete affairs. The prohibitions enable the things with which God is wrathful, and which are sins, to be recognized. Forbidden in the first place was the profaning of the Sunday. He who disregards Sunday forgets and dishonours God. There follows drunkenness, then quarrelling, which includes going to law. Also included are lying, evil gossip, reviling, cursing and swearing, ostentatious dress such as shows itself in wearing expensive ornaments, together with selfishness and irresponsibility in money affairs (like the taking of usury and the borrowing of money without care to repay it). Then those amusements and diversions which cannot be undertaken in the name of Jesus are forbidden, as well as books and songs of a similar kind, and superfluous or disparaging speech. But Wesley did not merely lay down prohibitions. Under the key phrase, 'Doing good', an echo of his Oxford days, he required, as the essential activity of the societies, that they should perform the works of mercy commanded by Jesus,[19] as well as exhort and show pastoral concern for those who stood in need of it. The limitation is noteworthy. Wesley was giving a warning against a type of inquisitiveness and desire for power which forces its way crudely into the affairs and secrets of other people: in other words, he was simply urging them to be tactful. The reference to the works of mercy included a warning against the view characteristic of enthusiasm, that a person ought to do good only when he inwardly feels free to do so, an attitude notoriously represented by the Herrnhut idea of 'stillness'. In the third section it was expected as a matter of course that members should share in services of the Word and Sacrament, personal and family prayer, Bible reading and fasting. Whoever failed to submit to these scriptural rules, or neglected them, was in the first place to be reported to the leader, then warned and borne with for a season. If he did not then repent, the fellowship was no longer to be concerned with him.

In the bands all this was presupposed. Their questions centred around fundamental matters at a deeper level. For the members of the bands John Wesley's own experience of conversion was made the basis of the questions. For this reason these were in part expressed in the actual words of Scripture:[20] Have you the forgiveness of your sins? Have you peace with God, through our Lord Jesus Christ? Have you the witness of God's Spirit with your spirit, that you are a child of God? Is the love of God shed abroad in your heart? Has no sin, inward or outward, dominion over you? Do you desire to be told openly and plainly of your sins, whatsoever we think and hear concerning you, whatsoever fears we have concerning you? Are you yourself desirous at all times and in all things to be open with us? These questions were to be asked as often as occasion offered, but the following four were binding for every meeting: What known sins have you committed since our last meeting? What temptations have you met with? How were you delivered? What have you thought, said, or done, of which you doubt whether it be sin or not?

In this case also all the questions revolve around the question of sin, but while in the case of the societies they are on the level of the law, with the bands they seem to be concerned with the Gospel. It was not any longer a matter of avoiding sin, but of overcoming it. They concern the forgiveness of sins, assurance of salvation, and the conquest of temptation. They are governed, not by the imperative but by the indicative, not by the mandate but the actuality, by the promise rather than the commandment. So they assume a developed stage in the Christian life, which reflects a more highly developed self-awareness. Yet this advance does not imply perfection. The members of the bands were not Christian perfectionists; it is probable that they were not even on the way towards it. Their questions show remarkable sobriety, the realism of what has been attained and what is unattainable, and an atmosphere of contending for a goal which is not itself in doubt. The inexorable and penetrating exploration of conscience, which Puritanism had effected, in this case came to its finest expression.[21]

Nevertheless this theoretical and theological co-ordination through the opposition and mutual succession of law and gospel was not in practice realized all the time. An indication of this is seen in the directions given to the bands on 25th December 1744.[22] In them Wesley also took the bands back to legalistic concerns, since they are about the same commonplace prohibitions as the Rules for the Societies. They enjoin Sunday observance, in a puritanical way forbid the drinking of alcohol and the smoking of tobacco, and condemn the immoderate wearing of necklaces, rings and ear-rings. They require honesty and trustworthiness in work, and forbid speaking behind a person's back. They call for quite concrete good works, such as almsgiving to the greatest possible extent. They warn that all who are seen to be sinning should be reproved with the love and meekness of wisdom, and that the members themselves should be patterns of diligence, frugality and self-denial.

From such austerity a disciplinary practice followed of its own accord. Those who sinned deliberately or who involuntarily fell into faults of this kind, and regarded them lightly, as well as those who were on the whole negligent or indolent, Wesley separated from the society for a time as penitents, and he met with them on Saturdays for a special service. All the hymns, exhortations and prayers were adapted to their circumstances, and the threats and promises of God's Word were directed to bringing them back again.[23] Wesley regarded the serious use of this whole system as very important, and not for nothing has it been said that Methodism became what it did through the class system. Naturally the question as to the practicability of such a method of Church discipline has been raised in this case, as always. Was it really possible to keep such a watch on all the classes, so that the genuine members could be separated with any certainty from the false? John Wesley unconditionally affirmed that this was the case. He himself examined the classes from time to time and demanded from himself courage and steadiness, and from the class-leaders common-sense and honesty. In his sober way he put a limit to what could be done. He resolutely renounced any claim to look into men's hearts, and was content merely to observe their way of life. His realistic statement of the case is noteworthy: the essential course of a person's life is perhaps not always clearly discernible, but it would be far more remarkable if it could be hidden. On the basis of this insight he held it to be unnecessary to claim, what apparently some enthusiastic followers ascribed to him, that miraculous gift of early Christianity, the discernment of spirits.[24]

In spite of all his diffidence he found, almost to his own surprise, that he was in a situation essentially similar to that of early Christianity, and in a candidly Pauline manner he saw himself as the born leader and pastor of all his societies.[25] In this situation he required from the band to which he himself un-bosomed himself inviolable silence, and he expected that every member would submit to the directions of his minister in all matters of secondary importance.[26]

All this gives an impression of a dictatorial severity. Was this the tendency of Wesley's communities? Had not a person to expect that he would give up more than he would gain, and as a consequence experience an increasing separation from his fellows? This point of view fails to recognize their real purpose. In reality John Wesley's concern was for a true fellowship, in its original, early Christian strength, and he deplored nothing so much as lack of love.[27] The existence of the societies could only be justified when they became centres of love.

As the movement grew Wesley himself could not any longer get through all the work; so he created a further office. In addition to the class-leaders and band-leaders, he had already appointed the stewards, to look after all the financial concerns.[28] Wesley reduced their number from sixteen to seven under the clear influence of the overseers of the poor in the Acts of the Apostles. When he did this—it was on 4th June 1747[29]—the quarterly income from the money the members had to give amounted to more than £300, and the weekly contributions for the poor and sick to about £8; these were by any standard considerable sums, of which a regular account had to be kept. But at the same time the stewards had a pastoral responsibility, since they had to inform the minister, John Wesley himself, if a rule of the society was not strictly observed, and to tell the lay-preachers in love if there was anything amiss in their doctrine or life. Here can be seen once again the essentially pastoral purpose of the whole structure; he guarded against the stewards being misunderstood as merely financial officers or policemen. Wesley showed in this a wisdom whose significance was only to become clear in the modern period of the bureaucratic Church. While he required the stewards to tell the lay-preachers of any blameworthy behaviour, he trained them to show ordinary tact. The rules which he gave them clearly show this feature, an as it were automatic pedagogic function, although they are only concerned with financial and social tasks. In the first place he exhorted his fellow-workers to be frugal and moderate, and then conscientious, whilst he forbade them to contract any debts or to spend any more than they receive, even if it is with the best of intentions in helping someone who is in need. He warned them against dilatoriness in paying accounts, and desired that everything be settled within a week. No one seeking help was to be given a harsh word or even a sour look. They should rather place themselves in the situation of the poor and so deal with them as they would God should deal with themselves.[30] 'Do not hurt them, if you cannot help', ran the rule. Finally they were not to expect thanks from any man.

In connexion with the office of steward John Wesley had in mind the sick as well as the poor.[31] He knew well what a great part sickness occupies in human life, how much it causes the sufferers to ask questions about God, and how much physical need requires physical help. So, as he said in 1748, he had made medicine the diversion of his leisure hours for twenty-six years, and just before his North American appointment he did this systematically, having had an apothecary and a surgeon as advisers in the circle of his acquaintances. He separated the care of the sick from the office of steward and created the new office of sick-visitor, who was to see his patients three times a week. In this instance too he combined care of the body with that of the soul in the closest possible way,[32] and he himself shared in this service by dispensing medical remedies, which he had apparently produced with his apothecary and doctor. In this activity he had surprising cases of healing.

Even all this was not sufficient. He required assistance in his own characteristic work, that of missionary preacher; it proved impossible for him and his brother Charles, especially after they had separated from George Whitefield, to undertake the whole of the work. As early as 1738 and 1739 John Cennick and then Joseph Humphreys were active as lay-associates.[33] Their occasional use developed into a permanent feature. The new office of lay-assistant or helper was thus created, or it would be better to say, was brought to awareness, and from then on gradually received its precise character, not only in its actual form, but also in John Wesley's own mind.[34] In this case also the whole thing developed gradually, even if it was not without design. The arrangement becomes evident in the Minutes of the early Conferences from the years 1744–8, which exist in two versions; in the original transcript of John Bennet, one of the leading lay-preachers, who was originally a lawyer, as well as in the revised abstract by John Wesley himself.[35] A comparison of the two yields several important conclusions. The variation in the names is revealing. First they are called lay-assistants, later, evidently under stronger scriptural and early Christian influence, helpers, and finally lay-preachers.[36] This reflects Wesley's Anglican view of ministry and his ecclesiastical upbringing, which caused him to feel strongly against parity in the preaching of the Gospel by ordained and unordained preachers. In line with this the introductory question at a conference in London on 29th June 1744, referred quite explicitly to this point: Are Lay Assistants allowable? The answer is equally pointed: Only in cases of necessity. Their duties are the same as those of the minister, that is, John Wesley himself, and indeed are not really differentiated from his. The lay-assistant then, when the minister was absent, had to look after the congregation, or as Wesley put it in the words of Scripture, 'to feed and guide the flock'. That meant expounding the Bible every morning and evening, meeting the societies, the bands and the leaders every week in separate gatherings, visiting the classes monthly, except those in London and Bristol, hearing and deciding all differences, and seeing that all the other office-bearers, such as the leaders, stewards, schoolmasters and housekeepers, fulfil their duties. Wesley expected each of the assistants to be diligent, wasting no time, and serious, avoiding anything frivolous, and he went so far as to forbid laughing as much as cursing and wanton swearing. He was to touch no women, and under no circumstances was he to show his affection for them in those ways which were customary, even such as were usual when expressing apologies.[37]

If all this seems harsh in its inexorable puritanical self-discipline Wesley also required the assistants to be generous in relation to their fellow-men. Evil reports were not to be believed, but, since they were to act as judges, they were first of all to take the side of the accused. In the same way they were forbidden to speak evil of anyone, because that would eat as a canker; instead they were to keep their thoughts within their own breasts, until they came to the person concerned. Then of course they were to speak openly about the thing they believed to be wrong, and not to retain any ill-feeling. The same spirit of concern for others is seen in the warning not to affect the gentleman, since the assistant had as little to do with this character as with that of a dancing-master. It is possible, but not provable, that this observation was made with Count Zinzendorf in mind, since in the same context he mentions him;[38] if opportunity offered the Count was known to assert his position as a nobleman. Therefore the assistant was not to be ashamed of doing anything, including the fetching of wood, the drawing of water, or the cleaning of his own or his neighbour's shoes. They were forbidden to take money. Apostolic poverty was to guard against the foolish charge that lay-preachers become rich by the Gospel. On the other hand food and clothing might be accepted. He must report the contracting of a debt. Punctuality was a duty, as also was the keeping of the rules, which he may not himself improve. Finally it is said: 'Act in all things not according to your own will but as a son in the Gospel.' Obedience to John Wesley is expressed in similar terms as the obedience of Timothy to Paul. So the early Christian trait in the tone of the document is corroborated, and it is only with the recognition of this conformity with the New Testament that the imperious austerity, the certainty and the self-assurance in Wesley's attitude are to be understood.

The lofty ideal which is evident in these requirements was derived from a desire to become 'holy for the Lord'.[39] A corresponding feature is seen in the last of the rules of a steward, when he was reminded that he was the servant and not the master of the helper.[40]

The Rules of an Assistant reflect the spirit not only of early Christianity, but also of a monastic puritanism. They could be compared with rules of many Orders. In spite of this Wesley later found it necessary to sharpen a few things in them. Thus he demanded under the first point, the division of time, that the lay-assistant should not stay anywhere longer than was absolutely necessary. In order to make the relationship with women quite clear he forbade the assistant to take any steps towards marriage, until he had consulted with his brethren.[41] On the other hand the rigour was softened when in the later version of the Rules the prohibition against taking any money was omitted. Also in other respects he softened down their formulation both then and later, so as to let it be seen that Christian love and its expression were as important as the seriousness of the whole concern.[42] In the same way he gave the position of the lay-assistants greater precision and a higher significance. He dropped the limiting clause which said that they were only allowable in cases of necessity, and defined their character more clearly as extraordinary messengers of the Gospel in contrast to the regular ministers, the clergy of the Church of England.[43] How much lies behind this bare statement can only be seen when Wesley's deep concern for the rich tradition of the Anglican doctrine of the ministerial office is also taken into account.[44] The words testify to a deep personal disclaimer by the Anglican churchman, and express a corresponding regard for the newly-created office. It was Wesley's wish that the extraordinary messengers should provoke the regular clergy to jealousy, that is, spur them on to greater zeal. Nevertheless they were not to stand in their way, but to serve precisely those who would not be reached by the normal procedure. Therefore Wesley placed the preachers on a level with the Anglican ministers, without actually saying so. He could not give them a higher position, and it was only for rhetorical effect that he closed this section with the words, 'But how hard is it to abide here! Who does not wish to be a little higher? suppose, to be ordained!'[45] At the same time this made a clash inevitable.[46] This not only concerned the office and the work of the Holy Spirit, and with the tension between His free and restricted activity, but also with the content of the ministerial office. For the Anglican, even if neither its liturgical and sacramental character, nor its character as a priesthood, were stressed in the eighteenth century as they had been in the seventeenth, the significance of this office did not lie unequivocally, as in Methodism, in preaching and pastoral care. So John Wesley challenged the Church of his day, and he was able to do this with such, pointedness, that he asked, as if in accusation, 'Where in the present Church of England is there to be found a true Christian fellowship?' To the related charge, that he was creating a schism, because he divided Christian from Christian and Church from Church, and so destroyed the brotherhood, he replied with all the rudeness of which, in his radicalism of faith, he was capable: 'These were not Christians before they were thus joined. Most of them were barefaced heathens. Neither are they Christians from whom you suppose them to be divided. You will not look me in the face and say they are. What! drunken Christians! cursing and swearing Christians! lying Christians! cheating Christians! If these are Christians at all, they are devil Christians, as the poor Malabarians term them. Neither are they divided any more than they were before, even from these wretched devil Christians. They are as ready as ever to assist them and to perform every office of real kindness towards them. If it be said, "But there are some true Christians in the parish, and you destroy the Christian fellowship between these and them," I answer: "That which never existed cannot be destroyed. But the fellowship you speak of never existed. Therefore it cannot be destroyed." Which of those true Christians had any such fellowship with these? Who watched over them in love? Who marked their growth in grace? Who advised and exhorted them from time to time? Who prayed with them and for them as they had need? This, and this alone, is Christian fellowship; but, alas! where is it to be found? Look east or west, north or south; name what parish you please; is this Christian fellowship there? Rather, are not the bulk of the parishioners a mere rope of sand? What Christian connexion is there between them? What intercourse in spiritual things? What watching over each other's souls? What bearing of one another's burthens? What a mere jest is it, then, to talk so gravely of destroying what never was! The real truth is just the reverse of this; we introduce Christian fellowship where it was utterly destroyed. And the fruits of it have been peace, joy, love, and zeal for every good word and work.'[47]

This harsh criticism meant that John Wesley had to lay all the more weight upon real fellowship in his own communities. This applied also to the lay assistants or lay preachers. None of them was permitted to stand on his own like a minister, and it was in this that Wesley saw an essential difference between them and the Anglican order. The whole point and justification of their position lay in the fact that they worked together, supported each other, and were subordinated to himself and his brother.[48] Perhaps also the undeclared background to this was the original Christian pattern of Jesus, who sent out his disciples two by two.[49]

Alongside of class or band, and yet superior to them, the

lay-assistant, helper, or lay-preacher became the leader, the real corner-stone in the structure of Methodism. An indication of the importance which John Wesley gave him is shown in the little matter of his being required to keep a journal; this emphasized the fact that here was to be both an account of his activity for those above him and a means of spiritual growth for its author. In this also he assimilated the assistant to his own pattern, and referred him to that classic guide to the exercise of the ministerial office, the *Gildas Salvianus* or *Reformed Pastor* by Richard Baxter, from which he emphasized above everything the need for visiting people in their homes. He supported this with the sad observation that personal and family religion were in a very low state.[50] It is understandable that he was uneasy in his mind about the directions he had given, and what he ought to do for the education of these preachers. He put off the plans he had for a seminary; instead there was a discussion at the first conference about what books they ought to read.[51] It is a very surprising selection. First because an unusually large place is given to the ancient classical writers: among them were Sallust, Caesar, Cicero, Terence, Virgil, Horace, Plato, Epictetus, and the Greek Epigrams; then the Humanists, Erasmus, Castellio and the Spanish poet Hieronymus Vida. These are followed by the early Christian Apostolic Fathers, Ignatius and the classic devotional writer, Ephraim the Syrian. The representation of the Anglican tradition is notably weak, consisting only of Archbishop Ussher's Sermons. Then there is George Buchanan from the Scottish Presbyterian Church, Pascal from French Catholicism (to whom John Wesley had probably first been introduced in childhood by his mother), and Johann Arndt, Francke and Böhme from German Pietism, the last-named being really the representative of August Hermann Francke in England. In addition, the almost unknown authors Duport, Test, Nalson and Gell are named;[52] then in conclusion there is a recommendation of those Tracts in which John Wesley himself made available for his people abstracts from the Christian tradition as a whole.[53]

What does this remarkable inventory show? Obviously John Wesley set out to do two things. His associates were to acquire a tolerable general knowledge of those basic ancient writings which were used in the English schools of the period. On the other hand their knowledge of Christian literature was to embrace an unusually wide ecumenical selection, which would introduce them in a quite unprejudiced way to valuable Roman Catholic, Presbyterian and Pietist books. Such breadth of outlook stands in noteworthy contrast to the monastic and Puritan austerity which governed the Rules. Wesley showed himself accordingly a wise educator, who knew how to use both features and to give scope to each in its proper place. Yet the importance of this perhaps hastily drawn-up list ought not to be over-estimated, particularly as before all the books referred to stood the Bible itself; and Wesley expressly confessed that he was a man of *one* book.

However, Wesley was sufficiently realistic to know that the principle advocated by many lay-preachers, that they should read only the Bible and nothing else, led with certainty to their decline, to say nothing of the fact that such a point of view rendered preaching superfluous. He was quite clear about two things: first, that the biblical message could not be isolated or applied to the present situation merely by purely private and personal study of the printed word; and second, that it required a dialogue with the cultural consciousness of the time to become living, however weakly developed or poorly equipped that consciousness might be. He would not tolerate a primitive, mechanical biblicism. Consequently he strongly opposed the high-sounding claim that a man might be exclusively concerned with the study of the Bible; he recognized this as rank enthusiasm. He desired the assistant to devote five hours a day to assiduous and concentrated reading. He saw the greatest danger in idleness, and regarded this as responsible for the failure of the lay-preachers, especially in Ireland. If anybody objected that he had no taste for reading, Wesley answered curtly that he must either contract it or return to his trade.[54] After prolonged consideration it was decided that a preacher was not to continue in his former occupation alongside his work as a preacher.[55] Also Wesley declared categorically that he would no longer preach in those Methodist societies which were not willing to maintain their preachers.[56]

In spite of this his preachers remained unsophisticated men. Wesley openly recognized this and defended their lack of learning with the most powerful evidence he knew, the example of the early Christians. He quoted in this connexion Acts 4^{13} in the Greek: as Peter and John, precisely as uneducated men, caused a sensation by their witness to Jesus Christ, so the same ought to apply to His workmen today. If anybody objected to him that he was exalting himself in that he was placing himself alongside the apostles, he had to declare that every preacher of the Gospel, indeed every Christian, must show this likeness. The apostles had given an enduring example of the Christian life and work, and similarity to them only shows the seriousness which characterizes a Christian's profession in the present time. And God has clearly enough acknowledged their work, then as now. But if Wesley admitted the imperfect equipment of his people in their general education, he resolutely denied that they were ignorant in the important things; in practical Christianity, in theological matters which concern their own lives and are confirmed by them, they are superior to the majority of candidates for the ministry.[57] Because of this he rigorously kept the direction of the lay-preachers under his supervision, and commissioned his brother Charles to this task. The repeated immoral behaviour of his workers confirmed the need for this. But John Wesley, following the early Christian pattern, left open the possibility of their being accepted again, if they declared themselves repentant.[58] At the same time he fought more than anything against the idleness which led to bad, confused preaching. Also the danger of more refined vices such as effeminacy or becoming a busybody did not escape his keen notice.[59]

How important Wesley thought all this was and how well he understood the large view-point from which to see small things is shown perhaps by the words which he addressed to the preachers in Leeds in 1755: 'It has been affirmed that none of our present preachers are so much alive as they were seven years ago. I fear many are not. But if so they are not fit for the work, which requires much life. Otherwise your labours will be tiresome to yourself, and of little use to the people . . . But let your conscience be the judge. Who of you is exemplary, so much alive to God, so as to carry fire with Him wherever you go? Who of you is a pattern of self-denial in little things? Who of you drinks water? Why not? Who of you has not four meals a day? Who of you fasts on Friday? Why not? Who of you goes through his work willingly and diligently, on no account disappointing the congregations? Who visits the people on Mr Baxter's method?[60] Is your heart in the work wholly, not giving way to indolence or unconcernedness, not yielding to the fear of men?'[61]

Twenty-two years later he wrote to the preacher Alexander Mather: 'The danger of ruin to Methodism does not lie here. It springs from quite a different quarter. Our preachers, many of them, are fallen. They are not spiritual. They are not alive to God. They are soft, enervated, fearful of shame, toil, hardship . . . Give me one hundred preachers who fear nothing but sin and desire nothing but God, and I care not a straw whether they be clergymen or laymen; such alone will shake the gates of hell and set up the kingdom of heaven upon earth.'[62] So in the true manner of Pietism he put all the emphasis upon the personal condition of the holders of office. It depended on them how the Christian message and the Christian life fared in the world.

All things considered John Wesley was bound to give the highest importance to these lay-helpers, and that meant that he also had jealously to guard their reputation. In the large number of attacks which he had to answer, many concerned them, and Wesley scarcely ever became so passionate as in their defence. An open letter 'To a Clergyman', printed in Dublin in 1748,[63] which begins straight-way with the statement that he has neither the leisure nor inclination to enter into formal controversy with his opponent, refers immediately to the most pertinent analogy, that of the doctor, and bases this on the fact that it is a matter of life and death. Can you name one doctor, asks Wesley, who has obtained his doctor's degree and qualified, and has not practised for years, who heals nobody, and indeed hastens the death of some people, should they come to him one day? *Medicus est qui medetur*, he is a physician who heals. What is the use of an authority to practise without results? The position is exactly the same with a clergyman. His scriptural name is minister, which means servant, one who serves so as to bring others to eternal life and salvation. A clergyman who helps nobody through the years to this, who rests upon the official nature of his office, or who shows his unfitness for saving souls by preaching false doctrine, is of no value. Each one has to be servant of eternal life, and woe to him who hinders a layman because he cannot produce evidence of an examination in theology or certificate of ordination. He brings upon himself the suspicion that he has nothing to do with souls apart from his own advantage, and he will have to give an account on behalf of those whose salvation he has neglected.

In 1769 a clergyman at Waterford, George T. Fleury, applied to the Methodist lay-preachers Paul's warning in Acts 20[29, 30] about grievous wolves which would enter in among the flock.[64] Wesley

H

answered the abuse by showing how little his opponent knew about the Methodists and how greatly he was subject to irrational phantasies. At the same time he referred expressly to the open letter of 1748 in order not to have to repeat what was long ago shown to be untrue. Further he represents himself and his preachers in terms of deliberate irony as friends of his opponent who passionately desire for him nothing so much as eternal salvation.

Finally Wesley took care to ensure that the authority of his helpers should be taken into consideration as well as their limitations. He was able to strengthen each one in his position as well as instruct him about his limitations. The class-leaders were responsible to the assistants, and the assistants to John Wesley himself. The assistant could seek the advice of the class-leaders, but he was not obliged to do so. It was the duty of the stewards to deal only with temporal affairs. An essential element in Wesley's skill as a leader lay in this strict regulation of the spheres of responsibility and the energy with which he sought complete clarity on these points.[65]

How were Wesley's work and movement to continue? The problem was sufficiently urgent for a Conference of fellow-workers to be called, and it is perhaps a matter for surprise that this occurred as early as June 1744, six years after John Wesley's conversion and five-and-a-half after the beginning of his evangelistic activity. The idea seems to have come to him almost at once, when with Richard Viney—the man who in his restless desire for Christian fellowship moved to and fro between the Herrnhuters and early Methodism[66]— he read Zinzendorf's account of his Pennsylvanian synods. When Viney wanted to learn more about Wesley and his principles, Wesley on his own initiative invited him to a discussion about his work; it was arranged that this should take place in London on 25th June 1744.[67] The preliminary agenda, which Wesley himself drew up, was divided into the three sections of doctrine, practice and discipline. Under the first the basic points about justification, sin and entire sanctification were to be discussed. Practice included first the relationship with the Church of England, particularly obedience to the bishops, and then the procedure of the Methodists, the itinerancy of the preachers contrasted with a permanent ministry in one place. One question raised the point whether there ought to be any more preaching in those places where church buildings were at their disposal, and where friendly relations with the Church of England existed. It was further desired to clarify the question of field-preaching. But also the founding of new societies and the expansion of the movement in England were to be discussed. A very important point concerned the lay-helpers. The usually so confident John Wesley asked: Are they allowable, and are they really unblameable men? He then put down the point as to the possibility or necessity of taking over elements from the organization of the Herrnhuters, and so strikingly demonstrated the dependence of his system upon theirs, even in individual features.[68]

It is noteworthy that he also refers to the Quakers in this connexion as another possible source, so little prejudiced was this Anglican churchman. Further he wished to discuss whether they could have a 'better oeconomy in temporals'.

Under Practice he raised first the question about the duty of bearing arms. In this matter also the influence of Herrnhut is clearly to be seen; had not the Brethren once left Georgia under Spangenberg and emigrated to Pennsylvania, because they did not wish to be compelled to use arms in the colonial war of England against the French, Spaniards and Indians?[69] The next question considered the lawfulness of going to court and swearing oaths, and thus the traditional problems of the Anabaptists and the Mystical Spirituals, with their strong emphasis upon the early Christians, emerged. The answer given was contrary to the opinions of this tradition: the bearing of arms and going to law were considered to be possibilities, if not the duty, of Christians. These decisions were based upon what they believed to be the attitude of primitive Christianity. The last subject to be discussed was whether they could unite any further with Whitefield or the Moravians. Finally there came the question of a further Conference.

This draft by Wesley is instructive for several reasons. It shows the unconditional precedence given to preaching before all the other activities, and this applied to its content as well. This man of great missionary activism was at the same time a responsible theological thinker. Dogmatic principles were to be expressly discussed in detail, a fundamental treatment of every point was provided for, and frankness was definitely required as a duty. All other points were subordinated to the questions of doctrine and brought into relation with them. The whole enterprise was governed by a spirit similar to that which informed the Church orders of the Lutheran Reformation, in which all the injunctions sprang from a similar consideration, that of creating the best conditions for the proclamation of the Gospel.[70] The agenda further reveals the continuing spiritual connexion with Moravianism, and this connexion could have been established in external ways. Finally it makes it clear how unfinished everything still was, and how varied the development could be. John Wesley had a thoroughly fluid programme, and what is more, he was prepared to question everything. The same thing is seen in the fact that already he had invited Richard Viney to state all his objections against what he himself had written or organized, so that they could be discussed at the Conference.[71] All this does not sound like dictatorship, although it would be incorrect to assume that this was excluded for ever. Rather, John Wesley's assurance is shown in his ability both to encourage and to accept reproof.

When the Conference actually met, one of the first points to be considered was whether any lay-helpers were to be admitted in addition to the six ordained Anglican clergymen who were present.[72] This accordingly raised the problem of the legal equality of ministers and helpers within the growing Methodist movement. Already it was clear that it would have to be decided in a positive way in the course of time. Put in another way, Methodism would have to proceed to its own ordinations. For the time being a distinction was made. The lay-helpers were to be invited to the proceedings only as the others thought proper. Straightway another question followed, one directly concerned with discipline: how far was each of those present willing to submit to the unanimous judgement of the rest? The answer stated: in speculative matters everyone must follow his own conviction; on practical points they must submit as far as they could without wounding their consciences. So from the beginning John Wesley introduced into the Conference the principle of unanimity, and in so doing invested the Methodist movement with a weapon of great strength. The Conference of the preachers became the symbol of its unity. Closely connected with this was the duty not to divulge anything which was said about people, which was also decided at the outset. Only the very highest consideration, the preservation of God's honour, could suspend this decision.[73]

The Conferences, which from then on were held annually, became increasingly important. All questions which arose were discussed at them, and first place was always given to doctrinal matters, even if increasing time had to be given by the members to the relationship with the Church of England. Wesley kept the character of the preaching movement strongly based on biblical and dogmatic principles. At the second Conference in 1745 at Bristol a further division in the organization of the lay-preachers was made. Superintendents were appointed, and from then on they were the only ones to be described as 'assistants', while 'helper' was used for the lay-preachers. The assistants had to exercise oversight of the helpers, for whom a further injunction was added to the twelve Rules already in existence. It stated: 'You have nothing to do but to save souls. Therefore spend and be spent in this work. And go always, not only to those that want you, but to those who want you most.'[74] Thus once again the pastoral point of view, which was the basic feature of the whole structure, was sharply underlined. The third Conference, which likewise met in Bristol in 1746, recognized the arrangement of circuits (still a feature of Methodism), which were at the time seven in number. The various assistants and helpers were appointed to stations, with the qualifying note, 'as far as we can yet see'. The mobility of the preachers of the Word was consequently assured as a definite arrangement. John Wesley had for long given an example of this; now it was also clearly applied to his fellow-workers. A Methodist preacher was essentially not bound to one congregation, and he was independent of it. He was a travelling preacher in the service of the Gospel, like the first apostles and the missionaries of the early Middle Ages.

At Bristol in 1746 they also discussed the important question of how a man's call to be a preacher could be tested. It was stated that the main consideration was whether as a result of his preaching others had genuinely received the forgiveness of sins and salvation by faith.[75] In this way the main content of Wesley's conversion was elevated to the position of the principle of preaching. As in Wesley's case the material content and the spiritual effects were intertwined. This did not mean that the question of the effect depended upon special results being produced, perhaps of an excitable nature, but it was required that a genuine test should be made by another lay preacher. He was himself to hear the candidate preach and afterwards to sound the other hearers, as well as to have a more searching conversation with the preacher on trial. In addition the latter had to write down the reasons why he was applying for acceptance as a preacher. The 14th Conference, held in London in 1767, under the impulse of this very point took up the matter of attempting to appoint a governing body for the whole movement.[76]

It was only natural that the question of the relationship of the plenary power of Conference to Wesley's own authority should be raised. Must not the one threaten the other? It says much for the frankness which obtained at the meetings that he should be directly asked: 'What power is this which you exercise over both the Preachers and the societies?' John Wesley replied: 'Count Zinzendorf loved to keep all things close; I love to do all things openly.' He then went on to relate how some of his people had asked him quite of their own free will to exercise pastoral oversight of themselves, and shortly afterwards three young men had offered themselves one after the other to help, in the words of Paul, as 'sons in the gospel'. This was the historical beginning of his authority. When the numbers increased the situation remained just the same as with these first three. It was he who personally built up the movement, and he himself appointed those who assisted in the preaching, pastoral oversight and financial administration. Those first three preachers had complete freedom to leave him at any time, just as he was in no way committed to them indefinitely. He then described the extent and content of his own position and said expressly: 'What is that power? It is a power of admitting into, and excluding from, the societies under my care; of choosing and removing Stewards; of receiving or not receiving Helpers; of appointing them when, where, and how to help me, and of desiring any of them to confer with me when I see good. And as it was merely in obedience to the providence of God, and for the good of the people, that I at first accepted this power, which I never sought, so it is on the same consideration and not for profit, honour or pleasure, that I use it to this day.' When it was objected that several gentlemen were offended at his having so much power, he replied: 'I did not seek any part of it. But when it was come unawares, not daring to "bury that talent", I used it to the best of my judgement. Yet I was never fond of it. I always did, and do now, bear it as my burden—the burden which God lays upon me—and therefore I dare not lay it down.'[77] Nor will he allow the objection that this is shackling free-born Englishmen, or setting himself up as a Pope. Nobody is forced to submit to him, and everyone can at any time leave him, but while anyone chooses to stay he does it under the same terms as when he first joined him. The Pope demands obedience from every Christian for God's sake, but he does nothing of this sort. What he affirms is something totally different: all preachers who choose to labour with him choose to serve him as sons in the Gospel. Once again the Pauline and early Christian pattern was shown to be the prevailing model for his action. For this reason he definitely rejected a democratic conference with majority decisions of all the preachers present; this could not be said to correspond to such a pattern.[78] When he conceded that perhaps after his death it was possible that such an arrangement might take place, his cautious words showed how foreign and lacking in appeal this whole idea was to him; he decisively rejected any responsibility for an experiment of this kind.[79]

It can be easily understood that the very rigid discipline, even if exercised with much wisdom, was foreign to the mounting political liberalism of the period, and earned for John Wesley the charge of showing the spirit of the Jesuits.[80] His order and his leadership were in direct opposition to everything that liberalism desired and strove after. John Wesley did not allow himself to be put out by the insinuations and accusations which grew into the suspicion that he wanted by his movement to bring help to the Roman Catholic Jacobite Pretender to the throne.[81] The everlasting problem of message and structure, faith and organization, was solved astonishingly early and with a remarkable awareness of its goal, so that its emphasis upon a strong union and mutual responsibility, its combination of authority and obedience in a necessarily limited fellowship differed not only in degree but also in kind from both the Anglican tradition and the Church orders of the Lutheran Reformation, and stood nearer those early Christian congregations which were under Pauline influence.[82] It was this awareness of primitive Christianity which sustained John Wesley in everything he did and demanded, and which gave him a dominating assurance. He knew that he had the New Testament on his side, and yet he kept far enough from it to give room for gradual development and for those circumstances which had changed since the time of the early Church. If his structure is compared with that which Count Zinzendorf put in hand, there stands out, alongside the similarities which arose largely through direct borrowing, one basic difference: Zinzendorf constantly changed the details of his system, as a plethora of plans ran through his mind and caused him continually to strive after improvements; the fellowship of the Brethren was for long subject to alteration and experiment. But it was quite different with Wesley. He pursued his course with a constancy which was at the same time certain of its goal, resolute and circumspect; yet he did not desist from calling into question what had been already attained.

Besides the hesitations and censure which dominated the scene, words of recognition and encouragement were also heard. The leading voice was that of the man whom Wesley had designated as his personal successor, John William Fletcher. On the opening day of the great Conference held in Leeds on 1st August 1775—it was the 32nd, and was for long the one which made the greatest impression—he invited Wesley point-blank, with great urgency and in 'bold modesty' to take a decisive step towards the further reformation of the Church of England, a reformation which its best members basically desired. And as if to overcome his reticence and to accelerate his progress, he reminded Wesley that he had for long acted as a reformer, and that he ought now simply to complete the task. Fletcher in the first instance called for a stronger exercise of the Church's discipline, which so far as the Church of England was concerned had almost fallen into disuse; following that there should be a cleansing of its doctrine in the 39 Articles, Homilies and Liturgy from specks of Pelagian, Calvinist and popish dirt. To bring this about the Methodists should take the lead as a fighting society. To this end they must unite; all members of the movement in Great Britain, Ireland and America would have to constitute themselves a united society which would look upon itself as the daughter-church of the Church of England; the recognition of this character should be given by the Anglican authorities, the two archbishops and the bishops. This would be in the interests of the Church of England itself, for only in this way could it be defended against the attacks of the dissenters. The 'methodist' Church was called to be the educator of the 'unmethodized' Church. The preliminary requirement of this plan was the ordination by the Anglican bishops of the suitable Methodist lay-preachers. If this were refused the two Wesley brothers should on their own accord bring about an independent Church of England. The preachers would be bound by obligation to the most spiritual part of the Prayer Book, the 39 rectified Articles and the decisions of the Methodist Conferences. Its great and basic task—and it must be made visible far and wide—was to preach the grace of God in the justification of sinners against the moralism of the Socinians, the justice of God against the predestinarian capricious God of the Calvinists, and the doctrine of holiness against the whole world and worldliness.[83]

It is not difficult to recognize the great guiding principles of this plan. It can be seen as a draft which was both revolutionary and conservative, dynamic and institutional,[84] and one in which everything was to be subservient to the proclamation of the message. Its aim was the reformation of the whole Church by the message itself; everything organizational and all its suggestions for forming a Church were determined by this point of view.

In doing this Fletcher was giving precise form to a suggestion made by the lay-preacher Joseph Benson. Benson had been greatly disturbed because many Methodist preachers were not equal to the demands which had to be made on them, and so failed to realize the hopes set upon them by John Wesley and the other brethren. He had therefore proposed that all should undergo an examination which should seriously test their capabilities, exclude the unsuitable, and send those capable of improvement to Kingswood School, which had been opened by Wesley, there to undertake intensive study of the Bible, English writers in divinity, Church history and the history of England. The best qualified should be immediately ordained as ministers by the brothers Wesley, Fletcher and other presbyters of the Anglican Church; the others should be ordained after a period of training, as soon as they showed themselves competent. The whole plan, combining the features of a school so far as its purpose and scope were concerned, amounted to an intensive system of adult education,[85] from which all formal educational subjects like languages were purposely excluded. John William Fletcher's design of making the Methodist movement serve as a substitute for the whole Church went far beyond this limited plan for education in the technical sense.[86]

What did John Wesley himself have to say about this? He kept silent. So far as we know he avoided taking up any position. He read the letters to the Conference, and asked that they should be openly discussed. The conversation showed that most of the objections against the preachers were without foundation. In this way the plan to change the method of testing them came to nothing.[87]

It is possible to see the founder of the Methodist movement in this instance as inflexible and limited in outlook. Ought he not to have recognized that there was a spirit at work which fundamentally understood his design to re-awaken and give form to primitive Christianity, and which was willing to undertake just this? Perhaps John Wesley perceived this, and perhaps both his private approval and his personal difference of outlook were seen in the caution and the freedom with which he handled the Benson-Fletcher proposal. He was sufficiently practical to distinguish between the situation at the time and what might happen after his death, and sufficiently discreet in himself and his exercise of authority not to bind the future. It may be that he actually wanted John William Fletcher to be his successor for the sake of this plan. In the exercise of such a limitation, and in the capacity to leave the question open, true greatness lies.

What was finally accomplished by this design is seen principally in the stability of the Methodist movement and in its development into a Church with a distinctive ethos. At the same time it can be observed in small individual features, chiefly in the internal formation of the lay-preachers. Among the many examples which could be quoted, we refer to the *Journal* of William Holder, which only exists in his own handwriting, and which in this natural, non-literary form provides authentic evidence.[88] William Holder lived from 1740–1810, and was therefore a generation after Wesley, and as such more open to the strength of his influence than an older man would have been. He must have joined the Methodist movement either in 1764 or 1765 and a few years afterwards he became a lay-preacher. The fragment of his *Journal* gives a glimpse of the years 1768–70. He came from Painswick near Birmingham and was originally a tailor; from the beginning he was a very straightforward person. His notes give a picture of the struggle of faith in all its victories and defeats, its limitations and disappointments, its successes and troubles. The whole record is characterized by two main features: self-examination and spiritual conversation with likeminded folk. If the origins of the first lay in the Puritan investigation of conscience, the second came from the Methodist class-meetings. The religious societies of Horneck were in this way developed and considerably added to, for unlike these, which existed for training in churchmanship, the class meetings concentrated on the personal.[89] Thus William Holder's *Journal* starts with the meeting of a class on 12th October 1768. There he met an unknown man from near London named John Valton, who in a moving way revealed to him his spiritual experiences, and so became his friend. The first conversation brought the two men so close to each other that Holder would have been able to take the heart of the other into his own breast, as he somewhat colourfully expressed it. What Valton told him about himself he took as a comment on his own experiences which had occurred three or four years previously, and he was seized with a powerful longing for a present inner movement of the Spirit. He was aware that the 'tender conscience', a favourite expression of the literature of conscience, ruled in him and made him doubly on his guard against any disturbance which hindered his progress to the one thing which was needful. Fears tormented him; above all he could see no end to sin, and he recognized with dreadful clarity that this would always be so. And yet he felt impelled to strive after a sinless life, and not only that, but also to believe firmly that it was attainable, not through human activity, but as the miraculous intervention of God, who by His all-powerful Word makes mountains into valleys.[90] There appears here that faith which can remove mountains, related quite concretely to personal existence before God. Exalted feeling and temptation, peace and deep disturbance, alternate with each other. William Holder was athirst for a pure heart, and he received a love for God, struggling against unbelief. In the midst of such experiences, which both lifted him up and cast him down, he fled to the refuge of prayer, and joined the little group, the band. His soul was filled with a deep happiness, although sometimes it was drowsy and almost dead, even while he was preaching.[91] Afterwards the prayer of the group brought him inner peace, and so he looked upon the fellowship of the band as a welcome opportunity for experiencing God's nearness. The desire for a divine nature and for holiness, and the absence of these because of the constant attacks of the adversary; the presence of the divine love and peace, but also the allurements of unbelief; these things alternate with one another.

On one occasion, after he had spent twenty minutes in private prayer and felt himself assured, he heard the sermon of another leading lay-preacher, John Pawson. The sermon destroyed his assurance and threw him naked and empty upon God's mercy. He asked himself if he were not a great hypocrite. He heard the promise: 'If you can believe now, you will experience salvation from God', but he did not have the power simply to believe. Another evening he went to a love-feast, a service for the exchange of personal experiences, at which he openly confessed the struggles and perplexities in his soul and in this way obtained freedom. He writes in his *Journal*: 'Satan was very active, but the Lord brought all his undertakings to nothing.'[92] On yet another occasion he felt so filled with the love of God that he wished to melt as wax in the fire. This condition lasted for quite a while, especially during prayer. But then he was once again thrown back into uncertainty, and when he opened his Bible at Matthew 12[43] he applied to himself, since he stood in danger of spiritual pride,[93] the parable of Jesus about the evil spirit, which returned with more evil helpers into the cleaned and re-decorated house after having been expelled. In a band meeting he was able to tell the members of God's willingness to save them, if they were prepared to give up all things for Him.[94] Every time the experience of fellowship strengthened his faith.[95] Since he was repeatedly attacked by temptations before and during his preaching he asked himself whether God wished to suggest to him that he should give it up, so that he might not be deceived about a power which he did not possess. In prayer he wrestled with God about it. When he then opened the Bible he found Isaiah 66[9]: 'Shall I bring to the birth, and not cause to bring forth? saith the Lord: shall I cause to bring forth, and shut the womb? saith thy God.' He took these words to be a confirmation of his activity, and a command to continue preaching, and so delivered himself from the Donatist danger of making the message dependent upon the personal faith of the preacher.[96] It was a similar situation to that in which Peter Böhler had urged John Wesley to preach faith until he had it,[97] and the advice given was also the same.

So it runs through the whole of the *Journal*. The spiritual history of the preacher William Holder is a series of temptations and deliverances, a continuous education in watchfulness over the personal life of faith, which was nourished by study of the Bible, prayer, self-examination, preaching, and conversation in the bands and classes. It is in many respects a reproduction of John Wesley's conversion, lasting through the years. This is particularly so in the case of the entry for 27th March 1769, where Holder after deep depression experienced the assurance of sins forgiven as personal consolation, felt himself conqueror over all temptations, and obtained the conviction that according to Romans 8[28] these temptations served what was best for him, but that the certainty he had was independent of all inward impressions like joy and jubilation.[98] To be sure several favourite turns of phrase constantly recur in the *Journal*, like: 'I felt great nearness to the Lord in prayer',[99] 'I found greater rest in my soul'[100] and 'My peace flowed like a stream';[101] so the whole work takes on something of a stereotyped form. Nevertheless this does not destroy its genuineness, but rather shows that it was the product of a man of uncomplicated authenticity who had a limited vocabulary and ability in expressing himself.

If an autobiography of a woman, like that of Elizabeth Johnson,[102] is examined, the contents prove to be similar, with great emphasis upon feeling. The particular characteristic of her *Diary* is that it takes the form of prayer to God, and it contains also extracts from letters, including one to John Wesley.[103] In this book a personal concern for the truth of salvation is taken to its limits: Help me or I am undone![104] Take me and do with me what Thou willest! Let me be wholly Thine![105] Leave me not, Lord, I fly to Thee, for Thou knowest how weak I am![106] This is the tone of the book.

In these instances the unsophisticated life received its mark of nobility. In spite of much which runs according to type, the individual plain man found his uniqueness and status by interpreting his personal history as lived under God. This was also the meaning and the importance of the Herrnhut way of life. Both movements made their contribution towards the development of autobiography, and the appreciation of it.

Preaching and pastoral care were both the origin and object of the whole Methodist structure, and they remained its determining point of view. They prevented the rigid organization from becoming top-heavy, which, had it occurred, would have led to mere formality. Systematic design and organized growth, direction and spontaneous development were united as the spirit of fellowship and nurture of the individuals. It was the taking seriously of the most important element in the individual's spiritual life, his relationship to God, which caused every member of the Methodist fellowship to become aware of being neither over-valued nor over-ridden. Further it conferred upon all the proud conviction that this form of fellowship had restored primitive Christianity. In this way John Wesley introduced into the main stream of history the attempt to make the spiritual impetus of primitive Christianity fruitful for the present by giving it an appropriate external form. This tradition extended from the coenobitic monasticism of the Eastern Church, through the whole of western monasticism, to the Waldensians, Hussites and Anabaptists, and from them to the Pietists and their precursors in the mystical spiritualists. In each case the ideal was understood somewhat differently, and so the attempts were always tackled in different ways. Wesley's efforts and way of doing it establish his claim, both through the uniqueness of the whole and its individual features, to an independent position in this history.

FOUR

John Wesley's Relationship to the Church of England

JOHN WESLEY was an ordained presbyter of the Church of England, and he was always conscious of himself as such. That Church remained his true home. His relationship to it affected his whole life, his missionary and pastoral activity as well as his theology, the building up of his societies and his liturgical attitude, his preaching as well as his writing and his pastoral correspondence. Its treatment in a separate chapter is bound to be incomplete because it ran through every relationship in which he was involved and in which he unexpectedly found himself. It ran through his controversy with the Moravians and similarly with his polemic against the Deists and Socinians. Accordingly it has a profoundly tragic note. His unfriendly relationships with Anglican bishops and writers could never really become polemical. They were always apologetic, determined by an inner bond of unity. His college fellowship in the University of Oxford gave him the right to preach anywhere,[1] and at the same time relieved him of any connexion with a particular congregation. This was a providential preliminary condition of his evangelical movement, which did not overthrow the parish system of the Middle Ages but strongly modified it, in that it supplemented it by itinerant preaching and restored to it certain early Christian and medieval features.[2]

On the other hand it could have been foreseen that this relationship would also lead to conflict with the Church of England. The evangelical movement exercised at least a silent protest against the official representatives of the Christian faith. Its note of challenge made this inevitable, and John Wesley was the last man to weaken this. On the contrary he denied that the Church of his time had any ability to create real fellowship.[3] An Anglican minister like Vincent Perronet (1693–1785) at Shoreham in Kent, who during thirty-nine years supported John Wesley, advised him, and reorganized his own parish in accordance with Wesley's principles, besides giving his two sons as lay-preachers, was a unique case. It is understandable that Charles Wesley should have given him the title, 'Archbishop of Methodism'.

From the beginning difficulties emerged. The conversations with Bishop Gibson in London and Bishop Butler in Bristol were inoffensive enough, but both soon afterwards believed that they had to warn against the enthusiasts. Gibson himself wrote against the Moravians, to whom he reckoned the brothers Wesley belonged, and forbade the clergy of London to admit Methodists to their pulpits. Butler instructed the young minister Josiah Tucker to write a theological caution against the Methodists.[4] But John Wesley did not have to look as far as the official authorities; there were open criticisms from among his own family and circle of friends. His elder brother Samuel put it with biting sarcasm in a letter to their mother: 'As I told Jack, I am not afraid the Church should excommunicate him (discipline is at too low an ebb), but that he should excommunicate the Church.'[5] The mother of his friend James Hutton considered that his statement that he had only become a Christian at his conversion was very extravagant.[6] Of his Oxford companions one, James Hervey (1714–58), from whom he had not expected such an attitude, opposed him, and this was particularly painful. Hervey had at one time in Oxford actually enthusiastically admired Wesley. As late as 1747 he praised the kindness with which the great teacher had received the simple students. It is not surprising that when hostility was shown to Wesley in the university he had been unconditionally on his side and steadily defended him. His steadfastness in the difficult situation in the New World had elicited from him further admiration. To Hervey, Wesley's approach to the heathen seemed like Noah's exit from the ark: a new land, full of promise, lay before them both, although it was full of uncertainty. Indeed he crowned this paean of praise by avowing that everything which he himself was and had was due to the surpassing excellence of his master. He called him the friend of his studies and the friend of his soul, the friend of all his valuable and eternal interests.[7] Precisely because he valued him so highly he watched the new movement with the closest of attention. But the more keenly he observed it the more it caused him to be uneasy. The doubts about it, which he probably expressed in writing, have been lost in their original form, but John Wesley's reply of 20th March 1739 fully makes up for this.[8] This is one of his most important letters, and it must therefore be treated fully, not only so far as its contents are concerned, but also for its implications.

The way in which Wesley begins is noteworthy. He recognizes in the first place the freedom with which his correspondent treats him. The best way in which he can thank him is to use the same openness. He then joins with him in a prayer that God will sanctify them both and lead them into the whole truth as it is in Jesus Christ. In this way he established from the first a foundation which was rooted in their common faith and was at the same time genuinely human. All the controversial points which followed were based upon it. Everything which divided them assumed this ultimate unity, and rested upon it. In this way he removed any personal bitterness from what was of necessity a matter of sharp controversy. He then proceeds to discuss the actual points of dispute. The primary place is given to the question as to whether John Wesley could really claim to be a Christian—denied by Hervey. Apparently Hervey had tried to place Wesley in a dilemma by saying that his activity was irreconcilable with the character of a Christian. Wesley counters this excessively sharp attack with the forthright confession that he is not a Christian, but only strives to become one. The name of Christian always had for him, even in his youth and now perhaps more than ever, the full splendour of an unattainable crown.[9] At the same time he underlines this lowly description of himself by using Pauline expressions which only served to make his situation more serious. His intention was not to avoid any personal challenge, but rather to point out that in everything he has undertaken he has been moved by the desire to be a Christian, and the conviction that he was bound to do anything which served that end. In this way he was able to hold together in the most intimate way both command and intention. It was on this principle that he had set out for North America and later visited the Moravian Church at Herrnhut, and on the same principle he was now ready to go to Abyssinia or China or wherever God should call him. Once again it is the missionary idea which drives him on. As to the advice that he should settle in his college at the university, he replies abruptly that it is very clear to him that he has no place there. He has not been given any work of supervision, nor entrusted with any students. So seriously, so strongly, and so precisely had his conception of vocation developed that it was not sufficient for him to belong in a general way to his college; he needed the directly appointed task and

I

some pressing necessity for him to be convinced about his path of duty. The other possibility, the second part of Hervey's proposal, was that he should accept a cure of souls. To this Wesley replies that the time would have come to consider this when one was offered him. In this instance too he required a definite task and call, one which he could not evade.

The discussion at this stage proceeded to the real point of contention, and so came to the heart of the matter. Hervey believed that for the time being Wesley should remain inactive, and reproached him for assembling in peculiar groups Christians who were not his charge, and for concerning himself with people who were not in a parish belonging to him. He maintained that on 'catholic', that is, general Christian, principles, this was unlawful. This caused Wesley to express himself with the utmost pointedness: he asked Hervey whether he recognized any catholic principles other than scriptural; for himself only these had any weight. According to these it was not difficult for him to justify his evangelistic activities, for God commands him clearly in Scripture, according to his power, to instruct the ignorant, reform the wicked, confirm the virtuous. If men forbade him to do this in a parish which belonged to another minister, then that would be an instance of the classical early Christian situation which raised the question whether God or man should be obeyed. Not content merely with this example from the New Testament of Peter at a great moment of decision, he immediately cited another: Paul's confession of unconditional adherence to his missionary commission, 'A dispensation of the gospel is committed to me; and woe is me if I preach not the gospel.' In this way he summoned to his defence the highest conceivable, unanswerable authority. If then, he continued, there exists an obligation to mission, it can only be exercised in those areas which—in one form or another—are divided out and arranged in definite parishes. Even the heathen in Georgia, from whom he had recently come, belonged either to the parishes of Savannah or Frederica. According to Anglican Church order John Wesley was quite correct, for the congregations in North America were under the jurisdiction of the Bishop of London. At the same time his words once again reveal the absolutely decisive role which the missionary idea had come to occupy in his understanding of his whole work and of his place in it. Paul's words (1 Corinthians 9[16]), in which he speaks of the unavoidable necessity laid upon the preacher of the Gospel, were used by John Wesley again when a few months later he had the interview with Bishop Joseph Butler in Bristol.[10] In this connexion the difference between the Church at home and the mission-field was entirely discounted; the parish is a mission-field and the mission-field is a parish. It was in these terms that John Wesley, speaking like an early Christian missionary, addressed the Anglican parish clergyman James Hervey, in these terms that he expounded the New Testament over against the historically developed form and legal status of the medieval parish system, which was still in existence in the eighteenth century. It was not only a case of setting revolution against tradition or the needs of the situation against the status quo, but even more it was the original dynamic of the Church itself which was showing itself with elemental force. All that the canon of scripture as the absolute standard had meant in the history of Christianity was here being applied to the immediate situation.

It is in this connexion that John Wesley uttered the words for which he has become so well known: 'I look upon all the world as my parish; thus far I mean, that in whatever part of it I am, I judge it meet, right, and my bounden duty to declare, unto all that are willing to hear, the glad tidings of salvation. This is the work which I know God has called me to; and sure I am that His blessing attends it.'[11] He is motivated by this more strongly than anything else. He knows that, as the servant of God, his activity has God's clear command behind it. And in this connexion he found it necessary to refer once again to the text which had inspired him when working with the Oxford undergraduates—St Paul's words about doing good to all men whenever we have opportunity (Galatians 6[10]). This provided John Wesley with the connecting-link with his own personal way of life. God's providence, which has bestowed upon him the unique ecclesiastical position of an ordained college Fellow, but without actual employment, concurs with his own words. In that it has set him free from all distracting duties it points him directly to the devoting of himself to the one task of 'doing good'.[12]

But what if this 'good' is not recognized as good? What if the man who does it is evilly spoken of on all sides? What then? Against this objection John Wesley emphasizes, as at Oxford and in Georgia, that persecution which the disciple meets for Jesus Christ's sake is the surest sign that he is following the right way. Indeed at this point he goes over from defence to attack, and expresses the fear that Hervey has fallen victim to Satan's temptations, because he has forgotten the basic principle of the Christian faith, that there is no other way for the follower of Christ than the way of the Cross. Contempt and censure by the world are an essential part of Christian existence.

In this way Anglican feeling for the Church and evangelistic activism clashed sharply with one another. If the contrast between the two were to be expressed as the choice between a positive way of acting or inactive waiting then John Wesley's character would be correctly portrayed. He could not simply remain idle. But the basis of this was not an inborn impulse to be on the move or an inward urge always to be busy, but a consciousness of the early Christian duty to preach the Gospel. At the same time the letter shows—and in this the two correspondents were at one again—an equally concrete conception of the meaning of vocation. The position of a Fellow, which was a survival from the monastic organization of the university, associated with the mendicant system of learning, was in John Wesley's eyes not an accidental arrangement of fate but a present commission from God. The contents of this commission, however, he derived from the New Testament. The belief in providence, characteristic of Pietism, expressed in many German autobiographies, and seen especially in August Hermann Francke's views about his orphan-house, also governed Wesley's thinking. It was a living testimony to the fact that the whole of life, even to the apparently most trivial detail, lay under God's direct dominion. It is quite possible to maintain that had John Wesley not become a Fellow of Lincoln College at Oxford there would not have been a Methodist revival movement of the distinctively evangelistic character which it came to have.

The importance which John Wesley himself attached to this letter is seen by the fact that he repeated the main points from it to his brother Charles on 23rd June 1739. In this he emphasized his point of view, especially about the question of refusal of permission from a bishop. His answer was that he must unconditionally obey God and if necessary suffer for it.[13]

Nevertheless even with this latter possibility in mind Wesley held to a firm connexion with his Church and used every opportunity to emphasize it. Already in his discussion with the Herrnhuters over the office of 'monitors' his different standpoint as an Anglican showed itself. Originally he supported the strict Anglican catholic view that the three-fold order of bishops, priests and deacons was God's will, and argued that in all questions the greatest possible obedience should be given to his Church.[14] He could still extol the bishops in the words of the Revelation of St John as the angels of the Church, the stars in the right hand of God.[15] He not only used the liturgy of the Church, the Book of Common Prayer, but took its details so seriously that in accordance with the original version of 1549 he divided the Sunday service in 1736 at Savannah into three separate parts, the morning service at five in the morning, the Communion at eleven, and the evening service at three.[16] In addition he constantly defended the Prayer Book,[17] and even in his old age vigorously protested when his fellow-worker Thomas Coke changed two or three small things in it.[18] He rejoiced when he discovered clear indications that the members of his movement adhered to it. Thus in a London Methodist society the weekly fast according to the Anglican order was strictly observed by the majority of the members. John Wesley expressed the wish that this should be done by members of the Church of England in general, especially by those who declaimed against himself.[19] With an insistence which is almost wearisome he warned against leaving the Church, and nipped in the bud everything which threatened a move in this direction. No question recurs so frequently in his correspondence as this.[20] He was thoroughly persuaded that it was God's will at that time to restore the Church of England to health by means of his movement. Accordingly he could only see in separation from it a new heresy—indeed, more than that, treason against a God-given task. When his friend John Gambold went over to the Moravians he said that nobody who went away would prosper.[21] At Athlone in Ireland he declared almost with satisfaction that the Methodist society had declined as soon as some members left off going to the Anglican services.[22] In controversy with one of his most unpleasant critics, the clergyman John Baily of Kilcully, near Cork, in Ireland, he said that he would not give him the pleasure of leaving the Church, but that he would remain in it under all circumstances, if only to reprove those who betray her with the kiss of Judas.[23]

After seven years of strife at the beginning of his evangelical activity Wesley set out in a letter, written on 11th March 1745, to the aforementioned friend, the clergyman Vincent Perronet, a sort of peace proposal.[24] In this he gave in the first place a review of the unhappy course which relations had taken. In the beginning the Methodist preaching had started with its unusual subjects, summarized by Wesley as inward, present salvation, attainable by faith alone. The result was that they were forbidden to preach in most churches, and so they preached in private houses, and when there was insufficient room, in the open air. This led to the storm breaking out. There was a flood of propaganda by word or writing against the Methodists from the clergy. When the people who had been won by the Methodist preaching desired care and nourishment, and Wesley took them with his own folk, opposition against him increased. If they had been first reproached as heretics and schismatics, false teachers and self-seekers, they were now called papists, enemies of the state, rebels and conspirators. The strict discipline which they practised among themselves, which excluded those who did not live according to the Gospel, was made by some of the bishops the occasion for fresh private and public attacks. As a consequence clergy stirred up the people to treat the Methodists as mad dogs, particularly in Staffordshire and Cornwall, but also in other places. This was the state of things at the present. Were they to remain so? Could the breach be healed? Wesley asked whether, in view of the increasing flood of popery, deism and immorality, they could not stand together? Naturally it must be clear that the Methodists could not discontinue their preaching nor give up their societies, for the personal salvation of a great many people depended on both. Methodism without the form in which it had been built up would be lost. Wesley wished to promise one thing, namely that his people, in spite of all that had happened, would behave with reverence towards those who were the regular servants and overseers in the Church of God, by which he meant the Anglican clergy and bishops. Nevertheless he did not go on—and this distinguished him from the attitude which was traditional in the Church of England—to promise obedience towards the bishops. Proudly he disclaimed all right to preach in those churches to which he and his friends could not be admitted without scruple of conscience. All the more he required the cessation of that ecclesiastical oppression which prevented well-disposed clergymen from admitting him into their pulpits. And he expected that the Methodists should not be condemned unheard, or pilloried and slandered as heretics without being seen. Finally he expressed his strong wish that clergymen should stop stirring up the mob against them.

All this implied that Methodism would continue, and that it ought to be recognized by the Established Church as a renewing force; also that Methodism itself would define its own preaching and constitution; and finally that the Church of England and Methodism would proceed along different ways to the same end, both working for the overcoming of ungodliness. They ought to do this in a spirit of mutual respect and tolerance.

This may not appear to be very much. It was at all events honest, reasonable, and realistic. Wesley could probably not have gone further at that particular time. In no sense did this one letter express all that he felt about his relationship with the Church of England. But at a moment of extreme tension, when embitterment could have led to hasty conclusions, he was with dignity and resoluteness watching over the internal and external status of his movement, and at the same time offering the hand of a reconciliation which was neither submission nor palliation, appealing to what was held in common and not omitting the note of love. At the same time the letter as a whole was cool and self-assured.

As a sort of supplement to this there is another letter, which he wrote nine months later to his shifty, unreliable, vain brother-in-law, Westley Hall, who was a confirmed woman-hunter.[25] He too had gone over to the Moravians. As a result the members of the Methodist society which he had led definitely separated from the Church of England and made life unpleasant for all who did not accompany them, principally Hall's own wife, Wesley's sister Martha. Wesley examined Hall's objections against the Church of England. When he attacked the apostolic succession of bishops, the divine constitution of the priesthood, and the threefold order of the ministry (bishops, priests and deacons) as a papist system, John Wesley defended these basic orders. In his view there was no biblical evidence against them. Although he condemned the prevalent abuses in the Church of England, he denied that they belonged to the essence of the Church as such. He regarded them as accretions, which could be as unessential as the baroque ornaments in Westminster Abbey. He considered it his duty to obey the bishops in all matters in which they enjoined the clear commands of God or justifiable ecclesiastical directions, although not when they misled by exerting merely their own bare wills. His judgement was that the distinctive features of his own movement, field-preaching, lay preachers, the rules given to the Methodist societies, in no way contradicted the Anglican Church laws. There was therefore no reason to separate from his mother-church, merely because bishops and clergymen acted arbitrarily against people they supposed to be in opposition.

It can be seen how far Wesley was from all forms of sectarian egoism. With every justification he could claim at the age of 82 that for forty years he had opposed all idea of his followers separating from the Church;[26] and when Edmund Gibson, the Bishop of London, once asked why the Methodists did not leave the Church, he could only answer that it was because they conceived it to be their duty to remain in it.[27] To be sure Wesley rejected the purely formal authority of the Church office-bearers, and defended the lay-preachers by comparing them with doctors. He argued that it was not education or approbation which makes a doctor, but ability. In the same way study and ordination are not evidence that a man is a physician of the soul, but effective results. Therefore he betook himself to the dangerous course of justifying by success. The Methodist preachers, he wrote, have brought it about that drunkards, thieves, sabbath-breakers have become orderly, religious men; they have won souls for eternal life. Therefore they have established their right.[28] Behind this lay an appeal to primitive Christianity; did not St Paul refer to the congregation as his letter of commendation?[29] In a similar way it could be inferred that regularly appointed clergyman of the Church of England who are unable to show any similar results from their labours have forfeited the right to their office. Nevertheless Wesley himself in the heat of the dispute was hardly aware of this unhappy conclusion. For him all the emphasis lay upon the general responsibility of every Christian for the spiritual welfare of his fellow-men, and this could not be confined to official holders of office. Looked at in terms of the New Testament, he desired to restore the full sense of the word 'servant' (diakonos).[30] It was always primitive Christianity which was for him the norm.

Wesley knew how to turn the tables upon people. In February 1740, when the Ordinary of Newgate reproached him by saying vehemently that he was sorry that he had separated from the Church, Wesley retaliated by quoting Article 20 of the Church of England

which defines the Church as a congregation of faithful people, wherein
the true word of God is preached and the sacraments duly administered. In the light of this it was not he who had left the Church
but those who disregarded God's basic truths, be it by their beliefs,
their teaching or their lives. These were the people who cared nothing
for justification by faith or salvation, who thought only on things of
this world and its pleasures, who loved money, clothing and self-
indulgence, who gave themselves over to such vices as adultery and
drunkenness, or who administered the sacraments indifferently to
ungodly persons.[31] Wesley's reply was characteristic of a Pietist who
was loyal to the Church.

This way of looking at the Church, the ministry and preaching,
which was concerned chiefly with their purport and their results,
largely dominated his conception of the nature of the Church. He did
not recognize a formal authority. The point which officials in Church
and state were always making, the irregularity of the Methodist open-
air preaching, lay-preaching and organization of societies, not only
struck him as a merely superficial argument, but conflicted with his
view of God's purpose in creating the Church. Every officer of the
Church, and indeed every disciple of Jesus, ought to be impelled by
the words, 'Woe is me, if I preach not the gospel!' For this reason—
and only because of it—the societies had developed, but it had been
a necessary process. The Methodist preaching and organization of
societies had brought salvation to people; could the same be said of
the regular ministry and order of the established Church of England?
According to the principle of formal lawful status the Reformation
of Martin Luther would never have been permitted to come into
being, and the Church would have gone down in error. Wesley
declared: 'Whoever today supports the doctrine of justification fulfils
the true end of the Church of England, but whoever obstructs this,
acts against this,' and he appealed definitely and with special reference
to his own situation, to the fact that his Oxford college, Lincoln,
was founded expressly for propagating the Christian faith and extir-
pating heresies.[32] From every point of view he felt that he was
justified.

The movement to separate from the Church in his own societies
was a different matter. Sometimes he found a desire for separation
among only a few members;[33] but often there was a violent movement
which made itself openly felt,[34] in which perhaps fanatical preachers

fanned the flames.[35] Rejection of an organized Church in the name
of a spiritual religion, which used the parrot-cry 'Babel', was also
sometimes at work, especially among the adherents of Whitefield's
great patroness, Selina, the Countess of Huntingdon.[36]

Although he held so strongly to the bond with the Church of
England he did not treat it as unconditionally binding. His attachment to the Church had its limits in the truth. When Charles Wesley
expelled one of the members of a Methodist society because he did
not attend worship in the Anglican Church, he vigorously criticized
this step, and attacked his brother's ideas about ordination. A difference of opinion about Church organization ought never to have
such far-reaching consequences. Otherwise he, John Wesley, would
have to admit that in his brother's eyes he was one who had separated
from the Church, and he counted it an honour that he was the
fifteenth in the nonconformist line of the Wesleys.[37] To his friend
Samuel Walker, the clergyman in Truro, he said clearly that if the
essence of the Church of England consisted of her orders and laws
and not of her worship and doctrines, then indeed separation from
her was a genuine possibility for true Christians. By this he was not
making any decision about himself or his movement, but was only
suggesting that those who left the Church of England might have had
considerable grounds for doing so.[38]

It was therefore a question of the truth of doctrine which in the
last resort lay behind this problem, and it was this which made it
necessary that the members of the Methodist societies should have
a concern about the truth of what was preached. So John Wesley
noted in the year 1788 that his members in his birth-place of Epworth
had an insuperable aversion to the worship of the parish church
there because the minister did not preach the true gospel.[39] In the
end everything depended upon doctrine.[40] John Wesley welcomed
the statement that the Church of England was free from the reproach
of holding the doctrine of predestination, which he regarded
as heretical,[41] and he advised his followers to go out of a church
if it was preached, although it is noteworthy that he qualified
this by saying that the hearers should quietly leave during that
particular sermon but should be present again on the following
Sunday.[42]

In one of his earliest exchanges with his Anglican fellow-clergymen
John Wesley clearly laid down his basic position. This took place on

13th September 1739. The name of his correspondent is not known, but perhaps it was a certain Howard, with whom his brother Charles had had sympathetic contact.[43] On the first question as to wherein he differed from the Church of England, he replied that so far as he knew, in nothing. What he preached were the doctrines of the Church of England as they were clearly laid down in its prayers, articles and homilies. His correspondent then asked in what points he differed from the other clergy of the Church. Wesley answered that he did not differ at all from those who adhered to the doctrines of the Church, but only from those who dissented from it. He then outlined these differences very exactly. For those clergy from whom he was conscious of differing, justification was either the same thing as sanctification or something which followed it; according to his own understanding it was antecedent to sanctification. He heard the other clergy speak of our own holiness and of good works as the cause of our justification, whereas he saw its cause exclusively in the death and righteousness of Jesus Christ. The basis of justification on the part of man could only be faith. He indeed might produce good works, but they are not required for justification itself. As he saw it, sanctification or holiness meant for the other clergy something external and also outwardly perceived, namely good behaviour, the doing of no harm or helping the neighbour and the maintenance of a regularly ordered Church life, making use of the normal means of grace. For him on the contrary, sanctification was something inward through and through, and he did not shrink from using in this connection the greatest and most pregnant words; holiness was for him the life of God in the soul of man, a participation in the divine nature. It comprised having the same mind which was in Jesus. It was a restoration of the divine image. Consequently the new birth could not be, as the others understood it, something external, limited to the act of baptism, or at best consisting in a change in the way of life from outward wickedness to outward goodness. The new birth must be an inward event, a complete change of the deepest nature from an image of the devil into the image of God, from the love of the creature to the love of the Creator, from earthly, sensual feelings and desires to heavenly and holy ones; in a word, a change from the spirits of darkness to those of the angels of light. In all these sentences the notes of the Pauline doctrine of justification resound in closest connexion with the concerns of the new birth, in that characteristic combination between

Luther and Pietism such as the Herrnhut Brethren, taught by Count Zinzendorf, had handed on to Wesley. Wesley now argued strongly for this position himself, not only in the sense that it was his own point of view and experience, but that it was the actual truth, about which there could be no compromise. There was a simple alternative. Either the other Anglican clergymen with their moralistic synergism were correct, and if so he himself had been found out as a false witness before God, or he had taught the truth, in which case they were blind leaders of the blind.

But this was not all. John Wesley was proud of the fact that in the year 1764 there were, besides him and his brother Charles, at least thirty-four Anglican clergymen who taught the same doctrine, namely the three principal points of original sin, justification by faith, and holiness of heart and life. This encouraged him to propose again to the Anglican clergy in general that there should be a union which would be a fellowship of conviction and work based upon respect for one another. This went further than the peace proposal of 1745, since it was intended to be a genuine alliance of trust and love.[44]

The question as to whether the Methodist societies should separate from the Church of England, and as a step towards this hold their meetings during the times of the Anglican services, was one to which the Methodist Conferences had to give their attention, and they always, in agreement with Wesley, declared decisively against it. Especially important in this connexion was the London Conference of 1788.[45] At times there were proposals to compromise, as at Bristol, where in 1786 they agreed not to bring about any separation so long as John Wesley was alive, or in Dublin in 1789 where they decided they would go to the Anglican service once a month.[46] Wesley also thought it was important not to offend against Church order, although he explained this order according to his own interpretation. Thus he was pleased to emphasize that the laws of the Church said nothing against open-air preaching.[47] He kept an open eye for those abuses which were outside the main scope of doctrine and preaching, and which were present in the Church, such as the accumulation of several livings by one man, so that the clergyman was never in the parish which was entrusted to him, or the questionable nature of the contemporary university education when it was allowed to count as the only necessary qualification for ordination.[48] Furthermore he did not believe in the unbroken succession of bishops from the time of the apostles; he considered it an unprovable fable.[49]

It is not surprising that two of his fellow-workers, Joseph Benson and in association with him, John William Fletcher, actually invited him in 1775 to become the reformer of the Church of England. They proposed to him a programme of reform and reorganization which would have given the Methodist circuits the official status of a select Church within the whole Church and would have recognized John Wesley constitutionally as a special bishop of the Anglican Church. The reformation itself—and in this they correctly understood their leader—should include matters of doctrine. The Pauline message of the justification of sinners by grace alone through faith in Jesus Christ should again be made central in the Church's preaching. At the same time Christian perfection as the fulfilling of the law ought to be made obligatory, and all forms of antinomianism and the indolence associated with it or established by it should be excluded. An attitude of loyalty and respect towards the Church of England ought to be maintained. Benson and Fletcher held that principally changes in the liturgy were necessary; but they also found deficiencies in the 39 Articles and the Homilies, those model Reformation sermons from the sixteenth century. The points of true Christian preaching they laid down clearly and distinctly: as preaching about grace it was to be directed against the Socinians, as preaching about the righteousness of God it was to be opposed to the Calvinists, as preaching on holiness and sanctification it should be against the whole world.[50] The explanation of these various opposed characterizations must be sought in the following points: as humanists the Socinians were ethical fanatics, aiming at self-salvation. By such a classification Benson and Fletcher were also attacking the general humanistic enlightened circles within the Church of England, those which stood for faith in man and his possibilities, as well as the Socinianism itself which was growing within the nonconformist churches.[51] The Calvinists by their emphasis upon double predestination seemed to reduce God to a partial tyrant. This reference was to the Presbyterians. The world in general in its self-sufficiency was in conflict with God's holiness and sanctification through Jesus Christ. They avoided pointing a finger at any definite Church; it was not Churches but doctrine which was condemned.[52] The Churches had to test how far they were themselves guilty in this respect. Fletcher was of the opinion that Methodism, the new and relatively independent daughter-church of the Church of England, was doing away in its own sphere with all recognized abuses and errors and was thus setting up its new form as the future model for the whole Anglican Church. At the same time, because it maintained intact its relationship with the Church of England, it was to protect her against the unjust attacks of the dissenters. In this context Fletcher understood the word 'methodist' in a formal way; a 'methodized' church for him meant a reformed church, and so he contrasted 'methodist' and 'anglican' as reformed and unreformed. The Methodist Church thus became the improved form of the Church of England.[53]

What did John Wesley say about this well-considered proposal? Unfortunately we do not possess any direct comment by him about it. He went only cursorily into the associated suggestion that the preachers should be tested with great care. This was an important point, because it included within it a decision about the equal value of the Methodist and the Anglican preachers.[54] Apparently he was not concerned to regulate finally and definitively the relationship of his Church to the Church of England; rather he left everything still in suspense. This could also be put in the following way: he hoped to the last that the Church would allow itself to be summoned by his preaching and its effects to a state of order. Throughout he desired to be its reformer, and in this sense his associates correctly understood him. But he differed from them in that he wished to be this without a programme of reformation. The similarity with Luther's attitude to the Church which he brought into existence should not be overlooked, even if the judgement of the two men turned out to be radically different. From 1520 onwards Luther distinguished between the Church of Christ and the Church of the Pope,[55] but to the end Wesley felt that he belonged to the Church of England.

This is once again confirmed by an important letter, which shows how constantly he himself was personally concerned about the question of separation. In 1755, before the annual Conference, which met at Leeds, he engaged in a discussion with his brother Charles about a book which had appeared nine years earlier. Its author, Micaiah Towgood, a nonconformist minister from Exeter, stated the reasons for his continued separation from the Church of England. The book had raised a controversy in which the Church of England clergyman John White, from Ospringe near Faversham, had defended the Anglican point of view; to this Towgood had replied. John Wesley read all this and conceded that Towgood had given an impressive statement of his position and written a most virulent satire on the Church of England. But he had not convinced Wesley, and that not perhaps so much because his objections were inconclusive but because he did not agree with the spirit of the author. He contrasted him with the most obvious example from the past, Richard Baxter, who one hundred years before justified separation in an entirely different spirit, and at the same time sorrowfully deplored it. Baxter's words expressed love; but from Towgood only bitterness and animosity were heard.[56] Yet Wesley's relationship with the author was in no way confined to a study and judgement of his words. Three years later he wrote him a personal letter and invited him to consider the following points:[57] He had maintained that his separation from the Church was not because of his own inclination but a feeling of duty and that it necessarily followed from his obedience to Jesus Christ, the only lawgiver in the Church; for the Church of England required the observance of certain customs which Jesus did not command. John Wesley took Towgood at his word and asked him where in the New Testament Jesus Christ had forbidden His Church to introduce certain ceremonies for worship. Certainly when ceremonies, resulting from the absence of corresponding injunctions in the New Testament, are by nature of secondary importance, it ought not to be a matter of faith to observe them. On the other hand Christian humility actually requires obedience to the direction of the Church in these small matters.[58] When Towgood contested the right to obedience of every authority in the organization of the Church by reference to the sole authority of Jesus, and appealed to Jesus's command not to call any man master,[59] adding to this His sharp distinction between ecclesiastical and worldly orders, he was forgetting first of all that the supreme ruler could and must have subordinate helpers.[60] Thus John Wesley decisively rejected the fanatical and utopian character of this protest, which was a repetition of that made at the time of the Reformation by Thomas Müntzer shortly before his death.[61] He rightly pointed out that in giving his warning about calling men master Jesus intended to guard against the misunderstanding about spiritual leadership which had been developed by the rabbis at that time. They had looked for an unconditional submission to their judgement in all religious questions. Nobody in the Church of England in Wesley's time laid claim to such pretensions.[62]

Up to this point John Wesley was obviously in the right against the very superficial one-sided arguments of Towgood.[63] His position became more difficult when he distinguished between the Church of Jesus Christ and the Church of England as a particular society or group, and he allowed that the latter could have rules for admission and exclusion which were different from those which Jesus Himself gave for the whole Church. In this he took over the distinction between the universal Church and a part of the Church which had certainly been current since the scholasticism of the Middle Ages. Nevertheless more important than the unnoticed connexion with this tradition was the fact that he was defending almost without question the Church of England even in its canonical aspects. This was a measure of his loyalty to it.

At the same time he did not compromise his own position or that of his movement. The question was posed in the year 1757. Some Anglican clergymen who had been well-disposed to him and who had opened their parishes to his activity, of whom Samuel Walker of Truro was the most outstanding, cherished the understandable wish that once the Methodist societies were founded by him in their parishes Wesley would hand the societies over to them and withdraw his preachers. He roundly refused to do this. He vigorously disowned the prerogative of the parish system of the Established Church, and inquired defiantly: 'But (to go a little deeper into this matter of legal establishment) does Mr Conon or you think that the King and Parliament have a right to prescribe to me what pastor I shall use? If they prescribe one whom I know God never sent, am I obliged to receive him? If he be sent of God, can I receive him with a clear conscience till I *know* he is?'[64] So he rejected on principle the claim of the institutional Church and broke down one of the main supports of the Anglican system. He could even record the sarcastic comment that to be merely an Anglican clergyman without connexion with the Methodists was good advice for anyone striving after preferment, but bad counsel for one wanting to go to heaven or wishing to do good to others on earth.[65]

Perhaps at this point the question can be raised which is sometimes asked: how would events have turned out if Wesley had been offered a bishopric in the Church of England? Would he have taken it and, with the considerable freedom which the office provided, would he have made his diocese, after Benson's and Fletcher's plan, into a model and nursery for the whole Church? Probably he would have declined it for more than one reason. His parish was the world. This was more than a matter of words. The conditions under which he did his work were fundamentally those which he desired. He would certainly have found a bishopric of the type which was common at the time a restriction upon him. Moreover he looked upon his own position as fundamentally episcopal, exercising oversight in the New Testament sense of the word.[66]

We look back once again to his letter of 20th March 1739, to James Hervey. Hervey had asked him how his free activity stood in relation to the ordered structure of the Anglican organization of the clergy and their parish boundaries. This was only superficially a matter of externals, for behind it lay the deeply-rooted Anglican historical consciousness which, in its realistic attitude to the natural order, to this day looks upon the historical way as a permanently essential feature of the mission of Christianity in this world.[67] When John Wesley made the decision to look upon the limits, which Hervey wished to know he had observed, as a mere human contrivance, he stepped outside the realm of this consciousness, and it was a sign of the seriousness of the decision that he quoted as a reason the clearest word of command from the early Church. In view of the divine compulsion and the total obligation of the apostolic commission, what could be said for the precise division of the inhabited world into distinct geographical entities? Wesley looked upon the whole world as his parish. This does not mean, as can be crudely misunderstood, that he claimed for himself the right, after the manner of the medieval mendicant orders, to break into the regular spheres of the clergy and seduce people from their churches, but it did imply that wherever he was he was to be a living herald of the message. A Christian is always on active service. Wesley always believed that ordination did not bind a person to one place or to a particular congregation, but that it was essentially universal. It is basically mission. From the time of his visit to Georgia the idea of mission permeated his understanding of the ministerial office. The mission-field is the congregation and the congregation is a mission congregation, because the situation of 'the old man' before the gospel message does not differ in any material way from that of the heathen: both stand in need of the new birth.[68]

Although John Wesley had always thought of doctrine as the

K

essential feature of the Church, the organization of the latter was never a secondary matter. Following Anglican tradition he saw the bishop's office at the head. It has already been stated that originally he thought of this in a catholic way, but on 20th January 1746, Lord Peter King's *Account of the Primitive Church* became of revolutionary and fundamental significance for him. He had to concede, in spite of all the prepossessions of his strict Anglican upbringing, that this writer had demonstrated clearly the original equality of bishops and presbyters, that is, priests. The Church of England had thus not followed Scripture at this point. Further it seemed to him proven that each Christian congregation was fully a Church, able to exist independently of others. Accordingly there was opened to him perspectives which approximated to the opinions of Presbyterians and Independents (Congregationalists), that is, the main types of nonconformist churches. Immediately prior to this he had been strongly at variance with his brother-in-law, Westley Hall, who had joined the Moravians, over this very question, and he had maintained that the Anglican three-fold order of bishops, priests and deacons was derived not only from the early Church but from primitive Christianity, which implied that it was held by canonical authority.[69] Lord King's interpretation remained his own to the last, and in particular it was responsible for his attitude in the question of the North American ordinations.[70]

It was in connexion with this that Wesley in 1780 made a last attempt to co-operate in a regular way with the authorities of the Church of England. He requested the Bishop of London, Dr Robert Lowth (1710–87), to ordain for North America a trusty Methodist preacher, John Hoskins. The bishop was a learned student of Hebrew poetry, well known both for the depth of his scholarship and for his attachment to the Church; fifteen years previously he had replied in moderate and yet strong terms to a literary attack made upon him by William Warburton, the Bishop of Gloucester, which had called forth Wesley's admiration.[71] Hoskins, as a result of his conversion at Bristol in 1746, became a Methodist, and introduced Methodism to Newfoundland in 1774, first as founder and teacher of a school, and then, because no services of worship were held, as reader of Wesley's sermons and the services in the Book of Common Prayer. Thus there had been a case of exceptional need, which he tried to remedy, and this was the point from which Wesley began. Now the elderly founder of Methodism saw a similar situation, but of far greater urgency; he felt that he had not long to live, and he reminded the bishop that he had been in North America. Therefore it was his wish that the colonies should have competent church-leaders, duly appointed, so that the Christians there, in difficulties as a result of the war and without leaders, could be cared for. He reminded the bishop that he had already ordained some young men for North America, but asked him whether they were really qualified for the problems of this particular area. He emphasized that, in spite of the high value he, with the bishop, gave to theological knowledge and proficiency in ancient languages, suitability for the ministry at that time did not depend upon these but upon knowledge of the Scriptures and readiness to be dedicated to the work of pastoral care. Discreetly but firmly he asked the bishop whether he could deny that many men had lost their direction. In this way he reminded Dr Lowth of his duty but left no doubt that in fact he himself would attend to it if the appointed Church official were to fail.[72] The bishop did not reply, and so the ordinations of Methodist preachers for North America by John Wesley followed, and this was a decisive step towards Methodism becoming an independent Church.[73] But John Wesley could plead that he was driven to it by necessity. On the other hand he had unmistakably put pressure upon the bishop, and by urging the ordination of a layman had reduced the importance of theological education for the office of preacher—and that with one of the most scholarly churchmen of his age! Of course the bishop ought not to have remained silent. The confused nature of the situation, which came out clearly in this case, was typical of the early period of Methodism. In principle it left every way open, but in fact led to hasty actions, which themselves created further difficulty.

On the question of the ministry Wesley was fortified by Bishop Edward Stillingfleet's *Irenicon*, because it showed that the episcopal form of Church government, although valuable, was not prescribed in the Bible.[74]

Twenty years after the beginning of the great revival Wesley gave a clear and comprehensive account of his reasons against separating from the Church of England, and we shall hardly go astray if we see in it his true intention. It was a sign of his sense of reality that he considered the question from the practical point of view rather than the theoretical. He rejected separation because it would have served only the enemies of God and divine truth, for by means of it the dispute would be felt not only within Methodism but by all people, while at the moment all were able to live with each other in peace— quite different from what had been the lot of their forbears, who would have been grateful for such a time of peace. Further he urged that if separation occurred, the Methodists, with their assurances of loyalty to the Church, would appear as liars, and this would have resulted in destroying their whole missionary activity. Furthermore the plan for a new Church would absorb endless time and energy. The previous experiences which England had known of Church separations were in his view thoroughly discouraging. They only confirmed people in their prejudices about the office of clergymen and advanced them not a single step in holiness. The same thing was also true of countries outside England. It was clear to him from the history of the Church since the Reformation that those who remained in the Church, in spite of its clearly recognized faults, acted as leaven. In this connexion he referred to Johann Arndt in Germany and to the Puritan Robert Bolton in England. For him the peculiar glory of the Methodists lay in the fact that they could do and suffer all things for the brethren's sake, indeed, that their love grew, the less it was returned by others. For that very reason separation would contradict the very purpose of God. God has sent them to the lost sheep of the Church of England, and they are not the founders or leaders of a new sect; they are His messengers to those who bear the name of Christian but who in heart and life are heathens. Their task was to call these people back to that from which they had fallen, to real genuine Christianity. Wesley revealed himself in this section clearly as one who was giving expression to feelings associated with membership of a national Church, to natural association with his homeland, and to love for it. He felt that he and his people had an obligation to England, and he referred to the tears which Jesus wept over Jerusalem as well as to the apostle Paul's readiness to be sacrificed for his brethren. If the Anglican clergy were failing in their pastoral duty this gave nobody the right to show a pharisaic pride, but rather it summoned them to show compassion and increased zeal in the exercise of a similar responsibility.[75] Contempt, sharpness, bitterness, could do no good.[76] Therefore Wesley urged remaining in the Church, and actually gave a warning against visiting dissenting services, because this would lead to alienation from the Church of

England. He further warned against imitating the tones of dissenting preachers and the length and language of their prayers; obviously such phenomena indicated a weakening of the connexion with the Church of England. All these points implied that a Methodist would never speak contemptuously of the Church, nor make fun of it, nor exploit its failings.[77]

There can be no doubt that John Wesley always felt that he was a member of the Church of England, and he never contemplated severing the connexion. At the same time his modesty prevented him from characterizing himself as a reformer of the Church, or from adopting any such posture. When his friends Benson and Fletcher not only thought of him in this role but urged him on as one destined to fulfil it, Wesley rejected their counsel. He desired to be nothing other than a messenger of God, a herald of the truth, a servant of souls, even if he thought of this service in actual fact in terms of exercising control. Neither could he allow that any real difference existed between himself and the Church of England over doctrine. On the contrary he still held to the statement made in his early years that for him the plain ancient faith of the Church of England was none other than what was being decried under the new name of Methodism.[78] On the other hand he perceived very clearly the advantages which would accrue to himself and his movement by remaining within the Church. There would be the existing stable organization, the right to preach which came from ordination, the freedom and the right to criticize, and the possibility after all of winning over to himself a section of the Anglican clergy. From this standpoint the oft-discussed question as to whether he was a 'high' churchman in a liturgical and sacramental sense can be resolved. He felt that the Church of England was his home, and the idea of separation never seriously attracted him, although at times he could rather pathetically use it as a threat. He genuinely loved its liturgical and lawful order, in which he had grown up, and he approved of its aim to reproduce the ancient Church,[79] which he extended to the limits of restoring primitive Christianity. He partook of its sacraments with all the fervour of a faithful believer.[80] Yet he did none of these things in a self-consciously artificial or fanatical way. One thing is certain; he was one of those who took seriously the Church as a divine reality upon earth, and he had nothing in common with the dominant liberal Erastianism,[81] the piety of which was largely confined to an external ecclesiasticism. Wesley was concerned with personal faith, the meeting with God through Jesus Christ, rebirth and the new man. Should it have become a point of dispute he would have reckoned the spoken word, preaching, superior to the sacrament without the word, or to a liturgy which consisted of expressions perhaps no longer understood. His movement was essentially a preaching movement and a movement of pastoral care. Its centre of gravity was in proclamation, and everything which concerned organization moved around the circumference. This organization gave to proclamation a place in which to contain and secure its outworkings.

But Wesley was never faced with this clear alternative. Word and sacrament, proclamation and prayer, were for him still the natural unity such as they had been in primitive Christianity, the early Church, the Middle Ages, the time of the Reformation, and the old Anglo-Catholicism of a Lancelot Andrewes and the Caroline divines.[82] In this respect his attitude was not modernist like Joseph Butler and the whole rationalist theology of the eighteenth century; rather he was a traditionalist—but in the original sense of one who definitely grounded himself upon Scripture.

A closer look reveals that the way in which Wesley determined his relation to the Church of England was repeated in his understanding of the essential situation of the Church of Jesus Christ in the world at large. He was convinced, and perceived that this was the most important point, that its task in the changed situation was mission. Accordingly the concept of mission which he held from his youth onwards retained its dominant significance for his activity. Mission stands in a polar relation to institutionalism, yet Wesley understood this not really in terms of opposition but as a complementary relationship, even if it were one which acted as a criticism and a check upon itself. The Church of England was an institution and ought to remain so, but its purpose lay in the proclamation of the message, in the word of mission, and in the structure which resulted from this. John Wesley saw quite clearly that the institution in the modern age did not have the capacity to exist on its own, since it was not a self-sufficient entity; rather it required to be definitely and constantly legitimized by a higher authority. That authority is quite simply the Word, which called the institution into existence. John Wesley's greatness lay in the fact that he succeeded in carrying this through, despite every temptation in his own ranks to treat it absolutely and more conveniently as a mutually exclusive alternative—an Either-Or. Thus in him institutionalism and dynamic vitality, tradition and present reality, were held together, and not, as would have been easy, divided into an opposition between two historical periods.

FIVE

The Opposition

THE PREACHING of the Methodists quickly called forth opposition and resistance.[1] Usually this began with the clergy of the Church of England for they must have felt that their position was being challenged, if not impugned, by the new movement. John Wesley and his helpers were in effect a sign that the previous work of the Church had largely failed, both in the content of its preaching, in the way it treated people, in individual pastoral care and congregational life. It would have required superhuman self-abnegation on the part of the regular clergy simply to have accepted this.

The opposition took many forms. It ranged from the use of brutal force to highly skilled theological argument. The degree to which the Anglican clergy were able to influence the mob was astonishing; they could actually order them, when they wanted, to set upon the Methodists. By 1741 John Wesley's unpleasant experiences with the rabble had begun in the environs of London. While preaching in Deptford some people screamed as if half-mad.[2] Shortly afterwards, on Shrove Tuesday, a fight broke out; men shamelessly tried to behave indecently towards the women in his societies and were ordered by a constable to keep the peace. Wesley was struck to the ground; whereupon several spirited Methodists seized two of the assailants and shut the doors.[3] In Long Lane[4] and Marylebone Fields[5] stones hailed on Wesley, and in Charles Square in Hoxton disturbers of the peace tried to drive an ox into the crowd.[6] When he had finished preaching at Chelsea on the nature and necessity of the new birth, a dissenting teacher, who did not disclose his identity, asked him in Latin what his name was, and when he did not reply, triumphantly derided him before his companions and said, 'Aye, I told you he did not understand Latin!'[7] Then the rumour was circulated that he had been fined twenty pounds for the illegal sale of spirits, and that he was keeping two Popish priests in his house. The story was circulated that he had received large sums of money from Spain in order to raise a party among the poor on behalf of that country, and that when an invasion took place, they would give military help.[8] At Breage in Cornwall a clergyman in 1745 said from the pulpit that John Wesley had been expelled from his college in Oxford for misbehaving himself, and that since then he had been out of his mind.[9] Nothing was too absurd to be brought up and believed.

On 21st May 1743, while preaching from the steps of the town hall in Wednesbury near Birmingham, his brother Charles was pelted with stones and knocked down. This place came to have a dismal notoriety. In October of the same year John Wesley was himself violently seized, and he expected to be thrown into the river; but he was wonderfully protected. Immediately after this, in October 1743, he published a series of statements about these experiences under the challenging title, 'Modern Christianity, Exemplified at Wednesbury'.[10] The Methodists there had not only been attacked on the streets, but people had forced their way into their houses, broken their windows, damaged their furniture, and had even dragged women and children at night from their beds. John Nelson, one of the soundest lay-preachers, originally a stonemason by trade, was forced to see fanatical women ill-treat his pregnant wife in an ugly way and so bring about a miscarriage, as a result of which she suffered for the rest of her life.[11] It seems that in this place for the first time a definitely planned rising, with appointed ringleaders, took place.

From the early years onwards the continuous outbreaks of persecution did not cease, but John Wesley refused to allow this to arouse his animosity; instead, it drove him to prayer. It shows how deeply he was rooted in the liturgical life of his Church that he should end his account of the affairs at Wednesbury with a prayer, consisting largely of quotations from the Psalms and the New Testament. He submitted himself completely to God's will and prayed for the genuine humility which opens the mouth not in complaint but to the praise of the Lord. He desired to be faithful even to death on the cross. So he attained full freedom, an ability to rise above anything which others did to him or took away from him.[12] Six years before, on his return to England from Georgia, he had felt a similar readiness to glorify God in deed, suffering or death.[13]

Such readiness could not possibly mean for so active a nature as John Wesley's that he was not prepared to defend himself. A significant example of this was the letter he wrote on 11th March 1745 to

'a Clerical Friend'.[14] In this he combined self-esteem and consciousness of duty with an understanding of the opponent's position. While
he appealed to the Anglican sense of objective commission and was
sympathetic to their feeling for legal discipline, he continued his
argument skilfully. For his own part he abandoned nothing of what
was characteristic of Methodism; his method was to put everything
which was in dispute in the form of questions. In this way he was
able to demonstrate impressively how carefully he had thought about
every aspect of his movement, and how every feature of its structure
had developed as part of one organic whole. In no way did he himself
appear as an initiator or organizer; everything was shown to have
developed naturally. He had acted merely as the instrument in what
had been happening; he was a servant, not the leader. He had obeyed
intrinsic necessities.

Even this important document, in which he was reacting comprehensively against attacks, calumnies and persecution, shows the
leading place he gave to the message. It shows him as preacher, and
at the same time reveals how little he allowed himself to be embittered. He was still freely and without hindrance dedicated to the
service to which he had given himself.

But he applied to his opponents the same rigour as that with which
he examined himself, and he allowed only the circumstance and the
message to occupy the role of judge. He refused to exempt them from
anything. It was not to the unrestrained mob that he attributed all the
animosity but to the clergy, who ought to have known better. With
all the esteem he had for the bishops he could still recognize that there
rested on them the responsibility for the lamentable disorder as well
as for the increase of Popery, unbelief and immorality. He did not
shrink from accusing them, even if in a veiled form. But more important than these reproaches was for him his reference to the real task,
that proclamation of the true message and its prosecution in the
Church and among the people.

The appeal had little success. The attacks continued. The most
serious came from the pen, in larger theological discussions and in
shorter newspaper articles. The favourite expression which was used
to dismiss Methodism in the eighteenth century was 'enthusiasm'. It
appeared in one of the earliest polemical writings, namely in *Common
Sense or The Englishman's Journal* of 19th May 1739.[15] How accu-
rately the anonymous author expressed the feeling of the time is

shown by the fact that straightway two magazines printed it.[16] In this article, which bore the significant heading, 'The pernicious character and tendencies of the Methodists', it was contended that they were hopeless fanatics, as morally wanton people and therefore dangerous enemies, whose sole concern was to better themselves—a typical judgement from the century of reason and education. Immediately, however, an attorney also entered the lists, and in the same magazine, *Common Sense*, set forth a detailed and ironical discussion of enthusiasm.[17] He protested that he too was a follower of reason, and understood by enthusiasm opinions which were at variance with a sound faith and which endangered the order of the State. He reckoned the doctrines of God's free grace, the new birth, predestination and reprobation, were of this kind, because they attributed to God the odium of unrighteousness and in this way spread immoral ideas of God among the people.

This assertion betrays the fact that the writer did not have John Wesley, but George Whitefield, in mind. And in fact it was the latter who caused the greater stir. In spite of this the writer argued with all the resoluteness of a man of the Enlightenment for freedom of conscience, which also included freedom to err. If according to protestant conviction the Bible was the basis of religion, then its interpretation was open to individual protestants, and it was impossible to lay down in general one particular line of exposition. Should anyone wish to do that then the Methodists must be compelled to conform to the belief of the Church of England; this, however, would be religious slavery and would certainly bring political slavery in its wake—an anticipation by the author of the situation in modern authoritarian states. Interference with the Methodists and in particular with the views of Whitefield would therefore be justified only if it were carried out with force and if it were desired to set up a religious dictatorship. Such a thing could, it is true, threaten the stability of the State. The opponent of the Methodists had not been able to produce proof of any principles of slavery held by them, nor of anything which led to such. On the contrary what he was demanding led rather to slavery, for what he advocated was the persecution of those who thought differently; and of all the principles of slavery that was the worst. It was necessary to ask why he himself did not oppose features in the Church of England which showed the same tendency, such as unconditional submission to the law of the Church, independence of the clergy from secular authority, and the exaggerated system of ecclesiastical legislation, especially the plenary powers of the episcopal courts. He was a blind persecutor of sects, and his case against the Methodists was that they were also a sect and by toleration of them the number of sects was unnecessarily increased. In fact, however, the sects were nourished by the idleness and indolence of the clergy. The writer did not shrink from asserting that if only those on his side had a little of Whitefield's zeal and energy for the faith probably nobody would need to get excited about the number of sects in England. But since the life of a missionary was strenuous, irksome and unproductive, he was not surprised that the clergy expected the civil authority to hand over to them completely the task of conversion, so that they themselves could get on with more profitable undertakings. On the other hand the existence of a number of sects prevents any one of them from setting itself up as absolute. Nothing was so beneficial as mutual criticism, and the state and society could only rejoice when they held each other in check by these means. Of course he also granted that the English would be an extremely fortunate people if they possessed only one religion, without any slavish tendencies. This end, however, could only be attained if everybody followed natural religion and practised the exposition of Holy Scripture solely according to such principles. Thus, according to the point of view of the writer, natural religion was the saviour from all troubles and difficulties. The chief short-coming of the critic of the Methodists lay in the fact that he was not critical enough. He did right to expose and severely criticize all their obvious, rightly condemned improprieties and tendencies, and also those of the official Church of England. Only so would freedom and reason maintain themselves against spiritual tyranny. It is very questionable whether the Methodists, and John Wesley in particular, were really helped by this sort of defence which failed to perceive their true spirit and which condemned their basic doctrines as unwholesome.

In the following period satirical references to John Wesley and Methodism constantly appeared in the form of isolated remarks, which, however, show the movement being persecuted as it grew. Thus the *Craftsman* of July 1739 carried the announcement that John Wesley, to the great sorrow of his followers, had been summoned to Lincoln College, Oxford, in order to fulfil his prescribed period of residence.[18] At the same time the following comment upon his sermon in the Fleet prison appeared in *Common Sense*: 'The prisoners were obstinate, and would only believe that he had power over heaven's door if he first opened their prison doors.'[19] Another time a case of suicide was attributed to the excessive importance given to repentance by the Methodists, because a well-to-do bootmaker took his own life immediately after returning from the Foundery, where he had listened to John Wesley preaching.[20]

On St Bartholomew's Day, 24th August 1744, the anniversary of the restoration of the Anglican Church system in 1662 after the Great Revolution, John Wesley preached in St Mary's Church, Oxford. It was the usual sermon on Church and Christianity in the life of the people but the newspaper *Lloyd's Evening Post* could not find words sharp enough to censure him for offending, to the point of insulting, his listeners, because he compared city and university with Sodom and declared that in them not a single Christian and scarcely a morally serious person was to be found. Just because the higher dignitaries in State and Church refused to silence such enthusiastic misleading of the people, it was to be hoped that at least the university would now act.[21] A satirical poem in the year 1751 described the Foundery in London, Wesley's headquarters, as a hospital for the insane.[22] It was in similar vein that Methodism was represented as a popular movement for making credulous spirits ignorant.[23] This would appeal to the enlightened spirit of the age, since this in its radical form tried to show that religion was an imposture on the part of priests.[24] In the year 1776 Methodism was called as a matter of course 'Father of superstition' and described as notoriously ruinous for weak souls. Its chief sin consisted in the fact that it caused all innocent pleasures to be suspect and that it created for its followers a world of tears and groans, anxiety and distress, as alone pleasing to God. It thus set itself in direct opposition to the apostolic summons to be joyful. Joyfulness was the best way to health. Methodism must therefore be condemned as dangerous to health. If religion were essentially the mother of all that is worthy, hopeful and joyful, its debasement by the Methodists into a matter of fear and trouble must be deplored. The writer of this article sarcastically asked therefore that attempts should be made to convert only those who from the Methodist side could be compared with Saul the persecutor of Christians; on the other hand he warned those who worked with tender and convincing means of proof against making use of serpent's venom.[25]

It was clear that John Wesley's conservative political attachment gave rise to fresh attacks. These reached their climax in the opposition aroused by the sentiments he had expressed to the American colonies.[26] The movement for independence originated as is well known from the fact that the colonials were forced to pay taxes on behalf of the homeland. Samuel Johnson, that embodiment of typical English middle-class opinion in the eighteenth century, wrote a pamphlet entitled *Taxation no Tyranny*. John Wesley, who in the first instance had adopted a position more in favour of the Americans,[27] was persuaded by Johnson to change his opinion, and he borrowed from the pamphlet with a freedom which surprised the younger man. Johnson did not take this ill, but he closed the incident with a grandiloquent gesture. He was proud that he had won over to his point of view this great national figure.[28]

After Methodism had become established in North America, the rejection of independence by its leader could serve only to weaken its naturalization in the New World, particularly as it was a clear case of a change of mind. But it is also significant that Wesley encountered opposition in his native land. Under the pseudonym 'Americus' a critic, a Rev. John Erskine,[29] expressed great amazement concerning the late change of the minister into the politician, about which he could not refrain from making the cynical comment that apparently even the most perfect of men had not only heavenly but also earthly interests. Then he derided John Wesley's description of his pamphlet as a 'Calm Address', since the whole activity of the leader of the Methodists showed a quite different tendency and testified to the victory of enthusiasm over prudence. How could he suppose that following the recent history among his followers of palpitations, transports, visions of angels and devils, presumptions of the consummation of physical marriage with Jesus Christ, he would find listeners when he appealed to reason? With everything that he says he only demonstrates that the world of constitutional law and political logic are foreign to him. This is not to be wondered at in the case of a man who has been accustomed since his youth to discuss exclusively questions which avoid demonstration by human reason. As a consequence his statements betray an astounding ignorance of the historical suppositions of present-day America. Wesley completely overlooks the fact that the first settlers were refugees, desirous of escaping from the persecution by the established Church under the

Stuarts; for he depicts the character of the colony in such a way as to suggest that a right was granted by the Crown to peaceful citizens in England to settle in North America for profitable undertakings. Why, asks 'Americus', were the rights of freedom kept back from free men, and thus freedom before the law violated? Why is North America denied what Ireland possesses? Apparently because the Crown hopes that the murmurings of discontent will die away on the voyage over the Atlantic ocean, and the Americans therefore fail to receive permission, like the Irish, to be oppressed at least by their own (even if corrupt) Parliament. When John Wesley argues for the present unjust state, he lays violent hands upon human dignity—and it is obvious that he has one eye upon a royal pension, while the other is directed to heaven. He has forgotten the word of his Master: 'Thou canst not serve God and Mammon.' 'Americus' does not forget to remind him expressly that it is bigotry, religious enthusiasm, which has alone and so often deluged the world in blood. 'It is when men fight for they know not what, when the object is hid in the clouds, or evaporated in dreams, that they become Savages and Brutes, and it is when they expect to be fed with Manna from Heaven, that they die of hunger in their camps, and give up the enterprise.'[30]

So this attack on John Wesley culminated also in the usual sentiments of the Enlightenment: religion is a deception by priests, supporting the ruling powers. It deprives a man of his rights in this world in the name of the other world. These objections appeared only in a moderate form, for it was not religion as such, but only that proclaimed by the Methodists, which was in the dock. John Wesley therefore could not be considered as a prophet, but at the most as God's servant. The consciousness of freedom, the faith in progress and the conviction of victory of this 'enlightened generation' not only went against political pessimism, which came from the conservative attitude and which was anxious to retain the outworn forms of the state, resting upon the experiences of former generations rather than forwarding the former qualities.[31] John Wesley and 'Americus' were motivated by different ideologies, and the opposition between Methodism and the spirit of the Enlightenment became in this instance as clear in the political field as it had been formerly in the theological. In the polemical literature on this question Wesley was accused of displaying Jesuitical distortions and a servile attitude, so that his chief opponent, the Baptist minister Caleb Evans, without any hope of converting him, set himself the objective of making his true character known to as many people as possible.[32]

It is understandable that the part played by lay-preaching in the movement was another favourite target for ridicule and censure. In 1760 the *London Magazine* contrasted the defective education of this clerus minor with the Anglican conviction that it possessed the most learned ministry in the world, in order to expose the whole infamy of the Methodist movement. This movement was not only felt as the greatest of insults to the century; it was offensive to the Church of England also, and indeed to the Reformation as a whole. Much speaking without meaning, outward activity punctuated with noisy violence and all sorts of foolery—this was how the Methodist preaching appeared to the critic who did not fail to draw attention to the contradiction into which John Wesley fell with his own demands, since he had desired clergymen to have a knowledge of the basic biblical languages, philosophy and history.[33] Another could only conclude from John Wesley's action that he was a Quaker and separatist in Anglican clothing, using his office to betray the Church to its enemies with the kiss of Judas, an ambitious, power-seeking tyrant who kept his lay helpers in ignorance so that he could rule over them as pope without opposition.[34]

Still fiercer shots were fired. A satire, *The Fanatic Saints or Bedlamites Inspired* (1778) sought in a spiteful manner to bring together everything which had been advanced against John Wesley. Hypocrisy and folly support the building of Methodism; Jesuitism and Machiavellianism are its inner character. Under the banner of the definite rejection of the pope people are more degraded and enslaved than ever they were under Rome. The class-leaders, who are often women, act as spiritual spies, so as to lighten the task of the chief leader in ruling over souls. In the most abject way he enters into alliance with the political powers and plays their tunes in order to summon people to murder their brethren, a reference to Wesley's approval of the English war against the North American colonies. In this way he denies his God and deifies the king. He leads his followers astray into irrational enthusiasm, with the result that, under the delusion that they are saved by faith alone, they leave their ordinary occupation, neglect their duty of caring for their families and hand over to him their last penny. Under the guise of unity he contrives nothing but separation and division. According to the requirement of the moment he can be either severe or tender, appear strict with troublesome people, act graciously towards love-sick women, to whom, although he is over seventy, he devotes himself all too intimately. While he teaches his own people to climb up John Bunyan's Jacob's ladder, he knows how to secure himself against loss in earthly pleasures. Since he understood how to place himself in the centre he is given excessive veneration and this enables him to find believers for every falsehood. He flatters the vanity of the uneducated in that he raises them to the position of preachers, and trains them by a virtuous mimicry to be deluded about their hollowness. The watchword 'faith without works' gives him and his followers the right to throw off all real seriousness and give themselves up to pure enthusiasm.[35] No wonder that the same author, who kept his anonymity, devoted his next slanderous writing against John Wesley to the subject of 'Perfection', in *A Poetical Epistle Calmly addressed to the Greatest Hypocrite in England*.[36] In both pamphlets he gave John Wesley the nickname Cantwell, and used it at every opportunity, altogether 212 times. Wesley's watchword of Christian perfection was fully employed in the sense of perfecting all that was common and base in the name of Christianity. Methodism appeared as the completion of Roman Catholic, Jesuitical degeneration. It was recorded against John Wesley that his chief offence was that he had cast off his 63-year-old wife after he, who was actually in love with a poor young girl, had married her as a rich widow. The reproaches which this libel brought against him were similar to those in the former work: concupiscence, wantonness in his relations with women, which was said to be a sign of sinless perfection, the suppression of all moral seriousness amongst his followers through the preaching of the forgiveness of sins and the certainty of election; covetousness, which extracted the last farthing from the pockets of his people; lust for power, which revealed him to be a successful adept in that which was characteristic of the Vatican; fawning devotion to the king and thirst for blood, which heedlessly murdered the life of the citizens of Britain in an unjust war through his 'Calm Address to the North American Colonists', continual lying and hypocrisy without parallel. In brief there were no crimes of which he was not regarded as capable. If from the Foundery, the London headquarters of the movement, the truth were to be published in historical tracts, similar to his religious ones, the hosts of fallen girls and the tricks of bankrupts would decrease

L

and fewer cries of the insane be heard in the lunatic asylum of Old Bedlam. The author did not scruple to charge John Wesley with having illegitimate children, and he put him on the same level as the monster of the Roman renaissance, Cesare Borgia, 'in faith an angel, in deed a beast'. Wesley and his movement were in his eyes a danger to the community, and it was not possible to oppose them too strongly. The year 1778 produced seven attacks of this kind—and this was forty years after the beginning of the great movement of evangelization. The emblems which decorated these writings were also significant. John Wesley was depicted as a wolf, a fox, and as a lion in the form of a lamb sitting in a triple crown; he has a key to the entrance to heaven, which alludes to his pretended claim, and a mousetrap, which refers to his skill in leading astray the unsuspecting.

Another satire bore the title: 'Toothless, he draws the teeth of his flocks.' Wesley is represented in this as a fox in a master's gown with bands, bending over, employed in drawing out teeth.[37] A further abusive writing shows him as a serpent.[38] Finally his consecration as bishop is represented as being performed by the half-naked goddess Murcia sitting on a throne, by which Venus is meant, and Wesley kneels at her feet, again with a fox's head—he, the chosen one, having supplanted two other candidates, Romano, who represents the Roman Catholic Church, and Simonio, who stands for spiritual avarice, simony.[39] Wesley's relationships with women in particular engaged the lively fantasies of his opponents. Thus in 1775, when Wesley was 72 years old, the Tête-à-tête Portraits were published, showing the pious preacher in an intimate attitude with a pretty young woman, the daughter of a public prosecutor.[40]

But much more serious were the attacks based upon theological and ecclesiastical arguments. It was part of the structure of the Church of England, as well as its historical experience, that the bishops should exercise the function of warding off heresy, or of recognizing and fighting against dangerous symptoms in the Church. It cannot be said that they were either slow or negligent in undertaking this task against early Methodism. The bishop of the capital city in which the centre of the movement lay—if not from the beginning yet soon afterwards—was Edmund Gibson (1669-1748),[41] who was by then an elderly man of mature judgement. In his youth he had seen the advance of Roman Catholicism at Oxford, and in London the immorality of the Court in sexual matters, drink and gambling. He thus seemed to be the right man to hold a healthy midway Christian position. As the bishop with jurisdiction over the North American colonies he had examined John and Charles Wesley in a friendly way on 20th October 1738 and 21st February 1739; on 1st August 1739 he had composed a pastoral letter for his diocese, in which he gave a warning against both indifference and over-zealousness in matters of faith. He was careful to avoid condemning the movement as a whole. In the following period he closely watched its progress. His chief source was apparently George Whitefield's *Journal*, the chief feature of which seemed to him to be religious enthusiasm. The result was that he turned sharply against the move-ment in 1744, but made no distinction between it and the Herrnhut Moravians.[42] The Methodists, he wrote, ought to leave the Church, since they have broken all the rules of ecclesiastical obedience. The use of lay-preachers, the erection of their own meeting-places, their open-air preaching, and their reception of the Holy Communion in churches other than their local ones, contradict the basic Anglican parish legal system;[43] this particular point was also made by Gibson with ruthless insistence against the dissenters.[44] Instead of joining the trusted, inner-church fellowship movement of the Religious Societies, John Wesley and George Whitefield had to associate themselves with the foreign sect of the Moravians. On 20th August 1744, Gibson had held an unsuccessful conversation, troubled by language difficulties, with the Herrnhuter Wenzeslaus Neisser, the memory of which was apparently still with him when he turned against the Methodists.[45] Finally he feared that the importance which the Herrnhuters and the Methodists gave to justification would blunt the readiness to accept moral responsibility. He found it significant that Whitefield had raised strong objections against *The Whole Duty of Man*, a devotional book which gave classical expression to the Puritan spirit within the Anglican Church during the seventeenth century, and was only willing to grant that at best it was 'man's half duty'.[46]

In Gibson's objections there sounds the voice of the true eighteenth-century Anglican churchman, yet as a mediating, and in the last resort untheological, person he did not go beyond the commonplaces of his time. The second bishop, who concerned himself directly with John Wesley, Joseph Butler of Bristol, was a very different character, a genuinely independent thinker. He, however, did not deal with the matter himself, but entrusted it to a young clergyman, Josiah Tucker.

This man, who later made a name for himself as one of the economists of the eighteenth century,[47] showed himself in this instance to be an outstanding thinker. He set about the task he had been given with deep seriousness and approached it from both an historical and a systematic-theological angle. He did not confine himself to the most obvious features of the Methodist movement, but penetrated to its essential principles. He traced the fundamentals of the Methodists to the writings of William Law, discovering in them a unique combination of Arminian and Calvinist doctrines. Their central point, he maintained, was the new creation. While Calvinism asserts the complete ruin of the original creation in man, Arminianism preserves a significant remnant of the image of God intact. On the one hand Law takes over the pessimism of Calvinism in its judgement on man; he looks upon him flatly as an evil animal. On the other hand he maintains that at the fall a new principle became operative in him, a redeeming power, which makes his restoration possible.[48] In Law's language this is the inner gospel, the Christ within us. Tucker, following the thought of the Enlightenment, identifies this with the awakening of conscience, the interest in virtue and a feeling for morality. Sanctification amounts to improvement, and, in a way which Tucker obviously approves, man possesses a power to bring it to effect. This feature derives from Arminianism. Sanctification means the constant improvement and refinement of talents for the good, and not a once-for-all endowment with a miraculous capacity, not a change into a perfect condition, but a gradual process, which is realized by degrees with the help of divine grace. So Jesus becomes the real father of the new man, although in a spiritual sense, just as Adam was the real and actual parent of the old man in his perverseness.[49]

Tucker claims that the Methodists did not possess the ability to penetrate into the basic pattern and tensions in the thought of William Law, and Whitefield, fresh from the university, with an inadequate and superficial knowledge of Law's system, preached the urgent necessity of the new birth. The effect of his preaching was like a rebirth of Calvinism, although he himself was ignorant of this. Since, however, Presbyterians favoured his preaching he was grateful to them, and himself became more and more inclined to the Calvinists. On the other hand in Pennsylvania he was strongly attacked by other Presbyterians, in the main because, basing himself upon Law, he promised to his followers participation in the divine nature; indeed he actually baptized them into the nature of the Father, Son and Holy Ghost.[50]

So much for Whitefield, who because of his aggressive tactics generally claimed greater attention. In the case of the Wesley brothers Tucker, by quoting in detail from John's *Journal*, confirmed their dominant relationship with the Moravians, but at the same time emphasized that John had never seriously freed himself from William Law's basic principles. This is seen in his teaching on justification and sanctification. In this he still holds that a perfection without sin, not merely without intentional malignity, but even without failure due to weakness, is attainable, while on the other hand with Christian David he calls for justification along with humility. This is almost the same as saying that a sinful condition still persists after conversion. Even so John Wesley teaches that the 'Christ in us' follows on the 'Christ for us', or in other words that real personal righteousness, which completes the righteousness of Christ, is essential for justification.[51] Consequently in spite of all the subsequent Herrnhut superstructure Law remains the foundation of his system, and there is a similar relation between them as with the Catholic Church and the faith of the early Christians.[52] It is characteristic of the spirit of the eighteenth century that Tucker should represent the Herrnhut precepts as 'dreamings'.[53] Thus he arrived at the remarkable conclusion that John Wesley, in virtue of Law's superior influence, hit upon correct conclusions starting from erroneous—Herrnhut—presuppositions.[54] In this way he on the one hand discredited the Methodists as illogical thinkers, and on the other granted their moral seriousness—a position which in the midst of the whole anti-Methodist polemics showed remarkable independence of judgement, and merited a place of its own. Perhaps the reason why it was destined not to bear fruit was its very complicated pattern of ideas. Neither through its methodology and its general tenor, nor in its conclusion could it serve the needs of the age, particularly as in the last resort it provided at least a justification of John Wesley. In the course of a few pages there was the recognition of something extremely important, and it was expounded with real originality of thought.

An attack in the *London Magazine* in the year 1760, which selected the two central points of the new birth and sin, went very much deeper. With reference to the first[55] the whole argument rested on the point that people in the England of that day were Christians and therefore needed no rebirth. The concept only applied to Jews and pagans of the first generations in the history of the Church. The author recognized only two basic kinds of people: the depraved and the virtuous. Accordingly he could only understand rebirth as consisting in a moral change in the way of life. Since, however, with the passage to Christian faith the decision for virtue had been made once for all, there could be no fresh change. John Wesley's call to the new birth must be understood by his contemporaries as a provocative claim, implying that they were not Christians, just as the baptism of John the Baptist implied that the Jews of his time were in fact proselytes. To the writer everything hinged upon the fact, in view of the doctrine of inspiration, that the difference between early Christianity and the eighteenth century should be properly clarified. Even if everything that was said in the New Testament rested upon an equal divine authority, it must not be used in the same manner. He went even further in his historical criticism. It was also necessary sharply to distinguish between the words of Jesus himself and their record by his disciples, that is, the theology of the Church. For this reason the new birth as a whole was to be excluded as a subject for preaching by the Church of the present day. At the same time the writer carefully and with theological precision sought to show that it was a valid element in baptism for the eighteenth century. He demonstrated in this way with unmistakable naïvety how easily ecclesiastical institutionalism became satisfied with itself, constantly appearing as the consequence of a culture pressed upon people by the national established Church. He was expressing the common feeling of his time. In such a situation it was not possible for the intention and task of a movement of re-awakening to be recognized as a manifestation of genuine Christianity.

The second subject, sin, was treated in an equally superficial way.[56] The author, who called himself Philanthropos, selected as his particular point the equation of God and reason. He saw in rationality God's highest characteristic. The essence of sin must therefore be any action which goes against the purpose and the declared will of the highest Being. Since this is reason, sin is any offence against reason, and as Philanthropos further supposed that the original reason is adequately portrayed and manifested in human reason, he was led to assert that whoever acts against his reason, or indeed is led astray by passion, prejudice or the search for worldly gain, is a sinner.

It was very significant that in neither case was anything directly said about Methodism, to which reference was only made through the treatment of its themes; these were handled in a devious manner. The first time they were dismissed altogether, and in the second instance the basic concept was so changed in meaning that it resulted in a complete inversion of the original sense. Thus in this case the polemic appeared in the form of an assertion of the spirit of the age in opposition to the rebirth of primitive Christianity.

What the eighteenth century really stood for is seen in few places so clearly as in the 'moral weeklies'. This new style of publication, by means of which the leading intellectuals communicated with the people, possessed the merits of immediacy, unpretentiousness, and a closeness to everyday affairs. Accordingly they invaded the sphere of church preaching and instruction. In 1750 Samuel Johnson, who reflects his age most faithfully, founded *The Rambler*. In this paper his own opinions only were allowed to appear between the lines of the gossip and other ephemeral material. With typical English diffidence he hoped that those readers whom he was not able to please would at least not be wearied, and if he were not commended for the beauty of his works he would at least be pardoned for their brevity.[57] In this way he was able to provide a constant education in reflection and in the responsible conduct of life. Even if the requirement of historical truth was not to be applied to what was written, nevertheless moral probability was demanded. The 'idea of virtue' must shine forth as a genuine human possibility. Moral and spiritual maturity go together, and wickedness is at the same time an infallible sign of spiritual narrowness.[58] Thus many surprising and valuable ideas were found among the opinions, as for example the sentiment that the small effect a man's decease has is not only a warning against too great self-esteem, but also a reminder that we should not tyrannize over each other.[59] As a consequence religion is thought of in relatively narrow terms, and is given a predominantly ethical character. How much is possible in any situation is shown by reflection on solitude, an idea which shows the influence of Boethius. Solitude is extolled first as a condition which is fertile for the acquisition of understanding and facility in judgement. Then in solitude a man undertakes self-examination. He inquires after God's will, and so directs his attention to the future instead of the present. The reward promised for virtue and the punishment threatened to vice become more important to him than pleasures and desire, and so he is able to withstand life's temptations. He recognizes how well the apostle describes the human situation when he compares it with the war-service of a soldier, for he arms him for the struggle between morality and sensuality. The real goal of all religion is virtue. An ecclesiastical institution has no purpose other than to strengthen and renew the resolve to virtue. Solitude is then essential to cut out the seductive allurements of the external world. The truly wise man and the real moral combatant is the solitary man.[60]

This conception of religion knew nothing of sin, or the deep-seated failure of man before God's claim. The preaching of the Methodists understandably seemed strange and foolish to a century which had been taught such ideas.

In the same magazine Mrs Elizabeth Carter wrote expressly about the subject of 'religion'.[62] She recounted her views in a dream full of symbolic images.[6¹] A woman veiled in black, with many wrinkles on her face and scourges in her hands, commanded her to follow. She led her into a deep, deserted valley, and wherever this woman trod, the grass withered. Her foul breath disseminated bad fumes and the sky grew dark. Then she turned and said, 'Retire with me, O rash unthinking mortal, from the vain allurements of a deceitful world, and learn that pleasure was not designed the portion of human life. Man was born to mourn and to be wretched . . . Fly then from the fatal enchantments of youth and from social delight, and here consecrate the solitary hours to lamentation and woe. Misery is the duty of all sublunary beings, and every enjoyment is an offence to the Deity, who is to be worshipped only by the mortification of every sense of pleasure, and everlasting exercise of sighs and tears.' Completely desolated by this first distressing experience, the authoress turned herself about and saw the form of another woman, quite different in appearance. Endowed with the charms of youth and beauty, her eyes sparkled with brightness and strength; her whole countenance and demeanour were love and inner peace. At her appearing the clouds disappeared and the heavens brightened, the grass again became green, and the whole region around was changed into a garden of rich flowers. Then she introduced herself with these words: 'My name is Religion. I am the offspring of Truth and Love, and the parent of

Benevolence, Hope, and Joy. That monster from whose power I have freed you is called Superstition; she is the child of Discontent and her followers are Fear and Sorrow. Thus, different as we are, she has often the insolence to assume my name and character, and to seduce unhappy mortals into thinking that we are the same, till she, at length, drives them to the borders of Despair, that dreadful abyss into which you were just going to sink.

'Look round and survey the various beauties of the globe, which Heaven has destined for the seat of the human race, and consider whether a world thus exquisitely framed could be intended as an abode of misery and pain. For what end has the lavish hand of Providence diffused such innumerable objects of delight, but that all might rejoice in the privilege of existence and be filled with gratitude to the beneficent author of it? Thus to enjoy the blessings he has sent, is virtue and obedience; and to reject them merely as means of pleasure, is pitiable ignorance or absurd perverseness. Infinite goodness is the source of created existence; the proper tendency of every rational being, from the highest order of raptured seraphs, to the meanest rank of men, is to rise incessantly from lower degrees of happiness to higher. They all have faculties assigned them for various orders of delights.'

'What,' cried the authoress, 'is this the language of Religion? Does she lead her votaries through flowery paths, and bid them pass an unlaborious life? Where are the painful toils of Virtue, the mortification of penitents, the self-denying exercises of saints and heroes?'

'The true enjoyments of a reasonable being,' answered the other, mildly, 'do not consist in unbounded indulgence, or luxurious ease, in the tumult of passions, the languor of indolence, or the flutter of light amusements. Yielding to immoral pleasure corrupts the mind, living in sensual trifling debases it.' She went on to say that whoever would be truly happy must devote his whole strength to it in careful and regular exercise. He must honour the perfection of his Maker, and give practical proof of his goodwill to his fellow-creatures. He must be guided by self-control and a sense of responsibility. If he has done wrong he must submit willingly and wisely to grievous and strict exercises, which Nature imposes through healing arts and which morality prescribes for his education. No despair overwhelms him, no terror or fear of hell worries him. His path always leads upwards. All things can become better, and even the deepest humiliation is only the door to the most elevated hopes. No difficulty is insurmountable. In patience and trust he depends upon the Sovereign of the universe and yet by himself he comes through all undertakings. Silent resignation to the will of the Creator, ready accommodation to its inscrutable ways, are the noblest form of self-denial and the source of the most exalted transports.

The sphere of human virtue is not the solitude of the monastic cell, but ordinary social life. Only by living together, by the daily conquest of difficulties, by consideration for people and human relationships, does the Christian grow. Suffering is not a duty, nor is pleasure a crime. But when the first becomes necessary for spiritual development, it is undertaken without complaint, and where the second is a danger to the inner man, it is renounced as a matter of course. Moral education for true humanity is the content of religion. It comes both from personal effort through strong-willed endeavour on the part of a man himself, and also from encounter with the outer world, which as the place of destiny and human relationships possesses a compelling strength.[63] The Christian and the hero belong together.[64]

The spirit of the Enlightenment is here seen in its clearest form. It is not surprising that the same publication could use the word 'repentance' and make it synonymous with a 'change of life'.[65] In this way the Enlightenment became one with Pietism, and was able from this point to develop a limited but mistrustful appreciation of the work of Methodism, without agreeing with its fundamental basis.

In a manner similar to that adopted by the author of the article on the new birth in the *London Magazine* of 1760, the Archdeacon of the diocese of Essex, Thomas Rutherford, attacked the transferring of early Christian practices into the present, such as was done by the unlearned itinerant preachers among the Methodists. In the days of the apostles the office of preaching had a completely different function from what it had now come to possess in the present-day Church of England. The apostles were instrumental in first making known the message, and they did not have at their disposal any philosophical tradition upon which to draw, while the prophets of the old covenant only prophesied the Coming—they did not cause it. In between, a rich theological literature had developed, of which the Church needed to avail itself in order to fulfil its task.[66] In true Anglican fashion the sanctification of tradition was in this way advocated so that the Methodist claim of restoring primitive Christianity might be disallowed. But this was not sufficient. Rutherford further contested the right of John Wesley to appeal to an inner assurance, said to be derived from the Holy Spirit, which yet avoided further testing, because it had its central point in indeterminate 'feeling'.[67] In contrast to this he argued forcefully that the Holy Spirit imparts clear directions and demonstrates Himself in clear virtues. These are the fruits through which, according to Paul (Galatians 5[22]), the Spirit attests His presence.[68] Accordingly there is no need for any special assurance of forgiveness or of adoption. The promise of God, that He forgives sins, is sufficient. The fact that Jesus gave his disciples the Lord's Prayer as a model is more important than Paul's idea of assurance, in which the Spirit of God speaks directly to believers (Romans 8[15, 16]). Rutherford rejects the cultivation of religious subjectivity. He was concerned with the objective act of salvation and God's saving promise, which must be allowed to stand alone in their seriousness and majesty. In this way he was able to appear as the representative of orthodoxy. At the same time he referred, after the manner of the Enlightenment, to the condition which the individual must fulfil in order that God's offer might become a reality.[69]

A favourite subject of attack was the question of sin and perfection. Thomas Whiston undertook a careful consideration of the Methodist opinions,[70] and it was his treatment of actual righteousness which showed his different point of view. In the spirit of the eighteenth century and of Anglican theology he wished to avoid the over-evaluation and self-validation of man, as well as his disparagement. Consequently he could not speak of the annihilation of the divine image in man, but only of an impaired likeness and a ruin, which can still call forth admiration and respect. In his view the miserable condition, which Paul describes in chapter 7 of the Epistle to the Romans, applied only to the unredeemed sinner, and in Platonic fashion he described the conflict which goes on in him as a struggle between body and soul. The two must once again become one, and this becomes a possibility through the crucifixion and resurrection of Jesus. The soul once again receives its immortality.[71] William Law, whom like Josiah Tucker he saw as the spiritual father of Methodism, went too far when he was unwilling to grant to fallen man any good at all. He actually makes him out to be a devil.[72] According to Whiston the erroneous doctrine of justification of the Methodists is in line with this. He grants that they are correct in denying that a man can be justified because of works done, but to set aside his plea to be such on the basis of works still to be done leads directly to antinomianism and disregard for law.[73] The new birth, to which he comes, and the new man, which proceeds from this, are not completely foreign to the earlier nature, but are a continuation of it.[74] Whiston opposed miracles with all the force of a man of the Enlightenment, but at the same time as a churchman he desired to accept the biblical teaching. Therefore for him everything was to proceed as far as was possible in a natural, organic and ethical manner. His conception of salvation was determined by the idea of development and the principle of analogy. He was opposed to making a breach between the old and the new man, and claimed there was a connexion between them; this connexion was not a sudden transition from one to the other, but rather a gradual process. His theology was governed by the idea of natural development, typical of the Enlightenment. Sin became atavism, and sanctification was the higher, true nature of man—ideas which were worked out at a much deeper level in Schleiermacher's *The Christian Faith* (1821). He was being quite consistent when he charged the Methodists with arrogating to themselves the supernatural gifts of the Holy Spirit, instead of cultivating the natural ones.[75]

Owing to the elevated tone of this controversial theological writing, when viewed as a whole, it occupied a unique position. In those cases which dealt with basic themes and kept to matters of fact, the objections advanced were generally milder. An anonymous pamphlet, consisting of four pages, written in 1763, declared in nineteen 'humble Quaeries' its opposition to the claim that a Christian could attain sinless perfection, not only on the ground of scripture texts like Romans 3^{20}; 7^{17}; 1 John 3^4 and 5^{17}, but also that nobody ought to maintain that he loves only God and fulfils all His commandments.[76] The author feared that antinomianism would be the inevitable consequence of the Methodist position, and he wished to know whether its representatives really no longer felt any temptations. If they claimed this to be the case, then it must be further asked whether that feeling was a trustworthy experience. Behind this was the serious question as to whether Pharisaism was not the real sin, in that man no longer stood in need of God. But it was not in fact pursued to this limit. On the contrary this seriously-intended caution thereafter came to nothing, because it went on to charge the movement with responsibility for a notorious mentally disturbed non-commissioned officer named Bell.

Much more frequently the opponents were content merely to brand the movement with names. As has been noted these were primarily the accusations of enthusiasm and fanaticism, favourite epithets of the time. Between 1749 and 1751 an anonymous book appeared in three parts, comparing Methodists with Papists. The author was George Lavington (1684–1762), Bishop of Exeter, who had already made a name for himself as a violent opponent of the Methodists.[77] When at the beginning he declared that in view of the growing unbelief and the increasing immorality of the time he would be prepared to welcome a reform movement in the Church, this was only in order to emphasize the more strongly that this could never take place on the basis of enthusiasm.[78] The model of a detested type of enthusiastic sect he found in Montanism,[79] and accordingly he attempted to find the characteristic features of that movement repeated among the Methodists. Of course he had to admit that they had not yet reached an equal level of madness, and so the comparison could not really succeed. In addition the realization of the programme which had been announced left much to be desired. Lavington let the comparison with the Montanists drop, although it had scarcely been given more than a mention, and he proceeded to set the Methodists alongside the Roman Catholics since this promised to be a more profitable line. In this connexion Francis of Assisi, Dominic, Ignatius Loyola, Antony of Padua, Catharine of Sienna, and St Teresa were lumped together in a somewhat motley historical succession, but as characteristics common to Wesley and all of them he discovered a passionate love for God and man, a burning zeal to save souls, and a rock-like determination in all undertakings to serve the higher honour of God. In each case the actual means employed was open-air preaching done by wandering brothers who acknowledged responsibility to no earthly authority and who would therefore necessarily create confusion.[80] Like the Catholics, the Methodists demand a religion which shows itself in outward appearances. They require a mournful countenance, strictly defined conduct in speaking or silence, and a disdain for all recreation. They disallow diversions, gambling and amusements, they cultivate an unnatural yearning for persecution and martyrdom, indeed for death and hell.[81] Of course they do not succeed in attaining the heights of Roman Catholic saints. While

Francis of Assisi hoped to die as a martyr at the hands of the Egyptian sultan, Antony among the Moors in Africa, and Ignatius Loyola among the Turks, Wesley and Whitefield were content to be with the Indians in the civilized British colony of North America.[82] They completely forget that Jesus himself condemned such a desire for the glory of martyrdom. Does it not say in the Lord's Prayer: lead us not into temptation? And does not the Saviour command his disciples, when persecuted, to flee from the city in which they are threatened into a safer one (Matthew 10^{23})? What a great contrast this is to the Methodist-Catholic self-mortification, and how far Wesley and Whitefield are from early Christianity, to which they constantly appeal, when they boast of their stoical insensibility to pain and torment or cherish an unnatural desire for it.[83] Further indications of enthusiasm are the sudden conversions, an essential part of their system. They ascribe to the Holy Spirit phenomena which are due to diseased and over-strained nerves.[84] The deluded idea of Christian perfection, which they have taken over from the Moravians, raises the question: at what point do these haughty heaven-stormers intend to call a halt? Do they not compare themselves with Prometheus, who stole the holy fire from heaven? Their baseless appeal to their own revelations makes them so headstrong that neither rational demonstrations nor scriptural statements have any effect on them. In the darkness of their infallibility they put themselves forward as being like the early Church at the first Pentecost. But storms and earthquakes as proofs of the reality of God have nothing essentially to do with Christianity. It was among the heathen that they were believed to testify to the presence of divinity, as can be read in the works of Virgil and Ovid.[85]

In this way Lavington believed that he had established his claim that Methodism and Popery were similar in type. Of course he admitted that it was a case of unconscious and unintentional agreement. The Methodists were not actual pupils of the Roman Catholic fanatics, or their envoys. But their principles and their design, so far as enthusiasm can be said to have a design, led them to the same goal.[86]

Lavington was not a young man when he wrote all this. When the book appeared he was 65, and it serves as the last declaration of a convinced adherent of the Enlightenment, who saw in the new movement the denial of the ideal he had cherished for a lifetime, and the most serious danger for the future. John Wesley answered him clearly and sharply,[87] whereupon Lavington brought out a third part, which was directed particularly at Wesley, and which was more severe than the first two sections. Lavington made use of that part of Wesley's *Journal* which had already been published, covering the period between September 1741 and October 1742, the chief subject of which was the breach with the Moravians. Lavington, who all through dismissed Wesley as a vain braggart, inquired scornfully why he suddenly lost his taste for them and reviled his truest friends as his most evil enemies.

The answer which Lavington gave was because they had become his rivals. Whereas formerly Herrnhut had been the home of genuine Christians, now Wesley could not do enough to bring out their hypocrisy, their denial of God's commandments, and their accommodation to the world. Count Zinzendorf had stolen from him his best followers; this was the secret of the whole matter. The only point now was which of the two was the greater.[88] If the principles of the Moravians were really so bad, why had Wesley adopted them and been so happy with them?[89] The fact was that it was after the separation that he had clearly deteriorated morally. Lavington did not scruple to charge him with gross debaucheries. Wesley and his disciples had once been holy men, who spoke no unprofitable words, who slept on the ground, but who now were not merely not satisfied with a warm bed, but required bed-fellows in them. This is the way of all sects. Like the 'Family of Love' of Heinrich Niclaes in the sixteenth century they end up with the worldly enjoyment of sex, and this mixing of holiness and licentiousness results in something merely offensive.[90] However blameless Methodism may have been at the beginning it has now developed gradually and unscrupulously into a system of solemn deception.[91] One cannot hand over to its followers the Holy Scriptures because they handle them in such a wanton way, and by their own secret conversations with God, their visions and their marvels, they set them on one side. They compare themselves with the prophets and the apostles, even with Jesus Christ Himself. Pride, vanity, and lack of love to the rest of mankind are the marks of their leaders. Unruly behaviour, strange paroxysms, and the outpourings of a sick brain are interpreted as signs of holiness. The path to the goal of perfection leads through immorality, indifference towards the authorities, unbelief, atheism, and mystical 'abandonment', despair and madness, while an imaginary new birth is called forth by means of torments which call to mind the pains of a woman in labour.[92] The mystical experiences of Antoinette Bourignon are taken as the model by which the Methodists are portrayed, and in order to demonstrate again the similarity with Catholics, the pains of the new birth are described as anticipations of purgatory.[93] According to Lavington, John Wesley surpassed his instructress in one feature, that is, in cunning. She predicted the final judgement would be within the next three years. Wesley was more shrewd. He avoided giving any precise time, and so could announce it constantly. The consequence of this was the increasing licentiousness of his followers.[94]

If he complains that the churches are closed to him, he should be asked if he really believes that the Anglican clergy would allow themselves and their teaching to be derided from their pulpits. It is reported of Mohammed that he had a vision in which he saw his opponents climb into his place and jump around like monkeys. The Anglican clergy had seen this picture more often, and not only in a dream.[95] In this way the elderly bishop descended to spiteful accusations. The book leaves the reader with an extremely painful impression, and is fittingly succeeded by the vulgar satires of the year 1778.

Four years later Lavington entered the lists against the Moravians, whom he compared with the Gnostics and all their excesses.[96] This attack was in general an echo of his objections against Wesley and Whitefield, but at the same time was a strengthening of his former effusions in that he saw in the Moravians the roots of Methodism.[97]

It is a cause for surprise in one sense, and yet in another not so, that a dignitary of the Anglican Church, one of its leading bishops, at the same age of 64, twelve or thirteen years later could bring little more against Methodism, and that in scarcely a more polite way. William Warburton (1698–1779), Bishop of Gloucester, who in his day possessed a European reputation, and whose great work on the Old Testament was referred to by Lessing in his *Erziehung des Menschengeschlechts*,[98] wrote in 1762 specifically against Methodism in a two-volume book on the doctrine of grace or the office and operations of the Holy Spirit.[99] He too traced it from William Law and the Moravians; but he did not stop there; he proceeded to develop his own point of view from a thorough examination of John Wesley's *Journal*. He was at pains to demonstrate that Methodism attracted to itself discord. He strongly rejected Wesley's view that the reverse had been true at the beginning. Rather it was his combination of faith and zeal, typical of an enthusiast, which was responsible for the strife. His presumptuousness in claiming to possess extraordinary prophetic and apostolic powers, and to stand in a particular relationship to the Holy Spirit, is very debatable. When one compares with this the words of the Epistle of James (3^{17}) it becomes clear that it ties in with strife and disorder, not with the 'wisdom that is from above'. Wesley's whole method lacks the one quality which according to the will of Jesus ought to be placed first in religion, namely, sagacity. Jesus Himself had referred to it in His debates with the leaders of the Jewish people, as the treatment of the question of His authority proves (Mark 11^{27ff}).[100] The Gospel is the message of peace. Peace can be maintained only by sagacity. Therefore the Gospel also can be preached correctly only with sagacity. When John Wesley tries to trace back his difficulties to the work of the devil, this is a very easy way out, one which anyone can take. When foolishness takes control there is no need to bring in any devil. This can be gathered from John Wesley's own behaviour. How can he maintain that he preaches the old, simple religion of the Church of England, and at the same time ignore its recognized ordinances, as when he disregards parish boundaries, holds meetings in unrecognized places and at improper times, or attacks the civil and ecclesiastical authority?[101] How can the violation of peace among men serve to advance the divine peace? When he appeals to the word of Jesus, that He has not come to bring peace but the sword, he exchanges what was merely an unusual situation in the life of the Gospel for its normal form of existence. It is the heavenly proclamation of peace among men which describes the real and lasting result which will flow from it.[102] But what can one expect from a fanatic? Men of his stamp are possessed of a delusion, and so they fail to perceive the reality of a Christian country before their eyes, seeing only heathens or idol-worshippers before them, the princes and lords of this world, who desire to suppress the word of life. So they have to reject good order, and raise both the authorities and the people against themselves. Peace and fanaticism are completely opposed to one another. Peace is the cure for fanaticism and fanaticism the end of peace. The leaders of sects must either themselves attack or be attacked, either themselves persecute or raise persecution against themselves. So the

M

Methodists are unrest incarnate and personified. Order does not fit into their view of the world. They are justly ranked with the revolutionaries of Cromwell's time, and the Puritans were their spiritual fathers. During the powerful reign of Elizabeth I they did not dare to come into the open, but hid their opinions. Under the weak and confused rule of Charles I they threw off their masks and called themselves quite appropriately 'Independents', those who were disdainful of all authority. In such a situation the murder of the king easily came about. Whoever reads the accounts of that sad and disgraceful period of British history will agree that the speakers of that time not only thought of a persecution and martyr halo as did the present-day Methodists in their journals, but also that they used the same theological language about faith, grace, salvation, new birth and justification. Their obsession with the life of feeling and its expression in a particular spiritual jargon correspond to one another precisely. Would it also result in the same explosive consequence? On this point Warburton believed he could reassure his readers. John Wesley was unlucky in his particular period of time, because it was unfriendly to persecution and maintained complete freedom of conscience. Wesley desired persecution but it would not come at his behest. Consequently his undoubted qualities as leader of a sect could unfortunately not become effective. A prudent and responsible authority undoubtedly forced Methodism to moderate itself.[103]

When one considers John Wesley one is reminded in many ways in the first place of Oliver Cromwell, and then of Ignatius Loyola. All three sect-leaders combined blind zeal and deceit in the most skilful manner, so that they themselves believed in it. Since Wesley admittedly studied the biography of Loyola, there is no need to be surprised at the similarity between them.[104] They both possess the same lust for power and dissimulation.[105] They boast about miracles and heroic deeds, and yet at the critical moment are cowardly, as John Wesley's disappearance from Georgia proves.[106] In order to complete the tale, on the way he even dissuaded some Swiss from settling there, and in this way robbed a British colony of many worthy and necessary hands.[107] His use of the lot is the crowning-point of his superstition, since according to Augustine it was copied exactly from the heathen practice of antiquity.[108] No wonder that anxiety and dark narrow-mindedness in their style of living follow those who seek such things. Laughter is thought a sin, and a solemn resolution against it is made.

Among the Moravians there is strife over the question as to whether a newspaper may be read.[109] Ought one therefore to be surprised that in the meetings cries of religious madness are heard?[110]

Warburton winds up his general attack on John Wesley's character with the summary claim that he has now torn away the mask from the deformed face of fanaticism. Since the time when Elijah perceived the Spirit of God, not in violent tumults but in quiet whispers, man has in general been disposed to treat Him seriously, and such distortions as the Methodists perpetrate only serve to confirm this. Therefore it is a Christian duty inexorably to show the way, as he has done, in the interests of true religion. He is convinced he has to proceed as conscientiously as possible. For this reason he has taken his points exclusively from John Wesley's *Journals*. Nobody would be able to charge him with having failed to take as a starting-point the genuine Methodism visible in the person of its founder; he has not faulted the movement simply because of the misguided effusions of some little lay-preacher. He has taken the Methodists, especially John Wesley, at their word; and since they claim to be faithful members of the Church of England he has said less of their doctrines and more by way of criticism of their method and general bearing. It has not been his concern to deal with precise theological definitions or scholastic distinctions of doubtful concepts, such as the new birth, original sin, irresistible grace, justifying faith, election, reprobation, or the worthlessness of good works before God, but rather with their vigorous method, in order to dispose of these types of belief.[111] For he is convinced that an enthusiastic way of preaching even of a fundamental apostolic truth causes more harm in human society than a restrained and thoughtful presentation of erroneous doctrines or innovations. Violent emotion or the stirring up of emotion is always evil. It is significant that from the beginning of its history the Gospel has always been proclaimed in strict subjection to authority. When today the Methodists have recourse to mass-meetings in the open-air this is said to mean that there is a great hunger for God's word. How can one dare to do such an injustice to the regularly appointed ministers of the Church, as if they had neglected their duty? Must this not cause in them a deep depression? And what is proposed as an alternative? This alleged new birth, with its infernal lamentations, is bound to act as the jumping-off ground for opposition to the normal preaching of the Church—quite apart from the fact that it provides the opponents of religion, the radical deists, with a welcome point of agitation and a justification for their rejection of the Christian faith. For these reasons the Methodists are not harmless, poor misguided folk, but dangerous, noxious persons, who, when all things are taken into consideration, threaten the collapse of that alliance between Church and State which Warburton in another connexion praised so highly;[112] nor did they put anything convincing in its place.[113]

The basic feeling and the dominant way of looking at things at that time were rarely expressed so clearly as in this example. Everything is brought together here. Antiquity's principle of reason and order, revived by the humanists, permanently introduced into the Anglican tradition in the sixteenth century by Richard Hooker and understood in a cosmic and institutional form, given practical expression in the seventeenth century in the Puritan ideal of sobriety and associated in the eighteenth century with the thought of a common humanity, this it was which furnished Warburton with his leading thoughts. He is entirely devoted to their prosecution, and will allow nothing to contradict them. Enthusiasm and fanaticism are the most severe indictment he can bring against any attitude. They cannot be treated lightly because he fears they will overthrow everything that is enduring and has been proved so by history. For this reason he did not attack the content of the Methodist preaching; he was satisfied to make the formal charge that it was conducted in a revolutionary manner. But in doing this he was contesting its basic assumption, namely that the task of Christianity in the modern world is that of mission. He rejected Wesley's diagnosis of the modern world, namely that it was Christian in name only and in practice followed quite other standards. The difference of viewpoint was fundamental.

What was John Wesley's attitude to all this? How did he conduct himself as an apologist and polemic? He pursued the laborious path of careful analysis of separate items and examined the arguments of his opponents point by point. In this way he safeguarded the principle of justice with minute precision, and so incurred the danger of getting lost or exhausted in details. From the outset he stressed the fact that he was not interested in this kind of writing, and referred to the saying that God made practical divinity necessary, but the devil controversial. The defence of his own person, his teaching and his movement, he found not only an uncongenial task, but also an unusually difficult one, although it was something he was unwilling to neglect.[114] It was a task he had always had to undertake, beginning from the early correspondence with Richard Morgan in 1732–4, while he was at Oxford.

The first occasion of such defence after his own conversion and the beginning of the revival was his reply to Josiah Tucker's pamphlet on the principles of Methodism.[115] In its opening sentences he expressed the fear that he would fall by his own spirit, especially as the many examples from controversial literature, and particularly theology, all show a tendency to self-assertion, wilful misrepresentation, and a concern to exploit the opponent's weaknesses. Not only do they show these characteristics, but, far worse, the attendant necessity to act in this way. Polemical and apologetic writing is writing under compulsion, and it does honour to John Wesley that he undertook the task as an advocate of freedom. But he viewed the situation in a more serious light. Polemics and apologetics result in our offending against the fundamental Christian obligation to love our neighbour. Does a man cease to be my neighbour because he defends a different opinion? Ought I not to treat him as I would wish him to treat me —and not as he actually treats me? Am I not forbidden to repay with the same coin as that with which I am paid? Ought I not to cast the mantle of love over my brother's nakedness, rather than take advantage of it? But who does this? Who thinks of acting like this? Certainly this does not mean that we should avoid all discussion of opposed viewpoints. But who is there who keeps strictly to the question, without striking at the person? Wesley is determined to attempt to do this in his discussions and thus maintain the basic Christian qualities of humility, forbearance, patience and friendship.[116]

He groups Tucker's objections under three short sentences. They are that he, Wesley, believes that justification is by faith alone; that he believes sinless perfection is attainable by Christians; and that he believes inconsistencies. This statement of the case is characteristic of John Wesley. Although he follows his opponent's progression of thought as closely as possible, he does this only after he has set out the point of the discussion in his own way. He does this as simply, clearly, and basically as possible. This gives him a double advantage. Once the subject of discussion has been determined, it follows that this central point shall rule the treatment from the start. Methodism is concerned from first to last with the justification of sinners before

God. John Wesley develops from this the classical Pauline and orthodox teaching about justification and does not neglect to emphasize that it also satisfies the justice of God, since Jesus Christ fulfilled the necessary work in our place. At the same time he brings out the point that man's faith as such is not able to justify the believer. It is God alone who accomplishes this in Jesus Christ. God takes sins away. Such a faith is much more than a holding that something is true, even though it may begin in this way. A bare belief that something is true, without application in personal life, is believed by the devils also. Genuine Christian faith goes far beyond this. It produces not only assurance of personal salvation, but also love for God and readiness to serve Him by obeying His commandments.

This much John Wesley says about justification, and the next question is sinless perfection. On this point Tucker had vigorously charged him with inconsistency, for in his preface to the biography of Thomas Haliburton, which he wrote immediately after his return from Germany, he had contradicted all his earlier statements. In his reply Wesley underlines clearly and decisively two points: content and place in time. On the second of these points Tucker had said that Wesley was convinced that perfection in the sense of complete freedom from ignorance or mistakes in things not essential to salvation, or as growth beyond temptations or weakness, cannot be attained on earth, but that nevertheless a victory over known and deliberate sin is possible. But Wesley was said to regard the actual time as a subordinate question. The content is much more important. What then is Christian perfection? In his reply Wesley vigorously keeps to the claim that a Christian can appropriate to himself all the great statements of Scripture, especially those of the apostle Paul, the Epistle to the Hebrews, the First Epistle of Peter, the Letters of John, and the Psalms.

He has the mind which was in Jesus Christ (Philippians 2[5]).
He has clean hands and a pure heart (Psalms 24[4]).
He is sanctified in body, soul and spirit (1 Thessalonians 5[23]).
He does not commit sin (1 John 3[9]).
He walks in the light (1 John 1[7]).
He is crucified with Christ (Galatians 2[20]).
It is not he himself who lives, but Christ lives in him (Galatians 2[20]).
He is holy, as God is holy (Leviticus 19[2]).
Everything he does is done in the love of Christ (Colossians 3[14, 17]).

He proclaims the excellencies of Him who called His own from darkness into His wonderful light (1 Peter 2⁹).[117]

Thus it is clearly seen that Wesley was faithful to the Bible in taking seriously what the Old Testament and the New Testament say about the new man. The Bible becomes its own witness and evidence to the life of the Christian. Quite consistently John Wesley quotes as the source for his convictions nothing apart from it. True, he had read William Law's writings at Oxford, but, he insisted, only after he had been there eight years. What importance can be given to them in the light of the fact that he devoted several hours a day to the Bible in its original languages? That is where the origins of his thought are to be sought. It is the Bible which left its impress upon him.[118] After that it is true that the Herrnhuters had been his teachers, beginning with his voyage to Georgia in 1735 up until his conversion in London in 1738. But he had not followed them slavishly. Indeed he only believed his counsellor, Peter Böhler, after his own study of the Scriptures confirmed what his friend said.[119] He constantly turned to the Bible itself. It was the Bible which, in an important difference of opinion between Count Zinzendorf and Peter Böhler, made him agree with the little man and disagree with the greatly admired Count. The latter had said to him that a man could be justified without knowing it. Others may know he is justified by the indications he gives of a new life, namely power over sin, the seriousness of his love for the brethren, and his hunger and thirst after righteousness, and they ought in a given case to make such a valid judgement about a fellow-Christian. On the other hand Böhler was of the opinion that a man has a clear awareness of his own justification, even if it does not occur straightway and in full strength. Wesley was clear about this on the evidence of the Bible.[120]

Concerning the doctrine of justification itself, according to Wesley's answer, Tucker had incorrectly reported his point of view when he attributed to him the opinion that real inner righteousness was essential to justification. This was by no means the case. For Wesley, real, inner righteousness results only from justification. It belongs to the spiritual state of perfection, but not to the actual state which establishes justification. So Wesley contends with all his strength on behalf of the 'Christ given for us'. He agrees with Luther and Melanchthon against the Nüremberg reformer Osiander, who wished in the Catholic manner to make the actual indwelling of the Holy

Spirit, the Christ in us, necessary to the efficacy of justification. It was Christian David to whom John Wesley in this instance quite rightly appealed.[121]

On this point he found it necessary to put Tucker right, and so refute his last statement in which he had said that he, John Wesley, had contradicted himself. In order to explain this more precisely, he alluded to his conviction that the new birth, the reality of the new man, actually begins with justification, but that only sanctification brings the higher state of the new birth. Perfection is the culmination of the process.[122]

The difference between Wesley and Tucker is seen once again clearly and sharply at the conclusion. The Anglican churchman is concerned basically with sanctification, and only a little with justification. Sanctification was more congenial to the primarily ethical interest of the humanistic Enlightenment. Wesley on the other hand regards justification as a divine act as the decisive point. Sanctification follows upon it.[123]

The impression left by the first controversy is that Wesley undertook the task in fact with very great objectivity. He makes no accusation, nor does he defy the whole ethical consciousness of the age; there is no irony, but only straightforward adherence to the Bible and a simple mode of self-expression; yet at the same time there is a clear grasp of the essential difference and a sure estimate of its consequences. Tucker's view that Wesley had spoken in a contradictory way about justification must be adjudged an error.

Three and four years afterwards John Wesley turned his attention with greater detail to another Anglican clergyman, the London vicar Thomas Church.[124] This man had published in 1744 *Remarks on Wesley's Journal*, which had appeared in the same year. In the first place he had found fault with Wesley for becoming so friendly with the Moravians, in whom the England of that day saw, as in the case of the Huguenot Cevenne prophets, the 'Church in the wilderness', a particularly shocking example of religious enthusiasm.[125] Then, like Tucker, he had attacked John Wesley's teaching on justification, because it overstressed faith and minimized morality. Finally he accused him of enthusiasm, because he followed his own impulses and ecstasies rather than the judgement of reason and the clear directions of God. John Wesley acknowledged in the first place the objectivity and eirenical spirit of his critic, as well as his readiness to promote the honour of God in his writing, and he welcomed the opportunity of stating his own convictions with great clarity. There would be nothing in his own way of writing which would spoil the atmosphere. The style of the letter is marked by clarity, firmness and veracity, and in addition it uses a rich variety of expression, thus avoiding bare uniformity. It is easy to believe, as he says, that he has not found any form of dissimulation necessary.

After the introductory remarks Wesley attempts to refute his correspondent point by point, and so expresses his overwhelming impression that Church's censure of his doctrine of justification must raise a justifiable doubt about Church's own understanding of this subject. Church apparently concedes—as Abelard had done—that works, especially those done before repentance, are able to cancel sins.[126] On the other hand he encourages sinners, even when they still continue in their sin, because the hope endures that they will receive help from on high to purify themselves in their serious moral endeavours.[127] It is clear that both objections against the Pauline-Reformation conception of justification, as maintained by John Wesley, have their common origin in ethical concern. Therefore in spite of their different orientation they have a unity. Wesley meets his correspondent with an important distinction; for justification man requires to do nothing beyond recognizing his sinfulness and incapacity for good, and from this he automatically passes on to repentance. The all-important attitude is faith, which, however, is no performance. It is a different matter with the final judgement, if a man is to stand with honour before God. For this, complete holiness is necessary, purity from all sins. God makes demands *after* justification, not before it. Good works have their place, *after* justification not before it. This is quite intelligible because justification awakens moral energies in the believer, and therefore the final judgement is according to works.

Church was afraid that justification by God's grace alone, offered in the Word and received by faith, only increases on English soil the prevalent irreligion and wickedness, since it serves to confirm it. Thus he raises against Wesley the objection that he is laying snares in the path of ordinary people Instead of carefully tending the last remains of religion and seriousness, he is rooting them out with his view of cheap grace. According to Church the same tendency is seen in John Wesley's view of the Lord's Supper, which stresses one-sidedly its character of a free gift on the part of Jesus, and underplays the requirement of preparation for it. The only thing a person needs to bring with him to this feast is a consciousness of his own sinfulness and helplessness. All he needs to do is to wait upon the gift of God.[128] Wesley contrasts with this the fact that it was in his societies in London, Bristol and Newcastle that the members resolved to live in obedience to God and to lead more holy lives than when they had been unacquainted with the Methodist preaching [129] It is precisely his teaching about the growth of faith which Church attacks; this faith begins with the assurance of the forgiveness of sins and the adoption of sonship, and then proceeds to perfection in love, and is, in fact, the very opposite of what Church alleges it to be. As to the point about Holy Communion, John Wesley considers it a genuine misrepresentation of the facts of the New Testament that it has become usual in the Anglican Church to rule it out from being a means of conversion. His experience with the Methodist societies has shown him how this ordinance actually awakes in man the resolve to belong wholly to God and to obey Him in all things. The awareness of one's own lost state awakens like nothing else the desire for true holiness and Christian perfection.[130] It is apparent that at this point also there was once again a fundamental contrast between a moralism and synergism in the relationship between God and man, which dominated Church and the Anglican Church in the eighteenth century, and Wesley's conception of the free grace of God. Since Church bases his attacks on Wesley's *Journal*, Wesley emphasizes that this gives an account of facts and experiences, not the results of his own favourite doctrines. The reporter himself was generally surprised by the facts. If he showed preference for one particular meaning that was only because he was willing to see and make visible the finger of the divine care.[131] So far as his relationship with the Moravians went, he stated clearly why he separated from them and wherein he deviates from them. He agrees with them in the basic doctrine of justification through grace alone. He differs from them in the understanding of holiness, which they consider as not necessary, and in the estimate of the means of grace, which they neglect.[132] He rebuts the charge of stoical insensibility, which Church had made against him, and affirms that this refers to his own astonishment over a case of real Christian readiness for suffering, which he was able to see in a certain woman.[133] The same thing applies to his alleged dependence upon ecstasies and singular spiritual experiences, and a naïve identification of his own personal desires with God's will. None of this corresponds with the facts, nor does he think that the future will admit charges of this kind. He is concerned with soberness of spirit, yet nobody, not even Church, can deny that sensible impulses belong to the nature of faith. Love for God and for the neighbour, peace and joy in the Holy Spirit, are examples of such inner experiences.[134] Thus there was no point made by his opponent which John Wesley neglected; he took notice of everything; but it was the doctrine of justification by grace alone, received only through faith, which remained the leading consideration. In this particular discussion the basic Reformation attitude of the Methodist preaching was once again affirmed.

The second and longer letter which John Wesley sent to Church was even more conciliatory in tone. He did not wish to regard him as an opponent, but rather as a friend.[135] Accordingly the letter contains an unusual number of deeply personal expressions. In the introduction Wesley once again asks in a quite general way, as when he replied to Josiah Tucker in 1742, whether polemical and apologetic undertakings, which necessitate the maintenance of one's own standpoint, do not lead to an unchristian attitude.[136] The letter is concerned with the same subjects as the first, principally with the Moravians. Church simply could not understand how John Wesley could differentiate between attitudes in his treatment of this community. He thought that one must either accept them in their entirety or completely reject them. Wesley again objects against him that his *Journal* is an account of the facts, and that the facts never followed a consistent pattern. Among the Moravians he found both openness and dissimulation, friendliness and harshness, ecclesiastical discipline and lawlessness. Men like Christian David and Michael Linner and many others were completely free from any kind of guile. Of such he could only give the best testimony.[137] His complaint is in general against Philipp Heinrich Molther and August Gottlieb Spangenberg, because of their fateful mystical teaching about stillness. Such stillness leads to contempt of worship, of the sacraments, and particularly of holiness; in other words, to pride and libertarianism.

Similarly in answer to Church he stressed that it was only Count Zinzendorf himself who denied such a thing as a growth in holiness, and he did so only once, in the heat of a dispute. Such a charge could not be levelled against the Moravian community as a whole.[138]

In this connexion Wesley protests against the unfair way in which

Church quotes his words. He has cited them in an incomplete form, torn them out of their context, and inverted them into negative statements in place of the obviously intended positive sense. It is only in this way that he arrives at the conclusion that statements contradict one another.[139] At this point Wesley proceeds with a carefulness which is painfully exaggerated almost to the point of being a philological criticism of the text, and attacks his opponent with greater precision. In what follows he takes the sentences apart as with a sharp knife and examines their logical form.[140]

The second group of questions concerns justification. Church had charged Wesley with requiring for it too little in the way of preliminary qualifications—and too many afterwards. For justification he demands only faith, but for the final judgement sinless perfection. In actual fact, however, the resolution to obey God is a condition of justification. Wesley replies, as he always did in discussions about this subject, that since the content of justification is the forgiveness of sins, and its form declaration and promise, there can be no answer from the side of man other than believing acceptance. That this immediately gives rise to a desire to keep God's commandments is to be understood as a matter of course. But this is not to be understood as a condition—and that means as a human performance—prior to the act of justification, since this would destroy its whole logic and threaten its character as a gift.[141]

A consequence of the doctrine of justification is John Wesley's teaching about sinless perfection, criticized by Church and many others. He stated once again that all religious thinkers agree on one point, namely that the completion of the process of sanctification, which God the Holy Spirit, that is God Himself, effects, is sinlessness, and that only people who are completely made holy will enter God's eternal kingdom. It is only over the question of the time when this occurs that they differ from one another.[142] Church had cited two actual incidents from Wesley's account of his experiences as consequences of his teaching about sinless perfection, wishing to exploit them, and so Wesley was under the necessity of putting him right. The first was due to a glaring misunderstanding. Wesley had quoted in his *Journal* the visionary and ecstatic experience of a certain Mrs Jones, as a sign of the power of the devil, but Church, presuming to follow Wesley's meaning, had understood it as a manifestation of God.[143] In the other case Wesley had expressed his astonishment that a man was able to give God unbroken praise while suffering in bed from the most severe pain. His surprise did not spring from what he considered an instance of human victory over self, much less, as Church suggested, from stoical insensibility. On the contrary Wesley was amazed at the power of the love of God, which so completely filled a man's heart that the natural feeling of pain was submerged.[144]

A further complex of controversial points had to do with Church order. Quite understandably Church had accused Wesley of contravening this by his irregular preaching wherever there was a congregation, thereby repeating the charge made in the year 1739 by James Hervey; to this charge Wesley had made his famous reply—that he looked upon the whole world as his parish. This time he replies in different terms, referring to his ordination. This did not take place for any definite congregation, but for the whole Church of England. In so far as any particular place was in mind, he was appointed to Lincoln College, Oxford. The statutes obliged him—and he quoted the actual words of the original text which stemmed from the Middle Ages—'to overturn all heresies and defend the catholic faith.'[145] He took this obligation very seriously, and he was content with it. For this reason he preached the true Christian faith in every place that was open to him. He always obeyed the Church authorities, and was only released from this obedience when their directions contradicted Scripture. Moreover Church had charged him with having pretended to an unlawful authority over his societies. Wesley rejoined that his position was due to their own wishes.[146] When finally Church quite generally and seriously charged him with having caused disturbances and divisions in the Church, he had to reply that he was not guilty. He conforms to the teaching and ordinances of the Church.[147] Moreover he declared that he was ready, should better methods for the proclamation of the Gospel be discovered, to choose them.

It is noteworthy that Wesley says only so much. He might easily have gone on to point out that others who opposed him were the cause of troubles; it was those who failed to preach the primitive Christian gospel who contravened the order of the Church. Yet he avoided saying anything like this. He did not go over to the attack. He only replied to the points about which he was questioned, and even this he did in a very concise way. It is obvious that he regarded such a reserve as one of the highest duties of a peace-maker.

He then came to the most serious accusation—that of enthusiasm. He has to refute the charges that he allows his conduct and mode of life to be directed by visions and ecstasies, and that he claims the enjoyment of a divine help which is given in particular for himself alone in special revelations and directions.[148] He declares that it is simply untrue that he describes opposition towards himself to be the same as withstanding the Holy Spirit, or that he regards his own actions directly as God's work.[149] There remains his use of the lot as a means of obtaining scriptural directions in difficult situations or when decisions are doubtful. In this case John Wesley embarks upon a broad and careful discussion. The lot has never been used indiscreetly or simply as an oracle. It was always preceded by a detailed discussion, when the reasons for and against a particular decision are set out and considered. If it seems to those interested that the reasons on both sides are equally cogent, recourse is had to the scriptural lot.

Church also regarded it as a mark of enthusiasm that Wesley attributed cases of sudden illness or death to God's judgement. Wesley admits the charge that this is what he maintained, but similarly he does not shrink—to the horror of his rationalistic age—from attributing it like the early Church to the demons.[150] If there is such a thing as possession by evil spirits, the unusual phenomena seen in the Methodist meetings immediately become understandable. As a consequence a true conflict between God and the devil can be recognized, and God, who so immediately manifests Himself, must be praised for His help.[151] Over this point Wesley is inflexible almost to harshness. What were his reasons?

For once his sense of reality drove him to this. This attitude was more than accommodation to unalterable facts; it must rather be called a form of obedience to God. Reality cannot and may not be avoided, for God constrains a man to recognize it.[152] In such a case Wesley's typical programme for living takes control, namely, the restoration of primitive Christianity. In this way actuality and the programme come together to form a complete unity, although usually in history they lie so far apart, and most often stand in opposition to each other.

Church had also described as enthusiasm Wesley's conviction that he himself had been suddenly freed from sickness and pain through prayer. Church concluded from this that the leader of the Methodists ascribed to himself miraculous powers. Once again Wesley had to put him right. He denies the deduction, but affirms very strenuously the healing power of prayer as such. It went against every expectation, his own most of all, and indicates the omnipotence and freedom of God. One must humble oneself before it. In order to meet his opponent Wesley proposes to examine in detail all the experiences to which objection has been made, and to note down some of the statements of those who were concerned.[153] The question as to whether God wills to perform further miracles in the future or will do so, Wesley, in accordance with his basic point of view, has to leave open. It is a matter for God alone. Miracles are, as Church maintains, in no sense indispensable to the Methodist movement. Its effects are not derived from them. Indeed people in this day will turn away from them as in other ages, and in like manner reject them as logical demonstrations of the truth. Is not this seen clearly enough in the example of the prophets and of Jesus himself? Abraham's word applies in this case: 'If they hear not Moses and the prophets, neither will they be persuaded, though one rose from the dead' (Luke 16[31]).[154] The intrinsic value of the teaching of the Methodist movement is in no sense guaranteed by miracles but only by Scripture, reason, and, if necessary, antiquity.[155]

On the other hand we do not know any reason why God should have confined His miracles to any particular period. There is nothing in either the Old or New Testament to suggest this. It is undoubtedly a fact that the deceptive wonders of the devil will continue, so long as this world and his rule within it endure. Why should we think that God, the lord of history, has capitulated to him and is less active than His adversary?[156] Nevertheless the real point of contention lies deeper. It concerns the fundamental question as to whether the astonishing effect of the Methodist movement was itself a miracle of God. To this Wesley replies confidently in the affirmative. In his own words it is 'a great and extraordinary work' that so many habitual sinners have been brought by the Methodist preaching of justification, new birth and cleansing from sin, to the love of God and obedience towards Him. A profound change in their way of life has truly happened in many folk. A sufficient number of people could testify to this. The real miracle with them is in the power of God's word. It is not because the Methodists, who are the least of the servants of God, preach it that the effect takes place, but because it is the true Word of God. But now it has pleased God to bless His Word in the mouths of Methodists and in the new preaching movement.[157] What Wesley demands is the simple recognition of this fact, but he knows very well that he is really asking too much of Church. Has not his opponent reproached him with the fact that on well-nigh every side he glorifies himself without justification and to excess, and that he speaks continually about himself and his own people?

For this reason the question about Wesley's self-praise becomes a new section of the letter. In this connexion he gives a noteworthy review of his preaching activity in general. He divides it into four significant periods. From 1725 to 1729 he preached a great deal, but in general saw no fruit; the reason for this is clear to him. He spoke neither of repentance nor of believing the Gospel, since he took it for granted that he was speaking only to believers and therefore the majority stood in no need of repentance. When between 1729 and 1734 he emphasized repentance more strongly he saw a little fruit. In the years 1734–8 faith in Jesus Christ became his theme more than before, and accordingly he found he had even more fruit. But he only saw the full effect after 1738, when he spoke continually of Jesus Christ, and made him the first and last subject of his preaching. Since then his preaching has followed completely the line of Jesus's opening message: the kingdom of God is at hand, repent and believe the gospel (Mark 1[15]). The response has been overwhelming. The word of God ran and spread as fire among the stubble. Everyone asked: what must we do to be saved? After which they witnessed: by grace we are saved through faith. Wesley then asked his friends whether he should keep silent about the powerful movement which had arisen; or should he make it known? They were for the latter, especially as the whole thing could not now be concealed. For this reason from time to time he published his *Journal*. According to Church's judgement that must be either enthusiasm or sheer self-glorification; enthusiasm, if he ascribed the result to God, self-glorification, if he said anything about his own part. What then can he do to avoid censure? Only keep silent. But this he cannot do. Were he thus to seek to please men he would not, in Paul's words (Galatians 1[10]), be the servant of Christ.[158]

There follows a very moving passage in which John Wesley opens his heart. Church appears to have no idea of his condition. How does it really appear to one who has been called by God and who is part of a unique preaching movement? Like Paul he is obeying a commission. Necessity is laid upon him. He has no desire at all to be further active in it. This is not because he foresees all the misfortunes which will meet him: shame, reproaches, loss of friends, loneliness and affliction; but much more because he knows himself only too well. He wants to cry out, 'O Lord, send by whom Thou wilt send, only send not me! What am I? A worm! a dead dog! a man unclean in heart and lips!' Alongside the greatness of the commission he is aware of his own failure, and it is precisely when he recognizes that he has certain capabilities that his judgement of himself becomes more severe. For God will require an exact account of the talent entrusted to him. When the work of the Lord prospers in his hand he is most of all watchful over himself, for God, God alone will be praised. He desires to keep silent, so as not to sin by speaking falsely, but his heart burns within him. It is with him as with the apostles Peter and John, who replied to the High Council: 'For we cannot but speak the things which we have seen and heard' (Acts 4[20]). So he declares what he must declare. If anyone calls this boasting, he cannot help it. A higher Judge will decide.[159]

Alongside this assessment of the movement and its originators was a more important question, one which led to the heart of the controversy: is England a Christian country? If it is, then obviously there is no need for such a preaching of repentance, with its prophetic primitive Christian radicalism. Had not England been won for the Gospel long before John Wesley himself saw the light of day? Therefore does not history testify against the new movement and its presumptuous claims?

The answer demands in the first place a precise survey of the situation. Nobody can deny that the people of England are called 'Christian'. They are all baptized, a considerable proportion of them attend worship and partake of the Lord's Supper. But none of this is sufficient to prove that they are really genuine Christians. How is it with the hearts and lives of the English people? Does Jesus Christ and His commandments and example rule there? Some live in open sin, others only seem to present a favourable picture. Their souls are full of other impulses, pride, self-indulgence and lusts, ambition, hatred, anger, malice and envy. If this means being Christian, how does it differ from hypocrisy? And even apart from these people, where are those who have the mind which was in Jesus Christ, who

N

follow His example, who have renewed their souls after the image of God, or who are holy as He is? Doubtless there are a few such, but they are very thinly scattered. Is there any meaning in calling England a Christian country because of them? Is Jesus Christ really honoured by such a description? Does it recommend Christianity to others, such as Jews, Mohammedans, or the avowed heathen?[160] On the contrary must it not confirm the heathen in their way of life, since the life of Christians is in no sense different? Therefore it is necessary to look beyond ecclesiastical institutionalism and come to the missionary situation, when it will be recognized that it is the God of this world who deceives men by making them think of England as a Christian country.[161]

A Christian England is then, in the eyes of Wesley, an illusion. This is the real point of difference between himself and the Anglican churchmanship of his day. The name of Christian, resting on the guarantee of a purely institutional national Church, was for him no Christianity at all. He was the first to recognize clearly in the modern age that the task of Christianity in the world is mission, and to draw the immediate practical deductions from this. At this point the heritage of his early attempts at mission in Georgia came to fruition.

Since the question of the Christian character of England was not given a satisfactory answer by his opponent, Wesley found it necessary to undertake a further investigation. It must be shown that the claim that the Methodist preaching proclaims the full Gospel is justified. Is it a true insight that Christianity has nothing to do with half-measures or with externals only, but that it requires the response of the whole man? Or do the Methodists belabour their hearers with favourite but misleading opinions? Wesley demonstrates the rightness of his preaching in the following way. He states the three main points on which the movement is based. They are repentance, faith and holiness. He calls these the porch and the door of religion, and religion itself, thus showing that they are indissolubly connected with each other.

Repentance comes first. The process of becoming a Christian begins when a man is terrified about his own sins—not so much by their number or frequency, nor even by becoming naturally accustomed to them, all of which is bad enough; the deepest fear really concerns the nature and content of sin. Man is terrified because he sees that it is essentially opposition to God. He accuses himself, and trembles before eternal damnation. There arises from the depths of his being a cry for deliverance. He desires to go on living, to begin anew, and yet knows that he has forfeited his life before God. So he is tortured by the anxious question whether a new beginning is in any way possible. Having described repentance in these terms, Wesley asks Church directly whether he has himself experienced it. It means being suspended between shame, consciousness of guilt, fear, doubt, and the elemental will to live, which clings to God.

Only against this background can the full force of faith be seen. It means much more than assent to the statements of the Bible or a general recognition of their truth. The devil also believes in this way. Faith is personal certainty and confidence that God has saved the believer, through Jesus Christ, from eternal damnation.

But even with this the full perception of the meaning of Christian salvation has not been reached. According to the example used, faith opens the door into the actual sphere of salvation. The full statement of the content of Christian truth is in Wesley's words, which he shared with the eighteenth century, reserved for 'religion'. This is used as a short summary for the two chief commandments of love for God and neighbour. Love is the alpha and omega of Christianity. God loves mankind in the first place, mankind which is lost and condemned, preoccupied with itself, imprisoned in the world, and despairing. He opened the way of love for them. The love of God, which takes up its abode in men and assumes a form, becomes the actual elixir of life, the remedy for all the evils of a disordered world, the cure for all the miseries and vices of men. It spreads abroad peace and joy and brings forth all virtues.[162]

This account of the Methodist preaching in shortened form carries great conviction. Wesley showed particular astuteness moreover, because he did not write his defence of it in his own words; to a large extent he selected words and phrases from the Homilies of the Church of England, and so reminded Anglicans of basic truths which had long been forgotten. The Homilies, written by Cranmer, Ridley and Latimer and other evangelically-inclined theologians of the sixteenth century, served as model sermons of the reformed faith, and were an official document of the Anglican Church. In this way Wesley gave a striking demonstration of the correctness of his faith.

But this did not bring him to the end of his reply. There was a further question raised by Church. This asked whether in the last seven years, the great years of Methodism, more serious Christians (that is, faithful Anglicans), or more godless, real sinners had been won for the new movement by the preaching of Wesley and his helpers. This was a reference to the complaint commonly made by the official Church against this new type of evangelical movement, that it was simply drawing away faithful members of the Church and leading them astray, instead of gaining people who were outside the life of the Church. In the first place Wesley says it is impossible to give an answer for England as a whole, for the simple reason that there are no means available for finding out the facts. He therefore proposes instead to select important areas, which can be taken as representing central points of the Methodist movement. He names Kingswood near Bristol, Newcastle, London, Staffordshire and Cornwall, and finally parts of Wiltshire and Somerset near Bath, where new work had just begun. If one were to inquire of the miners in these places or the tinners in Cornwall what kind of lives they had lived formerly as compared with the present, one would find out that the number of those who had been despisers of God, thieves, brawlers, drunkards and lascivious was much greater than those who had been good-living people. Although Wesley might be able to satisfy his correspondent on this point, he does not believe, as the other does, that he would be able to convince his opponents of the error of their objections. Church had said that should Wesley be able to show that in fact the majority of members of the Methodist movement were previously good-for-nothing people who were now truly taught and educated to keep God's commandments and to love God and their neighbour, then all his opponents would be silenced with one blow. Wesley knew that he must go on his way without being disconcerted by praise or blame, assent or accusation, and he was determined to go on alone.[163]

Finally he turned to Church's complaint that he and Whitefield had abused the Anglican clergy, including the best and highest. His case was that they, the Methodists, had preached against blind leaders who had forgotten the message of the Holy Spirit as part of Christian truth, and had acted as if there were not a Holy Spirit. About this Wesley can only say that their complaints and accusations are supported by their own painful observations, the sermons they have heard, and the books they have read. He dare not keep silent about error and sin, otherwise he would be equally guilty and have to perish along with sinners. He also refrains from entering a counter-claim by quoting examples of abuses against the Methodists from members of the Church. They shall die and be forgotten.[164]

This long letter is an impressive document and a masterpiece of its kind. The leader of the Methodist movement, greatly disturbed and constantly provoked, certainly put himself to a great deal of trouble. Yet that was the smallest feature. There runs through the writing a personal warmth which becomes a personal appeal to, and pastoral concern for, his correspondent, as well as personal confession. A severe, flatly inexorable adherence to the facts characterizes the writing. Every sentence is carefully considered. His own conviction remains unshaken. He does not take back one iota. He believes that he is called to a service from which there is no remission. God's will, God's work, God's blessing, lead him in his activity and they vindicate that activity. One might venture to say that the close logic with which he proceeds is reflected in the closeness and clarity of the actual expressions. The wealth of ideas expressed in the letter is brought into a compact form. Although many individual points are discussed, the inner unity and the main line of argument are always maintained. The basic points come out clearly and insistently: the illusion of a Christian England as the false assumption of his opponent, together with Wesley's calm determination to give it up; and the understanding of the Christian message under the leading idea of justification. Corresponding to this is his consciousness of mission, which rests not upon any special personal revelation or suitability, but upon direct obedience to the Word, which has demonstrated its all-conquering power over him. Finally the letter indicates his conviction that this Word works miracles, transforms men, and calls into existence love for God. None of this is a matter of theory, but the record of facts. Theorizing belongs to his opponent and actuality to him. Once again the whole proceeding is governed by his life-purpose, the restoration of primitive Christianity. In this letter it is brought into immediate harmony with the facts themselves. It is no longer raised as a challenge, but has become an actual and unusual occurrence in history.[165]

Shortly afterwards John Wesley crossed swords with Edmund Gibson, the Bishop of London. This polemical encounter affected him deeply, for Gibson had originally repeatedly shown himself an understanding friend of the new movement. In particular when John

197

Wesley had explained to him what he understood by Christian perfection he had replied, 'Mr Wesley, if this be all you mean, publish it to all the world.' This had occurred in the year 1740. Now, seven years later, the whole situation was quite different. He had issued a pastoral letter to the clergy of his diocese, in which he urged them to preach with all their power against the Methodists, because they were confusing the people and circulating pernicious doctrines. In between he had published anonymously in the year 1744, *Observations upon the Conduct and Behaviour of a Certain Sect, usually distinguished by the name of Methodists*, and this revealed that he had already moved from his former position.[166]

The bishop's admonition of 1747 has not survived, and we have only John Wesley's reply to it.[167]

Gibson had given vent to a whole series of objections against the Methodists. A number were the same as those made by Church, but others went further. It is noteworthy that the man who was the great student and compiler of Anglican canon law, who was known as Doctor Codex, should expressly omit the matter of the relationship of the Methodists to Church order and concentrate upon doctrines.[168] In his view, their chief error, giving rise to such dangerous consequences, was antinomianism, and their next assertion was in line with this, namely that Jesus Christ has done everything for mankind, leaving them nothing to do except believe. He said further that the Methodists allow themselves to be led by sudden impulses, which they think are revelations of the Holy Spirit. They are persuaded that they are justified in a moment, instead of going through a long process of purification. They suppose that they can attain to sinless perfection, and they disregard the clear statements of the Bible, which assume that the whole of mankind is subject to sin. Wesley further dishonours the Lord's Supper because he requires nothing from those who partake and proffers everything to them as a gift from God. This contradicts moral seriousness, such as is enjoined by Christ, and leads to an intolerable pride, as if the Methodists possessed a higher holiness with which they were able to supply their followers. The worship of the Anglican Church is said not to be sufficient. Her clergy show less zeal in the care of the souls entrusted to them than the Methodist lay-helpers. It is expected that the members of the peculiar movement will attend their meetings so frequently that they can no longer fulfil their duties at work or at home. This implies that the extremely rigorous requirements clearly differentiate them from others by their holiness. In all these ways the Methodists lead ignorant people astray; they also trouble and cause distress to the Anglican clergy. The latter have naturally defended themselves and brought to the attention of the Methodists their errors. This had indeed for a time somewhat restrained their presumptuous claims, but had not really ended them. Consequently they must be expressly cautioned against them. They tear down instead of building up; they undermine the regular ministry of the Church instead of supporting it.[169]

In such reproaches there speaks the convinced yet anxious prince of the Church. His concern was on other grounds quite understandable. As bishop of the capital city he had striven with very great zeal to raise the moral standards of the population, especially on account of the contrary influences which emanated from the Court of the Hanoverian kings. Precisely because at first he had been well-disposed to the Wesley brothers, his disappointment was now the greater. Did it not seem that they cut across his purposes? Would he not have to carry into his grave his early hope for them?

John Wesley's reply was very different from that which he had given to Thomas Church. All through it shows signs of irritation. Right at the beginning of the letter the bishop must have been offended when Wesley remarked that it was his custom not to reply to charges made against him for things he had not done, or for teaching which he did not give, but then went on to say that in the case of the highly eminent author he must make an exception, for to keep silent would look like contempt. This was tantamount to saying that it was not Gibson the man or theologian, nor the weight of his arguments, which merited a reply, but only the person who was Bishop of London. In this way Gibson was driven to see a certain frivolity in the forming of Wesley's judgement, and this fundamentally offended his sense of ecclesiastical responsibility. In point of fact this was also John Wesley's opinion. He treated the picture which Gibson had painted of his person, views, and activities, as a gross misrepresentation in every way. But very rarely did he attempt to rectify its many mistakes. On the contrary he charged the bishop with not having taken the trouble to read his writings about particular doctrines and problems. At only one point did he go into detail, and that was in connexion with the teaching about the sinless perfection of Christians. By a series of quotations from St Paul and St John he explains his answer. He regards it as a matter of taking seriously the great personal confession of the apostle, that Jesus Christ lives in the believers and they in Him. Once again his essential purpose becomes evident: he wishes to restore primitive Christianity directly in the present. He took this even further and gave it the sharpest possible expression, by asking whether God fulfils His promises. Whoever weakens these particular statements from the New Testament casts doubt upon the trustworthiness of God Himself. Therefore it is not in any sense a matter of men and their possibilities, as if one could speak about enthusiastic extravagance; rather, God's truthfulness is at stake.[170] At this point the letter reaches the high water mark of its true value. Moreover John Wesley asks the bishop whether it can be justified from a Christian, or even from a human, point of view, that he should act towards him in the way he has done. Instead of bringing clear accusations he has advanced baseless rumours, which are without foundations. Finally he ironically inquires whether perhaps the Methodists have obtained a monopoly of all sins and errors, so that they alone must be treated as enemies of the Gospel—as if there were no Deists or Roman Catholics.[171] The fundamental misconception, which he has to refute, is that the Methodists aim at making proselytes. They are not a sect who entice Christians from one Church to another, but faithful Anglicans, who wish to remain such.[172]

During the years 1745–8 John Wesley exchanged six long letters with an anonymous correspondent who called himself simply John Smith. It is probable that this common name hid the identity of the man who at the time was the Bishop of Oxford, and who later became Archbishop of Canterbury.[173] Wesley recognized in him a worthy and sagacious opponent, one who had carefully considered his inquiries and objections.

Of the points raised in the first letter[174] Wesley puts first in order of importance the claim of the Methodists to reproduce the circumstances of primitive Christianity and to perform primitive Christian miracles. John Smith wishes to have evidence of this. He gives a reminder of the need for caution and expresses the doubt as to whether Wesley has not allowed himself to be imposed upon by designing men or hysterical women. The alternative was put as sharply as possible: either there has been deception, perhaps self-deception, or Wesley and his helpers are entitled to the same implicit faith in themselves as was given to the apostles. If such were so nobody would seriously oppose them. Wesley vigorously contradicts this view of the question of authority, since it is based upon a false presupposition. The implicit faith given rightly to the apostles was in no sense due to their miracles. There was a quite different factor by which they had to measure their statements, namely the written Word, that is, the Old Testament. Wesley and his followers are bound by the same standard in the present. They have no authority other than Scripture.

A second point is the language the Methodists use. Wesley agrees with his correspondent that basically it is right to use the most common words, but he goes on to give the highest value to those which are closest to Scripture, a consequence which follows naturally from his acceptance of Scripture as his authority. He gives important examples of this. He uses the word faith in the sense of the Epistle to the Hebrews as 'the evidence of things not seen' (Hebrews 11^1), and speaks of salvation through faith as contrasted with salvation by good works, which he finds is still the commonly accepted idea just as it was in the time of the New Testament. In general the careful observer at the present time would have to admit that the erroneous doctrines of the past and the present are remarkably similar, as his opponent has allowed as a matter of course, and that early Christianity and the present have fundamentally the same religious goal and the same religious attitude. Moreover the language of Scripture is also that of the Church's tradition, and it is impossible therefore to cast it aside. If it sounds unfamiliar this merely betrays that the spirit of the present is foreign to the Bible.

Nevertheless all this was only a preliminary skirmish. The important issue came with questions of doctrine. John Smith thinks that Wesley's doctrines are not founded on Scripture, and Wesley goes into details. First he takes faith. Smith had attributed to Wesley the view that faith is a supernatural gift, which comes upon the recipient like a miracle at a fixed moment, instead of being a rational assent to a clear statement and a moral disposition which perceives its import, and which can only be attained by the exertion of all one's powers—a view which reflected the moralistic thinking of the very temperate Enlightenment. Wesley's reply was surprisingly accommodating, in that he largely admits the way his opponent expresses himself. He also agrees with the point the latter had found lacking, namely that faith is rational assent, since for him faith is just this, a rationally responsible assent to the truth of the Bible. Further, faith is for him a moral virtue, in the same sense as hope and love. From this it follows that men ought to exert their utmost strength and industry to attain faith. Up to this point Wesley appears to follow the course of his opponent's thinking well-nigh to the point of glossing over the difference between them. But he changes his line of argument with the final decisive assertion and opens up the chasm between them when he says that faith, like every Christian grace, is properly supernatural. It is an immediate gift of God. God normally gives it through the means of grace which He has ordained. It is evident that Wesley was at pains to concentrate upon the decisive point among all that his contemporaries found unusual and alarming in his preaching, and to confine himself to that. Nobody should be able to accuse him of theological wilfulness, or, even less, of superiority to the Church of England. The discussion went on in this manner. Wesley even conceded to his opponent that although faith is generally given in a moment, this does not happen arbitrarily on God's part; it takes place with a certain regard for the inner preparedness of the recipient.

John Smith had further objected that Wesley imagined that it was necessary for a person to have a clear assurance of salvation in the sense of assurance of the forgiveness of sins, and that this was likewise bestowed at a definite moment. For his part, evidently on the ground of the average experience of numerous Christians, Smith believed that such assurance grew gradually and took effect unnoticed in the heart. Again Wesley accepts as much as he can. It may well happen that the assurance of the love of God as surrounding the individual takes effect gradually and silently in him. But this is in no sense the universal rule. If John Smith is able to call upon perhaps ten or twenty pious witnesses, he can set against such people twelve or thirteen hundred persons, of whom he has precise knowledge, who can all point to the day when—in the words of the Epistle to the Romans[175]—the love of God was shed abroad in their hearts. If John Smith wishes to say that all these are liars, that is his affair. He, John Wesley, cannot do this with a good conscience. On the whole the central question in the whole dispute seems to have been whether faith has a clearly defined beginning. Wesley is only able to declare that his opponent has not distinguished sharply enough between the origin and the continuance of faith. Smith's plea for the organic development of faith, as being invisible and without demonstration, can be accepted only for its growth, not for its origin. Moreover, John Smith had charged him with associating the inability to sin with the beginning of faith, that is, with the assurance of salvation. To this Wesley replied that he distinguished between 'having sin' and 'committing sin'. He in no sense claims that sin ceases with the beginning of faith. It is true he is convinced that a Christian, if he exercises due regard, can through perfect love to God, arrive at the position where he commits no sins in the outward sense, that is, no open act of sin. The root of sin, of course, still remains within him.

Wesley goes on to say that he is glad that his correspondent agrees that particular texts of Scripture are not to be picked out to establish opinions or used as proof-texts, but should be interpreted according to the general tenor of the Bible. It is precisely this principle, however, which makes it undeniable that the Bible teaches that we are saved through faith, and not through hope or repentance or holiness. Therefore, in view of this central position given to faith, he is bound to ask whether John Smith holds that faith is the gift of God in no higher a sense than earthly riches are, or whether he believes that Scripture regards both gifts as of equal importance. He must directly contradict him if he gives the nature of faith precisely the same meaning as full and practical assent to truth. This is not the teaching of the Bible. According to it, the saving faith of a Christian is a divine conviction of invisible things, together with a filial confidence in God's love. It is quite possible for somebody to be thoroughly convinced of the truth of the statements of the Bible, so that his daily life is influenced to a certain degree, and yet not have one grain of real faith.[176] It is to be noted that John Wesley thinks of faith in a completely personal way, something concerned with salvation. He contends for that comprehensive conception which understands it as the revolutionary and all-embracing internal living action of the man born anew of God. It was his own conversion-experience which was reflected in his words.

The deep concern which he showed about the actual content of faith became a personal matter when he turned to the question as to whether he was not putting forth singular opinions of his own. That was certainly not the case. Naturally, like everybody else, he has his favourite tenets, but he has never represented them as the main doctrines of the Christian religion. He could demonstrate what he

has preached, but his opponents take pleasure in emphasizing subsidiary points as central ones, and in keeping absolutely silent about
the main message of his preaching, against which they are unable to
raise any objections. His appeal to his hearers has always been: love
is the fulfilling of the law. This point his adversaries have wilfully
failed to hear, and only attack him for asserting that such love is
bestowed upon the believing man at one single, definitely ascertain-
able moment. Even if he is convinced of this, it has never been his
main point. He has insisted upon love to God and to men; this has
sufficed. Likewise, when he has spoken about justifying faith, he has
always stressed the fact that repentance is its presupposition and
obedience its consequence. People have also malevolently stopped
their ears to this, in order to be able to cry: A heretic! a heretic! Yet
he preaches not opinions, but the biblical message, and when anyone
objects that he answers his opponents only with naked Bible texts
rather than with reasons, this is in itself an indirect justification of
his method, quite apart from the fact that he has not hesitated to
argue for a true explanation and exposition of the Bible texts he has
used, and which have been given various interpretations. Finally he
was at equal pains to answer the objection that it is of no account
that he should be in agreement with the Church of England of the year
1545, since what matters is the Church of the year 1745 and whether
he is in agreement with it. To this Wesley replied with some heat that
it is bad enough when Anglican clergy subscribe to the reformed
articles of belief and standard sermons, the 39 Articles and the Book
of Homilies, without believing in them in their hearts, and added with
bitter irony that he must have been blind when, charged with
deviating from the Church, he had believed that reference was being
made to those basic doctrines laid down at the time of the Reformation.

The letter sounds a whole scale of tones and is so lively that one
can feel the inner emotion of the writer. Diplomatic skill, clarity of
thought, resolute determination, and the effort to remain true to
Scripture, together with passionate devotion to the truth, were
combined with a charitable desire to be accommodating. But the
latter is the dominant impression. Wesley asks his correspondent
to reprove him if he deserves it, and to instruct him in a way which
he can receive, and assures him that he will be grateful for both.

John Smith's reply was not long in coming. It was sent two months

later, on 27th November 1745, and Wesley answered it in a conciliatory way at the end of the year 1745.[177] Along with John Smith
he refused to endow quite natural happenings with miraculous
character, such as were alleged to have happened in the Methodist
meetings. All the more, therefore, he guarded against claiming that
such presumed miracles, which were nothing more than effusions
of over-excited nerves, especially of women, should serve as confirmation of his teaching. This was rather to be established by the
Bible, or further by the Articles and evangelical Homilies of the
Anglican Church, which originated from the time of the Reformation.
Again he felt that he was one with his correspondent in agreeing that
it was better to avoid obsolete scriptural expressions. But he could not
in any way regard words like 'salvation', 'justification', or 'faith' and
'works' as coming in this category. Nor could he allow that 'spirit'
and 'flesh' were synonyms for 'Christianity' and 'Judaism'. If John
Smith believes that nobody in the Church of England today proffers
external service in works in the place of internal holiness, he is greatly
in error. He, John Wesley, could attest of himself that he had done so
for twenty years. Similarly he knows a sufficient number of people
who think they have fulfilled their duty to God by going to church
and receiving the Sacrament, instead of practising righteousness and
mercy. On the other hand several deists and at least one atheist have
been converted by the preaching of faith working by love and the
exposition of an outward religion which springs from within. All
these are facts which have to be recognized out of respect for truth.
It is exactly the same with the so-called infallible witness of the Holy
Spirit. This is in no sense infallible. Nor has he, John Wesley, used
this word. It was John Smith who introduced it into the discussion.
But just as little may one as a matter of course doubt people's assertions that the Holy Spirit has assured them of their faith, or explain
this experience as pure fantasy. Augustine's words in his *Confessions*
may serve as a classic example of this; by taking a deep look into his
inner self he discovered something other, quite different from his own
Ego, superior to heaven and earth. It was the eternal, changeless light
of God, that which demonstrated Himself to the observer as God
Himself.[178] The description of faith as a God-given, inner conviction
of things invisible, which John Smith had given, he could himself
accept. When his correspondent called faith the originator of all
Christian practice, he would prefer to call it the producer of all

Christian holiness, for everything depends upon an inner equipment, not upon external action.

The same sense of realism requires that one should take seriously the testimony of those men who through faith have passed from fear and sorrow to unspeakable joy and true peace, who discovered their heart to be filled with the love of God, and all this in a moment, in a sudden change. But when the Methodists are charged with holding singular doctrines such as unconditional predestination, perceptible inspiration through the Holy Spirit, and sinless perfection, he can only make the following reply: he has never preached unconditional divine predestination, and although George Whitefield has done so, he, Wesley, must renounce all responsibility for it. It is true that he and every Methodist preacher contends for inspiration through the Holy Ghost. But what is meant by this? They mean that the Spirit of God fills believers with righteousness, peace and joy, with genuine love for God and men. This is the heart of his message, and indeed the source of his Christian position, such as was given to him from the time of his conversion on 24th May 1738.[179] The Holy Spirit is the author of faith, and apart from this a Christian cannot understand his existence. If the opponents of the Methodists deny this operation of the Holy Spirit, they deny the Christian faith as a whole, and concerning this there is found to be contention among people.

In this way John Wesley demonstrated that for him it was all or nothing. Methodism was not a particular type of Christian organization, but the proclamation of the truth of God.

Once again, after almost two months, the next reply came, but on this occasion Wesley gave himself more time.[180] John Smith had condemned zeal in faith, and Wesley understood this as the zeal which did not spring from love. He thanks Smith for his warning against fanaticism, which he takes seriously. Yet he must point out that a greater danger for himself lies in the opposite direction. His inclination is towards academic laziness and lukewarmness. He must therefore ask whether it is not part of the task of love to arouse sinners out of their sleep, rather than leave them to wake up in hell. As for the rest, he was forced to go over nearly everything again, because his correspondent had taken none of his points. John Smith had set him alongside the Quakers, and Wesley vigorously repudiated this, principally because for him the two sacraments of baptism and the Lord's Supper were so important. The question which lay behind this was probably, from John Smith's point of view, the main issue. It concerned Wesley's way of speaking about the inspiration which the Methodists allegedly claimed. Wesley put it thus: there is a truly miraculous working of the Holy Spirit. But he straightway added that what is referred to is that creative activity of God, with which He fills every true believer with righteousness, peace and love. Wesley had therefore expressed himself completely in Pauline terms, but Smith objected that this was not the point he had intended. His protest was not about the fruits of the Holy Spirit but about the manner and method of His perception by the individual. This was the point at which he perceived the Methodists to be deviating from a healthy type of teaching.

As to the question of the manner of the Spirit's working Wesley deliberately gives no answer, but confines himself to the Pauline statements, thus implying that he was not concerned to appeal to any particular inspiration of the Holy Spirit. Nor did he accept any responsibility for an apparently mentally-disturbed preacher—who appeared in London condemning all bishops, prelates, priests and deacons—even if he was said to have called himself a Methodist. As for the rest, he continues, he looks upon faith, even if he extols it so highly, not as the end, but as the means to the Christian life. The end is rather love. In love everything is comprised. If John Smith will give the palm to that view of religion which radiates the strongest and farthest-reaching love, he is in agreement. According to the words of Jesus it is not ignorance but neglect of love which excludes from heaven, and yet he cannot possibly recognize the average Christianity, which he meets daily in the Church of England, as the fulfilment of the divine will. If a person imagines that going to church, the occasional giving of alms and some sort of prayer, will suffice, he is fundamentally deceiving himself. The demand which John Smith, according to Titus 2^{12}, had put forward, namely to live soberly, righteously and godly, in this world,[181] is quite impossible apart from the new birth and the total conversion of the whole man. The recognition of this belongs to the first elements of Christianity. Talk about the fruits of the Spirit, which people had said was in Wesley an extravagance and an aberration, is really the decisive point and quite essential. He is persuaded that without God a man can do nothing, and he cannot understand how anyone should desire to begin the Christian life without this certainty, especially as his natural existence every day reminds him of his dependence upon the Creator.[182] Whoever thinks he is able to rely upon his natural faculties will find himself in radical error. He will have to offer external works as a substitute for inward holiness, and he will remain a man of compromise, one who loves the world, money, pleasure and approbation and who in no sense advances to full surrender to God. So he is unaware that he is walking on the broad way of destruction, and he lulls his soul with a false promise of life. Such a nominal Christianity, to which John Smith, without being aware of it, is really attached, such an aversion against the full conversion of the individual ego into the image of Jesus Christ, is the cancerous sore of the present age. When finally John Smith raised against him the typical objection of the ecclesiastical leader, that the activities of the Methodists were destructive of all Church order, Wesley replied that he ought to pursue the point further and inquire into the significance of Church order in general. Is it not to bring men from the power of Satan to God, and to build them up in His fear and love? Would not this change be the restoration of true order? Church order has value only as it serves this end. Did it fulfil its purpose in those places where he has been at work with his people, among the tinners in Cornwall, the keel-men at Newcastle, the colliers in Kingswood and Staffordshire, or among the drunkards, scoundrels and harlots in London? In no sense, for they remained what they were. They went resolutely on in bondage to their hard master, although near them in St Luke's church and St Giles's the normal Church order continued with regularity. Only the 'disorder' of the Methodists brought about any change. Through this these people began to be serious about God, to fear and love Him, and to keep His commandments. It was not the lack of order which kept them for so long under the power of the devil, but lack of love for God. Where both the knowledge and love of God were present true order would naturally appear. But where knowledge and the love of God fail the most complete apostolic order is less than nothing.

Thus the second letter presents the same picture as the first. Wesley wrote hopefully but positively, and insisted in passing beyond the discussion of individual points to the consideration of the main claims of Christianity. For this reason he was disappointed when he received the next reply.[183] He missed in it the seriousness which he thought the subject demanded. John Smith tried to indicate certain contradictions in Wesley's letter, which Wesley briefly discussed. The most important of these was Wesley's assertion that the witness of the Holy Spirit to adoption could for a time disappear, leaving the soul open to doubt and temptation. Wesley ascribed this to the working of Satan, and, contrary to his opponent, asserted that the human soul was the arena of the conflict between God and the devil. As to the main point Wesley expressed the question correctly, that is, he formulated it biblically. Smith had rejected the Methodists' claim to inspiration as Quakerish enthusiasm. Wesley inquired whether there is a perceptible witness of the Holy Spirit, and in claiming that there was, appealed to Romans 8[16], where the Holy Spirit testifies to believers of their adoption as children of God. Rather than being upset by the comparison with the Quakers, Wesley replies: so much the better, if both teach scriptural truth in this important matter. The real difference between him and John Smith consisted in the fact that for Smith the Holy Spirit must always be something extra-ordinary, known apart from daily experiences and manifesting Himself in miracles, whilst for Wesley He belonged to the normal inner life of a Christian. If his correspondent will not accept the statement of Romans 8[16] that the Spirit of God testifies to believers their adoption as children of God, the reason most likely lies in the fact that he is not aware of this fact himself. Therefore, instead of canonizing his own ignorance he ought to pray to God that He will teach him this important truth.

The other question which Smith regarded as important concerned ecclesiastical order and disorder, and he defined this more precisely with reference to lay-preaching. Wesley strenuously defended his lay helpers, because the content is more important than the form, and everything depends upon bringing people into contact with the real message of the Gospel. In this way the proper assignment of those who have been converted to the care of the regular clergy became possible. When John Smith made reference to such a famous example as the Calvinist Thomas Cartwright (1535–1603), who had been forced out of his Cambridge professorship in 1570 because of his polemic against the Church of England and its constitution, Wesley could in no sense agree with the unfavourable judgement of his opponent Edmund Grindal (1519?–83) that he had done more harm than good during his lifetime. It is simply incorrect to place him on the same level as the German Anabaptists; rather the Puritans of that

age ought to be regarded as the most learned and pious men in the
Church of England, men who had been driven out only through lack
of understanding and spite. It was analogous to the fact that he
himself, after the failure of the regular physicians, had in the past
months cured six or seven hundred poor folk by means of his own
simple remedies. If Smith objects that the regular Anglican clergy
occasion far fewer troubles, he must be reminded of the word of
Jesus, 'He that gathereth not with me scattereth' (Luke 11[23]). A
minister without spiritual life, says Wesley very pointedly, one who
converts nobody to Jesus Christ, is the murderer-general of his
parish.[184] Indeed he does not shrink from naming the two incumbents
of the London churches already referred to, Dr Bulkeley of St Luke's
and Dr Galley of St Giles's, although induced to do so by his
correspondent.

The opinion of John Smith, that the success of the Methodist
preaching was due to the attraction of its novelty, Wesley resolutely
disallows. He has never immediately experienced results. Rather he
has had always to exert himself for long periods; in that very town
of Newcastle he had asked himself after 120 attempts whether he
had not laboured in vain. To the objection that he had no call to be an
itinerant evangelist he replies that he is persuaded of the contrary
and that God's blessing on his work is an abundant proof. He is
certain that although, as John Smith implies, pride and vanity dwell
in his heart, they are not the motive behind his preaching, and should
he cease from this, he would hear the words of condemnation at the
Last Day: 'Cast ye the unprofitable servant into outer darkness,
where is weeping and gnashing of teeth.'

The next correspondence took place in the months of June and
July 1747. John Smith had reproved John Wesley for too freely
threatening people with hell, and Wesley retorts boldly that he
desires to keep the two oceans of heaven and hell ever before his eyes
while he stands on the isthmus of this earthly life.[185] Once again the
point at issue is the present reality of the Holy Spirit. John Smith
had followed the view expressed by the Bishop of Lichfield and
Coventry, Richard Smallbroke, who in a pastoral letter had issued a
general warning against enthusiasm, stating that an inner testimony
of the Holy Spirit was confined to the early days of the Church.
Wesley opposed this on biblical grounds. He filled his letter with
detailed explanations and refutations of individual points, and

expressed the hope that they would both move towards a greater understanding of each other.

It is possible to wonder whether anything was gained from continuing this correspondence. The writers went round in circles. A final exchange of letters took place in March 1748.[186] In his letter Wesley adduced as the strongest support of his interpretation of Paul's words in Romans 8[16] the last words of his father upon his death-bed: 'The inward witness, son, the inward witness, that is the proof, the strongest proof, of Christianity.'[187] As for the rest, he reminded his correspondent that the conversion of sinners to repentance and to a new life of obedience to God should be recognized as real facts and as miracles, as the New Testament does. When John Smith charged him with assuming an apostolate for England Wesley confidently accepted it; indeed he was prepared to go further and extend it to Ireland, France, Europe, Asia, Africa and America, or wherever he saw men running towards hell. John Smith also derisively taunted him by saying that in his view Paul, with all his infirmities, might more reasonably be looked upon as an inspired prophet than John Wesley, who imagined himself to have attained to sinless perfection. Wesley replied that he knew himself well enough to be aware that he was as yet far from this height, although he strove to love God with all his heart, soul and strength. He lived in the conviction that God would at last forgive and reward him, and that was enough.

When one considers the whole correspondence the leading impression gained is that John Wesley was at pains to establish a real encounter with a correspondent who was himself serious and well-disposed. He was very patient with him and did not allow himself to be annoyed at the repetition of subjects which had already been thoroughly discussed. He combined sober objective exposition with an urgent solicitation which became a pastoral appeal, having the last judgement in prospect. The Bible, and supremely the Pauline letters, contain the Word. They were the sure ground from which he argued and the authority to which both men have to subject themselves. Taken as a whole the dominant impression is that of a desire for understanding, the hope of convincing his correspondent, and the certainty that in their ultimate concern of causing Christian truth to prevail and spread abroad, they were one with each other.

John Wesley's attitude to George Lavington, the bishop of Exeter, was completely different. With this man who had publicly abused him Wesley employed above all an ice-cold logic. Point for point he thoroughly examined the accusations which had been made, and established either that they could not be included—as the bishop had maintained—under the phenomena of enthusiasm or fanaticism, or that he contradicted himself in that his sentences often fell foul of the elementary rules of grammar, the use of language, or the requirement of intelligibility. Further he complained that the bishop frequently supplied no reasons for his assertions and that he did not understand the things with which he dealt. His conclusion could be summed up by saying that his opponent had acted on the common principle: throw as much dirt as you can and some will be sure to stick.[188]

Under the first group of those things which were falsely included under the subject Wesley ranks the charge that he has provoked the Anglican clergy and attributed this to the command of the Holy Spirit. Against this he states in the first place that he is not guilty, and secondly that neither his alleged calumny nor the attribution of it to the Holy Spirit is enthusiasm or fanaticism. It is on the contrary a very conscious, deliberate, not to say ordinary, piece of dexterity. The same goes for the charge that he has put on a sanctified appearance, avoiding laughter or levity, in order to draw followers to himself. But again this cannot be called enthusiasm, let alone fanaticism; rather it is action directed to an end. It is not otherwise with his enthusiasm for martyrdom, for according to Lavington this gives the expectation of a higher reward in eternity.[189] In the same way the charge that, like the Papists, he has only a seeming contempt for money while in reality he hankers after it, is false because it mistakes realistic calculation for enthusiasm.[190] Under the second characteristic of contradictory statements Wesley discussed Lavington's introductory charge that the Methodists, like the papists of the counter-reformation, because of a derangement of spirit conceive of a general reformation of the Church, in which motives of genuine piety could be said to play a part. In reply Wesley asked: how can sincere piety arise from a 'configuration and texture of the brain'?[191] Further, he attacked Lavington's whole method. Frequently he dissects and distorts Wesley's sentences, so that with the best will in the world no sense can be found in them.[192] When he comes to speak of conversion and to develop every kind of false opinion about it, he reveals the fact that he understands nothing about it; and

Wesley declines to make any attempt to explain its meaning to him.[193] He abandons him as hopeless. Similarly he declines to instruct him about Christian perfection before he has learned a little heathen honesty.[194] Moreover the bishop does not seem to him to be particularly well informed about the Old and New Testaments, since he is unable to recognize Wesley's biblical allusions.[195] The bishop's dealings with Wesley make it a good thing that he concealed his name as author, or he would be obliged to hide his face from every man of candour or even common humanity.[196] He consciously tells falsehoods, particularly about Wesley's relationship with the Moravians, although he knew better; his object was only to attack Wesley.[197] Wesley then discusses a series of separate points, which Lavington had distorted, and in spite of his low opinion of his opponent, whom he exhorted to have a scrupulous regard for the dignity of the episcopal office,[198] gave some explanations of points of doctrine, in particular of the relationship between justification and regeneration. This was a matter of destroying an erroneous meaning, one which suggested that they were instantaneous, contemporaneous events.[199] As to the rest he acknowledges that he was guilty of two charges. The first concerned his youthful decision not to laugh or behave with levity. This he countered by asking Lavington if he could think of fulfilling 'in laughter' Paul's injunction that a man should show himself worthy of his calling in all circumstances of his life as a servant of God (2 Corinthians 6[4,10])? As for the rest, however, he does not lay down any definite prescriptions, but leaves each free to decide according to his own insight. It is a matter of doing all things to the honour of God.[200]

He agreed that he sees and esteems the Methodist revival as a real and great work of God, for in a short time, and in limited areas, thousands have been summoned to repentance and conversion. Large parts of Britain and Ireland were previously covered with vice and indifference towards God, but now it is very different. In the hearts of countless people faith and love towards God are once again a reality. Naturally the God of this world, the devil, has not been able to endure this. According to his well-known devices he has attempted to check the movement by attaching to it a nickname, so that it should be condemned unheard. Now every scribbler, unencumbered by understanding, good nature, or modesty, can raise a laugh against those he cannot confute, and run down those whom he dare not look in the face. In this way he earns cheap applause, at least from people of his own kind, especially when he lumps Methodists and Papists together.[201]

If the letter as a whole is considered it must be said that Wesley imparted a snub which could scarcely have been sharper. Any possibility of mutual understanding was ruled out.

Shortly afterwards the third part of the bishop's controversial tract appeared. Wesley's letter of 27th November 1750,[202] which was an answer to it, is richly coloured, extending from calm correction of facts and biting irony to pastoral admonition, both challenging and accusing, addressed to his opponent. In the first section he discusses in very great detail a single instance, from which through repetition in addresses to the clergy of his diocese, the bishop had made capital against the Methodists. John Wesley was said to have driven a woman into such a state of terror by threatening her with hell and throwing doubts upon her assurance of salvation that she had been forced to break off all connexions with the Methodists; furthermore, the latter, in their shameless impertinence, had desired that she would support them for nothing. In his reply to these charges John Wesley described the occurrence down to the last detail and demonstrated his innocence. It all amounted to a bland piece of defamation, and Wesley could only express his astonishment that the bishop could believe rumours of such a kind.[203]

He then went on to treat his adversary with incomparable ridicule, rendering him helpless. To his great satisfaction Wesley saw that the third part of the tract was fundamentally different from the first. The bishop had not returned to the earlier method of procedure, nor had he gone into Wesley's vindication; consequently he had abandoned the accusations. Further, apparently under the influence of the reply, his tone is markedly changed. Now Wesley no longer has before himself the babblings of a fool who obviously finds pleasure in making fun of all the basic Christian truths, to the applause of the Deists. The treatment shows an increase of seriousness by a few degrees and a lessening of shameless self-confidence. This shows how right Wesley had been to reproduce, hesitatingly and as little as was absolutely necessary, his opponent's manner of writing; rather he had concerned himself with not damaging by improper treatment the dignity of the subject, namely the basic Christian truths.[204] Further he has to ask the bishop whether indeed he has not exerted himself unnecessarily? Are the Methodists really more than a fly on the wall or a partridge in the field? From the tract, Wesley argues, one can get no impression other than that of overwhelming meaninglessness. Furthermore, against whom does the bishop summon the ministers of all denominations, particularly those of the Established Church, to pursue the Methodists to the point of death as people who are not worthy to live upon the earth? The effects of their activity are seen clearly in the Counties of Cornwall and Devonshire, and the fact is that preaching of the Methodist sort has never led to riots in England. One is forced to ask: would it be a satisfaction to the bishop if a religious persecution were to rage throughout the land like that of the Middle Ages or Cromwell's time, or if the Methodists were burned at the stake like dangerous heretics? Would this promote the honour of the Church or of the British people? Would it be any advantage to the Protestant cause?[205]

According to the general tenor of the tract there is no doubt that the bishop would answer, Yes. For, as Wesley says, in this way the horrid consequences of the Methodist preaching would be prevented. Therefore everything depends on the point: what are the consequences of the Methodist preaching? They have been working now for a year in the bishop's diocese. Let any man go there, to Liskeard in Cornwall and to Tiverton in Devonshire, and inquire what sort of people their followers were a year before. Let anyone find out what are the main doctrines the Methodists have been preaching this twelvemonth. Let anyone examine what effects these doctrines have had upon their hearers. He will find that the greater number of the Methodist people were previously wicked men, that they laid hold of love to God and neighbour and obedience to God's commandments, and that they have since exercised themselves in living according to this pattern. If that is not God's work then Wesley confesses that he does not know what to call it. He then even applies to himself the words of Jesus (and at this point his tone towards the bishop becomes almost threatening): 'He that despiseth me despiseth Him that sent me' (Luke 10[16]). So he must go on his way and do all those things with the talents entrusted to him, so that men may come to the true Christian knowledge of God, and the love and fear of God, unconcerned by the opinions of others. True faith, righteousness, peace and joy in the Holy Ghost are the objects of his work.[206]

Once again the point which stands out most clearly in the whole affair is the appraisal of the Methodist revival. Wesley could only repeat what he had previously declared as his basic conviction about this. He was not afraid of a literary repetition; he transcribed as his concluding words a section of his letter to Thomas Church.[207]

The same question prompted Wesley's last controversial writing against Lavington, the long letter of December 1751, which was intended to occupy itself only with the second part of the bishop's tract.[208] In this Wesley made it clear point for point that Lavington's accusations of Roman Catholic thought, experience, practices and usages, especially those of a mystical kind, were quite insufficiently based. The bishop had for the most part contented himself with vague similarities and incidental likenesses. He had indiscriminately set separate points alongside each other. Thus he had often treated John Wesley's *Journal* in a highly arbitrary way, mainly by taking sentences out of their context or quoting them in a manner which made no sense. The total result was that he said nothing about an inward relationship with God and recognized as 'faith' only an external churchmanship or a morality of good works. As a consequence John Wesley once again was forced to tell him that he was completely ignorant of spiritual experiences such as the conflict with Satan, the struggle for faith and its assurance, the new birth by God's Spirit.[209] It was sufficient to make him bring an indictment against John Wesley that Wesley recommended Roman Catholic books, like the biography of Gaston Jean-Baptiste de Renty. He thereby showed that he was quite unaware that the Methodist leader had prepared his own edited extract of this book in order to rid it of certain objectionable features.[210] All the other points which Lavington raised— Wesley's pride and praise of himself on account of the rapidly growing movement, his doubtful concern for the truth, his tendency towards disagreement, his claim of special revelations, his lack of charity towards opponents, the quarrelsomeness of the Methodists among themselves, their complete contempt for authority and order, their despising of good works in favour of a mystical stillness which was supposed to be faith, and worst of all, their scepticism, infidelity, and atheism—all fall to the ground together.[211] These had been indiscriminately brought together, and most were misconceived. Lavington's conception of religion was merely that of a routine churchly Christianity, in which the individual needs to have opinions about nothing, let alone believe anything which is personally binding.[212]

Wesley brought the letter to an end with a sharp personal impeachment—and it is a letter in which he proved to the bishop most acutely his prejudiced judgement and his weakness in demonstrating the truth. He claims that the bishop's polemic not only seriously violates the command to love one's neighbour but also offends against all ordinary human claims of justice. He regards neither mercy, justice nor truth. He is moved by one purpose only—to vilify and to blacken. May God not lay to his charge all the malice he has poured forth, but show mercy to him, the merciless slanderer.

The letter was long, but so far as the actual argument went, concise and close. It was an open declaration of war and a definite act of defiance. There was combined in it contempt for the theological half-wit, the methodical bungler, the spiteful opponent, with the indignation of the faithful scriptural Christian, who showed condescending pity against the superficial man of the Enlightenment. After this nothing further could follow. Only a complete recantation by Lavington would have changed the situation.

Nine years later another Anglican, the London clergyman John Downes, delivered a brusque and biting attack against John Wesley.[213] He expressed his opposition to the Methodists in the form of a vigorous summons to his fellow-ministers to carry out their pastoral duties by protecting their congregations against the new false doctrines.[214] Accordingly this too was a case where theological questions were involved.

John Wesley took his critic at his word and subjected him to his own principle and procedure. While he claims to have carefully examined the doctrines of the Methodists, he has in fact completely failed to do so. He has read none of their writings or sermons, and he ought not to have dreamt of denying this for it is only by acknowledging it that he can enable his readers to understand why he has written in such a way. His authoritative tone is in peculiar contrast to his ignorance. He speaks not merely like an archbishop but like an apostolic vicar who has at his disposal full papal power. Thus he reproaches Wesley and his fellow-workers with having dreamt twenty-five years before, while still beardless divines, that they were called by divine inspiration with a special commission in a peculiar manner to great things. They carried this out with incomparable spiritual arrogance and became founders of the sect called Methodists. Wesley replied with irony that he sincerely regrets that he had not been able twenty-five years before to trust in the wise and paternal guidance of his opponent, in order to be able to avoid in time at least some part of his displeasure; it is, however, no longer possible to make up for that. He repudiates the supposition of an awareness of having been specially sent. The only dream they had—to use the language of his opponent—was the desire to instruct their pupils in Christian faith and learning and to teach a few prisoners the common principles of Christianity. Downes had further accused them of being docile followers of the Roman Church. They had taken over the pretension of being infallibly correct interpreters of the Bible. Wesley did not take this to be a joke, and he asked sharply in return in what way the Methodists were under obligation to the Church of Rome, how they had discharged this, and where they had ever claimed to interpret the Scriptures infallibly. Similarly he desired clear proofs for the claim that they appealed to special gifts of the Holy Spirit. In his *Journals*, of which his critic could have read no more than the titles (a fact he betrays when he states that his brother had written some of them), he, John Wesley, had expressly disclaimed anything of this nature. The only effects of the Holy Spirit to which he had laid claim were those common to all Christians.[215]

The next charge, that in Methodism all the early Christian heresies, Montanism, Gnosticism, Simonianism, Antinomianism and Donatism, are combined, Wesley could not take seriously. Only in passing does he refer to the fact that this list describes as many contradictions as there are words. Generalizations of this kind prove nothing; one must come to particulars. Why has he not added to his list of heretics the Carpocratians, Eutychians, Nestorians and Sabellians? All this is only dust to blind the eyes of ignorant spectators.[216]

Wesley on his part then attempts to go into the separate points. The first real objection was that the Methodists made the way to heaven too easy, in that they required only faith and not works. With such erroneous ideas as trust in Jesus Christ, without the trouble of serious moral effort, the libertines could get on very well and comfortably. The advocates of Valentinian gnosticism were those who required good works only from people of the lowest grade, but not from their own followers. The Methodists do precisely the same now. Wesley counters this by saying that Downes cannot yet be awake or be dealing with reality; he is dreaming, and fighting with spectres of his own imagination. What he, Wesley, really teaches can be read in his sermon of 1733 on the Circumcision of the Heart, or in his sermons on the Sermon on the Mount. In these he will quickly see that Wesley in no way lightens the way to heaven but rather makes it more difficult because he directs it at the inward man, seeking to lead him to both inward and outward holiness. The truth is that the Methodists in the last thirty years have had to listen to just the opposite objection, that they are too strict, too austere, and that they try to bring about an excessive righteousness, asking too much of themselves and others.[217]

Again when Downes says that Wesley makes man completely dependent upon God's sovereign will and reduces him to a mere machine, this simply does not tally with the facts. He teaches quite the contrary, and refers Downes to his tract on predestination, which he had written ten years earlier. Similarly the further accusation that the Methodists see in faith a supernatural principle which precludes judgement and understanding is without any foundation. They do not imagine that such an enthusiastic sentimentality is to be commended, nor certainly that it should be set up. Naturally faith is a divine gift, and as such is miraculous and supernatural. But by it reason is in no sense condemned, although faith cannot be based on it. Faith gives evidence of itself outwardly in moral works and inwardly in feelings. Outwardly it shows itself as approximation to the life of Jesus, inwardly as love, peace, joy, meekness, gentleness, or, in a word, as the fruit of the Holy Spirit, which Paul often, and especially in Galatians 5[22], describes.[218]

In his account of regeneration, as it is ostensibly taught by the Methodists, Downes mixes truth and error. Of course the Methodists believe that the new birth ushers in the actual, genuine life under God, as truly at the present as 1700 years before. But they do not make a law out of the external circumstances of a previous age. The new birth can be either an instantaneous experience or a gradual process. The physical accompaniments which have occurred in the Methodist meetings, are in no sense essential to it. It is completely without foundation that the Methodists propagate a Christianity of wild ecstasies, a claim which will bear no examination. Where, asks Wesley, has he ever said this; in which sermon, or in what writing, practical or polemical? There is no truth in it at all. On the contrary

he examines himself and his activity in the closest detail in the light
of the New Testament.[219]

When Downes maintains that they, the Anglican clergy, have one
advantage in particular over the Methodists, namely reason, Wesley
is prepared to let the evidence decide where clear insight and where
enthusiasm are at work. The argument in Downes's tract is no
evidence of the former. Similarly it is sheer nonsense to maintain
that he and his Methodists despise learning and knowledge. Of course
he is aware that many men make poor use of their learning; but the
New Testament does state that, while knowledge passes away, love
never fails.[220]

Wesley is also forced to reject the more practically-based objections.
It is untrue that the Methodist leaders consider themselves the only
true preachers of the Gospel. He knows full well that there are many
more in England and elsewhere. When they represent their revival
as the work of God this is fully in line with the biblical witness: the
regular action of the Church in preaching and sacrament is not to
be conceived under any other principle. Nor, as Downes suggests,
does he expect from his followers a blind faith or slavish dependence.
They agree with him so far as his preaching is in conformity with
Scripture; they reject what goes beyond it or deviates from it. The
accusation that they treat the Anglican clergy with contempt, abuse
them, and so dissolve the pastoral relationship between the clergy
and their congregations, is answered by John Wesley with the ironic
counter-question as to how the Methodists could dissolve what never
existed. For what takes place beyond the Sunday sermon and the
occasional saying of prayers? How wretchedly the Anglican clergy
fulfil the early Christian command to watch over the souls entrusted
to them, for whom they must one day give account. That the
Methodists vainly seek for harmony between Anglican sermons and
the standard Reformation sermons, the Homilies of Cranmer, Ridley,
and Latimer, is unfortunately all too true. He himself has heard a
sufficient number of sermons which flatly contradict the article about
justification.[221] But there are no spiteful, disparaging statements
about the Anglican ministers in his societies, and he has no use for
such weapons.

One final charge was often heard. It was the assertion that the
Methodists exploited their followers financially and asked and took
from them money, while 'believing' wives stealthily stole from their

'unbelieving' husbands. Wesley was in duty bound to declare that his conscience was absolutely clear on this point. He himself possessed sufficient for his moderate needs. The weekly contributions, which were freely given in his societies, did not come into his hands. The stewards who receive them are honourable people, trustworthy from every point of view. The accusation made against the women, that they passed on to him money without the knowledge of their husbands, Downes ought to prove. Otherwise he must bear the blame of being a friend of lies.[222]

Should Downes at the end wish to object that a few years before a greater man than himself had said the same about the Methodists, by which evidently William Warburton was in his mind, John Wesley answered mischievously that he ought not make unsuitable comparisons. A frog may swell himself out as much as he can, but he will not become an ox. As Wesley emphasizes by a quotation from Horace, everyone should know his own size.[223] Even although the whole affair was distasteful nevertheless even in this letter the personal opposition to his critic was regarded as less important than his instruction in the truth.

But how did Wesley treat the 'great man' among his adversaries, none other than William Warburton, the bishop of Gloucester?[224] From the very first word the difference between this and his treatment of Lavington is obvious. Wesley seizes upon Warburton's comment that in the service of religion buffoonery should be entirely avoided and makes this the main theme of his own discussion. The treatment ought to be as serious as death, for this is required by the importance of the subject as well as by the position of his critic, who was in many ways superior to him. The subject is not 'John Wesley', although Warburton had actually begun his attack in this way, but 'the office and operation of the Holy Spirit'. In this John Wesley has merely the role of an example.[225] The perceptive reader will already note that the leader of Methodism was treating the highly-esteemed bishop in an ironical way, in that he sharpened the latter's point and put his subject into its correct setting. The final sentences of the letter confirm this. After Wesley had summarized in an overlong discussion the whole of Warburton's points into what was in fact a minor work, he made the point that should the bishop do him the honour of writing again, he would be more serious.[226] Thus he treated the high prince of the Church with an inimitably fine ridicule, without showing bad form.

He retained this tone when he came to deal with the actual subject. Doubtless, he remarked, he is dealing with twice-cooked cabbage, to use the words of Juvenal. But the bishop has been pleased to repeat oft-heard accusations which he has answered a hundred times, and so he is constrained to repeat the replies. In the first place he will consider the question of his claiming extraordinary workings of the Holy Spirit. This is by no means the case. He claims for himself precisely the same endowment of the Spirit of God as that which the Scripture gives warrant for every Christian minister of the Word and Sacrament. When Warburton quotes against him the admonition of the Epistle of James (3^{17}) that the wisdom from above is first pure, then peaceable, gentle, and easy to be intreated, full of mercy and good fruits, without partiality and without hypocrisy, he must deny its application to such a situation. Warburton seeks to use it as a test for true and false prophets; but it is not meant in this way. In the original context of the Epistle it refers not to prophets but to Christians in general. As a Christian he of course accepts the admonition for himself, but he does this daily as a matter of course.[227] When Warburton further objects that he has laid claim to every apostolic gift, Wesley says that the lists given in the New Testament must be examined. The references are Mark $16^{17,18}$ and 1 Corinthians $12^{8,10}$. When the gift of working miracles mentioned therein is compared with John Wesley's *Journals*, it is clearly seen that not a single one of those referred to is present.[228] What remains after the accusation has been made is his, Wesley's, conviction that God hears prayers, that He equips a man who calls upon Him with special strength in an hour of need,[229] that the devil is a reality who tempts, troubles and misleads men,[230] and finally that God ordains judgements on evil men which from time to time become visible, but which are not under the power of man.[231] But all of this is in the Bible and belongs to Christian belief. Warburton had made the point against him, again through a false application of James 3^{17}, that what is decisive is not the content, but the form of preaching. The Epistle of James mentions under six characteristics only one which concerns the content, while all the others have to do with the form. Therefore Warburton had concluded that an enthusiastic manner of preaching works more harm than erroneous doctrine which is gently spoken. Wesley replies: since the whole Bible passage in its particular context refers not to preaching but to living, Warburton's argument is of no account. On the actual point he must continue to maintain that the decisive thing about preaching is its content, not its form.[232]

In the true spirit of the Enlightenment Warburton had charged the Methodists with violating the peace of the country by their intolerance. The wisdom from above is peaceable and peace-loving. Wesley acts violently, and behaves as the great critic amongst contemporaries and fellow-citizens. Zeal and the faith of a fanatic lead him astray to perform imprudent actions, all of which disturb healthy life. To this Wesley replies: if faith and zeal become words of abuse then Paul is the greatest of fanatics. For what was zeal to him if it was not burning love for God, and what was faith if not confidence in the invisible reality of God? It is evident how determinedly Wesley everywhere keeps to the New Testament. The cardinal point for his understanding of the meaning of faith is the opening sentence of the great chapter on faith in the Epistle to the Hebrews (11^1). He denies that he forgets prudence, in so far as it is truly Christian. When Warburton reproaches him with the charge that a sign of his lack of prudence is his indiscreet preaching in the open-air, since it is an offence against Church order and the parochial system, he replies that this form was precisely the right one for the colliers of Kingswood and Hanham Mount. Instead of creating disorder, as Warburton supposed, it has turned disorderly men into orderly.[233] If the reference to the persecution which the Methodists had to endure is a disturbance of the peace, then he must ask: who was it who in the first place brutally broke the peace? He could not leave out any mention of persecution, for he must witness to the truth and warn against those who are Christians in appearance only. The climax of Warburton's argument on this point was that he reproached John Wesley with having a desire for persecution. Wesley's short reply was that he desires peace, but expects persecution.[234] The further charge, that he shows no compassion to his opponents he firmly rejected, and he gave instances of very different behaviour on his part.[235]

One question of fundamental importance and of far-reaching consequence had been raised by Warburton, when he asserted that according to Paul in Ephesians 5^9 right opinions are at least a third part, and that the important part, of religion. From this it follows that reason has the decisive word in the faith. Wesley again contests Warburton's interpretation of the biblical reference, and proposes to the bishop a different exposition of the text, following Johann

Albrecht Bengel's suggested reading: 'Walk as children of the light' instead of Warburton's less well-attested text, 'children of the Spirit'. From this it follows that the qualities of goodness, righteousness and truth which follow ought not to be understood intellectually as referring to the Christian's ability to know, but to their way of living. The words 'walk in the light' are contrasted with 'walking in darkness'. Therefore this saying does not refer to the role or task of cognitive and judging reason in faith, but to the true conduct of life. The point thus remains, as Wesley had said in the sentence which Warburton had complained of, that right opinions are a slender part of religion, since God does not begin His work in the understanding but in the heart. The Philippian jailer believed before he was able to give a clear intellectual account of his faith.[236] This particular text does not refer to this problem of true and false doctrine.

Behind this whole question there lay the accusation of Warburton that Wesley had separated grace and reason from each other—as if reason were not a gift of grace, or grace were irrational. Therefore in his meetings he both favours and produces religious frenzies. Wesley replied that those members of his meetings amongst whom phenomena of this type had broken out were either already spiritually unwell, or they had experienced healing in the Methodist meetings, but that these had taken place, not through miraculous proceedings, but as answers to prayer. Moreover he grants to reason a favoured place in faith. There is no doubt that right opinions are a great help and false ones a great obstacle to faith.[237] And when Warburton charges him with despising natural religion, that is only because in an account of the Indians he had misunderstood descriptions of religious ideas for an account of 'natural religion'. It had been concerned with concepts natural to heathen religion and the customs which flow naturally from it.[238]

The problem of miracles was very important for so typical a man of the Enlightenment as Warburton. As a rational supranaturalist he found a solution in the opinion that miracles belonged to the early days of Christianity, making the claim that they were only a temporary expedient until the time when the institution of the Church became regularly established. This is the point which Wesley felt impelled to deny. He was convinced that miracles could happen just as well today as formerly, if God so willed. Nobody should put limits upon the Holy Spirit.[239]

Wesley had to attack the basic assumption, as he had done in the case of Thomas Church, using the very same words, that England was a Christian land, not in need of evangelization.[240] Throughout the whole of his book Warburton treated the subject of conversion, the new birth, and the sanctification and perfection of Christians with ridicule.[241] Wesley therefore tried to refute him by means of the authority of the Church of England itself. He quoted whole passages from the Homilies, the prayers in the Book of Common Prayer, and *Exposition of the Creed* by John Pearson,[242] one of the classic Anglican divines of the seventeenth century. In this way he set a leading churchman of the eighteenth century over against a leader of the seventeenth century, that classical period of Anglicanism. He intended to show that in sharp contrast to Warburton's thoroughly formal and formalized way of thinking, which placed the method of preaching above its content, and even attempted in addition to discredit the name of Methodist as an honourable description of the movement,[243] the real work of the Holy Spirit was completely different. This work can only be determined by what He does, and it penetrates much deeper and includes far more than Warburton has any presentiment of, for it is a new birth, a re-creation of the whole man. The cry of enthusiasm which is raised as soon as this subject is mentioned demonstrates how completely foreign to the Bible the age is. The abusive name is indeed only a convenient evasion for the ignorant, since it is quite impossible to eradicate the subject of the new birth from the Bible or the patristic writers.[244] With this last remark he touched his great opponent on a tender spot. What Church leader likes to hear the soundness of his scholarship called into question?

If one looks back once again at Warburton's attack from this point of view the question arises: what is to be said of the two men? On the one hand there was the discreet bishop, dedicated to the spirit of moderation; on the other, the fanatical leader of the Methodists who endangered public order and brought unrest to the whole country. Wesley's tone and handling of the facts were superior. He reacted to the irritating language of the accusation with light-hearted mockery and did not go into insulting charges like the comparison of himself with Ignatius of Loyola or the murderers of the king during the period of the revolution.[245] Faced with the generalizations in Warburton's attack he insisted upon going into actual events, and to the institutionalism of the contemporary state Church he brought the statements and outlook of the New Testament. Indeed in using the celebrated John Pearson as his ally he made it clear how much deeper and better this man from a hundred years earlier treated Warburton's subject, the work of the Holy Spirit. In this way he demonstrated to this opponent and the world at large who it was who really stood in the line of the Anglican tradition and which of them could claim the support of the one legitimate standard, the New Testament.

With the reply to Warburton the great apologetic and polemical writings of John Wesley came to an end. What followed was merely like an echo. The only remaining and fairly extensive theological controversy which took place brought no new points to light, nor did it clarify the old ones. This was John Wesley's reply to the attack which the Archdeacon of Essex, Thomas Rutherford, made in the year 1763, apparently dependent to a certain extent upon Warburton.[246] Wesley's answer was not made until five years later, and this considerable period of time is very revealing. The archdeacon's writing had not come to the notice of the Methodist leader. In spite of that he was too conscientious to allow the matter to lie as something belonging merely to the past. As usual he took seriously every single accusation. Rutherford had devoted three out of four of his charges to the clergy of his archdeaconry to warnings against the Methodists. He gave it as his opinion that they represented only themselves as faithful Anglicans, whereas in fact through their use of lay preachers and their condemnation of human learning in general they went against the basic inherited principles of the Church.[247] Their appeal to inner feelings, claimed to be the working of the Holy Spirit, their pretended inward assurances of the love of God, which are said to be reserved solely for them, go against reason and bring about a type of unrestrained enthusiastic Christianity.[248]

In the first place Wesley stated that it was upon his helpers, the lay-preachers, that he laid the burden of obtaining real knowledge. He certainly differentiates between this and that which is normally required in the theological tests for the Established Church. It is knowledge of the Bible. But through it his helpers should be more than a match for the Anglican candidates. There is no question of contempt for knowledge.[249] As to inner feelings, these do not refer to an uncontrollable enthusiasm, but to a genuine, persuasive transition from the doubt of sin to the joy and freedom of the redeemed children of God. Take that away and Christianity becomes an empty dead form,[250] which stands in contradiction to the New Testament. A rejection of reason is in no way associated with it. Finally Wesley went strongly over to the attack. He charged the archdeacon with having misused his highly responsible office, which provided him with so many fine opportunities. Instead of reminding the stewards of God's mysteries of their own inner dangers, which threatened them through lassitude and negligence, instead of calling them to make their life a living sacrifice to God and to seek the salvation of the souls entrusted to them, he has tried to prejudice them against their brethren and fellow-labourers. How will he make amends for wasting this opportunity of working for God?[251]

In spite of all their variations the attacks from the Anglican side were all characterized by a great similarity. From all the writings, speeches and newspaper articles came the same complaints about enthusiasm, exaggerated piety, fanaticism, lust for power and tyranny, excessive austerity or unrestrained lawlessness, hypocrisy, disparagement of the regular Church and its representatives, and more than all, and yet running through all, threats to the peace of the Church and disturbance of the public quiet. The memory of the Great Revolution a hundred years earlier was still living, and it affected the whole controversy. Very few really went into the doctrines of the Methodists, and when they did so it was nearly always merely to show the evil consequences which would follow for Church, state, society and individual lives. The majority were content to stress their complete novelty for their age, their absurdity for reason, and their uselessness for practical living. In addition there was a considerable amount for Wesley continually to answer about his discipline of himself. Although he sometimes let himself go and became sarcastic, biting, and rude, on the whole he kept much more to facts than his opponents. In every letter he penetrated to the real heart of the matter, as well as to the differences about fundamental points such as the Christian or unchristian character of England, and about the real central doctrines, which included the supreme authority of the New Testament. The radically missionary characteristic in his general view of Christianity also showed itself at this point, indeed it became clearer and sharper; mission for the nation as a whole was concentrated in the conversion of the individual, mission on the large scale implied new birth in individual experience. Here Wesley's programme for life reached its

deepest and characteristic fulfilment, the bringing back of the early
Christian energy into the present and accordingly the direct verifica-
tion for the truth of God's promises.

If it should be asked, in conclusion, what was the attitude to the
Methodist movement of the leadership of the Church, as personified
in the Archbishop of Canterbury, one answer is given and this answer
frequently occurs in the history of the Church; it is that the leadership
avoided a clear decision and manifestly let things largely take their
own course, adopting the attitude of Gamaliel: 'If this counsel or
work be of men, it will come to nought; but if it be of God, ye cannot
overthrow it' (Acts 5[38,9]). This was all the more the case since the
Archbishops of Canterbury at the time were men who were not much
above the average. Among the most important was John Potter
(Canterbury 1737–47), who ordained both John and Charles Wesley
when he was Bishop of Oxford, and who up to the last was well-
disposed to them. Thomas Secker (Canterbury 1758–68), the close
friend of Joseph Butler, came from a non-conformist background and
perhaps because of this did little officially about an independent
evangelical movement. From him alone there has been preserved a
concise official statement about Methodism, which fully confirms
this impression. In the second charge to his clergy from the year
1762 he referred specifically at the end to the movement.[252] In a
cautious way the Methodists are charged with wishing to practise a
very strict religion and with laying on the Anglicans severe blame
because they have departed from the true Christian doctrines and
precepts. At the same time they have themselves circulated unjustifiable notions as necessary truths. These have raised groundless fears
among good people and groundless hopes among bad ones. They
have given rise to perplexities, and amongst multitudes have raised
mistrust and prejudice against their proper ministers. So they have
produced first disorder in the Church of England, then separations
from it, and finally they have set up unauthorized teachers in their
own assemblies. These irregularities must be resisted, but with care.
They should not be driven into opposition by being called enthusiasts, fanatics or hypocrites. When extravagances are seen among
them, and can be proved, it is certainly admissible to speak strongly
against them, but this should be done without anger or bitterness,
and particularly without ridicule. Nobody should ever allow himself
to be driven into the position where he offends against a truth of the

Gospel, for that would give to them the advantage. The overruling requirement is to weigh every word and to treat them on their individual merits. Let those who are worthy amongst them be acknowledged, that they may be spurred on to earnest care for the common religion.

When these counsels were obeyed a great possibility for extension was in point of fact opened out to the movement, in spite of all the hostility. This was corroborated by its historical development.

Notes

Chapter 1: The Beginnings of the Evangelistic Movement: John Wesley and the Moravians

1. It was a particularly important group, meeting in the Minories in the City of London. In this street, which took its names from a French convent for nuns from the year 1293, Peter Sims the butcher lived. The group met in his house and was one of the type of religious societies founded by Anton Horneck, i.e. it was strictly Anglican and was probably in association with Holy Trinity Church. Cf. Edward H. Sugden, *John Wesley's London. Scenes of Methodist and worldwide Interest with their historical Associations*, 1932, 175–7. Cf. *Journal* II, 70–2. John Wesley frequently stayed with his old friend Jonathan Agutter at Charterhouse (see Vol. I, 68).

2. *Journal* II, 79f, Sept. 30, Sat. 1738, and *Letters* I, 259f, Oxon., Oct. 13, 1738, to Benjamin Ingham.

3. *Journal* II, 93. This was the first Methodist society of soldiers.

4. Cf. John S. Simon, *John Wesley and the Religious Societies*, 1921, 194–200. The rules are reproduced there 196–8 from Daniel Benham's *Memoirs of John Hutton*, 1856, 29–32. I made use of a contemporary manuscript in the Francke Archives in Halle: hIL1.

5. The same rules, especially the obligation to remain in the place, were drawn up on Oct. 13–14, 1742, at the establishment in North America of the Moravians at Bethlehem (Pennsylvania) by the community. *Bethlehem Diary* for the other half of the year 1742 under this date, manuscript in Moravian Archives Bethlehem (Pennsylvania).

6. Hitherto the importance of this point has not been sufficiently recognized. Wesley at no time went forward as a solitary individual; indeed he saw in the inclination to solitariness a temptation of the devil (cf. Vol. I, 219). The fellowship with his companions naturally became especially close in Georgia, and when they left the Isle of Wight on Nov. 3, 1735, they resolved: 'In the name of God, Amen. We whose names are here underwritten, being fully convinced that it is impossible, either to promote the work of God among the heathen without an entire union amongst ourselves; or, that such an union should subsist unless each one will give up his single judgement to that of the majority, do agree, by the help of God:

First. That none of us will undertake anything of importance without first proposing it to the other three.

Second. That, whenever our judgements or inclinations differ, any one shall give up his single judgement or inclination to the others.

Third. That, in the case of an equality, after begging God's direction, the matter shall be decided by lot,

John Wesley

C. Wesley

B. Ingham

C. Delamotte'

(Reproduced by Luke Tyerman, *The Oxford Methodists*, 1873, 10). Probably this engagement took place under Moravian influence, which was also true of the lot. On the other hand he was a very solitary person, who never found a completely intimate friend. Closest to him was his brother Charles, who acknowledged unreservedly what he owed him. Cf. his letter to John Cennick of March 1741, in John Wesley's *Journal* II, 434.

7. This leads to the intensifying of the consciousness of the cross and persecution, so that John Wesley could choose Acts 28[22] as a text for his sermon. *Journal* II, 293, Oct. 15, 1739.

8. The central significance of the idea of mission comes out strikingly in the important letter to James Hervey of March 20, 1739. *Letters* I, 284–7, especially 285, 286.

9. An example of this was the letter which John Clayton, then in Manchester, wrote to him May 1, 1738 (from the manuscript, privately owned, reproduced by John S. Simon, op. cit., 188f). It objected that he was departing from the sound principles of Anglican churchmanship when he preached without notes and offended by excessive use of words and lively gesticulation. It was the English feeling for moderation, which led him to fear for Wesley and censure him for 'self-sufficiency and ostentation', as if these gave an impression of apostolic appearance, whereas it only led to his becoming carried away by self-will and lust for power. Wesley's letter to Zinzendorf of Oct. 30, 1738, is revealing: 'for though a great door and effectual had been opened, the adversary had laid so many stumbling-blocks before it that the weak were daily turned out of the way. Numberless misunderstandings had arisen, by reason of which the way of truth was much blasphemed; and hence had sprung anger, clamour, bitterness, evil-speaking, envyings, strifes, railings, evil surmisings, whereby the enemy had gained such an advantage over the little flock that "of the rest durst no man join himself unto

them." But it has now pleased our blessed Master to remove in great measure these rocks of offence.' *Letters* I, 265.

On Nov. 16, 1738, John Wesley wrote somewhat disappointedly about the Holy Club to Benjamin Ingham and James Hutton (*Letters* I, 266f), saying that not all build upon the true foundation, but establish their own righteousness. He regrets that Charles Kinchin and Richard Hutchings, as he had done originally, laid too great weight upon the perceived feelings of assurance of salvation and its joy.

10. *Letters* I, 270, Oxon., Nov. 24, 1738, to Mr Fox; *Letters* I, 275, Oxon., Dec. 1, 1738, to James Hutton.

11. Samuel Berein, the assistant preacher of Friedrich Michael Ziegenhagen, the court-chaplain in London, wrote on Dec. 4, 1738, to Gotthilf August Francke in Halle, that 'a pretty large movement started in London through Mr Wesley and his friends, in particular through the doctrine of the assurance of sins forgiven and the state of grace, which of course is the same thing'. An English preacher, Bedford, had taken an opposed position in a public sermon, and accused his opponents of believing that a man has to be assured of the forgiveness of sins by an extraordinary revelation. He even considered that the witness of the Holy Spirit is something extraordinary, whereby not all Christians, 'but only those who had to testify to the truth through great suffering or even with their blood, were assured of their adoption' (manuscript in the Francke Archives Halle: hIL5). On Oct. 6, 1738, Wesley took to task Arthur Bedford, the chaplain of the Prince of Wales and of Haberdashers' Hospital in London (*Journal* II, 82), after he had written him a letter on Sept. 28 (*Letters* I, 254-7).

12. *Journal* II, 83-91, Oct. 9-14, 1738. The fact that it was this imperative which became the starting-point shows how far he was from the danger of a mechanical biblicism, which reduces the Scripture to an oracle.

13. Here is found again the significant juxtaposition of holiness and happiness. For the attachment to 2 Corinthians 5^{11} in German Pietism cf. Anton Wilhelm Böhme, *The New Creature*, in a New Year's Day sermon, 1719, on the text. Anton Wilhelm Böhme's *Sämtliche Erbauliche Schriften*, published by Johann Jakob Rambach, I, Altona 1731, 689-732.

14. This extreme negative judgement of the old man through the new is found in the first place in a basic book of early Puritanism, *The Practice of Piety* by Bishop Lewis Bayly of Bangor (Wales, *c.* 1600). Cf. my essay *Eigenart und Bedeutung der Eschatologie im englischen*

Puritanismus, Theologia Viatorum (Jahrbuch d. Kirchl. Hochschule Berlin) IV (1952), 224–51.

15. This agrees essentially with the view of Luther: the knowledge of sin comes from the Scripture (*Larger Catechism* 1529 *Vom Sakrament des Altars* 76.) *Die Bekenntnisschriften der Ev. luth. Kirche* (publ. by the deutschen evang. Kirchenausschuss 1930), 1952, 723, 1.

16. Wesley therefore anticipates with unusual clarity the transcendental apperceptive theology of Schleiermacher's dogmatics, which was derived from Kant. Wesley's position is one of the most impressive examples of that line which runs from Puritan analytical theology through German Pietism to Schleiermacher, and renders it apparent that he was the systematic fulfilment of Pietism. It is noteworthy how carefully Wesley considers each of the 'fruits of the Spirit' in Galatians 5[22]. He purposely singles out love and faith, because he obviously feels the strongest restraints in exercising them.

17. Cf. *Journal* II, 89, Oct. 14, 1738; II, 97, Oct. 29, 1738; II, 103, Nov. 23, 1738; II, 106, Dec. 3, 1738; II, 158, March 28, 1739, and frequently in the following period.

18. Cf. esp. the letter which he reproduces *Journal* II, 109–11, between Dec. 5 and 10, 1738.

19. Cf. the letter printed in *Journal* II, 108.

20. Cf. the Earl of Egmont's *Diary* (publ. 1920) under April 26, 1738, reproduced in *Letters* I, 365: 'Mr. John Wesley, our minister at Savannah, left with us his licence for performing ecclesiastical Service at Savannah, which we took for a resignation, and therefore resolved to revoke his commission. In truth the Board did it with great pleasure, he appearing to us to be a very odd mixture of a man, an enthusiast, and at the same time a hypocrite, wholly distasteful to the great part of the inhabitants, and an incendiary of the people against the magistrates.'

21. Ziegenhagen to Gotthilf August Francke, Kensington, Dec. 26, 1738, and Jan. 25, 1739: 'The collection sermons in London, which raised 45 pounds sterling, are to be repeated in Bristol. June 1, 1739: From a Tuesday sermon in the open-air 20 pounds sterling came in.' The manuscripts of the letters in the Francke Archives Halle.

22. Evidence of this is the self-examination of Dec. 16, 1738 (*Journal* II, 115f), which followed the same scheme as that of Oct. 9–14, but came to a much more depressing conclusion: 'therefore there is in me still the old heart of stone . . . Therefore there is in me still the carnal heart, the φρόνημα σαρκὸς . . . Again my desires, passions, and inclinations in general are mixed; having something of Christ and something of earth . . . Nor can I divide the earthly part from the

heavenly.' The self-examination of Jan. 4, 1739, *Journal* II, 125f, ends even more severely.

23. Cf. John L. Nuelsen, *John Wesley and das deutsche Kirchenlied*, 1938, 70–2. On the Spanish hymn cf. C. D. Hardcastle, *Wesley's Psalms and Hymns*, 1737–1825. *The Collections of Psalms and Hymns, Compiled by the Revds. John and Charles Wesley*, Proc. Wes. Hist. Soc. III (1900), 57–63. It deserves to be especially emphasized that at this time (from Sept. 20, 1738) J.W. sang as often as possible by himself and with other believers. The day began in this way at 5 or 6 o'clock; also on the course of a journey, such as the way to Oxford, or at evening meetings, singing played an important part (*Journal* II, 75; *Diary*–115; *Diary* Sept. 20, 1738–March 26, 1739). This was a Moravian influence.

24. *Journal* II, 121–125, Jan. 1, 1739. It is noteworthy that at this meeting seven Anglican clergymen were present. As early as Oct. 13, 1738, Wesley had expressed to Benjamin Ingham the hope that in a short while a great number of Anglican priests would believe (*Letter* I, 260: 'Indeed I trust our Lord will let us see, and that shortly, a multitude of priests that believe.'). On attacks during worship among the Moravians cf. *Fetter Lane and the English Moravians*, Notes and Queries, in Proc. Wes. Hist. Soc. IV (1904), 140ff, S.142.

25. Wesley does not cite, as might have been expected, in this connexion (*Journal* II, 125f) 1 Corinthians 13³, but this text is clearly in the background, especially as love according to Galatians 5²² is placed first. That he includes 'all the saints of the world' shows that in the last resort he is not concerned with his own ego but about the position of a perfect Christian. He is in this very like Clement of Alexandria.

26. *Journal* II, 137, Jan. 28, 1739: 'Two or three of our company were much affected, and believed she spoke by the Spirit of God. But this was in no wise clear to me. The motion might be either hysterical or artificial. And the same words any person of a good understanding and well versed in the Scriptures might have spoken.' Cf. as an example of an original work about the Camisards (the French prophets) the anonymous booklet: *A Cry from the Desert*, London, 1707, which reproduces extracts from the affidavits of the 'prophets', who had been examined by the royal commissioners John Edisbury and Richard Holford in March and April 1706. Much of their preaching had been about the prophecy of the fall of Babylon—the Roman Catholic Church, on the inexplicable mastery of the French language by uneducated women, and the nervous convulsions. For the German area cf. *Unschuldige Nachrichten*, 1707, 771–7; cf. further Anton Wilhelm Böhme in a letter to Aug. Herm. Francke on July 26,

1714, that is eight years after their first sensational appearance in England (Anton Wilhelm Böhme's *Erbauliche Briefe*, Altona and Flensburg 1737, No. XCVII, pp. 325–35). From this it is apparent that sexual motives were also at work. Böhme emphasizes in addition particularly their aversion to work (p. 329f). His final judgement (p. 332) is: 'Whether I should look upon these things as dangerous on account of these and other attendant circumstances, yet I love the good seedling which grows green in the midst of so many weeds.' A perceptive description and careful assessment is given in Ronald A. Knox, *Enthusiasm*, 1950, 356–71.

27. *Journal* II, 131f, Jan. 21, 1739; II, 240–2, Feb. 9, 13, 17, 1739.

28. Esp. characteristic is the letter to George Whitefield from London, Feb. 26, 1739, *Letters* I, 280. Cf. the one to the same, Mar. 16, 1739, *Letters* I, 281–4.

29. *Letters* I, 283, Mar. 16, 1739, to George Whitefield.

30. *Letters* I, 271, Oxon., Nov. 24, 1738, to James Hutton, I, 272, Nov. 26, 1738, to the same: 'Every man in my band is my monitor, and I his; else I know no use of our being in band.' Wesley refers to Leviticus 19[17]. *Letters* I, 274, Oxon., Nov. 27, 1738, to the same: 'I believe bishops, priests and deacons to be of divine appointment, though I think our brethren in Germany do not.'

31. It was said of Whitefield: 'If he will convert heathens, why does not he go to the colliers of Kingswood?' *Journal* II, 322, Nov. 27, 1739.

32. At about the same time John Wesley reproached Whitefield for not giving sufficient importance to the vote of the society and for expecting that it would capitulate to his own wishes. *Letters* I, 287f, Mar. 20, 1739.

33. For the description of Bristol cf. John S. Simon op. cit., 264–79: Bristol in 1739. On the colliers of Kingswood cf. G. M. Trevelyan, *English Social History* (1942), 3rd ed. 1947, 285.

34. *Letters* I, 288f, Bristol, Apr. 2, 1739, to James Hutton.

35. On all this *Journal* II, 156–68, Mar. 16 to Apr. 1, 1739.

36. *Journal* II, 175, Apr. 5, 1739; II, 179, Apr. 15, 1739.

37. This point is of decisive importance, for it shows that Wesley stressed the result and not the manifestations. He was anxious that the whole company, like the early Christians, should feel responsible for each member and that it should be all to the praise of God. Cf. the sentence: 'But we continued in prayer till "a new song was put in her mouth, a thanksgiving unto our God." ' *Journal* II, 180, Apr. 17, 1739.

38. *Journal* II, 180–2, Apr. 17–21, 1739; II, 184f, Apr. 26, 1739; II, 186, Apr. 30, 1739 (doctor); II, 187, May 1, 1739 (Quaker); *Letters* I,

305f, Bristol, May 7, 1739, to James Hutton (about John Haydon) *Journal* II, 189–92, May 2, 1739; *Letters* I, 308–10, May 10, 1739, to his brother Samuel (about John Haydon).

39. *Letters* II, 24f, Aug. 22, 1744, to Mrs Hutton.

40. *Letters* I, 301, Bristol, Apr. 30, 1739, to James Hutton.

41. *Letters* I, 290f, Bristol, Apr. 4, 1739, to his brother Samuel; *Letters* I, 308–10, Bristol, May 10, to the same; *Journal* II, 201–2, May 20, 1739; *Letters* VII, 207, near London, Jan. 21, 1784, to Mrs Parker: John Wesley argues that these attacks had been divinely-willed external signs of conversion for fifty years.

42. *Letters* I, 295f, Bristol, Apr. 9, 1739, to James Hutton.

43. *Letters* I, 301, Apr. 30, 1739, to James Hutton.

44. *Journal* II, 171, Extract from Whitefield's *Journal*, Apr. 2, 1739; *Journal* II, 239, Extract from the same, July 10, 1739; *Letters* I, 292, Bristol, Apr. 9, 1739, to his brother Charles; *Letters* I, 302, Bristol, Apr. 30, 1739, to James Hutton: *Letters* I, 305, Bristol, May 7, 1739.

45. See n. 6.

46. *Journal* II, 194–8, May 9, 1739; *Letters* I, 311, Bristol, May 14, 1739 to James Hutton.

47. *Letters* I, 338–40, Dec. 6, 1739, to Nathaniel Price, Bristol.

48. *Letters* I, 302f, Bristol, Apr. 30, 1739, to James Hutton; 305, Bristol, May 7, 1739, to James Hutton; 307f, May 8, 1739, to James Hutton; 312, May 14, 1739, to James Hutton; 323, July 2, 1739, to James Hutton.

49. *Letters* I, 319f, Bristol, June 7, 1739, to James Hutton; *Journal* II, 211–13, June 5, 1739.

50. *Journal* II, 216–22, June 11–17, 1739.

51. Cf. esp. Norman Sykes, *Church and State in England in the XVIII Century*, 1934, 392f; for the present, Roger Lloyd, *The Church of England in the 20th Century* I (1946), 6.

52. On James Hervey (1714–58) cf. Luke Tyerman, *The Oxford Methodists*, 1873, 201–333. James Hervey to John Wesley, Oxon., Sept. 2, 1736: *Arminian Magazine* I (1778), 130–2; the same Wheston near Northampton, Dec. 30, 1747, ibid. 134; the same Stoke Abbey, Dec. 1, 1738, ibid. 132f. John Wesley to James Hervey, London, Mar. 20, 1739; *Letters* I, 284–7.

53. *Letters* I, 328, July 31, 1739, to Dr Henry Stebbing.

54. John Wesley did not consider the conversation important enough to be recorded in his *Journal*, but only briefly in the *Diary*, which was written in cipher. The source for it is Charles Wesley's *Journal*, 1849, 208–9, reproduced in *Journal* II, 93, Oct. 20, 1738, n. 1

Curnock. Cf. Norman Sykes, *Edmund Gibson, Bishop of London* (1669–1748), 1926, 302f.

55. *Journal of Charles Wesley*, 1849, Feb. 21, 1739; *Journal* II, 143, Feb. 21, 1739, n. 1, Curnock, and Sykes, op. cit., 305.

56. How favourably Wesley thought of Cennick is seen in *Letters* I, 283, London, Mar. 16, 1739, to George Whitefield: 'In the morning our brother Cennick rode with me whom I found willing to suffer, yea to die, for his Lord . . .' and shortly before 'strong in the faith'.

57. Cf. the thorough investigation by H. McLachlan, *English Education under the Test Acts. Being the History of the Nonconformist Academies 1662–1820*, 1931, 16ff, 300ff (Lectures and Text Books).

58. Cf. Samuel Wesley, *A Defence of a Letter, concerning the Education of Dissenters in their private Academies* . . . 1704, esp. 50.

59. Joseph Butler, *The Analogy of Religion*, 1736. On the influence of Butler cf. esp. William Ewart Gladstone, *Studies Subsidiary to the Works of Bishop Butler*, 1896, 129–38. The idea of analogy between natural and revealed religion was prominent in English thought not only through the philosophy of the Renaissance but also through the close analogy between the first and second creation, worked out in the Puritan theology of regeneration. As an example cf. esp. Thomas Taylor, *A Man in Christ or a New Creature*, London, 1632 (3rd ed.), 42–6.

60. Cf. Joseph Butler, *Sermons* (*The Works of Bishop Butler*. New Ed. by J. H. Bernard), Vol. I, 1900, 6, 57.

61. Evidence for this is his treatment of the relation between self-interest and the common good, which is seen as a simple parallelism. Ibid. 27 (the text of the sermon is Romans $12^{4,5}$): 'And since the apostle speaks of the several members as having distinct offices, which implies the mind; it cannot be thought an unallowable liberty; instead of the body and its members, to substitute the whole nature of man, and all the variety of internal principles which belong to it. And then the comparison will be between the nature of man as respecting self, and tending to private good, his own preservation and happiness; and the nature of man as having respect to society and tending to promote public good, the happiness of society. These ends do indeed perfectly coincide; and to aim at public and private good are so far from being inconsistent, that they actually promote each other.' This is then considerably developed. The basic point of view agrees with John Wesley's parallelism between sanctification for the individual and for fellow-men. *Letters* I, 173, Dec. 10, 1734, to his father. Cf. Vol. I, 120.

62. Therefore many interpreters have over-stressed the sceptical trait in

his thought, the eradication of Deists' confidence in natural religion.

63. *Sermons* (Works ed. J. H. Bernard, I, 1900), 44ff, 58ff, 205.

64. Cf. Norman Sykes, *Church and State in England in the XVIIIth Century*, 1934, 186f.

65. There is still uncertainty about this. According to the Diary for May 26 and June 2, 1739 (*Journal* II, 205 and 207), John Wesley had 'communion' at Mrs Williams with 13 and 12 people. The Anglican clergy of Bristol refused the Sacrament to the members of the religious societies (J. S. Simon I, 1921, 311, 320). It seems that there was an administration to a limited extent in private houses after the early Christian pattern. In that case John Wesley's answer to Butler's question would have been a half-truth, but only half, because he had not actually administered it in the religious societies, but in private houses, and the bishop had not expressly included this possibility in his question.

66. Characteristic of this is, for example, the following anonymous pamphlet: *An Enquiry into the Ministry of the Presbyterians whether lawful or not?* as also into their way of Preaching in a *Letter to a Presbyterian Minister of the Kirk*, London, 1678, 1of: 'In the affairs of this World Ambassadors (you know) must not want their Credentials. How much less the Ambassadors of Religion? What? To reform the World, overrun with Idolatry and Superstition, and no appearance of your Authority for (11) so doing! To this you answer, That the powerful gifts and sanctity of those Persons were great tokens of their being inspired by the Spirit of God, and that the conversion of many Thousands from Superstition to Godliness was an undoubted Seal to their Ministry. This is the answer of all Dissen—(12)ters and Parties of what name soever. Independents, Anabaptists, Behemists, etc.'

67. Cf. Hermann Steinlein, *Luthers Doktorat*, 1912.

68. *Journal* II, 256, n. 1.

69. On Jan. 21, 1746, John Wesley recognized the excellence and thoroughness of the method of Joseph Butler's *Analogy*, but doubted its effectiveness on account of its profundity: *Journal* III, 232: 'a strong and well-wrote treatise, but, I am afraid, far too deep for their understanding to whom it is primarily addressed.'

70. Therefore I am not able to agree with John S. Simon's opinion (op. cit., n. 4, 314), which has become almost typical of English Wesley scholarship: 'It might have been possible, by a little frank and friendly conversation, to have reached mutual understandings which would have influenced the future of Wesley's work . . . The whole interview was an illustration of a missed opportunity.'

71. *Letters* I, 331, Bristol, Aug. 8, 1739; *Letters* I, 333f. James Hervey to Wesley, Aug. 21, 1739.

72. *Letters* I, 251f, Utphe, July 7, 1738, to Samuel Wesley; 262–5, London, Oct. 30, 1738, to the same; 274f, Oxon., Nov. 30, 1738, to the same; 279, (Jan.) 1739, to the same; 290f, Bristol, Apr. 4, 1739, to the same; 308–10, Bristol, May 10, 1739, to the same.

73. *Journal* II, 267f, Sept. 3, 1739.

74. On her cf. *The Life and Times of the Countess of Huntingdon* I, II, 1841. On Ingham's marriage cf. Marmaduke Riggall, *Richard Viney's Memorandum and Diary* 1744, Proc. Wes. Hist. Soc. XIV (1923), 14ff, 19; invitation of the Countess to John Wesley to go to Newcastle-upon-Tyne, *Letters* II, 14, Newcastle, July 12, 1743, to the Mayor of Newcastle.

75. John Whitehead, *Life of Wesley* II, 1796; cf. John S. Simon, op. cit., 326. *Journal* II, 273, Sept. 9, 1739. Wesley's numbers are exaggerated, and it is not possible now to estimate their correct amount; cf. Curnock, *Journal* II, 285, n. 1.

76. *Journal* II, 273, Sept. 9, 1739; 276, Sept. 14, 1739.

77. *Journal* II, 283–5, Oct. 1–5, 1739.

78. *Journal* II, 274, Sept. 12, 1739; 296, Oct. 20, 1739: 'I have seen no part of England so pleasant.'

79. Molther had arrived in England on Oct. 18, 1739. Many internal and external factors testify to the connexion with French Quietism, not least the fact that Molther came from Alsace, which belonged to France. The merits and shortcomings of quietist mysticism affected the age and German Pietism in August Hermann Francke and Gottfried Arnold (and later Tersteegen) most strongly.

80. *Journal* II, 312–16, Nov. 1–9, 1739. Cf. Gerhard Reichel, *August Gottlieb Spangenberg*, 1906, 104–18; on p. 105 it is excellently said: 'In this way his own past as it were once again returned on him; there was a final struggle between it and what was new in him, the Brethren. In a still deeper sense the years in Pennsylvania were to become years of apprenticeship.' Reichel emphasizes moreover the difference between Spangenberg and Molther, without characterizing it further. Wesley believed that the two were similar so far as doctrine was concerned.

81. *Journal* II, 345, May 30, 1740.

82. *Journal* II, 327, letter from an unknown writer to John Wesley, Dec. 14, 1739.

83. *Journal* II, 329, Dec. 31, 1739: 'Whereas I believe:
    1. There are degrees in faith, and that a man may have some degree of it before all things in him are become new—before he has the full

assurance of faith, the abiding witness of the Spirit, or the clear perception that Christ dwelleth in him.

2. Accordingly I believe there is a degree of justifying faith (and consequently a state of justification) short of, and commonly antecedent to, this.

3. And I believe our Brother Hutton, with many others, had justifying faith long before they saw you.

4. And, in general, that the gift of God which many received since Peter Böhler came into England—viz. "a sure confidence of the love of God to them"—was justifying faith.

5. And that the joy and love attending it were not from animal spirits from nature, or imagination; but a measure of "joy in the Holy Ghost", and of "the love of God shed abroad in their hearts".'

84. Daniel Benham, *Memoirs of James Hutton*, 1856, 47.

85. *Minutes of the Committee for finding the first Aim and Intention of our Saviour by the Awakening in England going under the name of Methodism, how and in what respects this Aim and Intention has been deviated from and in what manner it might best be restored again.* May 18, 1747. Archives of the United Brethren Herrnhut. Copy in John Ryland's Library, Manchester, Engl. MSS. 1037, published in part in Clifford W. Towlson, *Moravian and Methodist*, 1957, 132: 'Had Molther let J. Wesley be the head (the account goes on), and had he done all things under him, as his servant, he might have done with him what he pleased.'

86. Principally Gerhard Reichel, *A. G. Spangenberg*, 1906, 116f. Unfortunately the Herrnhut manuscript sources yield no clear picture of Molther and tell us far less than Wesley's statements; the latter remain the only close, clear description for it.

87. *Journal* II, 328–31, Dec. 31, 1739; 336, Feb. 21, 1740; 354f, June 22, 1740.

88. *Journal* II, 324–6, Dec. 8–13, 1739.

89. *Letters* I, 345, Aug. 8, 1740, to the Church at Herrnhut.

90. *Journal* II, 419, Jan. 28, 1741.

91. *Journal* II, 352, June 18, 1740; *Journal* III, 16f, June 3, 1742. Ingham for stillness. *Letters* II, 80–4, Sept. 8, 1746, to Benjamin Ingham concerned mostly with stillness, which Ingham held to.

92. *Journal* II, 418, Jan. 22, 1741; cf. esp. John Wesley's letter to Charles of Apr. 21, 1741: *Letters* I, 353f, and below.

93. *Journal* II, 349, 356, 259f, 361f, June 5–29, 1740.

94. *Journal* II, 349, July 16, 1740. Wesley reports that the example includes some further additions of a similar character, in which abstention from reading the Bible, prayer, reception of the Sacrament

and all outward works is recommended for the twice-born. This sounds like French Quietism.

95. *Journal* II, 365f, July 16, 1740; 371, July 22, 1740. From whom this direction originated cannot be established, nor whether it came from Herrnhut or Marienborn, nor indeed who this Mr Chapman was. Possibly Count Zinzendorf was behind it, for already in his *Eventual Testament to the Church* of Dec. 27, 1738, he had reckoned Wesley— with Spangenberg, whom at the time he mistrusted!—among the 'persons who ought to be named by us and treated with care'; cf. Gerhard Reichel, *August Gottlieb Spangenberg*, 1906, 110.

96. *Journal* I, 220, n. 1 (May 22, 1736): 'Molther, on Jan. 25, 1740, returned the translation with a suggested alteration in one verse—"O love, thou bottomless abyss". Wesley adopted the alteration, and the hymn passed into the English Moravian book.' There is no confirmation of this in Wesley's *Diary* or *Journal*. This strengthening of the original word 'Abgrund' (abyss) in verse 4 by Molther is evidence of his attachment to quietist mysticism.

97. *Letters* I, 345–51, Aug. 8, 1740. A preliminary to this was the short letter, sketched out, but not sent, in Sept. 1738(!) full of critical questions: *Letters* I, 257f.

98. This exists in German in the *Buedingische Sammlung Einiger In die Kirchen-Historie Einschlagender*, sonderlich Neuerer Schrifften, Bd. III (XVIII Stueck, No. XXVIII), 1745, 136–852, and is dated Marienborn, Oct. 5, 1740. It remarks ironically: 'Although we do not really know to whom he refers in the letter, since the address is to Marienborn, and the inside direction to Herrnhuth, but Herrnhuth, as we have said, is a centre established by the Moravian Church, but in no sense the Moravian Church itself, much less the Sedes Episcopalis, or such a congregation for which the Moravian Church organization has to account for.' *Buedingische Sammlung* III (1745), 851. I also used the English version in the archives of the United Brethren at Herrnhut R13A 17, 10a.

99. *Buedingische Sammlung* III, 1745, 838.

100. Ibid. 836.

101. Ibid. 837. At this point the German text is sharper. The English says: 'The greatest of all Saints may fall tomorrow into all manner of enormities, if he think himself something upon account of this "Holiness".'

102. Ibid. 841: 'Belief in miracles requires an absolute πληροφορίαν without the least doubt, faith leading to blessedness remains always the same in the heart and hangs essentially on the wounds of Jesus, but it is in the mind, especially following the present manner of

conversion or rather the hundred methods, which in our time are subject to all kinds of usage . . .'

103. Ibid. 844: Societät.

104. Ibid. 845: 'A church . . . would be a congregation of sinners, who had received grace, forgiveness of sins, in the blood of Jesus.'

105. Ibid. Here too once again the leading place of 'herrlichen Sünderschaft' in Zinzendorf's theology.

106. Ibid. 846f.

107. Ibid. 846.

108. Ibid. 849–51.

109. *Journal* II, 378, Aug. 21, 1740.

110. *Letters* II, 12, Nov. 17, 1742, to Martha Hall; on Cennick, *Letters* I, 355, and William Leary *John Cennick* 1718–1755, Proc. Wes. Hist. Soc. XXX (1955), 30–7.

111. *Journal* II, 407, Dec. 16, 1740; II, 426–34, Feb. 22–March 8, 1741. Wesley's small numbers: *Journal* II, 410, Dec. 26, 1740.

112. Whitefield's decisive letter on behalf of predestination against John Wesley's sermon on Free Grace at Bethesda in Georgia, Dec. 24, 1740, took as its basis Galatians 2[11] and so aggravated the situation (*The Works of George Whitefield*, 1771, IV, 51–73.) He also raised independently some strong points, cf. 63: 'What if the doctrine of election and reprobation does put some upon doubting? So does that of regeneration. But is not this doubting a *good means* to put them upon *searching* and striving; and that striving for a good means to make their calling and their election sure? This is one reason among many others, why I admire the doctrine of election and am convinced that it should have a place in gospel ministrations, and should be *insisted on with faithfulness and care*. It has a natural tendency to rouse the soul out of its carnal security. And therefore many *carnal men cry out against it*. Whereas universal redemption is a notion sadly adapted to keep the soul in its lethargic sleepy condition, and therefore *so many natural men admire and applaud it*' (My italics). These passages must have affected John Wesley.

113. On this cf. my examination: *Das Erbauungsbuch The Whole Duty of Man* (1659) *und seine Bedeutung für das Christentum in England*. Theologia Viatorum VIII (1961–2), 232–77.

114. *Journal* II, 421f, Feb. 1, 1741, cf. later II, 441, Apr. 4, 1741; II, 439f, March 28, 1741; on the whole subject also Luke Tyerman, *The Life of the Rev. George Whitefield*, London, 2nd ed., 1890, I, 463–76.

115. *Journal* II, 429–34, Feb. 24–March 8, 1741. This is how the scenes must be understood, which from John Wesley's generally restrained

words (II, 429: 'being determined that no disorderly walker should remain therein') are not very clear.

116. Cf. esp. Samuel Eberhard, *Kreuzestheologie, Das reformatorische Anliegen in Zinzendorfs Verkündigung* 1937, 117ff, esp. 149ff.

117. *Journal* II, 451–3, May 2–6, 1741; *Journal* II, 456f, May 15, 16, 1741.

118. *Journal* II, 460, June 2, 1741; 461, June 5, 1741; 463, June 10, 1741; 464f, June 11, 1741; 472f, July 4, 1741; 467f, June 15, 16, 1741. 'Antinomianism' became the leading objection which Wesley made against the Herrnhuters. In this he came exactly into line with the polemic of the Halle theologians against them. (Cf. ch. 8 and n. 40.)

119. *Journal* II, 483f, Aug. 1, 1741.

120. *Journal* II, 488–90, Sept. 3, 1741. *Büdingische Sammlung* III, p. 1026 to 1030 (XVIIIth Stück) 1745, Supplement XXIX. Only one misprint is to be corrected: *Journal* II, 489, Wesley: Omnino lis est de verbis, correct in Büd. Slg. III, 1745, 1028.

The opinion of J. E. Hutton (*A History of the Moravian Church*, London 1909, 300), that Zinzendorf's first question: cur religionem tuam mutasti? means: why have you left the Church of England? is contradicted by the tenor and course of the conversation, even if a possible meaning of the words, because religio(n) in the eighteenth century, especially for Zinzendorf, meant fellowship of faith.

121. Cf. Otto Uttendörfer, *Zinzendorfs religiöse Grundgedanken*, 1935, 85ff, for the whole subject.

122. *The Declaration of Louis, Late Bishop and Trustee of the Brethren Church*, London, March, 43, *Büdingische Sammlung* III (1745), 852f.

123. On this much-discussed question cf. esp. Hans Joachim Iwand, *Rechtfertigungslehre und Christusglaube bei Luther*, 1930, 55ff; Eduard Ellwein, *Vom neuen Leben*, 1932; Johann Haar, *Initium creaturae Dei, Eine Untersuchung über Luthers Begriff der 'neuen Creatur' im Zusammenhang mit seinem Verständnis von Jak. i, 18 und mit seinem 'Zeit'-Denken*, 1939, esp. 68ff; Wilhelm Link, *Das Ringen Luthers um die Freiheit der Theologie von der Philosophie*, 1940, 2nd ed. 1945, 90ff. They carry further Karl Holl's insights (*Die Rechtfertigungslehre in Luthers Vorlesung über den Römerbrief*, 1910, Ges. Aufs. I, *Luther*, 1932, 111ff) and tie in esp. with Rudolf Hermann's investigation in *Luther's These Gerecht und Sünder zugleich*, 1930. Cf. also Erich Seeberg, *Luther's Theologie* II: Christus, Wirklichkeit und Urbild, 1937, 96ff, 158ff; Erich Vogelsang, *Die unio mystica bei Luther*, ARG 35 (1938), 72ff; and finally the important work by Axel Gyllenkrok, *Rechtfertigung und Heiligung in der frühen evangelischen Theologie Luthers*, 1952 (strongly critical of Haar and more mildly of Link, 121). In this connexion cf. also John Wesley's account of a

new opposition to his doctrine of perfection, which he met in London in 1763, in *Letters* IV, 204, Norwich, March 10, 1763, to Samuel Furly: 'A notion has lately started up in London, originally borrowed from the Moravians, which quite outshoots my notions of perfection as belonging only to fathers in Christ—namely that every man is saved from all (inward) sin when he is justified, and that there is no sin, neither anger, pride, nor any other, in his heart from that moment unless he loses justifying faith.

How will you disprove this position? In particular, by what New Testament authority can you overthrow it? These questions have puzzled many poor plain people.'

This also shows that—twenty-two years after the breach—Wesley was still concerned with the doctrinal issue.

124. Cf. O. Uttendörfer, *Zinzendorfs christliches Lebensideal*, 1942, 86ff.

125. In the final review of this relationship, which John Wesley drew up in 1744, he distinguished the three things which he besought the Herrnhuters to give up, since they contradicted Scripture: with regard to doctrine he condemned Antinomianism, in the sphere of discipline their blind obedience, which led to treating men as gods, and in their practice untruthfulness to one another, *Journal* II, 499f, June 24, 1744. The leading place given to antinomianism is thus clearly demonstrated. Cf. on this also C. N. Impeta, *De Leer van de Heiligung en Volmaking bij Wesley en Fletcher*, Leiden 1913, 276ff.

Erich Beyreuther, *Zinzendorf und die Christenheit* 1732–1760, Marburg–Lahn 1961, 258–60, sets out the separation completely from Zinzendorf's point of view, and seeks to put the blame on Wesley, and puts the blame upon him much too easily and summarily for the controversial writings and evil reports. He fails to see the decisive significance of the doctrinal issue. Clifford W. Towlson and this second volume of the biography of John Wesley seek to answer his desire for a fundamental investigation of the part played by the Herrnhuters in the Methodist revival.

126. At this point I must differ from the considered judgement of Clifford W. Towlson, *Moravian and Methodist*, 1957, 116f, who sees the doctrinal differences in the main only against the background of personal opposition and mistrust.

127. John Wesley describes the meeting with him, the great authority of Bath on gout, on Dec. 15, 1741, in the following words: 'It being a hard frost, I walked over to Bath, and had a conversation of several hours with one who had lived above seventy, and studied divinity above thirty years; yet remission of sins was quite a new doctrine to him. But I trust God will write it on his heart.' *Journal* II, 517.

128. This is fresh evidence against the displacement of the evangelical conversion, as represented by Piette and Rattenbury, from its dominating position. Many separate points can be adduced also. I mention only the following. In his second letter to his bitter critic, Bishop George Lavington of Exeter, written in Dec. 1751, he picks out the verse of Johann Andreas Rothe in order to describe the basis of his confidence:

> Now I have found the ground wherein
> Firm my soul's anchor may remain—
> The wounds of Jesus, for my sin
> Before the world's foundation slain.

This was a typical Herrnhut way of expressing it. *Letters* III, 302. He entered into a detailed discussion on justification with his old friend James Hervey, *Letters* III, 371–88, Oct. 15, 1756. On Aug. 14, 1771, he confessed to the Countess of Huntingdon: 'I know your Ladyship would not "servilely deny the truth." I think neither would I; especially that great truth justification by faith, which Mr Law indeed flatly denies (and yet Mr Law was a child of God), but for which I have given up all my worldly hopes, my friends, my reputation—yea, for which I have so often hazarded my life, and by the grace of God will do again.' *Letters* V, 274.

129. J. W., *An Extract of the Life of Monsieur de Renty, a late Nobleman of France*, 1741, 27f.

130. Richard Ridley apparently wholeheartedly accepted Molther's view about mystical stillness (*Journal* III, 19, June 6, 1742). On the other hand a month earlier (*Journal* III, 5, May 8, 1742) he had shown John Wesley a letter in which Samuel Meggot, later a successful Methodist lay-preacher, complained because he kept to continuing sinfulness and daily forgiveness, instead of laying hold of the purifying power of the Saviour in a state of salvation. As a consequence he regards the sins of the regenerate too lightly, and could not even be sorry about them, because he can always turn to his Saviour. Meggot cannot share this point of view. John Wesley inserted the letter in his *Journal*, apparently in order to indicate the gross nature of Molther's antinomianism (*Journal* III, 5–8: the letter is dated May 3, 1742). Wesley (*Journal* III, 19) made Ridley responsible for the confusion which had developed among the members of the religious society in his own native Epworth. He must have felt very much that it was destructive of the work begun by his father.

131. Cf. Ingham's objection against the Herrnhuters in *Richard Viney's Memorandum* IX = Proc. Wes. Hist. Soc. XIV (1924), 99, Apr. 8, 1744; the Herrnhuter's complaint about Ingham, because he had

anything to do with Wesley, ibid. XV (1926), 194, June 23, 1744. Cf. Clifford W. Towlson, op. cit., 133f.

132. *Journal* II, 427, Feb. 22, 1741, Bristol: the point of departure was the difference over justification. 'Mr. Cennick answered, "You do preach righteousness in man. I did say this; and I say it still. However, we are willing to join with you; but we will also meet apart from you; for we meet to confirm one another in those truths which you speak against." I replied, "You should have told me this before, and not have supplanted me in my own house, stealing the hearts of the people, and, by private accusations, separating very friends." ' *Journal* IV, 415, Oct. 12, 1760: 'I visited the classes at Kingswood. Here only there is no increase; and yet, where was there such a prospect till that weak man, John Cennick, confounded the poor people with strange doctrines?' Cf. the moving letter which Charles Wesley wrote in March 1741 to Cennick (printed in John Wesley's *Journal* II, 434).

133. See below.

134. *Richard Viney's Memorandum (and Diary)* 1744, VII, Proc. Wes. Hist. Soc. XIV (1923), 51. John Wesley repeatedly expressed his suspicions to James Hutton and William Holland. Shortly after the breach, in a letter to Hutton written on Nov. 14, 1741 (*Letters* I, 362–4), he said openly that Spangenberg, Molther and their associates had acted contrary to justice, mercy and truth. For it was quite unfair that they should invade the sphere of another man's labours and remodel it according to their own way. In order to make the point clearly he asked them to imagine that he, having learned German perfectly, should set himself up in the neighbourhood of Marienborn or even Herrnhut itself as a preacher against the known teaching of the Count. He found it merciless that valued friends, with whom they had grown up, men like Gambold, Hutchings, Kinchin, and his brother-in-law Westley Hall, should have been alienated. Finally they had been treated insincerely. On Feb. 6, 1748 (*Letters* II, 115f), he lamented to William Holland his surprise that the Herrnhuters continued to regard and treat him as their real enemy; however, he has committed the matter to God now. Wesley wrote in similar terms to him in a letter of Apr. 20, 1748; while he sought peace they made war; although they did not believe a word he said his desire was that this should strengthen them in his love (*Letters* II, 145).

135. Ibid. (see n. 134), Proc. Wes. Hist. Soc. XIV (1928), 18: 'With Mr. Westley I spoke to this effect: That I was excluded ye Moravian Church for some difference between us about Church Government

after I had first resigned my offices and been declared by Lot to be an enemy to ye good order of God in His Church and a Satan.' Cf. also ibid. XIV (1924), 98ff. On his occupation, which Towlson, op. cit., 144, gives as tailor, cf. his own *Memorandum* I, Proc. Wes. Hist. Soc. XIII (1921), 79: 'The Present State of things within my Knowledge. Of myself. First, my Employ is stay-making which I took to ye 12 Octo^r last, after having done nothing at it from May 1742. I have but little to do, but as much as I desire: for to stick close to it, in the 1st place I am now no more able, and 2dly it does not agree with my health to be continually sitting and 3rdly I think I shall not abide long at it.' Cf. also ibid. V, Proc. Wes. Hist. Soc. XIV (1923), 14: 'To Br Gussenbauer I told my Intent of going to London next Monday night, but not with what Intent. On the way, I visited Lady Margaret (Ingham) at Aberforth.' Wesley gives a somewhat more detailed account of the conflict with Spangenberg, based on Viney's own narrative. According to it Viney had expressed his considerations against the demand for strict obedience already in Feb. 1743, a demand which was raised in the Brethren Church in the name and under the authority of the Count. At the same time he had offered to lay down his office of Vorsteher of the Brethren Church and to become an ordinary member. Spangenberg had refused this, and Viney remained Vorsteher.

In May 1743, at a conference of 'church workers', i.e., of office-bearers, he was invited to resign. Then without his presence the two questions were discussed for four hours, as to whether he was not from Satan and as such an enemy of the church, and whether his opposition to church discipline did not arise from anger, egotism and pride. He was then called in and asked whether he was convinced that his objections were without foundation. This he denied and desired that the question should be decided by lot. The lot agreed with him: his objections were right. After this there was peace for six months. In November 1743 the case was once more taken up. The Brethren once more conferred together and sent a brother to him in order to let him know that he had been excluded from the Church, because he came from Satan and had raised objections against it from anger, egotism and pride (*Journal* III, 121, Feb. 19, 1744). There is much to be said for this account, not least that Spangenberg emphasized the fact that the excluding was to be confirmed by the church, and therefore in the first place Viney's offer to resign from his position of Vorsteher was declined; it was the church which had to decide who belonged to it and who were to be recognized as officers, not the individual.

136. Cf. his revealing self-revelation, ibid. II, Proc. Wes. Hist. Soc. XIII (1922), 109ff, Jan. 3, 1744: 'The Bre[n] Teltchig and Holland and their wives' diligence is as a Glass wherein I see more of my deformities. Had I been so when I came here as Vorsteher (Warden) I might have avoided much hurt and have attained ye end of our Saviour's shewing me the things he did, but poor silly wretch that I am, the least thing that is present to my mind is enough to employ it and draw it from everything else, how much more those great things which at that time presented themselves; but it should not have been so, I ought to have been ye more diligent in Labouring among Souls and my fellow labourers according to Plan which our Saviour shew'd me was better than that I saw faults in, and should not have let everything drop and look only at that I saw amiss till I knew not what was right or wrong.' Ibid., p. 110, Jan. 8, 1744.

'I have spent this day to little profit, and indeed have many days and weeks. May ye Lord Jesus forgive me all my Faults and bestow that favour on me again as to give me opportunity of doing something in his Vineyard! My Soul longs to speak something of him to others, but have no freedom in Heart to Vissit any of ye souls here, or Liberty from ye Brethren to Preach . . . I was anew convinced of my Fault, my great Fault, in giving up my office and withdrawing myself from ye Labour among souls. Should I be for ever set aside and not allow'd to do anything more in ye Work of ye Lord, I must own ye sentence just, but o Lord who didst *Look* on Peter, *appear* to Paul, and whose name is Love, Have mercy and restore me to that Priviledge which I have justly forfeited.' (Italics in the original.)

The same VIII Proc. Wes. Hist. Soc. XIV (1923), 83, Fri., March 9: 'A Report is spread that a Mob intends to come from Halifax and Bradford to destroy ye Houses and drive away ye Persons of ye Brethren, for as much as it is Rumour'd that we are all Papists and enemys to the Government. This has filled some with fear, and I am one of those weak ones.'

The same XII Proc. Wes. Hist. Soc. XV (1925), 72, June 4, 1744, where he comes across Democritus (=Robert Burton): *Anatomy of Melancholy*. Cf. ibid. XV (1926), 124 and 192.

137. Ibid. V = Proc. Wes. Hist. Soc. XIV (1923), 19, Feb. 19: 'I could not live in ye world alone, but must have fellowship with children of God.'

VI = ibid. XIV (1923), 26, Feb. 20: 'I could not live without fellowship.' To James Hutton he said on Feb. 24–March 6, 1744: 'I told him "I was the most miserablest man in ye World, that I was like Noah's Dove save in its Innocency; that I could find no Resting

Place no more than she, and was perswaded never should out of the Church; that I had been a few days with Mr. Westley, but that neither my Heart nor Mind was with him, nor likely to be; that in this I had not so good fortune as Noah's Dove, for tho I had sought to be receive'd as well as I was able and was convinced yet ye Bre^n would not yet receive me." '

138. Cf. Proc. Wes. Hist. Soc. XIV (1923), 13; his impetus towards spiritual work, *Memorandum* II, Proc. Wes. Hist. Soc. XIII (1922), 112, Jan. 15.

139. Charles Wesley, *Journal*, ed. Thos. Jackson (1849) I, 201, March 20, 1740.

140. R. Viney's *Memorandum* IV, Proc. Wes. Hist. Soc. XIII (1922), 187, Jan. 23, 1744. *Memorandum* V, Proc. Wes. Hist. Soc. XIV (1923), 17, Feb. 11, 1744.

141. The same VI ibid. XIV (1923), 26.

142. The same I ibid. XIII (1921), 79f; the same II ibid. XIII (1922), 109f; the same V ibid. XIV (1923), 15, 17; the same VII ibid. XIV (1923), 49; the same XIII ibid. XV (1926), 123; the same XIV ibid. XV (1923), 190.

143. *Viney's Memorandum* XII, June 9, 1744, Proc. Wes. Hist. Soc. XV (1925), 78: 'I do not find any Inclination to go to London to Mr. Westley's Conference, nor indeed to have anything further to do with him. I cannot see any real fundamental Difference between ye Count and him: true, in appearance, in Doctrine and in Practice there is difference, but in the main *Aim* of both I can see none. They both seem to seek to be Chiefs over great Numbers of People, but neither of them will own it. Whether ye Lord will excuse this, or whether have this so for ye sake of carrying on ye Great work in ye world, I am unable to determine . . . Did I know that the Lord would have it so, then I think, I would soon join wholly with one of em and own it to be right, but as I question this and cannot look on their aims other than ye effects of Pride, I seem most inclined to live a retired Life without having anything to do with either.'

Ibid. XIV (1924), 198f: 'My Mind seem'd more easy to-night than for some time past. Mr. Westley and all his Matters have appear'd to me as only ye Affects of a Cholerick Complexion which pushes him on to do and seek after great and high things. He appear'd to me as proud and arbitrary as Count Zinzendorf, only that from certain principles he had learned to conceal or make it appear otherwise than it is, whereas ye Count appears as he is. I say thus it has appear'd to me for some days, therefore I found no desire to join with him nor ye Count, but to go home and live a quiet life without having anything to do with any of them. But now it appears thus: True he is of a Cholerick Complexion and so is ye Count, they are Bold, they seem to take much upon them; But perhaps they are fitter for ye Lord's purpose than others. A Melancholick person tho he is suspicious of himself and so appears humble, yet he has no Courage sufficient to carry on a great work, for should he but come into a Melancholy fit he presently lets fall his hands, yea perhaps runs quite away. The Phlegmatig has not understanding nor seldom honesty enough to skreen him from ye world's laying notorious faults to his charge, neither is he active. The Sanguine are active enough and have understanding, but then he is ficle and unstable, fond of new things. So that the Cholerick seem to have been chiefly made use of in great undertakings and seem the fittest, but they are men, and what is peculiar of them (viz.) Pride or haughtyness often appears, but they generally effect ye things they begin, and ye Lord do's not make use of angels to preach or act Visibly among men, so perhaps these sort are ye best among men for such undertakings. These thoughts made me have favourable opinion of Mr. Westley and ye Count notwithstanding their Pride, and I seem'd freed from all antipathy to them.'

144. The same I ibid. XIII (1921), 79f.
145. *Viney's Memorandum* V = Proc. Wes. Hist. Soc. XIV (1923), 19, Feb. 19, 1744 = ibid. XIV (1923), 26, Feb. 20, 1744, John Wesley's *Journal* III, 121f, Feb. 19, 1744.
146. *Viney's Memorandum* V, Proc. Wes. Hist. Soc. XIV (1923), 19, Feb. 19.
147. Ibid. and op. cit. 26, Feb. 20.
148. The same VII op. cit. XIV (1923), 54, March 3.
149. The same V op. cit. XIV (1923), 19, Feb. 19; on early Christian communism cf. the same op. cit. XIV (1923), 29, Feb. 22: 'Mr. Westley intended to have gone to see ye Quaker's Workhouse & I with him, but time would not admit. That is said to be ye best to take a Plan from of any in London. He told me of an intention he and some few have of beginning a Community of Goods, but on a plan which I told him I doubted would not succeed. Tis thus: each is to bring what cash they have and put it together. If any owe small Debts, they are first to be paid. Then each abiding in their Dwellings and following their Business as they do now, are to bring weekly what they earn and put it into one Common box, out of which they are again to receive weekly as much as is thought necessary to maintain their Familys, without Reflecting whether they put much or little into ye box.'

150. The same XI op. cit. XIV (1924), 200, May 31.

151. The same IX ibid. XIV (1924), 98, Apr. 3, 1744; p. 100, Apr. 13, 1744; Ingham's objection, p. 100, Apr. 13, 1744.

152. Ibid. 101, new popery; ibid 98, Apr. 3; 100, Apr. 13: 'I was almost come to this Determination: First, that the basis of their Church Govt. was no better, but might prove of more dangerous consequences than they of Rome, and therefore I would as soon join now with ye Church of Rome as with them.' Doubt as to whether the affair of the Herrnhuters was of God: *Viney's Memorandum* XI, Proc. Wes. Hist. Soc. XIV (1924), 195, May 27.

153. This desire constantly returned: *Viney's Memorandum* X, Proc. Wes. Hist. Soc. XIV (1924), 144, May 22; on this occasion his wife reminded him of the lot of Jan. 29, which directed him to Wesley; the same ibid. 195, May 27, 198, May 29; the same XII, Proc. Wes. Hist. Soc. XV (1925), 78, June 9. He considered Lightcliff near Halifax, May 22, Proc. Wes. Hist. Soc. XIV (1924), 144.

154. The same XIV, ibid. XV (1926), 192, June 19, 1744.

155. Ibid. 193, June 19, 1744. Wesley's later judgement about him: *Letters* IV, 36, Oct. 4, 1758, to Francis Okeley.

156. *Viney's Copy of Wesley's Conference Agenda*, Proc. Wes. Hist. Soc. XIV (1924), 203.

157. For this cf. Wesley's great letter to the Moravian Church in England of June 1744 (*Letters* II, 20–3) and the letter to Benj. Ingham of Sept. 8, 1746 (*Letters* II, 80–4) in which he opposed 'stillness' in the sense of silent waiting and rejection of the ordinances of the Church, and corrected various points of fact.

158. Cookham, Nov. 27, 1750, *Letters* III, 52–8.

159. London, Sept. 6, 1745, *Letters* II, 40: this very clearly indicates both sides, the connexion and the limitation. Also the great letter of Feb. 2, 1745, to Thomas Church, *Letters* II, 176–86.

160. *Letters* II, 20–3, London, June 24, 1744.

161. *Letters* II, 82, Sept. 8, 1746, to Benj. Ingham: 'There has not been one day for these seven years last past wherein my soul has not longed for union.' A little later, in Dec. 1746, he read the first part of the agreement which Johann Philipp Fresenius (1705–61) made in Frankfurt/Main with Count Zinzendorf and the Herrnhuters under the title: Bewährte Nachrichten von herrnhutischen Sachen (1746–1751), and attributed to him concern for truth, good manners and love for others. *Journal* III, 274, Dec. 8, 1746: 'He writes both like a gentleman and a Christian; with mildness, good nature, and good manners; and yet with all plainness of speech, so as to place their pride, guile, and various errors in the clearest and strongest light.'

162. *Letters* III, 52.
163. *Journal* III, 499, Oct. 20, 1750. Fifteen months before he had still doubted whether the printing of some passages from his *Journal* in the Büding Collection of church-historical writings (1742–4), which Zinzendorf had arranged, and as reported to him on July 18, 1749, by the German (Palatinate) minister Miller in Cork (Ireland), was a mark of goodwill or of evidence against himself. *Journal* III, 409.
164. *Letters* II, 175, Bristol, Feb. 2, 1745, to Thos. Church; *Letters* II, 83, Sept. 8, 1746, to Benj. Ingham.
165. *Letters* II, 83, Sept. 8, 1746, to Benj. Ingham.
166. On this cf. Clifford W. Towlson, op. cit., 137f. The title 'The Contents of a Folio History of the Moravians or United Brethren, printed in 1749, and privately sold under the title of Acta Fratrum Unitatis in Anglia; with suitable Remarks.'
    I cannot agree with him that it is on so much a lower level than Wesley's usual tone that his authorship is unlikely. This is another case where the question of doctrine is central. But the main thing is that the author shows himself so well informed about the Herrnhuters as only John Wesley could have been. It is conceivable that the clergyman Vincent Perronet from Shoreham, the friend of the Methodists, wrote it, with the essential assistance of John Wesley. On Perronet's authorship cf. Leslie T. Daw, *Two Polemical pamphlets. Did Wesley write them?* Proc. Wes. Hist. Soc. XVI (1928), 101–4. His argument that the Commentary could not have been written by John Wesley because it begins by praising him, is not in the last resort sound.
167. (J.W.) *The Contents of a Folio History of the Moravians or United Brethren* (op. cit., see n. 166), p. 46.
168. Ibid. 18, 34f, 57f. A year earlier John Wesley—most probably from his own pen—had criticized the Herrnhut hymns about the wounds in our Lord's side in the pamphlet *Hymns Composed for the Use of the Brethren—By the Right Rev. and Most Illustrious C.Z. Published for the benefit of all mankind. In the year* 1749, cf. on this Leslie T. Daw, op. cit., p. 100.
169. (J.W.) *The Contents of a Folio History* . . .
170. Ibid. 45.
171. Ibid. 43ff.
172. Ibid. 17, 14, 12.
173. Ibid. 32.
174. Ibid. 48.
175. Ibid. 48, 14, 51.
176. Ibid. 21.

177. Ibid. 50.
178. Ibid. 7.
179. Ibid. 42.
180. Ibid. 58f.
181. Ibid. 31f.
182. Henry Rimius: 1. *A Candid Narrative of the Rise and Progress of the Herrnhuters, commonly called Moravians or Unitas Fratrum*, 1753. 2. *A Solemn Call on Count Zinzendorf*, 1754. 3. *A Supplement to the Candid Narrative . . .* 1755. 4. *Animadversions on sundry Flagrant Untruths advanced by Mr. Zinzendorf*, as a supplement to No. 3.
Journal IV, 68, May 22, 1753; 72f, June 11, 1753; 86, Oct. 8, 1753. In the same year, in the hymnbook which he and his brother Charles together issued (*Hymns and Sacred Poems by John and Charles Wesley*, 1756, 14–16), he allowed the hymn of praise on Herrnhut, with the title 'God's Husbandry', beginning 'High on his everlasting Throne The King of Saints his Works surveys', to stand. Verse 9 runs:

> He prospers all his Servants' Toils
> But of peculiar Grace has chose
> A Flock, on whom his kindest Smiles,
> And choicest Blessings, he bestows:
> Devoted to their Common LORD
> True Followers of the bleeding Lamb,
> By God belov'd, by Men abhorr'd
> And Herrnhuth is the fav'rite Name!

In his own copy (in the Library of Richmond College, Surrey, near London) Wesley wrote the words: 'It *was*! But how is ye fine Gold become dim?'

It is not clear whether the anonymous pamphlet from this time, *Queries humbly proposed to the Right Reverend and Right Honourable Count Zinzendorf*, London MDCCLV, was by John Wesley (cf. Richard Green, *The Works of John and Charles Wesley. A Bibliography*, London 1896 (2nd ed. 1906), no. 169, who answers the question in the affirmative). In favour of this is the fact that it opens with a letter to James Hutton written on Jan. 7, 1755 (pp. 3–6), although it can also be pointed out that in the London *Daily Advertiser* Hutton had stated that the Count was willing to reply immediately to points which had been raised against him. Further evidence is the clear formulation of the questions into ten large groups, yet without excessive emphasis upon doctrine. Finally there is the frequent mention of the two friends John Gambold and James

Hutton, who had gone over to the Herrnhuters. On the other side there is the bringing up of historical points, especially from the differences of the Herrnhuters over the domination of Isenburg-Büdingen and the very negative general tenor. Clifford W. Towlson (op. cit., 146) is not able to come to a definite conclusion.

The Queries are arranged in the following way: the first group concerns the names applied to the Count and his Church. The first asks directly whether he allows himself to be called 'the angel of the church of Philadelphia' (after Revelation 3[7]) (p. 7). In the second group the doctrine of the Trinity is discussed (pp. 9–22), and the subordination of God the Father to the position of an executive instrument for the will of the Son is sharply criticized (p. 10), as well as the ascription of creation and sanctification to the work of the Son (p. 9); further the assertion that the Apostles had not baptized in the Name of the Triune God, that prayer to God the Father was an address to a God of wood or stone and that the preacher of God the Father preached the faith of Satan (p. 9). The opinion that the Holy Spirit was the wife of the Father, and the Mother of Jesus and the Church, who sympathized with the failings of believers in a motherly way and concealed them from the Father, is dismissed (p. 10), together with the whole theatrical view of the world and manner of speaking which were common among the Herrnhuters (p. 11f).

The third group is concerned with the way of looking at Jesus Christ Himself. In the Herrnhut method of speaking about Him he is brought down too much to human dimensions, His weaknesses are exploited and the records about Him fantastically exaggerated. Above all the Herrnhuters do this in their description of His temptation in the Garden of Gethsemane, although it also applies to His temptation by Satan, for whom He was hardly a match, because on one occasion He gave him an impudent answer and in other respects was only ready with a few wretched recollections from Scripture. So the Son of God is deprived of the honour which belongs to Him (pp. 13–15).

The fourth group, which concerns the Apostles, raises the objection against the Herrnhuters that they degrade these immediate friends and followers of Jesus to the position of the first corrupters of the Church—a monstrous exaggeration of their denial at the time of his arrest by the high council. The author of the *Queries* is at this point impressed by the agreement between such views and those of the popular deism of the time (pp. 15–17, the similarity with the deists Arthur Collins and Thomas Woolston, p. 17). The author further inquires whether the Bible is not too little used in the Herrnhut churches and declared to be unnecessary, and so dishonoured (p. 17), whether gross faults are not attributed to the records of the four gospels, and if the Epistle of James has not disappeared from Zinzendorf's New Testament (p. 16). Is it not the case that according to the Count the first Christians did not merit the name of a Church, but were a body of legalists? (p. 16).

The fifth section, the shortest but actually the most important, repeats the charge of antinomianism, the prohibition of good works (pp. 18f), and an intoxicating delight in the wounds of Jesus, such as was cultivated at Herrnhag near Büdingen (p. 19).

In the sixth section the Brethren are reproached for practising a superstitious veneration for the wounds in Christ's side and they are asked whether the holes in the side are God? (p. 20). But the Herrnhuters are not only fallen into idolatry in this way, they also pray to the angels and sing hymns to Mary. They do not only worship the image of Jesus, but Anna Nitschmann had also used her picture with the congregation at Fetter Lane in London (p. 21). The custom of putting flowers with the cross as an adornment of the altar is a mixture of superstitious and romantic madness, and the same applies to using elaborate candle lights at festivals. Had they learned this from Paul? (p. 22).

There follows a consideration of the characteristics of the Brethren. Is not an affectation of secrecy the basis of their Church? Therefore dissimulation and lies are part of their natural attitude. So John Gambold, Wesley's former friend in the Oxford group of students, maintained, in spite of his knowledge to the contrary, that Count Zinzendorf had not seen certain hymns against which objections had been raised, although he had actually written them (pp. 23f).

Also straightforwardness in their dealings with their fellows was questioned by the author of the *Queries*. Had not the Brethren trained their members who possessed wealth to borrow large sums of money and so ruined many? Had not one of them suggested to Mr Rimius that he should give him a certain sum in order to stop libelling him? (pp. 25–7).

In the ninth section the Herrnhut way of speaking about sexual matters, which went back to Count Zinzendorf, was discussed, particular attention being given to that type of marriage in which all sexual activity is regarded as representative of the work of Jesus for the soul, and from which all kinds of doubtful practices stem (pp. 28–30).

The last group of queries is concerned with the way in which the

256

Brethren respond to difficult questions. The author would like to know whether the Count has instructed the Brethren to ward off all accusations as lies or mere fabrications. Is his method of opposing outside complaints by the hymns of his followers a way of refuting them, or is it an easy evasion? (pp. 31f).

In conclusion the author, in a grandiloquent gesture, gives Count Zinzendorf the possibility of stating, by maintaining his own silence, that he, the author, is justified in his objections (p. 32).

Does this fit in with John Wesley? Is this style of going into details over the objections, even if grouped together and arranged under leading categories, characteristic of him? I am not convinced about this. Particularly it seems unlikely to me that he would exploit the follies of the Büding-Herrnhag testing period as is done in the book, although Rimius could have acted as the source of information for this. But Christian charity is completely lacking. Except in the harsh letter of farewell to his wife which he wrote on Oct. 2, 1778 (*Letters* VIII, 273f), he never expressed himself so implacably as here. Even the *Commentary on the Acta Fratrum Unitatis in Anglia* of 1750, for all its vigorous summons to return to the Bible and to submit to its judgement, ended on a decisively Christian note.

183. *Journal* IV, 86, Oct. 8, 1753.

184. *Letters* II, 54. A similar plan was in existence since the Conference of June 30, 1744, cf. John Bennet's *Copy of the Minutes of the Conferences* of 1744, 1745, 1747, and 1748. Publications of the Wes. Hist. Soc., no. 1, 1896, 18.

185. *Journal* V, 40, 42. Apparently several attempts at closer relations took place during the sixty years, cf. *Letters* IV, 162, London, Sept. 8, 1761, to his brother Charles: 'I doubt not the Moravians will be courteous. And I fear that is all.' The Moravian bishop, David Nitschmann, whom he got to know on the voyage to Georgia 1735–6, also once again came into his field of vision. On Dec. 11, 1762, he wrote to his brother Charles: 'I should be glad to see Mr Nitschmann. What is all beside loving faith!' *Letters* IV, 197. It is not known whether a meeting took place. Nevertheless there were still differences of doctrine, especially over the relationship between justification and sanctification. Cf. *Letters* IV, 204, Norwich, May 10, 1763, to Sam Furly (see n. 123).

186. *Journal* V, 441, Dec. 21, 1771; *Letters* V, 294, Dec. 26, 1771, to James Hutton; cf. also his brief, and on the whole friendly, correspondence with Peter Böhler in 1775, *Letters* VI, 140f, London, Feb. 18, 1775. On the other hand he warned against the Herrnhuters in a letter to Mary Bishop on Nov. 27, 1770, *Letters* V, 209, London:

'I could not advise our people to hear Mr. Shirley, but still less to hear the Moravians. Their words are smoother than oil, but yet they are very swords.'

187. On this cf. William George Addison: *The Renewed Church of the Brethren 1722–1730*, London 1932, 194–224; Towlson, op. cit., 157ff and Leslie T. Daw: *The Later Cordiality of Methodists and Moravians*, Proc. Wes. Hist. Soc. XVI (1928), 161.

188. In Addison, op. cit., 195; Towlson, op. cit., 158.

Chapter 2: The Progress of the Evangelistic Movement

1. *Journal* II, 333, Jan. 21, 1740; 453, May 7, 1741, cf. also the particular use of 1 Corinthians 12²⁶ᵃ: *Journal* II, 347, May 17, 1740; *Journal* III, 116f, Feb. 17, 1744.

2. *Journal* II, 515f, Nov. 7–19, 1741. The opinion about Eusebius: 'But so weak, credulous, thoroughly injudicious a writer have I seldom found', agrees in many respects with present-day critical and historical judgement, cf. esp. Walter Bauer: *Rechtgläubigkeit und Ketzerei im ältesten Christentum*, 1934, 13–16, 49f, 193–5, etc., except that in the meantime the particular point of view, of which Wesley realized nothing, has been recognized.

3. *Journal* II, 519f, Jan. 1, 1742.

4. *Journal* II, 517, Dec. 9, 1741.

5. *Journal* II, 527, Feb. 4, 1742.

6. For Kingswood cf. *Letters* II, 299, 1748, to Vincent Perronet; for London, *Journal* II, 536, Apr. 9, 1742.

7. For John Nelson *Journal* III, May 25, 1742.

8. *Letters* II, 14f, Newcastle, July 12, 1743, to the Mayor of Newcastle-upon-Tyne: 'When I was first pressed by the Countess of Huntingdon to go and preach to the colliers in or near Newcastle, that objection immediately occured, "Have they no churches and ministers already?" It was answered, 'They have churches, but they never go to them! and ministers, but they seldom or never hear them! Perhaps they may hear you. And what if you save (under God) but one soul?"'

9. Samuel Wesley to James Oglethorpe, Epworth, Dec. 7, 1734, MS. in the archives of the S.P.C.K. in London, MS. I/cr 2, pp. 105–7 (note in margin: Read Jan. 1735): 'Hond. Sir, I can't express, how much I'm obliged by your last kind and instructive Letter concerning the Affaires of Georgia. I could not read it over without Sighing (tho i have read it several times) when I again reflected on my own age and infirmities which make such an Expedition utterly unpracticable

for me; yet my mind works hard about it, and 'tis not impossible but providence may have directed me to such an Expedient as may prove more serviceable to your Colony than I should have ever been. (106) The thing is thus, there is a young man who has been with me a pretty many years and assisted me in my work of Job, after which I sent him to Oxford to my Son John Westley Fellow of Lincoln College, who took care of his Education. Where he behaved himself very well and improved in piety and Learning: then I sent for him down, having got him into double Orders and he was my Curate in my Absence at London, where I resign'd my small Living at Wroot to him, and he was instituted and inducted there; I likewise consented to his marrying one of my Daughters there having been a long and intimate friendship between them, but neither he nor I were so happy as to have them live long together, for She dyed in Child bed of her first Child. He was so unconsolable at her Loss that I was afraid he would soon have follow'd her, to prevent which I desir'd his Company here at my own house that he might have some amusement and Business by assisting me in my Cure during my Illness. 'Twas then, Sir, I had just receiv'd the favour of yours, and let him see it for his diversion, more especially because John Lyndal and he had been fellow Parishioners and Schoolfellows at Wroot and had no little kindness one for the other. I made no great reflection on the thing at first but soon after when I found that he had thought often on it, was very desirous to go to Georgia himself, and wrote the inclosed Letter to me on that Subject, and I knew not of any person more proper for such an Undertaking, I thought the least I could do was to send the Letter to your honour who would be so very proper a Judge of the Affair, and if you approve of it, I shall not be wanting in my Address to my Lord Bishop of London or any other, since I expect to be in London my Self at Spring to forward the matter as far as it will go.

As for his character I shall take it upon myself, that he is a good Scolar and sound Christian and a good Liver, has a very happy memory especially for Languages and a Judgment and Diligence not inferior. My eldest Son at Tiverton has some knowledge of him concerning whom I have writ to him since your last to me. My two other his Tutor at Lincoln and my third at Christ (107) Church have been long and intimately acquainted with him, and, I doubt not but they will give him at least as just a Character as you have done. And here I shall rest the matter, till I have the Honour of hearing again from you, and shall either drop it or prosecute it as appears most proper to your maturer Judgment. Ever remaining

Your Honours Most sincere and most obliged Friend and Servant Sam. Wesley Sen.'

10. John Whitelamb to J.W., June 11, 1742, *Arminian Magazine* I (1778), 183f: 'Dear Brother, I saw you at Epworth on Tuesday Evening. Fain would I have spoken to you, but that I am quite at a loss how to address, or behave. Your way of thinking is so extraordinary, that your Presence creates an Awe as if you were an inhabitant of another World . . .'

Ibid. 185, Whitelamb to Charles Wesley, Sept. 2, 1742: 'For, to be frank, I cannot but look upon your Doctrines, as of ill Consequence. Consequence I say; for to take them nakedly, in themselves, and nothing seems more innocent, nay good and holy. Suppose we grant, that in You, and the rest of the Leaders, who are Men of Sense and Discernment, what is called the Seal and Testimony of the Spirit, is something real: yet I have great Reason to think, that in the generality of your Followers, it is merely the effect of a Heated Fancy.'

On this J.W. makes the comment: 'No wonder he should think so. For at that time and for some years after, he did not believe the Christian Revelation.'

11. *Journal* III, 13–24, May 27–June 13, 1742.

12. *Journal* III, 54, Dec. 4, 1742; cf. *Journal* III, 81, July 14, 1743.

13. *Journal* III, 55f, Dec. 20, 1742.

14. *Journal* III, 61f, Jan. 2, 1743. The interpretation of these scenes is a further proof for the decisive importance of the conversion of May 24, 1738 (against Piette and Rattenbury). Moreover it limits the importance of the 'high-church' periods in Oxford and Georgia. Both the liturgical and sacramental usages, such as the preparation of the wine at Communion and primitive fasting, were practised by Wesley as approximations to early Christianity without their distinctive anglo-catholic emphasis.

15. *Journal* III, 525, May 11, 1751. Romley became insane and died in an asylum, ibid. 525f.

16. *Journal* III, 63f, Jan. 13, 1743.

17. *Journal* III, 67, Feb. 18, 1743.

18. *Journal* III, 69, March 12, 1743.

19. *Journal* III, 83, Aug. 22, 1743.

20. John Wesley, *Works* XIII, 1831, 236. To the Printer of the *Dublin Chronicle*, Londonderry, June 2, 1789 (=*Letters* VIII, 140f). *Journal* III, 78, May 29, 1743, does not mention this.

21. Charles Wesley, *Journal*, ed. Jackson (1849), 328, July 26, 1743.

22. J.W. *Journal* III, 89, Sept. 3, 1743, in Treswithin Downs (Cornwall):

'It was here first I observed a little impression made on two or three of the hearers; the rest, as usual, showing huge approbation and absolute unconcern.'

23. *Journal* III, 94, Sept. 20, 21, 1743: 'The beauty of holiness' is from Psalms 29^2, 96^9, 110^3, and became the description of the Anglican liturgy, probably especially through William Laud (1573–1645).

24. *Journal* III, 92, Sept. 12, 1743. In the original the contrast comes out very clearly: 'For what *political reason* such a number of workmen were gathered together . . . I could not possibly devise; but a *providential reason* was easy to be discovered.'

25. *Journal* III, 97, Oct. 2, 1743. Here reference may be made to his reflections on his evangelistic activity as a whole from Ireland on June 1, 1760: 'I have now finished more than half my progress, having gone through two of the four provinces. Who knows whether I shall live to go through the other two? It matters not how long we live, but how well.' *Letters* IV, 97, Athlone, June 1, 1760, to Dorothy Furly.

26. *Journal* III, 127–32, Apr. 4–16, 1744; 181–94, June 16–July 16, 1745; 256–64, Sept. 1–18, 1746; 377–80, Sept. 15–30, 1748. The scene in Falmouth, July 4, 1745, *Journal* III, 188–90.

27. *Journal* VIII, 3, Aug. 18, 1789.

28. Whitefield's *Journal*, March 8, 1739, cites J.W.'s *Journal* II, 223f, n. 1.

29. *Letters* I, 323, July 2, 1739, to James Hutton.

30. *Journal* II, 292–6, Oct. 15–20, 1739: on Howell Harris and his invitation to J.W., *Journal* II, 223f, June 19, 1739.

31. *Journal* II, 341f, Apr. 7–12, 1740; 505–7, Oct. 1–6, 1741; 532f, March 1–6, 1742; *Journal* III, 29, July 5–7, 1742; 76f, May 3–8, 1743; 133f, Apr. 20–8, 1744; 195f, July 19–25, 1745; 250–3, Aug. 11–22, 1746.

32. *Journal* III, 312–16, Aug. 9–23, 1747. On the history of this Evangelical-Lutheran congregation in Dublin cf. Julius Rieger, *Deutsche Lutheraner in Dublin* in the parish magazine of the German evangelical churches in England, *Der Londoner Bote*, 58 (1953), pp. 149–51. From 1689 there were two Ev.-Luth. army chaplains there, the Norwegian Ever Diderich Brinck and the German Esdras Markus Liechtenstein. In 1697 the latter became civilian minister for the Germans. The congregation had only twenty people, and met in Marlborough Street. The morning service was held in one of the Scandinavian languages, the liturgy was the Holstein, since Holstein at the time belonged to Denmark. A correspondence belonging to the years 1718–25 is in existence at the Dutch Ev.–Luth. church in

Amsterdam, which was carried on by the German Ev.-Luth. pastor Andreas Kellinghusen in Dublin, who was obviously from Holstein. He asked for help for building a church and for a church-order, and supported this request by his personal presence in Amsterdam on March 16, 1718. In Wesley's time Pastor Miller, who was a Halle Pietist, was working there (cf. J.W.'s account of his conversation with him, *Journal* III, 347, Apr. 20, 1748). There were 280 members of the Society, *Journal* III, 314, Aug. 17, 1747.

33. *Journal* III, 312, Aug. 10, 1747.

34. Cf. Charles Wesley, *Journal* (ed. Jackson, 1849) I, 457ff, Sept. 9 and following days, 1747. On Ireland cf. the exhaustive work of Charles Henry Crookshank, *History of Methodism in Ireland*, 3 vols., 1885–8.

35. *Journal* III, 337–53.

36. *Journal* III, 338, March 16, 1748, Dublin: 'Let this be a warning to us all how we give in to that hateful custom of painting things beyond the life. Let us make a conscience of magnifying or exaggerating anything. Let us rather speak under than above the truth. We, of all men, should be punctual in all we say, that none of our words may fall to the ground.'

37. *Journal* III, 340, Apr. 1, 1748, Clare.

38. *Journal* III, 340, Apr. 3, 1748, Athlone.

39. *Journal* III, 349, May 1, 1748, Connaught.

40. *Journal* III, 344, Apr. 10, 1748, Athlone

41. *Journal* III, 350, May 3, 1748, Birr

42. *Journal* III, 342, Apr 6, 1748, Tyrrell's Pass

43. *Journal* III, 338, March 14, 1748, Dublin; 341, Apr. 5, 1748, Tyrrell's Pass; 344, Apr. 10, 1748, Athlone; 351, May 8, ibid.

44. *Journal* III, 352, May 9, 1748, Athlone.

45. *Journal* III, 340, Apr. 1, 1748.

46. E.g. *Journal* V, 204, Apr. 15, 1767, Armagh.

47. *Journal* V, 203, Apr. 9, 1767. Cf. also *Journal* III, 340, Apr. 2, 1748 Athlone.

48. *Journal* III, 344, Apr. 9, 1748, Connaught; 347, Apr. 23, 1748; 353, May 11, 1748, Dublin, similarly *Journal* V, 136, July 13, 1765, Clare, after reading Richard Cox's *History of Ireland*.

49. *Journal* III, 348, Apr. 26, 1748, he read the biography of Patrick, which he describes as 'most correct'.

50. *Journal* IV, 161, May 6, 1756, Kilkenny; cf. also *Journal* III, 400, May 17, 1749: 'I met the class of soldiers . . . Most of these were brought up well; but evil communications had corrupted good manners. They all said from the time they entered into the army

they had grown worse and worse. But God had now given them another call, and they knew the day of their visitation.'

51. *Journal* IV, 395, June 28, 29, 1760, Sligo; 398, July 17, 21, 1760; 400, Aug. 7, 1760; 502, May 2, 1762; 505, May 30, 1762; 506, June 7, 1762; 507, June 13, 1762; 508, June 27, 1762; *Journal* V, 413, May 27, 1771; 501, Apr. 8, 9, 1773.

52. *Journal* IV, 505, May 30, 1762.

53. *Journal* IV, 161, May 6, 1756, Kilkenny.

54. *Journal* V, 505, return to Limerick and neighbourhood, esp. Clare.

55. *Journal* IV, 168f. On Philipp Embury, born of German parents from the Palatinate (probably 'Imburg') possibly in Ballingrane, who was the first North American Methodist, and who lived from 1728–73, cf. D. Am. Biogr. 6 (1931), 125f.

56. *Journal* IV, 275f, June 23, 1758, Courtmatrix.

57. *Journal* IV, 396–8, July 9–16, 1760, cf. also *Journal* V, 131, June 14, 1765, Ballingarane; 207, May 21, 1767, ibid. J.W. was also with the Palatinates on June 4, 1762, ibid., and on May 13, 1789, in Pallas.

58. A characteristic indication of this is that the report was able to circulate that in his old age he became a member of the Freemasons' Grand Lodge of Ireland (as I was kindly informed by Fritz Blanke of Zürich). In fact J.W. condemned and derided Freemasonry as foolishness, *Journal* V, 514, June 18. The report is based upon one of the same name who joined the Lodge in Downpatrick in Oct. 1788, cf. Proc. Wes. Hist. Soc. VII (1910), 163. On Apr. 22, 1772, W. preached in the Freemasons' Lodge at Port Glasgow, *Journal* V, 455.

59. To this belonged e.g. the lax observance of Sunday. It surprised him that a Roman Catholic priest who opposed Sunday work should warmly commend card-playing on this day. *Journal* IV, 503, May 13, 1762, Athlone.

60. The Cork riots in May and June 1749 were particularly serious. Nicholas Butler, with the approval of the mayor, incited a fanatical Roman Catholic mob against Wesley and his followers. Also through much rough treatment a pregnant woman was caused to mis-carry, and another whose clothes were torn received many wounds. *Journal* III, 409–14; 464f, c.f. also *Letters* III, 43f, Dublin, July 21, 1750, to Ebenezer Blackwell.

61. *Journal* VI, 105, May 10, 1776, Glasgow; 106, May 19, 1776, Aberdeen; 235, May 30, 1779, Glasgow.

62. *Journal* III, 522–4, Apr. 24, 1751. The connexion between the natural characteristics of a country, the mountains and national history, so far as they affected the different kingdoms, was first recognized by J.W. in the year 1770. *Journal* V, 367f, May 14, 1770.

Among the historical monuments he was particularly impressed by the magnificent royal palace (demolished in 1808) in Scone (*Journal* V, 258, May 5, 1768, and 363, Apr. 23, 1770). It reminded him of the words of Thomas à Kempis: *Sic transit gloria mundi*, which he translated freely as: 'So passes the dream of human greatness.'

63. *Journal* IV, 216–18, June 1–6, 1757.
64. *Journal* IV, 316, May 26, 1759.
65. *Journal* V, 111, Apr. 22, 23, 1765. They concerned the Eleven Letters of James Hervey against Wesley and the Methodists, which William Cudworth published in 1759 after Hervey's death with his own additions and probably against the wishes of their author. They were the most vicious disparagement to appear from a former friend of the Methodists.
66. *Journal* V, 168, May 26 and June 1, 1766.
67. *Journal* V, 366, May 8, 1770, in Arbroath.
68. *Journal* V, 171, June 23, 1766; 169, June 5, 1766, in Dundee.
69. *Journal* V, 171, June 18, 1766, in Glasgow. On the subject of participation in the Divine nature cf. my essay of the same name in the Festschrift for Paul Althaus, *Dank an Paul Althaus*, 1958, 171–201.
70. *Journal* V, 454, Apr. 18, 1772.
71. *Journal* VII, May 18, 1788, in Glasgow.
72. *Journal* V, 366, May 12, 1770.
73. *Journal* V, 363, Apr 20, 1770.
74. *Journal* VI, 19, May 17, 1774, in Glasgow; *Journal* VI, 239f, June 17, 1779, in Edinburgh; 502, May 5, 1784, in Aberdeen.
75. *Journal* VI, 240.
76. *Journal* VI, 499, Apr. 25, 1784, in Edinburgh.
77. *Journal* VI, 20, May 21, 1774, in Perth.
78. *Journal* V, 458, May 5, 1772.
79. *Journal* VI, 22, May 30, 1774.
80. *Journal* VI, 501, May 3, 1784.
81. *Journal* VI, 236, June 2, 1779.
82. *Journal* VII, 387, May 13, 1788, in Dumfries.
83. *Journal* V, 456, Apr. 28, 1772, Perth; V, 458, May 6, 1772, Arbroath.
84. *Journal* VI, 23f, June 4, 1774, Edinburgh. The reason was that one of his preachers, John Saunderson, was said to have gained power over a woman and extracted money from her. The prosecutor was fined and Wesley soon freed, not from prison but from a house near by.
85. *Journal* V, 365, Apr. 30, 1770, minister at Nairn; the same VI, 238, June 8, 1779; *Journal* VI, 108, May 21, 1776, Keith; 107, May 20, 1776, Banff: clergyman of the Episcopal Church.
86. *Journal* V, 455, Apr. 22, 1772.

87. On this cf. the excellent book by Dugald Butler: *Wesley and White-field in Scotland*, 1898; he calls attention to the importance for Scottish Presbyterianism of the permanent relationship of the minister to his congregation, even although it is a matter of custom rather than principle.

88. *Journal* I, 412, Dec. 22, 1737.

89. Concerning him cf. Nils Jacobsson, *Bland Svenskamerikaner och Gustavianer. Ur Carl Magnus Wrangels Levnadshistoria 1727–1786*, Stockholm. Diakonistyrelses Bokförlag 1953, on his visit to John Wesley in Bristol on June 14, 1768, pp. 200–6. Allan Parkman, *Carl Magnus Wrangel och anglosachsisk väckelsefromhet*. Kyrkohistorisk Årsskrift 57 (1957), 101–35, esp. 104–22. Wrangel as founder of the Societas pro Fide et Christianismo 1771 brought English piety to the notice of Sweden. On Nov. 16, 1769, John Wesley gave to the Lund Professor, Johan Liden, who had visited him shortly before in London, a precise account of the Methodist movement. *Letters* V, 154–6.

90. *Arminian Magazine*, 1784, 615. Wrangel's letter of Oct. 10, 1771, to J.W. ends: 'I beg you, sir, to remember me kindly to all your friends not forgetting dear Kingswood.'

91. *Journal* V, 290, Oct. 14, 18, 1768.

92. *Journal* V, 331.

93. *Journal* V, 350f.

94. *Letters* V, 177, Lewisham, Jan. 25, 1770, to Ann Bolton; 182, London, Feb. 17, 1770, to Lady Maxwell; 183f, Lewisham, Feb. 21, 1770, to George Whitefield; 212, London, Dec. 14, 1770, to Mrs Marston.

95. *Journal* VII, 23, Sept. 30, 1784.

96. *Journal* VII, 15, Aug. 31, 1784; on this cf. John L. Nuelsen, *Die Ordination im Methodismus*, 1935, esp. 98ff.

97. Cf. *Letters* VII, 191, Bristol, Oct. 3, 1783, to the Preachers in America; *Letters* VII, 238f, Bristol, Sept. 10, 1784, to our Brethren in America; *Letters* V, 212, London, Dec. 14, 1770, to Mrs Marston.

98. Who this Thomas Naisbit was and what his position was in the Society is not known.

99. *Journal* III, 97, Oct. 3, 1743.

100. Herder, *Adrastea. Sämtliche Werke* (Suphan) XXIV.
    Zinzendorf-Gedenkbuch, pub. by Ernst Benz and Heinz Renkewitz, 1951, 46.

101. *Letters* V, 174, London, Jan. 2, 1770, to Mary Bosanquet: 'I am more inclined to hope than fear.'

102. *Letters* V, 181, London, Jan. 30, 1770, to Dr Wrangel.

103. The question of evangelization in North America: Richard Boardman offers to go to America. *Journal* V, 331, 350, 330 n., 331 n.; VI, 377 n.; VIII, 124 n.

104. A good example of the dominant synergism is in the Bishop of London's (Edmund Gibson) Pastoral Letter for Aug. 1, 1739: 'A diligent attendance on the duties of the station wherein Providence has placed them, is in the strictest sense, the serving of God.' P. 18: 'Nor need they any other evidence besides those good dispositions they find in their hearts that the Holy Spirit of God co-operates with their honest endeavours to subdue sin and grow in goodness; nor that, persevering in their course, and praying to God for his assistance, and relying upon the merits of Christ for the pardon of all such sins, failings, and imperfections, as are more or less unavoidable in this mortal state.'

105. Cf. esp. *The Life and Times of Selina Countess of Huntingdon*, by a Member of the House of Shirley and Hastings, 1841, I, 12: 'Nothing awakened greater attention to their preaching than their quitting the universal habit of reading their sermons from a book, without any animation, and addressing extempore discourses to the congregation where they ministered.'

Chapter 3: John Wesley as Organizer of the Methodist Movement

1. *Letters* II, 292–311, to Vincent Perronet 1748 (without date) = *A Plain Account of the People called Methodists* (*The Works of John Wesley*, 3rd ed. 1830, VIII, 248–71); cf. esp. *Letters* II, 294: 'Thus arose, without any previous design, on either side, what was afterwards called a Society; a very innocent name, and very common in London, for any number of people associating themselves together.'

2. Cf. as a significant example of this: *Account of the Experience of Hester Ann Rogers and her Funeral Sermon by Rev. T. Coke*, New York 1832, esp. 19.

3. *Letters* II, 301, in association with *Journal* II, 528, Feb. 15, 1742.

4. *Letters* II, 297f.

5. *Letters* II, 299.

6. Cf. Vol. I, 231ff.

7. *Letters* II, 302, 300.

8. *Letters* II, 304: 'My design was, not only to direct them how to press after perfection, to exercise their every grace and improve every talent they had received, and to incite them to love one another more, and to watch more carefully over each other, but also to have a select

266

company to whom I might un-bosom myself on all occasions without reserve.'

9. At the same time it is important to note that the 'bands' were not original to Herrnhut, but, like the lot, came from the ancient Moravian tradition. It is noteworthy that this circumstance, to which Count Zinzendorf himself drew attention, has been so far universally overlooked. The Count originally had a different purpose. In the sense of the Lutheran tradition he had taken as the basis of the organization of his community an *external* factor, the house neighbourhood. The attention of the Moravian Brethren centred upon an *inner* factor, spiritual growth and acquired maturity, which were in line with early and medieval monasticism. The 'bands' are the Pietist corrective of Lutheran prosiness.

Cf. Ludwig Graf Zinzendorf, *Naturelle Reflexiones* (1747), p. 153f; 'The ancient community was divided into classes according to the proximity of the houses, and the Moravian Brethren arranged small companies amongst themselves according to the inner Profectibus, and these were called bands.' In spite of this the statement made by me in Vol. I, p. 231, about the origin of the bands on July 9, 1727, remains true. At that time they were applied to the whole Herrnhut community. Cf. Herrnhuter Diarium 1727 in Gottfried Schmidt, *Die Banden oder Gesellschaften im alten Herrnhut*, Zeitschrift f. Brüdergeschichte III (1909), p. 146f; and most recently Johannes Wollstadt, *Die Ämter im alten Herrnhut*, Theol. Diss. Leipzig 1965 (typewritten).

10. *Letters* I, 272f, Oxon., Nov. 26, 1738, to James Hutton.

11. *Letters* I, 274, Oxon., Nov. 27, 1738, to the same.

12. Cf. *Journal* I, 39, no date.

13. Cf. Otto Uttendörfer, *Alt-Herrnhut. Wirtschaftsgeschichte und Religions-soziologie Herrnhuts während seiner ersten zwangig Jahre 1722–1742*, 1925.

14. Cf. my article *Speners Wiedergeburtslehre*, ThLZ 76 (1951), 23.

15. *Journal* II, 429, Feb. 24, 1741, Bristol.

16. *Letters* II, 300.

17. Cf. John H. Verney, *Early Wesleyan Class Tickets: Comments and Catalogue*. Proc. Wes. Hist. Soc. XXXI (1957–8), 2–9; 34–8; 70–3.

18. Printed in John Wesley's *Works*, 3rd ed. 1830, VIII, 269–71, and in John S. Simon, *John Wesley and the Methodist Societies*, 1923, 100–3.

19. Matthew 25[31]ff.

20. *Works*, 3rd ed. 1830, VIII, 272f, *Rules of the Band-Societies* (Dec. 25, 1738).

21. Cf. my article, *Biblizismus und natürliche Theologie in der Gewissens-lehre des englischen Puritanismus,* Archiv f. Reformationsgesch. 42 (1951), 198–219; ibid. 43 (1952), 70–8.

22. *Works,* 3rd ed. 1830, VIII, 273f. *Directions given to the Band-Societies* (Dec. 25, 1744).

23. *Letters* II, 303. How close John Wesley came to the original German Pietism is seen from an undated letter by Johann Caspar Schaden (1666–98) to students (presumably in Halle). It runs: 'Let us be sober and consider well! we stick fast in many gross and subtle hypocrisies. The name of the so-called Pietists is by this time almost suspected, not so much by the world as by those who are chosen from the world to a righteous life in Christ Jesus. Most have the appearance of a godless life, but they deny its strength . . . (191) . . . The spirit of truth can do no other than rebuke the world. Hypocrisy and adulation come from the spirit of anti-Christ . . . It is unfortunately a great lack and fault that nobody has as yet sought to improve another by brotherly reprimand, or that nobody has been helped by such persuasion. This indicates that there is no true love of the brethren or fellowship or humility which can bring it about. Our meetings together ought to lead to such mutual edification. But you know, beloved, what happens with them now. Would it not therefore be good if you really met together in confidential love so that each could freely open his heart to the others?' (Johann Caspar Schaden's *Lehr- und Trostreiche Sendschreiben* 1721—included in J. C. Schaden's *Geistreiche und Erbauliche Schriften* III—pp. 190–5, LXVI. Letter, pp. 190f.)

24. *Journal* III, 284f, March 9–11, Newcastle: 'I examined the classes. I had been often told it was impossible for me to distinguish the precious from the vile, without the miraculous discernment of spirits. But I now saw, more clearly than ever, that this might be done, and without much difficulty, supposing only two things: first, courage and steadiness in the examiner; secondly, common sense and common honesty in the leader of each class.' By steadiness I take it that Wesley means trustworthiness of judgement, freedom from all partiality and the logical consequence of the whole attitude.

25. *Letters* II, 300ff. The appeal to early Christianity ibid. 294ff, 298f, 300, 303, 306.

26. Ibid. 304 (Section VIII, 3): 'No peculiar directions were therefore given to them, excepting only these three: (1) Let nothing spoken in this Society be spoken again. Hereby we had the more full confidence in each other. (2) Every member agrees to submit to his Minister

in all indifferent things. (3) Every member will bring once a week all he can spare toward a common stock.'

27. *Journal* II, 273, London, Sept. 9, 1739.
28. *Letters* II, 305f. Section X, 3, 4. On stewards cf. *John Bennet's Copy of the Minutes* (Publications of the Wes. Hist. Soc. 1), 1896, 16f. On all the following cf. Theophil Funk, *Die Anfänge der Laienmitarbeit im Methodismus*, 1941 (Beitr. z. Gesch. des Methodismus 5), 48ff.
29. *Journal* III, 300, June 4, 1747, in London.
30. Ibid. 301.
31. *Letters* II, 306f, Bennet 17.
32. Cf. ibid. 306 (Section XI, 4): 'It is the business of a Visitor of the sick,—To see every sick person within his district thrice a week. To inquire into the state of their souls, and to advise them as occasion may require. To inquire into their disorders, and procure advice for them. To relieve them, if they are in want. To do anything for them which he (or she) can do. To bring in his accounts weekly to the Stewards.' The precision is noteworthy.
33. The question as to who were the oldest lay-preachers in Methodism has been disputed. Against the older view, represented especially in the semi-official biography of the patroness of (Whitefieldian) Methodism, Selina, Countess of Huntingdon (*The Life and Times of Selina, Countess of Huntingdon*, by a Member of the Houses of Shirley and Hastings, 1841, I, 32f) that Thomas Maxfield made the beginning, Luke Tyerman, *The Life and Times of John Wesley* I, 1876, 274–6, whom I follow, argued strongly. The choice of Maxfield is understandable, because of his unusual gift for preaching and extempore prayer. John Wesley's mother was instrumental in restraining her son when he wanted to silence the young man, who had not been regularly called, from speaking in the meeting (cf. Thomas Coke and Henry Moore, *Life of John Wesley*, 1792, 219f; Henry Moore, *Life of John Wesley*, 1824, I, 507).

The problem of the date of Maxfield's debut as a preacher in the London Foundery, Wesley's main centre for meetings, is discussed with exemplary care by Frank Baker, *Thomas Maxfield's First Sermon*, Proc. Wes. Hist. Soc. XXVII (1949–50), 7–15. There are two possibilities, (a) at the end of Dec. 1740 or the beginning of January 1741, (b) Feb. 17, 1741. Neither would make him the first lay-preacher Cf. the careful discussion in Theophil Funk, op. cit., p. 119–31, with which I am in full agreement.
34. Only later was one lay-preacher appointed as Superintendent over the others. *Works* VIII, 319–21 (Minutes of Several Conversations 1744–89. The Large Minutes Qu. 40–4).

35. The comparison of the agendas of the early conferences, given originally by John Bennet and revised by John Wesley (Minutes of Several Conferences (The Large Minutes)), *Works* VIII, 319–21, gives an insight into the development.

36. 'Lay Assistants', Bennet, 15. 'Helpers', *Works*, 1830, VIII, 309; Twelve Rules of a Helper.

37. Bennet, 15: 'Touch no woman; be as loving as you will, but hold your hands off 'em. Custom is nothing to us.'

38. *Large Minutes*, Qu. 27 (*Works*, 1830, VIII, 310): 'Count Zinzendorf loved to hold all things close; I love to do all things openly.'

39. Bennet, 15, Qu. 3, A.2.

40. Ibid. 17, Qu. 7, A.7.

41. *Works*, 1830, VIII, 309. Later he puts prayer before the requirement of consultation with the brethren. Cf. George Latham, *The Twelve Rules of a Helper*, Proc. Wes. Hist. Soc. VII (1910), 82.

42. Latham, ibid. To be sure he only concentrates on the later modifications. Of the alterations made immediately the following two are noteworthy: Rule 4 ran originally: 'You know the judge is always allowed to be on the prisoner's side.' John Wesley substituted 'supposed' for 'allowed', Bennet 15. In Rule 12 the final sentence runs: 'Above all, if you labour with us in our Lord's vineyard, it is needful you should do that part of the work (which) we prescribe at those times and places which we judge most for His glory.' Wesley changed 'prescribe' for 'direct', Bennet 16.

43. *Works*, 1830, VIII, 309.

44. The strongest evidence for this is Wesley's constant preoccupation with Peter King's *Inquiry into the Constitution, Discipline, Unity and Worship of the Primitive Church* 1691 and Edward Stillingfleet's *Irenicum* 1659.

45. *Works*, 1830, VIII, 309.

46. His brother Charles saw this very clearly, even if not immediately; cf. his letter to the clergyman Samuel Walker of Truro, dated Bristol, Aug. 21, 1756, printed in Proc. Wes. Hist. Soc. XV (1925), 70f: 'Lay-preaching, it must be allowed, is a Partial separation, and may, but need not, end in a Total one. The Probability of it has made me tremble for years past and kept me from leaving the Methodists. I stay not so much to do good, as to prevent evil. I stand in the way of my Brother's violent Counsellors, the object both of their Fear and Hate . . . All I can desire of him, to begin, is

    1. To cut off all their Hopes of his ever leaving the Church of England.

2. To put a stop to any more new Preachers, till he has entirely regulated, disciplined and secured the old ones.
If he wavers still and trims between the Church and them, I know not what to do. As yet it is in his Power if he exert himself to stop the evil. But I fear he will never have another opportunity. The Tide will be too strong for him and bear him away into the Gulph of separation.'

47. *Letters* II, 295, to Vincent Perronet 1748. Once again it becomes clear from it what great significance the idea of mission and the experience of mission had all the time for him. Cf. my study, *Der junge Wesley als Heidenmissionar und Missionstheologe*, 1955, 40.

48. *Letters* III, 184, Bristol, Aug. 31, 1756, to Robert Marsden: 'These preachers are not ministers: none of them undertakes single the care of an whole flock, but ten, twenty, or thirty, one following and helping another; and all, under the direction of my brother and me, undertake jointly what (as I judge) no man in England is equal to do alone.'

49. Mark 6^1.

50. Bennet 16, Qu. 4: 'Should all our Assistants keep journals? By all means, as well as for our satisfaction as for the profit of their own souls.' Reference to Baxter's *Gildas Salvianus or The Reformed Pastor*, *Works*, 1830, VIII, 302f, 315. The *Gildas Salvianus* is in Richard Baxter's *Works*, ed. William Orme, 1830, vol. XIV, 273ff. On the Puritan family-theocracies cf. Levin Ludwig Schücking, *Die Familie im Puritanismus*, 1929.

51. Bennet, 17f, Qu. 14.

52. It is very difficult to assess the extent of John Wesley's reading in Christian literature. One often gets the impression that it was somewhat casual. Obviously he read everything he came across, and not only tried but succeeded in gaining a positive meaning from every reference. For the attention given to Pascal in his parents' home the account of his mother of a period of religious instruction with her daughter is revealing: *Mrs. Wesley's Conference with her Daughter. An Original Essay by Mrs. Susannah Wesley. Hitherto unpublished*, ed. G. Stringer Rowe, in *Publications of the Wesley Historical Society*, no. 3, 1898, 39.

53. He did this in the monumental publication: *A Christian Library* (50 volumes), 1749–55, the literary precursor of Everyman's Library and the issue of cheap editions. On this cf. Ferdinand Sigg, *John Wesley und die 'Christliche Bibliothek'. Einblicke in die verlegerische Tätigkeit des Methodismus im 18. Jahrhundert*. Schweizer Evangelist, 1953, 381–5.

54. *Works*, 1830, VIII, 315. Wesley was very critical on occasions of the education of his time; cf. *Journal* III, 284, March 4, 1747: 'This week I read over with some young men a Compendium of Rhetoric and a System of Ethics. I see not why a man of tolerable understanding may not learn in six months' time more of solid philosophy than is commonly learned at Oxford in four (perhaps seven) years.' On Wesley's efforts to educate his people cf. also Thomas Jackson, *Centenary of Wesleyan Methodism*, 1839, 114. Leslie F. Church, *More about the early Methodist People*, 1949, 47, and on the whole question also Alfred H. Body, *John Wesley and Education*, 1936, esp. 33ff.

55. *Works*, 1830, VIII, 314.

56. *Letters* III, July 20, 1751.

57. *Works*, 1830, VIII, 219f (*A Farther Appeal to Men of Reason and Religion*, 1745).

58. *Journal* III, 531–3, Bristol, July 8, 1751. *Letters* III, 69, Bristol, June 25, 1751; Charles Wesley's *Journal*, ed. Thomas Jackson (1849), II, 84, June 28, 1751; ibid. II, 101, July 10 and 11, 1754.

59. *Letters* III, 71, London, Aug. 3, 1751.

60. Richard Baxter (1615–91), Congregationalist minister at Kidderminster near Birmingham, chief representative of late Puritanism, highly respected by representatives of all ecclesiastical parties of his time. He wrote the classical work on pastoral theology, to which Wesley here refers, under the title: *Gildas Salvianus: The Reformed Pastor*.

61. *Letters* VI, 271, reproduced from Sutcliffe's manuscript *History of Methodism*, p. 468.

62. *Letters* VI, 271f, Bristol, Aug. 6, 1777, to Alexander Mather.

63. *Letters* II, 146–9.

64. *Letters* V, 243–51, Limerick, May 18, 1771.

65. Cf. esp. *Journal* V, 404–6, Dublin, March 29, 1771.

66. *Richard Viney's Memorandum* (*Diary 1744*), printed in Proc. Wes. Hist. Soc. XIV (1923), 19: 'I could not live in the world alone, but must have fellowship with children of God.'

67. Ibid. 204f, June 3 (1744). I must admit that this point is not conclusive. It is quite possible that John Wesley conceived the idea of a conference independently of Zinzendorf. Nevertheless the late point in time and the general dependence upon the example of Herrnhut seems to me to argue for this. There is no previous reference to the plan in Wesley's *Journal*; on the other hand Viney's *Diary* contains all the points necessary to explain the surprising invitation to one who was only half-committed. The completely naïve character of

Viney's notes are a further point in favour. In any case Viney printed the projected Agenda, op. cit., 201–3.

68. It is noteworthy that Clifford W. Towlson in his basic investigation in *Moravian and Methodist* (1957) overlooks this point.

69. Cf. Gerhard Reichel, *August Gottlieb Spangenberg*, 1906, 99.

70. Cf. *Die evangelischen Kirchenordnungen des XVI. Jahrhunderts*, ed. by Emil Sehling: Vol. I, 1902, 142f, ibid. 176f, 187, 210, 460, 507–9; Vol. II, 1904, 80f; Vol. III, 1909, 40f; Vol. IV, 1911, 30, 42f, 48 and 52, 292, 298, 329; Vol. V, 1913, 147f, 335; Vol. VI, 1, 1955, 14f, 22f. The point is especially clear in the Calenberg-Göttinger Kirchenordnung of 1542, ibid. Vol. VI, 2, 1957, 710–17; cf. also that of Riga 1530, drawn up by Johann Briessmann, ibid. Vol. V, 1913, 12f: 'Ceremonies should be none other than a public incitement to the gospel and faith'; cf. also my essay, *Die Reformation Luthers und die Ordnung der Kirche*, in *Im Lichte der Reformation* II, 1959, 5–31.

71. *Richard Viney's Memorandum* 1744 in Proc. Wes. Hist. Soc. XIV (1924), 205.

72. Bennet, op. cit., 7.

73. Ibid. On the ordination problem cf. the excellent monograph by John L. Nuelsen, *Die Ordination im Methodismus*, 1935 (Beitr. z. Gesch. des Methodismus 2).

74. *Works*, 1830, VIII, 310. In his monumental work *Histoire du peuple anglais en 1815* (which I used in the English translation by E. J. Watkin and D. A. Baker, 1924, 361, entitled *A History of the English People*) Elie Halevy maintains that the real, basic unit in the structure of Wesleyan Methodism was the circuit, headed by the superintendent, and not the society. The sources all make this improbable. As one devoted to early Christianity Wesley held to the principle of the congregation.

75. Bennet, op. cit., 35f (Headingley Minutes), also in John S. Simon, *John Wesley and the Methodist Societies*, 1952, 323f.

76. On this cf. John S. Simon, *John Wesley, the Master Builder*, 1927, 208f.

77. *Works*, 1830, VIII, 312, *Minutes of Several Conversations* 1744–89 (Large Minutes).

78. I regard this reason as absolutely decisive and regret that it has not yet been noted. As a restorer of primitive Christianity John Wesley becomes perfectly comprehensible at this point, and this explains his 'dictatorship'. The constantly recurring authoritative and monarchical character of the structure of the early Church, which sprang from the immediate, absolute authority of the charisma as a miracle, has been repeatedly emphasized. Cf. esp. Wilhelm Löhe, *Aphorismen*

über die neutestamentlichen Ämter, 1848–9 (*Ges. Werke*, hg. v. Klaus Ganzert V, I, 1954, 262ff); Rudolf Sohm, *Kirchenrecht* I, 1892, 54ff; Martin Schmidt, *Kirchenverfassung und Kirchenrecht im Lichte des Urchristentums*, Sächs. Kirchenblatt N.F.I (1937), 333ff; Hans von Campenhausen, *Kirchliches Amt und geistliche Vollmacht in den ersten drei Jahrhunderten*, 1953, esp. 27ff, who skilfully works out the uniqueness of the authority of Jesus (in spite of its difference from that of those he commissioned) as the true source for any understanding of the ministry. In an interesting way he comes to the same essential position as that occupied by Lancelot Andrewes (1556–1626), the father of the old anglo-catholicism. (Cf. Lancelot Andrewes, *Minor Works* (Library of Anglo-Catholic Theology), 1846, 351ff.)

79. *Works*, 1830, VIII, 313.

80. *Journal* III, 390, Feb. 5, 1749, at Hayes (Wiltshire); ibid. III, 404, June 2, 1749, at Bandon (Southern Ireland); *Gentleman's Magazine and Historical Chronicle*, 61 (1791), I, 250–3. Here too there is a parallel with German Pietism; Christian Ernst Kleinfeld wrote in 1726 a controversial piece, a public disclosure of those facts because of which he believed the Pietists were Jesuits.

81. *Journal* III, 129, April 7, 1744, at Rosemergy (Cornwall); III, 132, April 16, 1744, at Trewint (Cornwall); III, 191, July 4, 1745, at Wendron (Cornwall); III, 224, Nov. 8, 1745, at Bradbury Green (Cheshire).

82. John S. Simon, *John Wesley and the Methodist Societies* (1952, 105–113), shows in detail that Wesley's Rules did not fundamentally correspond to those of the religious societies in the Anglican tradition, but to the picture of primitive Christianity in the standard Anglican work by William Cave, *Primitive Christianity* (1672), against which Gottfried Arnold wrote his *Erste Liebe der Gemeinen Jesu Christi* (1696), because it idealized the situation inadmissibly (see esp. p. 6f); cf. also Erich Seeberg, *Gottfried Arnold, Die Wissenschaft und die Mystik seiner Zeit*, 1923, 240–2. The question as to the models for John Wesley's 'classes' cannot be decided with absolute certainty. Their immediate connexion with the Herrnhut 'bands' is clear. In spite of Simon at least something must have been owed to the religious societies of the Anglican Church (from 1678–9), if for no other reason than that John Wesley's father, Samuel Wesley, the Anglican rector of the village of Epworth in Lincolnshire, was their warm friend and promoter, as well as their adviser and organizer for the county. He was one of the first corresponding members of the Society for Promoting Christian Knowledge. Cf. his handwritten

letters preserved in the archives of the Society (now the publishers S.P.C.K.) in London (Abstract of Letters 1699–1701, p. 11, March 22, 1699) and Reports (MSS. Wanley ibid., pp. 186–94: An Account of the Religious Society begin (*sic*) in Epworth in the Isle of Axholm, Lincsh. Febr. 1, 1701/2 and ibid., pp. 145–53: An Account of a society of some of the Clergy and others in Lincolnshire for the promoting Christian Knowledg (*sic*)—with no date, but probably from the end of the year 1700). The reports of Samuel Wesley show that he at first despaired of forming from the congregation at Epworth a gathering of serious Christians according to the principles of the religious societies, and that it was after he read about a similar congregation at Romney in Kent that he founded a society. From his earliest childhood John Wesley was constantly reminded of such gatherings of decided Christians. He grew up from the cradle with the idea of classes. Henry Bett (*A French Marquis and the Class Meeting*, Proc. Wes. Hist. Soc. XVIII (1931–2), 43–5) wanted to derive Wesley's classes directly from the Roman Catholic brotherhoods of the French Count Gaston Jean-Baptiste de Renty from around 1640. It is correct to say that there was similarity in the object, but less in the form they took (on this cf. my article, *John Wesley und die Biographie des französischen Grafen Gaston Jean-Baptiste de Renty*, Theol. Viat. (Jahrb. d. Kirchl. Hochschule Berlin) V (1953–4), 213f. The rules of the religious societies are given in Richard Kidder, *The Life of the Rev. Anthony Horneck*, 1698, 13–16, and in Richard B. Hone, *Lives of Eminent Christians* II, 1850, 309–12, Garnet V. Portus, *Caritas Anglicana or An Historical Enquiry into those Religious and Philanthropical Societies that flourished in England betw. 1687 and 1740*, 1912, App. VI, pp. 255–8. In the following loyalty to the Anglican Church is emphasized (pp. 13f in Kidder):

III. That they chuse a Minister of the Church of England to direct them.

IV. That they shall not be allowed in their meetings to discourse of any controverted point of Divinity.

V. Neither shall they discourse of the Government of Church or State.

VI. That in their meetings they use no Prayers but those of the Church, such as the Litany and Collects and other prescribed Prayers; but still they shall not use any that peculiarly belongs to the Minister, as the Absolution.

VII. That the Minister whom they chuse shall direct what practical Divinity shall be read at these meetings.

VIII. That they may have liberty, after Prayer and Reading, to sing a Psalm.

IX. That after all is done, *if there be time left*, they may discourse each other about their spiritual concerns; but this shall not be a standing Exercise, which any shall be obliged to attend unto. (My italics!)

The last direction is especially revealing; pastoral conversation, which is given a subordinate position and which is not held to be essential, becomes central in Methodism.

When George Whitefield in 1744 maintained an identity between the Anglican religious societies and the Methodist, he did so to ward off an attack which described the Methodist groups as dangerous and objectionable innovations, but at the same time praised the religious societies (George Whitefield, *Works*, 1771, IV, 123–40, esp. 137). Apologetic of this sort cannot be used as evidence.

83. *Journal* VIII, 331–4, John William Fletcher to John Wesley, Thursday afternoon, Aug. 1, 1775.

84. One subordinate point shows how carefully the whole scheme was considered in the spirit of primitive Christian dynamism and Anglican institutionalism; the lay helpers are to be ordained as deacons, *Journal* VIII, 333.

85. *Journal* VIII, 328f.

86. It remained so, even though Benson (*Journal* VIII, 329) advocated ordination by John Wesley and thus raised him with his Anglican fellow-ministers to the status of bishop.

87. *Journal* VI, 73, Aug. 1, 1775, Leeds.

88. MS. in the Wesley Research Library, City Road, London. On the subject of the Methodist autobiographies cf. also T. B. Shepherd, *Methodism and the Literature of the 18th Century*, 1940, 141–62.

89. On this cf. Martin Schmidt, *Biblizismus und natürliche Theologie in der Gewissenslehre des englischen Puritanismus*, Archiv. f. Reformationsgesch. 42 (1951). It is noteworthy that the New Testament basis for the requirement to carry out the testing of conscience (2 Corinthians 13[5]), such as was always the concern of the Puritan theology of conscience, returns in Methodism (cf. *A Summary View of the Doctrines of Methodism occasioned by the late Persecution of the Methodists at Norwich*, 1752, 12f) and previously had served as text for the first conversations in the religious societies (cf. Josiah Woodward, *An Account of the Rise and Progress of the Religious Societies in the City of London*, 5th ed. 1724, 136). George Whitefield also made great use of it in his reply of August 1739 to the Pastoral Letter in which Edmund Gibson, the Bishop of London, warned against religious indifference and too much religious zeal at the same time; in connexion with the latter error he drew attention to ninety

references from Whitefield's *Journal* (George Whitefield's *Works*, 1771, IV, 6).

90. *Diary* of the late Mr William Holder of Painswick (Gloucestershire), 1768 until 1770, MS., p. 1, Oct. 13, 1768; p. 2, Oct. 17, 1768.

91. Ibid. p. 2, Oct. 19, 1768; p. 178, May 27, 1770.

92. Ibid. p. 3f, Oct. 23, 1768.

93. Ibid. p. 4f, Oct. 24, 1768.

94. Ibid. p. 5, Oct. 25, 1768.

95. Ibid. p. 52, March 27, 1769.

96. Ibid. p. 113f, Oct. 8, 1769.

97. Cf. Vol. I, p. 237.

98. *Diary*, p. 52: 'I have been Exceedingly Stript and grievously tempted all the Morning. I seemed not to have a Spark of Grace, and yet Astonishing! I did not doubt but I was in the favour of God; but was Sorely destroyed if Sin was not Destroyed for there was not any who enjoy's Deliverance from sin, but what felt more Happiness than my Self, and was not Tempted as I was; afterwards I was more stay'd on the Lord, could look beyond those Temptations and believe they would work together for my Good. In the Evening I met the Select Band and felt my faith much increased. I was greatly Confirm'd in the belief that Sin was Destroy'd and that these Temptations was no more than what was Consequent upon it, a proof that I had obtained that Grace.'

99. Ibid. p. 53, March 30, 1769.
    Ibid. p. 99, Aug. 24, 1769.
    Ibid. p. 101, Aug. 30, 1769.

100. Ibid. p 93, Aug. 2, 1769; p. 115, Oct. 10, 1769.

101. Ibid. p 67, May 21, 1769; p. 87, July 13, 1769.

102. An Account of Mrs Elizabeth Johnson, well known in the City of Bristol for more than half a century for her eminent Piety and Benevolence to which is added an Extract from her Diary (1799).

103. Ibid. p. 9.

104. Ibid. p. 35, June 2, 1750.

105. Ibid. p. 10.

106. Ibid. p. 59. Further rich material is contained in the series: *Wesley's Veterans. Lives of the Early Methodist Preachers told by themselves*, ed. John Telford, vols. I–VII, 1911–14 (which include autobiographies of thirty-six lay-preachers). Precursors were: *The Lives of Early Methodist Preachers*, ed. Thomas Jackson, 3 vols., 1837f; 2nd ed. in 2 vols., 1846; 3rd ed. in 6 vols., 1865. On the same subject cf. also Leslie F. Church, *The Early Methodist People*, 1948, 95ff, 149–83, in which, however, the scope is wider and all Methodists

are included. In the second work of Church, *More about the Early Methodist People*, 1949, chapter III, pp. 99–135, is devoted to the places where the men lay-preachers, many of whom were also class leaders, laboured, and chapter IV, pp. 136–76, to the spheres of the women lay-preachers.

Chapter 4: John Wesley's Relationship with the Church of England

1. This was always acknowledged in cases of dispute, cf. e.g. *Letters* III, 132, London, June 23, 1755, to Dr Sherlock, Bishop of London: 'Several years ago the churchwardens of St Bartholomew's informed Dr Gibson, then Lord Bishop of London, "My Lord, Mr Bateman, our rector, invites Mr Wesley very frequently to preach in his church." The Bishop replied, "And what would you have me do? I have no right to hinder him. Mr Wesley is a clergyman regularly ordained and under no ecclesiastical censure".'
2. Reference can be made particularly to the Waldensians and the Lollards.
3. *Letters* II, 295, 1748, to Vincent Perronet.
4. See the next chapter.
5. In Luke Tyerman, *The Life and Times of John Wesley* I, 1866, 286f.
6. *Journal* I, 479, May 28, 1738.
7. On Hervey cf. Luke Tyerman, *The Oxford Methodists*, 1873, 201–333. James Hervey to John Wesley, Oxon., Sept. 2, 1736, *Arminian Magazine* I (1778), 130–2: 'Rev. and Dear Sir, I have read your Journal, and find that the Lord has done great things for you, whereof we rejoice. Surely he will continue his loving-kindness to you, and shew you greater things than these. Methinks, when you and dear Mr Ingham go forth upon the great and good enterprise of converting the Indians, you will in some respects resemble Noah and his little household going forth of the Ark. Wherever you go you must walk among dry bones or carcases, among a People that are aliens from the life of God, buried in ignorance, dead in trespasses and sins. Oh! may the blessing of that illustrious Progenitor of ours, and of that favourite with the most High, be upon your heads! May you be fruitful and multiply, may you bring forth abundantly in that barren land and multiply therein! As for me I am still a most weak, corrupt Creature. But blessed be the unmerited mercy of God, and thanks be to your never to be forgotten example, That I am what I am.'
The same to the same, Wheston, near Northampton, Dec. 30,

1747, ibid. 134: 'Assure yourself, dear Sir, that I can never forget the tender-hearted and generous Fellow of *Lincoln* who condescended to take such compassionate notice of a poor Undergraduate, whom almost everybody condemned, and no man cared for his Soul.'

The same to the same, Stoke Abbey, Dec. 1, 1738, ibid. 132f, and the prefatory note to *Letters* I, 284–7.

8. *Letters* I, 284–7.

9. *Journal* II, 125f, Jan. 4, 1739; cf. *Letters* I, 62f, Nov. 25, 1730, to Mrs Pendarves; I, 66f, Dec. 12, 1730, to Mrs Granville.

10. 1 Corinthians 9^{16} is constantly used by John Wesley; besides the conversation with Bishop Joseph Butler at Bristol in 1739 cf. the important letter to the Earl of Dartmouth, Liverpool, April 10, 1761. *Letters* IV, 147.

11. *Letters* I, 286.

12. The fact that John Wesley constantly referred to this special regulation is of a piece with Luther's continual appeal to his doctorate as putting him under an obligation to engage in theological teaching and polemics. Cf. Hermann Steinlein, *Luthers Doktorat*, 1912.

13. *Letters* I, 322f, Bristol, June 23, 1739, to Charles Wesley.

14. *Letters* I, 274, Nov. 27, 1738, to James Hutton.

15. *Letters* I, 158, March 15, 1734, to Richard Morgan.

16. *Journal* I, 212f, Savannah (Georgia), May 9, 1736.

17. *Journal* III, 490f, Aug. 15, 1750; *Letters* III, 146, Bristol, Sept. 24, 1755, to Samuel Walker, *Letters* IV, 115, Dec. 1, 1760, to the editor of *Lloyd's Evening Post*.

18. *Letters* VIII, 144f, Dublin, June 20, 1789, to Walter Churchey.

19. *Journal* II, 291, Oct. 12, 1739, in London.

20. *Journal* III, 335, Holyhead, Feb. 27, 1748; *Letters* III, 36f, Bandon, May 22, 1750, to Gilbert Boyce; *Letters* III, 70, July 17, 1751; *Letters* III, 129–131, London, June 20, 1755, to his brother Charles; *Letters* III, 149–152, London, Oct. 31, 1755, to Thomas Adam; *Letters* III, 152, London, Nov. 20, 1755, to Samuel Walker; *Journal* IV, 186, Aug. 26 and 28, 1756, Bristol (Conference); *Journal* IV, 396, July 4, 1760, Limerick; *Letters* IV, 145, London, Apr. 2, 1761, to Dr Green; *Letters* IV, 303, Sligo, May 30, 1765, to James Knox; *Letters* V, 98, Swinfleet, July 19, 1768, to Thomas Adam; *Journal* VI, 90, Dec. 19, 1775, St Neot's (Kent); *Letters* VI, 268, Worcester, July 7, 1777, to Mr ——; *Journal* VI, 203, July 7, 1778, Dublin; *Letters* VI, 326f, London, Oct. 18, 1778, to Mary Bishop; *Letters* VII, Aug. 27, 1780, to Sir Harry Trelawney; *Letters* VII, 92, Nov. 19, 1781, to various friends; *Letters* VII, 163, London, Jan. 16, 1783, to Joseph Taylor; *Letters* VII, 213, Bristol, March 4, 1784, to William

Percival; *Letters* VII, 284, Plymouth Dock, Aug. 19, 1785, to his brother Charles; *Journal* VII, 112, Sept. 4, 1785, Bristol; *Journal* VII, 192, July 27, 1786, Bristol (Conference); *Journal* VII, 232, Jan. 2, 1787, London; *Journal* VII, 422, Aug. 4, 1788, London (Conference); *Letters* VIII, 80, London, Aug. 2, 1788, to Mrs Ward; *Letters* VIII, 92, Bristol, Sept. 20, 1788, to Mr ——; *Letters* VIII, 126, Dublin, March 31, 1789, to certain Persons in Dublin; *Journal* VII, 486, Apr. 12, 1789, Dublin; *Journal* VII, 492, May 4, 1789, Cappoquin (Ireland) *Journal* VII, 515, July 3, 1789, Dublin (Conference); *Letters* VIII, 152, Dublin, July 6, 1789, to Arthur Keene; *Journal* VII, 523, July 28, 1789, Birstall (Yorkshire) (Conference); *Letters* VIII, 186, London, Nov. 21, 1789, to William Black; *Letters* VIII, 224f, Hull, June 26, 1790, to Dr Pretyman Tomline, Bishop of Lincoln.

21. 'My belief is that the present design of God is to visit the poor desolate Church of England and that therefore neither deluded Mr Gambold nor any who leave it will prosper.' *Letters* II, 12, Newcastle-on-Tyne, Nov. 17, 1742, to his sister Martha Hall.

22. *Journal* V, 211, June 17, 1767.

23. *Letters* III, 289, Limerick, June 8, 1750.

24. *Letters* II, 29–32, Newcastle-on-Tyne, March 11, 1745, to a clerical Friend.

25. *Letters* II, 54–7, London, Dec. 30, 1745, to Westley Hall.

26. *Journal* VII, 112, Sept. 4, 1785, at Bristol. It was in this connexion that as early as Jan. 2, 1770, he commended to his fellow-worker, Mary Bosanquet, who later married his friend John William Fletcher, the rules of the Anglican religious societies in the following emphatic words: 'I suppose you have Instructions for Members of Religious Societies. I know nothing equal to them in the English tongue;' *Letters* V, 175, London, Jan. 2, 1770. He expressly and resolutely introduced the subject of the legality of the religious societies into the conversation he had with Dr Edmund Gibson, the Bishop of London, when he was accompanied by his brother Charles. *Journal* II, 93, no. 1, Oct. 20, 1738, in London (according to Charles Wesley's *Diary*).

27. *Letters* VII, 316, London, Feb. 21, 1786, to Thomas Taylor, VII, 332, Whitby, June 14, 1786, to Henry Brooke.

28. *Letters* II, 146–9, Tullamore, May 4, 1748, to a Clergyman.

29. 2 Corinthians 3^{1-3}.

30. *Letters* II, 148f: 'Will you object, "But he is no minister, nor has any authority to save souls?" I must beg leave to dissent from you in this. I think he is a true, evangelical minister, διάκονος, servant of

Christ and His Church, who οὕτω διακονεῖ, so ministers, as to save souls from death, to reclaim sinners from their sins; and that every Christian, if he is able to do it, has authority to save a dying soul.' Cf. on this question esp. the excellent selection and assessment by Theophil Funk, *Die Anfänge der Laienmitarbeit im Methodismus,* 1941 (Beitr. z. Geschichte d. Methodismus 5), 188ff.

31. *Journal* II, 335, Feb. 6, 1740. He was of exactly the same opinion in his old age and he also gave the same importance to the definition of the Church in Art. 20; cf. *Letters* VII, 285, Plymouth Dock, Aug. 19, 1785, to his brother Charles.

32. *Letters* IV, 146–52, Liverpool, Apr. 10, 1761, to the Earl of Dartmouth (afterwards the Colonial Minister).

33. *Journal* IV, 115f, May 18, 1755, at Newcastle.

34. *Journal* IV, 115, May 13, 1755, at Newcastle. *Journal* VII, 217, Oct. 24, 1786, at Deptford.

35. E.g. *Letters* III, 70, July 17, 1751, without place (fragment); III, 132, London, June 28, 1755, to Charles Wesley. *Journal* IV, 223, Normanby, Yorks, July 10, 1757.

36. *Letters* III, 132, London, June 28, 1755, to Charles Wesley; III, 135, London, July 16, 1755, to the same. In the spiritualistic tradition of Babel special attention should be paid to Paul Felgenhauer (1593–1677?) and Christian Hoburg (1607–75).

37. *Letters* III, 135f, London, July 16, 1755, to Charles Wesley.

38. *Letters* III, 146, Bristol, Sept. 24, 1755, to Samuel Walker.

39. *Journal* VII, 414, Epworth, July 6, 1788.

40. Particularly clear is e.g. *Letters* IV, 152, Liverpool, Apr. 10, 1761, to the Earl of Dartmouth: 'The doctrine of the Established Church, which is far the most essential part of her constitution, these preachers manifestly confirm, in opposition to those who subvert it.' Somewhat milder is *Letters* VII, 91–3, Nov. 19, 1781, to various Friends.

41. *Journal* V, 293, Nov. 19, 1768.

42. *Letters* VII, 98f, Lewisham, Jan. 9, 1782, to an unknown person.

43. *Journal* II, 274–6, London, Sept. 13, 1739. 'Courteous Mr Howard', as Charles Wesley calls him in a letter dated July 24 (no year), was a clergyman at Low-Leyton; cf. Selections from the Correspondence of the Rev. Ch. Wesley in: *The Journal of the Rev. Ch. Wesley*, ed. Thos. Jackson (1849), II, 210.

44. *Letters* IV, 235–9, Scarborough, Apr. 19, 1764, to various clergymen (between forty and fifty in number); cf. *Journal* V, 63 note); cf. also his opinion about William Barnard, Bishop of Londonderry in Ireland on May 3, 1758 (*Letters* IV, 19, Tullamore, May 3, 1758, to

Samuel Furly): 'He loves the Methodists from his heart, but he is not free from the fear of man.'

45. *Journal* IV, 115, Leeds, May 6, 1755; *Journal* IV, 186, Bristol, Aug. 26 and 28, 1756; *Journal* IV, 396, Limerick, July 5, 1760; *Journal* VI, 203, Dublin, July 7, 1778; *Journal* VII, 422, London, Aug. 4, 1788; *Journal* VII, 516, Dublin, July 3, 1789; *Journal* VII, 523, Leeds, July 28, 1789.

46. *Journal* VII, 192, Bristol, July 27, 1786; *Journal* VII, 482, Dublin, March 3, 1789.

47. *Journal* IV, 120, York, June 6, 1755, after reading Dr Sharp's Tracts on the Rubrics and Canons.

48. *Journal* VII, 173, Haxey, June 25, 1786; *Journal* IV, 373, Liverpool, March 20, 1760.

49. *Letters* VII, 284, Plymouth Dock, Aug. 19, 1785, to his brother Charles.

50. *Journal* VIII, 328–31, Madeley, July 12, 1775; 331–4, Aug. 1, 1775.

51. John Wesley's reply, *Letters* VI, 174f, Brecon, Aug. 18, 1775. On this cf. John McLachlan, *Socinianism in 17th Century England*, 1951.

52. This is the same position as the Lutheran Formula of Concord 1577 occupied in the controversy with the Calvinists (cf. *Bkschr. dt. Ev-KA*, 2nd ed. 1952, 756, 4). On the problem of reprobation cf. Hans-Werner Gensichen, *Damnamus. Die Verwerfung von Irrlehre bei Luther and im Luthertum des 16. Jhs.* 1955, 143ff.

53. *Journal* VIII, 332.

54. *Letters* VI, 174, Brecon, Aug. 18, 1775.

55. WA 6, 541; 565, 1. De captivitate Babylonica ecclesiae praeludium 1520.

56. *Journal* IV, 114, Apr. 30, May 1, 1755, Birstall, Micaiah Towgood, *A Gentleman's Reasons for his Dissent from the Church of England* 1746. Towgood replied to John White's *Three Letters* 1746 with the pamphlet, *A Dissent from the Church of England fully justified, Being the Dissenting Gentleman's Three Letters and Postscript Compleat,* 1746.

57. John Wesley to Micaiah Towgood, Bristol, Jan. 10, 1758, *Letters* III, 251–6.

58. *Letters* III, 253: 'Nor does all "the allegiance we owe to Him" at all hinder our "obeying them that have the rule over us" in things of a purely indifferent nature. Rather our allegiance to Him *requires* our obedience to them' (my italics).

59. Matthew 23[8,9].

60. Matthew 20[25].

61. Thomas Müntzer, *Hochverursachte Schutzrede und Antwort wider das*

Gaistlosse Sanfftlebende fleysch zu Wittenberg . . . (1524) in Thomas Müntzer, *Politische Schriften* hsgg. v. Carl Hinrichs 1950 (Hallische Monographien 17), 72, 90f. *Auslegung von Luc. 1 bei Karl Eduard Förstemann, Neues Urkundenbuch zur Geschichte der evangelischen Kirchenreformation,* 1842, p. 241f, see Karl Holl, *Luther und die Schwärmer, Luther,* 6th ed. 1932, 455, 2. *Ausgetr. Emplössung Politische Schriften* hsgg. Carl Hinrichs 1950, 21ff; cf. also the letter to the Count Ernst von Mansfeld of Sept. 22, 1523, *Briefwechsel* hsgg. von Heinrich Böhmer und Paul Kirn 1931 (Schriften der Sächs. Kommission f. Gesch. 34), 47f. In order to prevent misunderstanding I should point out that Towgood cannot in any sense be regarded as a follower of Müntzer. There are notable differences; in the first place the exclusive claim for Christ's rule by Müntzer is for the promotion of the revolutionary transformation of the world, while for Towgood it is confined to Church order. It is a matter of the relatedness of a certain type, which of necessity is repeated in the history of the Church.

62. *Letters* III, 252: 'We allow Christ does here expressly command to acknowledge no such authority of any, as the Jews paid their Rabbis, whom they usually styled either fathers or masters, implicitly believing all they affirmed and obeying all they enjoined.'

63. Ibid. 253: ' "However He alone has authority to fix the terms of communion for His followers or Church." "And the terms He has fixed no man on earth has authority to set aside or alter." (Assertions of Towgood.) This I allow (although it is another question); none has authority to exclude from the Church of Christ those who comply with the terms which Christ has fixed. But not to admit into the society called the Church of England or not to administer the Lord's Supper to them is not the same thing with "excluding men from the Church of Christ"; unless this society be the whole Church of Christ which neither you nor I will affirm. This society therefore may scruple to receive those as members who do not observe her rules in things indifferent, without pretending "to set aside or alter the terms which Christ has fixed" for admission into the Christian Church; and yet without "lording it over God's heritage or usurping Christ's throne".'

64. *Letters* III, 221–6, Penryn, Sept. 19, 1757, to Samuel Walker.

65. *Letters* III, 229, St Austell, Cornwall, Sept. 25, 1757, to Dorothy Furly: 'I think it was not you who advised poor Sam to be a mere regular clergyman un-connected with the Methodists. Certainly this is the best way to preferment; but is not the best way to heaven or to do good upon earth.'

66. *Letters* VII, 284, Plymouth Dock, Aug. 19, 1785, to his brother Charles: 'Some obedience I always paid to the bishops in obedience to the laws of the land. But I cannot see that I am under any obligation to obey them further than those laws require. It is in obedience to those laws that I have never exercised in England the power which I believe God has given me. I firmly believe I am a scriptural ἐπίσκοπος as much as any man in England or in Europe; for the *uninterrupted succession* I know to be a fable, which no man ever did or can prove. But this does in no wise interfere with my remaining in the Church of England; from which I have no more desire to separate than I had fifty years ago.' (Italics in the original.)

67. On the centrality of the parochial system in the Anglican view of the church cf. Norman Sykes, *Church and State in England in the 18th Century*, 1934, 392f; for the twentieth century Roger Lloyd, *The Church of England in the 20th Century* I (1946), 2nd ed. 1947, 6: 'For good or ill, the Church of England is inexorably parochial . . . The whole range of its activity is built on the foundation of its parishes . . . By a thousand ties of tradition, sentiment, economics, and, deepest of all, by the common human need to learn the art of love by loving first of all the thing you can see, the Church of England is wedded to the parochial system . . . The parish church is the executive unit of the whole Anglican Church. Missionary work in every scorched or frozen corner of the earth, all evangelism, and the cause of Christian education in every school, all ultimately stand or fall on the devotion of the English parish church.'

There is the same emphasis upon the office of the parish clergyman as the basis of the whole ecclesiastical action as early as John Wyclif in *De officio pastorali*, ed. Lechler 1863; cf. my article *John Wyclifs Kirchenbegriff* in der Gedenkschrift für Werner Elert, 1955, 93.

68. *Letters* I, 328, July 31, 1739, to Dr Henry Stebbing (Preacher at Gray's Inn in London). The deep feeling of this letter, written when John Wesley was 36 years old, is a clear expression of his view of his ministerial commission. In addition to the feeling of obligation which he had, his emotion becomes understandable also from the distinguished and influential position which Henry Stebbing (1687–1763) occupied. It was while in the same office that Frederick Denison Maurice was instrumental in setting in motion the social movement in the Church of England in the early part of the nineteenth century; cf. Maurice B. Reckett, *Maurice to Temple*, 1947, 1ff. Stebbing wrote against the Methodists in 1739: *A Caution against Religious Delusion. A Sermon on the New Birth: Occasioned by the Pretensions of the Methodists*. Within one year this sermon

passed through six editions! In 1745 he addressed to the Methodists the admonition: *An Earnest and Affectionate Address to the People called Methodists.*

Wesley replied in *Letters* I, 328: 'I do, indeed, go out into the highways and hedges to call poor sinners to Christ; but not in a tumultuous manner, not to the disturbance of the public peace or the prejudice of families. Neither herein do I break any law which I know; much less set at naught all rule and authority. Nor can I be said to intrude into the labours of those who do not labour at all but suffer thousands of those for whom Christ died to "perish for lack of knowledge". They perish for want of knowing that we as well as the heathen "are alienated from the life of God"; that "every one of us" by the corruption of our inmost nature, "is very far gone from original righteousness"—so far, that "every person born into the world deserveth God's wrath and damnation"; that we have by nature no power either to help ourselves or even to call upon God to help us, all our tempers and works in our natural state being only evil continually. So that *our* coming to Christ as well as *theirs* must infer a great and mighty change. It must infer not only an *outward change*, from stealing, lying and all corrupt communication, but a thorough *change of heart*, an *inward* renewal in the spirit of our mind. Accordingly "the old man" implies infinitely more than outward evil conversation, even "an evil heart of unbelief", corrupted by pride and a thousand deceitful lusts. Of consequence the "new man" must imply infinitely more than outward good conversation, even "a good heart which after God is created in righteousness and true holiness"—an heart full of that faith which, working by love, produces all holiness of conversation. The change from the former of these states to the latter is what I call *The New Birth*' (Italics in the original).

Cf. also *Journal* II, 296, Oct. 20, 1739 (after a preaching tour through Wales): 'I have seen no part of England so pleasant for sixty or seventy miles together as those parts of Wales I have been in. And most of the inhabitants are indeed ripe for the gospel. I mean (if the expression appear strange) they are earnestly desirous of being instructed in it; and as utterly ignorant of it they are as any Creek or Cheroke Indians. I do not mean they are ignorant of the name of Christ. Many of them can say both the Lord's Prayer and the Belief. Nay, and some, all the Cathechism; but take them out of the road of what they have learned by rote, and they know no more (nine in ten of those with whom I conversed) either of gospel salvation or of that faith whereby alone we can be saved, than Chicali or Tomo-chachi.' (Indian chieftains in Savannah, Georgia.)

69. *Letters* II, 55f, London, Dec. 30, 1745, to Westley Hall, and *Journal* III, 232, Jan. 20, 1746; cf. also Minutes of the Conference (1747) at London in *Minutes of the Methodist Conferences*, London 1862, 36.

70. *Letters* VII, 238, Bristol, Sept. 10, 1784, to brethren in North America: 'Lord King's Account of the Primitive Church convinced me many years ago that bishops and presbyters are the same order, and consequently have the same right to ordain. For many years I have been importuned from time to time to exercise this right by ordaining part of our travelling preachers. But I have still refused, not only for peace's sake, but because I was determined as little as possible to violate the established order of the National Church to which I belonged.'

71. Robert Lowth, *A Letter to Bishop Warburton*, 1765. Warburton had attacked Lowth in his great work on the Old Testament, *The Divine Legation of Moses*, 1737–41, to which Lessing gave an important place in his *Erziehung des Menschengeschlechts* (1780). John Wesley, *Journal* V, 153, Jan. 9, 1766: 'Thursday the 9th I read Bishop Lowth's Answer to Bishop Warburton. If anything human could be a cure for pride, surely, such a medicine as this would!'

72. *Letters* VII, 29–31, Aug. 10, 1780.

73. Cf. John L. Nuelsen, *Die Ordination im Methodismus*, 1935 (Beitr. z. Gesch. d. Methodismus 2), esp. 79ff. Unfortunately this otherwise excellent book overlooks the missionary idea as John Wesley's chief motive.

74. *Letters* III, 135, London, July 16, 1755, to his brother Charles; III, 182, Castlebar, July 3, 1756, to James Clark; IV, 146ff, Liverpool, Apr. 10, 1761, to the Earl of Dartmouth. The important book by Edward Stillingfleet, *Irenicon*, had appeared in 1659.

75. *Works*, 1830, XIII, 193–6, esp. 196: 'We look upon England as that part of the world, and the Church as that part of England, to which all we who are born and have been brought up therein, owe our first and chief regard. We feel in ourselves a strong στοργή, a kind of natural affection for our country, which we apprehend Christianity was never designed either to root out or to impair. We have a more peculiar concern for our brethren, for that part of our countrymen to whom we have been joined from our youth up, by ties of a religious as well as a civil nature. True it is, that they are, in general, "without God in the world". So much the more do our bowels yearn over them. They do lie "in darkness and the shadow of death": the more tender is our compassion for them. And when we have the fullest conviction of that complicated wickedness which covers them as a flood, then do we feel the most (and we desire to feel yet more)

of that inexpressible emotion with which our blessed Lord beheld Jerusalem, and wept and lamented over it. Then we are the most willing "to spend and to be spent" for them, yea, to "lay down our lives for our brethren".'

76. Ibid. 197: 'Contempt, sharpness, bitterness, can do no good.'

77. Ibid. 197–9.

78. *Journal* II, 293, Oct. 15, 1739, Abergavenny, Wales. That this point of view was actually understood is shown by the account of the Quaker Thomas Story, who was a friend of William Penn, of the Methodists on June 15, 1739, Proc. Wes. Hist. Soc. IX (1914), 141f: Their Teachers.

79. This is emphasized especially by R. Denny Urlin, *J.W's Place in Church History*, 1870, 68 etc., and *The Churchman's life of John Wesley*, 1886, and also later by John Ernest Rattenbury, *The Conversion of the Wesleys*, 1938, 168ff, and by Leslie F. Church, *The Early Methodist People*, 1949, 11ff; cf. also the collection of opinions: *John Wesley in Company with High Churchmen*, by an old Methodist, London, 2nd ed. 1870. With Urlin there begins the succession of energetic attempts to claim John Wesley for liturgical-sacramental anglo-catholicism. Against this James Harrison Rigg, *The Churchmanship of John Wesley*, 1878, 2nd ed. 1886, esp. p. 78, reacted sharply. The most significant interpretation of John Wesley along anglo-catholic lines is that of Rattenbury, *John Wesley's Legacy to the World*, 1928, esp. 175ff, *The Conversion of the Wesleys*, 1938, esp. 168ff, and *The Eucharistic Hymns of John and Charles Wesley*, 1948. From the stand-point of actual reunion is W. Sparrow Simpson, *John Wesley and the Church of England*, 1934.

80. Cf. on this esp. Rattenbury, *The Eucharistic Hymns of John and Charles Wesley*, 1948.

81. On this cf. Norman Sykes, *Church and State in England in the 18th Century*, 1926.

82. The theological and historical meaning of Lancelot Andrewes (1555–1626), the father of the older anglo-catholicism, in the history of the Church, can hardly be over-estimated; of recent works cf. Paul A. Welsby, *Lancelot Andrewes (1555–1626)*, London, S.P.C.K., 1958.

Chapter 5: The Opposition

1. Cf. Leslie F. Church, *More about the Early Methodist People*, 1949, II, Persecution and Triumph, pp. 57–98, where the emphasis is upon violent attacks. As early as Oct. 14, 1738, John Wesley wrote to

Herrnhut that most of the London churches were closed to him and his brother (*Letters* I, 261, Oxon., Oct. 14, 1738). It is particularly significant that after his sermon on Scriptural Christianity on St Bartholomew's Day, August 24, 1744, John Wesley was excluded from the pulpit of the University church because of his censure of the religious situation within the University. Cf. *Journal* III, 147, and further J. S. Reynolds, *The Evangelicals at Oxford 1735-1871*, 1953, p. 20f. On June 18, 1741, his friend John Gambold, whom he had consulted about the subject of his sermon in the University Church of St Mary, said that it was of no consequence, because nobody would in fact give him a fair hearing (*Journal* II, 468f). He over-rated the indifference.

2. *Journal* II, 423, Feb. 4, 1741.
3. *Journal* II, 424, Feb. 10, 1741.
4. *Journal* II, 425, Feb. 16, 1741.
5. *Journal* II, 452, May 3, 1741.
6. *Journal* II, 475, July 12, 1741.
7. *Journal* II, 486f, Aug. 25, 1741.
8. *Journal* II, 487, Aug. 26, 1741.
9. *Journal* IV, 133, Sept. 5, 1755, reviewing the past.
10. John Wesley, *Modern Christianity exemplified at Wednesbury*, printed Bristol 1745 (written 1743-4), *Works* XIII, 1831, 139-62. On the date of its composition cf. Richard Green, *The Works of John and Charles Wesley* (*Bibliography*), 1896, No. 72; cf. also *Journal* III, 98-102, 117-19.
11. John Nelson, *Journal* (1767) in *Wesley's Veterans*, ed. John Telford, III, 1911.
12. *Works* XIII, 1831, 162.
13. *Journal* I, 414, Dec. 28, 1737, Vol. I, p. 192.
14. *Letters* II, 29-32, 136f.
15. P.Q., *Of The pernicious Nature and Tendency of Methodism*, noted in Richard Green, *Anti-Methodist Publications issued during the 18th Century*, 1902, No. 5.
16. *The Gentleman's Magazine* and *The London Magazine* and *Monthly Chronologer* for 1739, 238-40 under the title *Of Enthusiasm and the present Practices of the Methodists*.
17. R.S., in *Common Sense or the Englishman's Journal*, Sat., June 30, 1739.
18. *Craftsman*, July 1739.
19. *Common Sense*, July 28, 1739.
20. *Lloyd's Evening Post*, Aug. 20, 1742.
21. Ibid. Sept. 4, 1744.

22. Ibid. March 5, 1751.

23. *Gentleman's Magazine*, Feb. 28, 1756.

24. Cf. esp. Charles Blount's indirect classification of Jesus with Apollonius of Tyana (*The Two First Books of Philostratus concerning the Life of Apollonius Tyaneus*, 1680); on this cf. the striking characterization by Gotthard Victor Lechler, *Geschichte des englischen Deismus*, 1841, 114ff; in general: Frank E. Manuel, *The Eighteenth Century Confronts the Gods*, 1959, esp. 47ff, 228ff, 311f.

25. Newspaper extract, 1776 (handwritten note on the year, without further date, the newspaper indecipherable. The author calls himself Horatio).

26. *Calm Address, Works* XI (1856), 76–86.

27. *Letters* VI, 160–64, Armagh, June 15, 1775, to Lord Frederick North.

28. Sam. Johnson's pamphlet has the title: *Taxation no Tyranny, an Answer to the Resolutions and Address of the American Congress*, 1775 (*Works of Sam. Johnson*, New Ed. in 12 vols., London 1806, VIII, 155–204). On J. Wesley's former attitude and that of Sam. Johnson cf. John S. Simon, *John Wesley, The Last Phase*, 1934, 71; and R. A. Knox, *Enthusiasm. A Chapter in the History of Religion*, 1950, 448.

29. Americus in *The Gentleman's Magazine*, 1775, 561. The handwritten piece from the collection of newspaper extracts on the early history of Methodism at Richmond College, Richmond, Surrey, bears the signature 'By Councellor Erskine'. This is John Erskine, 1721–1803, who was minister of Old Greyfriars in London; he advocated the alliance with North America and published the works of Jonathan Edwards and other American theologians. Cf. DNB VI, 850f. Nevertheless his theological and ecclesiastical inclinations were contrary to those put forward in the newspaper article.

30. *The Gentleman's Magazine*, 1775, 561.

31. Ibid.: 'But when men with a reasonable dependance on God and in an honest cause act upon human principles of justice and success, and in an enlightened age build a form of government on the experience of past ages, avoiding the bad and improving even on the best, the prospect is not so gloomy as you suggest. You are only a servant, not a Prophet, of God, and must therefore forgive my want of faith in your augurs.'

32. On this cf. the review in Richard Green, *Anti-Methodist Publications during the 18th Century*, 1902, Nos. 482–6, esp. Preface to No. 483.

33. *The London Magazine or Gentleman's Monthly Intelligence*, vol. XXIX, 1760, p. 471f.

34. Ibid. p. 587.

35. *The Fanatic Saints or Bedlamites Inspired. A Satire*, London, 1778, *passim*, esp. pp. 9, 13, 15, 25f, 29, 16f, 18, 34.

36. *Perfection. A Poetical Epistle Calmly addressed to the Greatest Hypocrite in England*, 1778, *passim*, esp. pp. 10, 11, 12, 15, 17, 19, 22, 23, 26, 30, 31, 34, 36.

37. British Museum. Department of Prints and Drawings. Catalogue of Political and Personal Satires, vol. V (1771–83), Nos. 4839–5630, by Mary Dorothy George; 1935, p. 302, No. 5494: 'Toothless, he draws the teeth of his flocks.' 1778.

38. Ibid. No. 5495: Wise as Serpents, 1778.

39. Ibid. p. 303, No. 5496: Reynardo's Consecration by the Goddess Murcia, 1778.

40. Ibid. p. 206, No. 5300: Series of Tête-á-Tête portraits.

41. On him cf. Norman Sykes, *Edmund Gibson, Bishop of London* (1669–1748), 1926, *passim*. On his relationship to Methodism, ibid. 302 to 332.

42. *Observations upon the Conduct and Behaviour of a certain Sect usually distinguished by the name of Methodists*, 1774.

43. On this cf. Norman Sykes, *Church and State in England in the 18th Century*, 1934, 392f. For the present day, Roger Lloyd, *The Church of England in the 20th Century* I (1946), 2nd ed. 1947, 6.

44. Cf. Norman Sykes, *Edmund Gibson* . . . 1926, 291.

45. Ibid. 326f.

46. Ibid. 316. On *The Whole Duty of Man* cf. my article, *Das Erbauungsbuch The Whole Duty of Man (1659) und seine Bedeutung für das Christentum in England*. Theologia Viatorum (Jb. d. Kirchlichen Hochschule Berlin-Zehlendorf) VIII (1962), 232–71.

47. Cf. Walter Ernest Clark, *Josiah Tucker, Economist* (Studies in History, Economics and Public Law. Columbia University, New York, XIX, 1), 1903, esp. pp. 22–36. R. L. Schuyler, *Josiah Tucker. A Selection from his Political and Economic Writings*, N.Y. 1931, 21–5. He was promoted because he had supported Robert Nugent in 1754 in the Bristol election. The latter afterwards strongly commended him to the first Duke of Newcastle, Thomas Selham Holles, cf. R. Nugent to Newcastle Aug. 1754 in Add.MSS. Brit.Mus. 32726 fol. 136, and N. Sykes, *Church and State in England in the 18th Century*, 1943, p. 168.

48. Josiah Tucker, *A Brief History of the Principles of Methodism, wherein the Rise and Progress, together with the Causes of the several Variations, Divisions, and present Inconsistencies of this Sect are attempted to be traced out, and accounted for.* Oxford, Printed for James Fletcher, and Sold by J. Rivington in St Paul's Church-Yard, London; and the Booksellers at Bristol. MDCCXLII, 8ff, 10.

49. Ibid. 11f.
50. Ibid. 12–17.
51. Ibid. 33.
52. Ibid. 40.
53. Ibid. 39: 'Mr. Wesley had never (strictly speaking) renounc'd Mr. Law's system by imbracing the Moravian *reveries*, but rather super-added those to his former plan. Just as the Church of Rome may be said to have done with resp. to the Orthodox and Primitive faith.'
54. Ibid. 45.
55. *The London Magazine or Gentleman's Monthly Intelligence*, vol. XXIX (1760), 545f.
56. Ibid. p. 354.
57. Sam. Johnson, *The Works*, ed. Arthur Murphy, 1806, IV, p. 5: 'It is one among many reasons for which I purpose to endeavour the entertainment of my countrymen by a short essay on Tuesday and Saturday, that I hope not much to tire those whom I shall not happen to please, and if I am not commended for the beauty of my works, to be at least pardoned for their brevity.'
58. Ibid. p. 25f.
59. Ibid. p. 37. 'It was, perhaps, ordained by Providence, to hinder us from tyrannizing over one another, that no individual should be of such importance, as to cause, by his retirement or death, any chasm in the world.'
60. Ibid. pp. 42–5.
61. Ibid. pp. 282–8.
62. Ibid. p. 284f. (Translator's note. At this point Dr Schmidt's text consists of quotations and paraphrases from an article in *The Rambler*, and he gives the original English version in this footnote. In order to avoid repetition I have incorporated the quotations in the text.)
63. How closely the general Christian feeling of the time is in this manner expressed is seen above all in the sermons of the Archbishop of Canterbury, Thomas Secker (1693–1768, from 1758 at Canterbury), who was a close friend of Joseph Butler. Cf. esp. Thomas Secker, *Works*, vol. I, 1770, 85f: 'Let us now proceed to the Duties, which we owe to our Fellow-Creatures. The Sense of these because they are of more immediate Importance to the Good of Society, God has imprinted with greater Strength in our Minds, than even that of our Obligations to himself. As it must be the Will of him, who is just and good to us all, that we should be just and good to one another; and from this Principle, as the Root, every Branch of right Behaviour springs: so he has planted in our Hearts a natural Love of Equity, a natural Feeling of kind Affection, a Natural Conscience, applauding

us when we violate them: and seldom do we deserve its Reproaches, but either at the Time, or soon after we undergo them. Consider but a little more particularly, what the mutual Duties of Men are: Honesty and Fairness in their Dealings, Truth in their Words, Friendliness in their Demeanour, Willingness to forgive Offences, respectful Obedience to Superiors, ready Condescension to Inferiors, tender Love to near Relations, Pity and Relief of the Poor, diligent Care to be serviceable to Mankind in our proper Station. Which one of These Obligations . . . can any pretend he was ignorant of or doubtful about?'

64. Ibid. p. 286: 'The christian and the hero are unseparable.'

65. *Repentance stated and explained* (1751) in Sam. Johnson's *Works*, ed. Arthur Murphy, 1806, V, pp. 246–52, esp. 249.

66. Thos. Rutherford, *Four Charges to the Clergy of the Archdeaconry of Essex*, 1763, pp. 2–5.

67. Ibid. pp. 15ff.

68. Ibid. p. 28.

69. Ibid. pp. 52–4.

70. Thos. Whiston, *The Important Doctrines of Original Sin, Justification by Faith and Regeneration* . . . 1740.

71. Ibid. pp. 3–7.

72. Ibid. p. 10f.

73. Ibid. p. 39f.

74. Ibid. pp. 54–6.

75. Ibid. p. 63.

76. *Some Quaeries humbly offered to those who profess sinless Perfection* (1763).

77. *The Enthusiasm of Methodists and Papists compared*, I, II, 1749; III, 1751. It is significant that in the same year 1749 a second edition of the two first parts became necessary. On the persecution of the Methodists in Exeter, 1745, cf. Leslie F. Church, *More About the Early Methodist People*, 1949, 65f. On the subject in general cf. Ronald A. Knox, *Enthusiasm. A Chapter in the History of Religion*, 1950, esp. 422ff.

78. '. . . A 3ᵛ an effectual Reformation of Manners and Propagation of the Gospel by all sober and Christian methods . . . this Great work will never be accomplished by an Enthusiastic and Fanatical head.' It is noteworthy that the two words 'enthusiastic' and 'fanatical' are used together as synonyms.

79. Ibid. A 2ᵛ he apparently obtained his knowledge of Montanism from Francis Lee's *History of Montanism*, 1709 (A 2ʳ).

80. Ibid. I, 10f.

81. Ibid. I, 18–26.
82. Ibid. I, 26f.
83. Ibid. I, 31–6.
84. Ibid. I, 40–4.
85. Ibid. I, 49–62.
86. Ibid. I, 10. 'It would not be understood to accuse the Methodists directly of Popery, though I am persuaded they are doing the Pope's work, and agree with them some of their Principles,—designing only to shew how uniformly both act upon the same Plan (as far as Enthusiasm can be said to carry on any Plan)—their Ideals fill'd with much the same Projects, driven on in the same wild Manner; and wearing the same badge of Peculiarities in their Tenets.'
87. See below.
88. George Lavington, *The Enthusiasm of Methodists and Papists compared* III, 1751, IX-XI.
89. Ibid. III, X, cf. II, 1749, 136f.
90. Ibid. III, XVIII.
91. Ibid. III, XXIV. 'Upon the Whole, I reckon it, Sir, my bounden Duty solemnly to declare—that I believe Methodism (however innocent in its Conception and Birth) to have been gradually and diligently nursed up into a System of solemn Imposture—that I see nothing in this Dispensation thus managed, but what lies in common with the most frantic and pestilent Fanaticism, that have so often poisoned the Christian World; nothing that is not drinking up the very Dregs of Popery in particular.' Lavington is apparently relying upon a false report that J.W. made an immoral proposal to a servant-girl. Wesley gave a detailed refutation of this in a letter of May 8, 1752, *Letters* III, 90.
92. Ibid. III, XXVf, cf. 282.
93. Ibid. III, 287–94.
94. Ibid. III, V-VII, 12, 30, 237.
95. Ibid. VIII.
96. George Lavington, *The Moravians Compared and Detected. By the Author of the Enthusiasm of Methodists and Papists compared*, London, 1755.
97. *The Enthusiasm of Methodists and Papists compared*, II, 1749, 138, 145.
98. Lessing, *Erziehung des Menschengeschlechts*, paragraph 24, also Wolfenbüttler, *Fragmente, Viertes Fragment*. Warburton, *The Divine Legation of Moses*, 1737–41 (*Works* 1–3, 1778).
99. Wm. Warburton, *The Doctrine of Grace, or the Office and Operations of the H. Spirit vindicated from the Insults of Infidelity and The Abuses of Fanaticism* (1762) in *Works*, 1788–94, vol. 4, 1788, 533–723.

100. Ibid. 608–38.

101. Ibid. 642.

102. Ibid. 642f. 'Nor will that fanatic Apology which is ever at hand, be any excuse for them in the commission of their disorders; namely, That the violation of peace amongst men serves to advance the peace of God; our blessed Master having himself declared, that he was not come to send Peace on earth, but a sword. Now the same Spirit which disposes them to apply to their own case all those declarations concerning the first extraordinary state of the Gospel, hinders them from seeing, that these words of Jesus respect only the accidental and transient struggle of the then expiring Powers of Darkness; but that the heavenly Proclamation of peace towards men, declares the genuine and constant fruits of God's good will to his Creatures: that the first only predicted the early fortunes of a suffering Church; and that the other described the essential nature, the eternal genius of an all beneficent Religion.'

103. Ibid. 643–5.

104. Ibid. 658–61.

105. Ibid. 666.

106. Ibid. 672–4.

107. Ibid. 673.

108. Ibid. 676.

109. Ibid. 610.

110. Ibid. 651–6.

111. Ibid. 680f.

112. *The Alliance between Church and State. The Necessity and Equity of an Established Religion and a Test-Law Demonstrated,* 1736, 2nd ed. 1748, 3rd ed. 1766—the classical apology for the Church of England in the eighteenth century, partly in opposition to Rousseau's *Contrat social—Works* 4 (1788), 1–331.

113. *Works,* vol. 4, 635.

114. *Letters* II, 174. The co-ordination of the devil with erroneous doctrine and its description as his own weapon against both the Church and God Himself, corresponds precisely with Luther's view. Cf. *Operationes in psalmos* 1519–21, WA 5, 530, 35. *An den christlichen Adel* 1520, WA 6, 447, 20; 448, 19. *Vom Abendmahl Christi, Bekenntnis* 1528, WA 26, 264, 1; 281, 11; 316, 11; 341, 26; 349, 33.

115. *The Principles of a Methodist. Written in 1740. Occasioned by a late Pamphlet entitled 'A Brief History of the Principles of Methodism'. Works,* 1830, VIII, 359–74. John Wesley was thoroughly aware of the significance of this innovation, cf. *Works,* op. cit., 359: 'this is the first time I have appeared in controversy, properly so called . . .'

In *Letters* II, 57, London, Dec. 30, 1745, to 'John Smith' he recognizes the difference between practical-theological, that is, positive writing and his apologetical-polemical: 'In writing practically I seldom argue concerning the meaning of texts, in writing controversially, I do.' In this way his careful precision is made into a principle.

116. *Works*, 1830, VIII, 360.

117. Ibid. 359–65.

118. Ibid. 366: 'It is "asserted that Mr Law's system was the creed of the Methodists". But it is not proved. I had been eight Years at Oxford before I read any of Mr Law's writings; and when I did I was so far from making them my creed, that I had objections to almost every page. But all this time my manner was, to spend several hours a day in reading the Scripture in the original tongues. And hence my system, so termed, was wholly drawn, according to the light I then had.'

119. Ibid. 366f.

120. Ibid. 367f.

121. Ibid. 371f. This confirms the account given in Vol. 1, pp. 291ff.

122. Ibid. 373f.

123. Ibid. 374; '"Gospel holiness", as Mr. Tucker believes, "is a necessary qualification, antecedent to justification." This appears to me now to be directly opposite to the gospel of Christ.'

124. *Letters* II, 175–211, Bristol, Feb. 2, 1745, and II, 212–76, June 17, 1746. On Thomas Church (1707–56) cf. DNB. His writing bore the title: *Remarks on the Reverend Mr John Wesley's Last Journal. The Divisions and Perplexities of the Methodists, and the many Errors relating both to Faith and Practice, which have already arisen among these deluded People.*

125. Cf. esp. Ronald A. Knox, *Enthusiasm*, 356–71 and 389–421.

126. *Letters* II, 193.

127. *Letters* II, 190.

128. *Letters* II, 202f.

129. *Letters* II, 195, 200f, 211; 200f is especially clear: 'You have preached justification by faith and works at Battersea and St Ann's Westminster; while I preached justification by faith alone near Moorfields and at Short's Gardens. I beseech you, then, to consider in the secret of your heart how many sinners have you converted to God? By their fruits we shall know them. This is a plain rule. By this test let them be tried. How many outwardly and habitually wicked men have you brought to uniform habits of outward holiness? It is an awful thought! Can you instance in an hundred? in fifty? in twenty? in

ten? If not, take heed unto yourself and to your doctrine. It cannot be that both are right before God.'

130. *Letters* II, 202; cf. also the repetition of this point in the second letter (June 17, 1746), *Letters* II, 231.

131. *Letters* II, 207–10.

132. *Letters* II, 186–201, 176–8.

133. *Letters* II, 203f.

134. *Letters* II, 204–6.

135. *Letters* II, 212, June 17, 1746.

136. *Letters* II, 212f: 'I never knew one (or but one) man write controversy with what I thought a right spirit. Every disputant seems to think, as every soldier, that he may hurt his opponent as much as he can: nay, that he ought to do his worst to him, or he cannot make the best of his own cause; that, so he do not belie or wilfully misrepresent him, he must expose him as much as he is able. It is enough, we suppose, if we do not show heat or passion against our adversary. But not to despise him, or endeavour to make others do so, is quite a work of superogation.

'But ought these things to be so? (I speak on the Christian scheme). Ought we not to love our neighbour as ourselves? And does a man cease to be our neighbour because he is of a different opinion? nay, and declares himself so to be? Ought we not for all this, to do to him as we would he should do to us? But do we ourselves love to be exposed or set in the worst light? Would we willingly be treated with contempt? If not, why do we treat others thus? And yet, who scruples it? Who does not hit every blot he can, however foreign to the merits of the cause? Who in controversy casts the mantle of love over the nakedness of his brother? Who keeps steadily and uniformly to the question, without ever striking at the person? Who shows in every sentence that he loves his brother only less than the truth? I fear neither you nor I have attained to this.'

137. *Letters* II, 217, 220.

138. *Letters* II, 214, 216.

139. *Letters* II, 216.

140. Esp. *Letters* II, 255f.

141. *Letters* II, 226f: 'Justification is the act of God, pardoning our sins and receiving us again to His favour. This was free in Him, because undeserved by us; undeserved, because we had transgressed His law, and could not, nor even can now, perfectly fulfil it.

'We cannot, therefore, be justified by our works; because this would be to be justified by some merit of our own. Much less can we be justified by an external show of religion or by any superstitious observances.

'The life and death of our Lord is the sole meritorious cause of this mercy, which must be firmly believed and trusted in by us. Our faith therefore in Him, though no more meritorious than any other of our actions, yet has a nearer relation to the promises of pardon through Him, and is the mean and instrument whereby we embrace and receive them.

'True faith must be lively and productive of good works, which are its proper fruits, the marks whereby it is known.'

Wesley's formulations approach very closely those of Luther, although the basic idea, that faith is the sole attitude which renders the honour due to God as the true One, while taking seriously His promise, is not reached.

Cf. also the concluding sentences, ibid. 227: 'I have only one circumstance farther to add—namely, that I am not newly convinced of these things. For this is the doctrine which I have continually taught for eight or nine years last past; only I abstained from the word "condition" perhaps more scrupulously than was needful, where the word "condition" is avoided, because it leads to error.'

142. Ibid. 226: ' "You make sinless perfection necessary after justification, in order to make us meet for glory." And who does not? Indeed, men do not agree in the time. Some believe it is attained before death; some in the article of death; some in an after-state, in the Mystic or the Popish purgatory. But all writers whom I have ever seen till now (the Romish themselves not excepted) agree that we must be "fully cleansed from all sin" before we can enter into glory.'

143. Ibid. 228–30.

144. Ibid. 231f.

145. Ibid. 236: 'Had the powers conferred been so limited when I was ordained priest, my ordination would have signified just nothing. For I was not appointed to any congregation at all, but was ordained as a member of that "College of Divines" (so our Statutes express it) "founded to overturn all heresies and defend the catholic faith".' The similarity with Luther's consciousness of obligation arising from his doctorate is apparent.

146. Ibid. 238f, esp. 239: 'so far as I governed them, it was at their own entreaty.'

147. Ibid. 240f.

148. Ibid. 240f.

149. Ibid. 244.

150. Ibid. 245–54.

151. Ibid. 252–4.
152. This is seen very clearly, when he comes to the next point, the discussion of healing by prayer, ibid. 256f: 'I acknowledge that I have seen with my eyes and heard with my ears several things which, to the best of my judgement, cannot be accounted for by the ordinary course of natural causes, and which I therefore believe ought to be "ascribed to the extraordinary interposition of God". If any man choose to style these miracles, I reclaim not. I have diligently inquired into the facts. I have weighed the preceding and following circumstances. I have strove to account for them in a natural way. I could not without doing violence to my reason. Not to go far back, I am clearly persuaded that the sudden deliverance of John Haydon was one instance of this kind, and my own recovery on May 10 another. I cannot account for either of these in a natural way. Therefore I believe they were both supernatural.

'I must observe that the truth of these facts is supported by the same kind of proof as that of all other facts is wont to be—namely, the testimony of competent witnesses, and that the testimony here is in as high a degree as any reasonable man can desire. Those witnesses were many in number; they could not be deceived themselves; for the facts in question they saw with their own eyes and heard with their own ears, nor is it credible that so many of them would combine together with a view of deceiving others, the greater part being men that feared God, as appeared by the general tenor of their lives.'

In what follows the following sentence is especially important: 'I believe God never interposed His miraculous power but according to His own sovereign will; not according to the will of man— *—neither of him by whom He wrought, nor of any other man whatsoever. The wisdom as well as the power are His, nor can I find that ever, from the beginning of the world, He lodged this power in any mere man, to be used whenever that man saw good'* (p. 257, my italics).

153. Ibid. 256–8, esp. 258.
154. Ibid. 258–60.
155. Ibid. 262: 'Let us consider this point yet a little farther. "What is it you would have us prove by miracles? The doctrines we preach?" We prove these by Scripture and reason, and (if need be) by antiquity.'
156. Ibid. 261, section 5.
157. Ibid. 263f, section 8.
158. Ibid. 264f.
159. Ibid. 265f.
160. This is a very revealing parallel to the programme of German

298

Pietism and Spener's *Pia Desideria*, where it is argued PD 36,38
Aland (Jews) PD 38,23 Aland (Papists) similarly by John Wesley
in the early *Letters* I, 251f, Utph, July 7, 1738: 'I grieve to think
how that holy name by which we are called must be blasphemed
among the heathen while they see discontented Christians, passionate
Christians, resentful Christians, earthly-minded Christians—yea (to
come to what we are apt to count small things), while they see
Christians judging one another, ridiculing one another, speaking
evil of one another, increasing instead of bearing one another's burthens. How bitterly would Julian have applied to these, "See how
these Christians love one another!" I know, I myself, I doubt you
sometimes, and my sister often, have been under this condemnation.
Oh may God grant that we may never more think to do Him service
by breaking those commands which are the very life of His religion!
But may we utterly put away all anger, and wrath, and malice, and
bitterness, and evil-speaking.'

161. *Letters* II, 266f.
162. Ibid. 267–70.
163. Ibid. 270–3.
164. Ibid. 273–5.
165. *Works* (1861) XI, 374.
166. *Observations upon the Conduct and Behaviour of a Certain Sect,
    usually distinguished by the name of Methodists* 1744, Green's *Anti-
    Methodist Publications* No. 164.
167. *Letters* II, 277–291, London, June 11, 1747.
168. Charge p. 7 in John Wesley, *Letters* II, 278.
169. Ibid. 278–87.
170. Ibid. 280: 'To declare this a little more particularly; we understand
    by that scriptural expression, "a perfect man", one in whom God
    hath fulfilled His faithful word—"From all your filthiness and from
    all your idols will I cleanse you. I will also save you from all your
    uncleanness." We understand hereby one whom God hath sanctified
    throughout, even in "body, soul, and spirit"; one who "walketh in
    the light, as He is in the light", in whom "is no darkness at all; the
    blood of Jesus Christ His Son" having cleansed "him from all sin".'

Further examples from German Pietism are the following: Philipp
Jakob Spener, *Pia Desideria* (1675), ed. by Kurt Aland, 3rd ed.
1964, p. 43, 31: 'If we look at the Holy scriptures we cannot doubt
that God has promised better things for His church here on earth.
We have in the first place the glorious prophecy of S. Paul and the
secret made known by him in Romans 11[25,26], that after the fulness
of the Gentiles be come in all Israel shall be saved. That therefore

if not the whole, yet a considerably large part of those Jews whose hearts have been hardened will be converted to the Lord. Also when the prophets of the Old Testament are properly studied, e.g. Hosea $3^{4,5}$, they are seen to allude to the same end. Then also the most eminent of our teachers from the ancient fathers of the church have testified to this mystery . . . If the Jews are to be converted, either the true church must exist in a more holy state than at present . . . or, by God's power a noticeable change and improvement of our church must take place . . .' Cf. also ibid. p. 48, 16f.

August Hermann Francke, *Nicodemus oder Tractätlein von der Menschenfurcht*, 3rd ed. 1707, p. 175–7: 'The eleventh chapter of the Epistle to the Hebrews gives the basis of such a view . . . It is not said that a faithful man is to do the same works as Noah, Abraham, Moses and others did, yet he is to imitate the faith of these men of God, and to evidence in power and deed such a faith in that calling and position in which God has placed him, and in those circumstances which happen to him daily; thus he has to ensure that he will see and experience in his faith the glory of the Lord, as the others did on their part.' (Translator's note: these extracts have been abbreviated.)

171. *Letters* II, 279–81.
172. Ibid. 288.
173. On this cf. the detailed discussion in John S. Simon, *John Wesley and the Methodist Societies* (1923), 3rd ed. 1952, 272–80. The letters of John Smith are in Henry Moore, *J. Wesley* II, 1824, 475–576.
174. *Letters* II, 43–51, Newcastle-upon-Tyne, Sept. 28, 1745.
175. Romans 5^5.
176. On this subject cf. John Wesley's great sermon, *Salvation by Faith*, which is considered later in this work.
177. *Letters* II, 57–65, London, Dec. 30, 1745–Jan. 3, 1746.
178. Wesley quotes from the Latin version of *The Confessions of Augustine* VII, 10, in *Letters* II, 60.
179. *Letters* II, 65: 'It is true that, from May 24, 1738, "wherever I was desired to preach, salvation by faith was my only theme"—that is, such a love of God and man as produces all inward and outward holiness, and springs from a conviction, wrought in us by the Holy Ghost, of the pardoning love of God; and that, when I was told, "You must preach no more in this church", it was commonly added, "because you preach such doctrine!" And it is equally true that "it was preaching the love of God and man that several of the clergy forbade me their pulpits" before that time, before May 24, before I either preached or knew salvation by faith.' It is deserving of special

notice that in this important apology and argument for his message
Wesley should refer to his conversion of May 24, 1738.

180. John Smith had written on Feb. 28, 1746, and Wesley replied on
June 25, *Letters* II, 68–79.

181. The important sentences are in *Letters* II, 71: 'I believe firmly,
and that in the most literal sense, that "without God we can do
nothing", that we cannot think, or speak, or move an hand or an eye
without the concurrence of the divine energy; and that all our natural
faculties are God's gift, nor can the meanest be exerted without the
assistance of His Spirit. What, then, do I mean by saying that faith,
hope, and love are not the effect of any or all our natural faculties?
I mean this: that, supposing a man to be now void of faith and hope
and love, he cannot effect any degree of them in himself by any
possible exertion of his understanding and of any or all his other
natural faculties, though he should enjoy them in the utmost perfection. A distinct power from God, not implied in any of these, is
indispensably necessary before it is possible he should arrive at the
very lowest degree of Christian faith or hope or love. In order to his
having any of these (which, on this very consideration, I suppose St
Paul terms the "fruits of the Spirit") he must be created anew,
throughly and inwardly changed by the operation of the Spirit of
God; by a power equivalent to that which raises the dead and which
calls the things which are not as though they were. The "living
soberly, righteously, and godly" in this present world, or the uniform
practice of universal piety, presupposes some degree of these "fruits
of the Spirit", nor can possibly subsist without them.'

182. This is a point where the influence of the book, *The Whole Duty of
Man*, based upon Titus 2^{12}, which was widely read and was so
typical of English piety, becomes evident. Cf. my article, to which
reference has several times been made, in *Theol. Viat.* VIII (1961–2),
232–77.

183. *Letters* II, 87–96, Newcastle-upon-Tyne, March 25, 1747.

184. *Letters* II, 95: ' "He that gathereth not with Me scattereth" more
especially if he be a preacher. He must scatter from Him if he does
not gather souls to God. Therefore a lifeless, unconverting minister
is the murderer-general of his parish.'

185. *Letters* II, 97–106, St Ives, July 10, 1747.

186. *Letters* II, 133–40, Dublin, March 22, 1748.

187. *Letters* II, 135.

188. *Letters* III, 259–71, Canterbury, Feb. 1, 1750, to Dr Lavington,
Bishop of Exeter.

189. Ibid. 264f.

190. Ibid. 261f.
191. Ibid. 260.
192. Ibid. 262f.
193. Ibid. 266.
194. Ibid. 266.
195. Ibid. 267.
196. Ibid. 263.
197. Ibid. 269.
198. Ibid. 269.
199. Ibid. 266.
200. Ibid. 261f.
201. Ibid. 270f.
202. *Letters* III, 45–51.
203. *Letters* III, 45–7.
204. *Letters* III, 47–9.
205. *Letters* III, 49f.
206. *Letters* III, 50f.
207. *Letters* III, 51, Section 16, *Letters* II, 273, Section VI, 9 in particular.
208. *Letters* III, 295–331.
209. *Letters* III, 299: 'In your seventh section you say, "I shall now give some account of their grievous conflicts and combats with Satan" (page 53). O sir, spare yourself, if not the Methodists! Do not go so far out of your depth. This is a subject you are utterly unacquainted with as with justification or the new birth.'

300: 'Well, but as to conflicts with Satan. "Nor can Mr. Wesley," you say, "escape the attacks of this infernal spirit"—namely, "suggesting distrustful thoughts, and buffeting him with inward temptations". Sir, did you never hear of any one so attacked, unless among the Papists or Methodists? How deeply, then, are you experienced both in the ways of God and the devices of Satan!'

301: 'As wildly do you talk of the doubts and fears incident to those who are "weak in faith" (sect. ix, p. 79, and c). I cannot prevail upon myself to prostitute this awful subject by entering into any debate concerning it with one who is innocent of the whole affair.'

301/02: 'That some time after, I "was strongly assaulted again, and after recovering peace and joy was thrown into perplexity afresh by a letter, asserting that no doubt or fear could consist with true faith, that my weak mind could not then bear to be thus sawn asunder", will not appear strange to any who are not utter novices in experimental religion.'

210. *Letters* III, 328.

211. *Letters* III, 330f.
212. *Letters* III, 309f.
213. *Letters* IV, 325–37, London, Nov. 17, 1759.
214. John Downes, *Methodism Examined and Exposed, or the Clergy's Duty of guarding their Flocks against False Teachers*, 1759.
215. *Letters* IV, 325–7.
216. *Letters* IV, 327–9.
217. *Letters* IV, 329–31.
218. *Letters* IV, 331.
219. *Letters* IV, 331–3.
220. *Letters* IV, 333f.
221. *Letters* IV, 334f.
222. *Letters* IV, 335f.
223. *Letters* IV, 337.
224. *Letters* IV, 338–84, Nov. 26, 1762.
225. *Letters* IV, 338f: 'Your Lordship well observes, "To employ buffoonery in the service of religion is to violate the majesty of truth and to deprive it of a fair hearing. To examine, men must be serious." (Preface, p. 11.) I will endeavour to be so in all the following pages; and the rather, not only because I am writing to a person who is so far and in so many respects my superior, but also because of the importance of the subject; for is the question only, What I am? a madman or a man in his senses? a knave or an honest man? No, this is only brought in by way of illustration. The question is of the office and operation in the Holy Spirit; with which the doctrine of the New Birth, and indeed the whole of real religion, is connected. On a subject of so deep concern I desire to be serious as death.'
226. *Letters* IV, 384.
227. *Letters* IV, 346: 'I desire to be tried by this test. I try myself by it continually; not indeed, whether I am a prophet (for it has nothing to do with this), but whether I am a Christian.'
228. *Letters* IV, 340–4.
229. *Letters* IV, 344.
230. *Letters* IV, 341.
231. *Letters* IV, 345f.
232. *Letters* IV, 350f.
233. *Letters* IV, 351f.
234. *Letters* IV, 353: 'But though I do not desire persecution, I expect it.'
235. The whole question discussed, *Letters* IV, 352–6.
236. *Letters* IV, 347.
237. *Letters* IV, 347f, 357.
238. *Letters* IV, 368.

239. *Letters* IV, 373.
240. *Letters* IV, 374–6.
241. *Letters* IV, 382.
242. *Letters* IV, 376–8: John Pearson, *Exposition of the Creed* art. VIII, II.
    Letters IV, 378f. Collects.
    Letters IV, 379–81 Homilies.
243. *Letters* IV, 350.
244. *Letters* IV, 382.
245. It is important that John Wesley imposed restraint upon himself. As his other controversies show, he could have adopted throughout a sharpness of language. Cf. his explicit statements, *Letters* IV, 420, to Sam. Furly, Norwich, March 10, 1763: 'I scarce ever yet repented of saying too little, but frequently of saying too much. To the Bishop I have said more than I usually do, and I believe as much as the occasion requires. But I spare him. If he replies, I shall probably speak more plainly, if not more largely.'
    Letters IV, 198, to Sam. Furly, Dec. 20, 1762: 'I think the danger in writing to Bishop Warburton is rather that of saying too much than too little. The least said is soonest amended, and leaves an ill-natured critic the least to take hold of. I have therefore endeavoured to say as little upon each head as possible. If he replies, I shall say more. But I rather think he will not, unless it be by a side stroke when he writes on some other subject.' *Letters* IV, 205, London, March 18, 1763, to the editor of *Lloyd's Evening Post*: 'To Bishop Warburton bringing particular charges, I have given particular answers, I hope to the satisfaction of every reasonable and impartial man.'
246. Thomas Rutherford, *Four Charges to the Clergy of the Archdeaconry of Essex*, 1763. *Letters* V, 357–69, Manchester, March 28, 1768.
247. Rutherford, op. cit., 1–13.
248. Ibid. pp. 15–33.
249. J.W. *Letters* V, 359–63.
250. *Letters* V, 363–8.
251. *Letters* V, 368f.
252. Thomas Secker, *Works* X, 4th ed. 1790, 279–84; cf. esp. the following extract, p. 279–82: 'It is peculiarly unhappy, that while we are employed on one Side in defending the Gospel, we are accused on another of corrupting it. I have not now in my View either the Church of Rome, or the Protestants who broke off from us a Century ago. The Methods of dealing with both have been long since prescribed, and I repeat them not: but intreat your Attention to the Movements of each, especially the former, if you have any of them

in your Parishes. But I mean to speak of Persons risen up in our own Times, and professing the strictest Piety: who vehemently charge us with departing from the Doctrines and slighting the Precepts of our Religion: but have indeed themselves advanced unjustifiable Notions, as necessary Truths; giving good People groundless Fears, and bad ones groundless Hopes; disturbed the Understandings of some, impaired the Circumstances of others; prejudiced Multitudes against their proper Ministers and prevented their Edification by them; produced first disorders in our Churches, then partial or total Separations from them; and set up unauthorized Teachers in their assemblies. Where these Irregularities will end, God only knows: but it behoves us to be very careful, that they make no Progress through our Fault.

Now it would not only be injurious, but profane, to brand, with an opprobrious Name, Christians remarkably serious, merely for being such: and equally imprudent to disclaim them as not belonging to us to let a Sect gain the Credit of them, and labour to drive them into it. Surely we should take, even were they wavering, or actually gone from us, the most respectful and persuasive Means of recalling such, and fixing them with us. Nay supposing any Persons irrecoverably gone, we should not be hasty to condemn, even in our Thoughts, either them or their Party, as Enthusiast or Hypocrites: whatever they are, it makes no Matter to us. And much less ought we to say of either worse than we are sure they deserve. When we are undoubtedly well informed of any extravagant Things, which they have asserted or done, it may be useful to speak strongly of them: but not with Anger and Exaggeration; which will only give them a Handle to censure our Uncharitableness, and confute us: but with deep Concern, that when so few Persons express any Zeal for the Gospel, so many of those, who do, run into Extremes, that hurt its Interests. Nor will Ridicule become our Character, or serve our Cause better than Invective. It may please those very highly, who are in no Danger of being proselyted by them. But what shall we get by that? Persons negligent of Religion will at the same Time be confirmed in their Negligence; and think, that all they need to avoid is being righteous overmuch. Tender Minds will be grieved and wounded by such illplaced Levity: and crafty Declaimers will rail at us with Success, as Scoffers denying the Power of Godliness. But if we let fall any light Expressions, that can be wrested into a seeming Disrespect of any Scripture Doctrine or Phrase, we shall give our Adversaries unspeakable Advantages: and they have shewn, that they will use them without Mercy or Equity. Therefore we must

guard every Word, that we utter, against Misrepresentations: be sure
to express, in public and private, our firm Belief of whatever
evangelical Truths border upon their Mistakes: and certainly be as
vigilant over our Behaviour, as our Teaching: encourage no Violence,
no Rudeness towards them; but recommend ourselves to them by
our Mildness, our Seriousness, our Diligence: honour those, who
are truely devout and virtuous amongst them, much more on that
Account, than we blame them for being injudicious, and hard to
please; and be full as ready to acknowledge the Good, they have
done, as to complain of the Harm; yet beware, of being drawn, by
Esteem of their Piety, into relishing their Singularities, and patroniz-
ing their Schism.'

Index